C000095517

Four Internets

FOUR INTERNETS
Data, Geopolitics, and the Governance of Cyberspace

Kieron O'Hara and Wendy Hall

OXFORD
UNIVERSITY PRESS

OXFORD
UNIVERSITY PRESS

Oxford University Press is a department of the University of Oxford. It furthers
the University's objective of excellence in research, scholarship, and education
by publishing worldwide. Oxford is a registered trade mark of Oxford University
Press in the UK and certain other countries.

Published in the United States of America by Oxford University Press
198 Madison Avenue, New York, NY 10016, United States of America.

Library of Congress Cataloging-in-Publication Data
Names: O'Hara, Kieron, author. | Hall, Wendy, 1952– author.
Title: Four internets : data, geopolitics, and the governance of cyberspace /
Kieron O'Hara and Wendy Hall.
Description: New York, NY, United States of America :
Oxford University Press, [2021] | Includes bibliographical references and index.
Identifiers: LCCN 2021014363 | ISBN 9780197523681 (hb) |
ISBN 9780197523704 (epub) | ISBN 9780197523711 (Online)
Subjects: LCSH: Internet governance. | Internet--Political aspects.
Classification: LCC TK5105.8854 .O43 2021 | DDC 384.3/34--dc23
LC record available at https://lccn.loc.gov/2021014363

DOI: 10.1093/oso/9780197523681.001.0001

9 8 7 6 5 4 3 2 1

Printed by Sheridan Books, Inc., United States of America

CONTENTS

FOREWORD

Predicting the future is never an easy task, given its inherent uncertainty. Old friends Wendy Hall and Kieron O'Hara have made as good a shot as possible by employing the tactic of exploring several possible futures based on experience and existing trends. We have examples of the Internet's manifestation in different geo-political settings and these have informed the four Internets envisioned in this thoughtful book. Among my favourite personal life theorems is #206: 'Everything is more complicated'. I think that may be the case here, as well.

The original Internet design envisioned a diverse collection of packet-switched networks held together by 'gateways' and a common set of protocols, starting with the Internet Protocol (IP) layer, which included a global addressing scheme that would locate a 'host' computer as to which network it was in and where it was attached to that network. The hosts and the gateways would be IP-aware although the underlying networks themselves did not need to be. In fact, in the original experimental implementation, the Arpanet, Packet Radio net, and Packet Satellite net were entirely unaware of the overlay Internet. Gateways between the networks encapsulated and decapsulated Internet Packets into and from the payloads of packets in the underlying networks. Internet packets were like postcards placed inside of envelopes for transport within a constituent network. Networks were not limited in geographic scope and could be local or global. The addressing structure was topological, unlike the country-coded telephone network.

It was assumed that any host could address an Internet packet to any other host in the system, implying universal addressability. This was considered essential because it was not clear from the outset which hosts might need to communicate with which other hosts, nor was it clear what applications might be needed or invented. A consequence of the latter idea is that the Internet packets had no information as to how they were transported—whether they were going over twisted pair copper, mobile radio, satellite, Ethernet, or some other bearer. Thus, when optical fibre appeared in the early 1980s, the

Internet packets were happily transported that way, without any change to the basic Internet architecture.

Moreover, the Internet packets were unaware of the applications they supported. From the protocol point of view, they simply were carrying a payload of uninterpreted bits to be delivered to the destination host computer. The host computer would interpret the payload to implement the application. A packet might contain part of an email message, bits of video or audio, a fragment of an image, part of a spreadsheet, and, later, portions of Web pages. This lack of application awareness was crucial to the Internet's rapid evolution of applications because the architecture of the basic Internet did not have to change to support new applications. The so-called end-to-end transparency of the Internet has served the application developers well. Implementers needed neither permission nor alteration of the Internet to invent a new application, with the possible exception that some applications required more transport capacity to be feasible. Thus it was that streaming audio, video, and video-conferencing required a substantial increase in transport bandwidth, mostly provided by optical fibre and more recent developments in high speed radio transmission, before they could be widely implemented.

The Internet architecture is layered with well-defined interfaces between the layers. These interfaces have been largely stable since the beginning of the Internet's design and this has been beneficial for two reasons. The first is that the lower interface of a new protocol benefits from being able to rely on the stability of its interface to the layer below on which functionality it depends. On the other hand, the new protocol may exhibit a new upper interface and functionality in support of new applications. So, for example, a Real-Time Protocol (RTP) may rely on the lower, unreliable User Datagram Protocol (UDP) in support of real-time speech. UDP does not guarantee orderly and complete delivery, unlike the Transmission Control Protocol (TCP), but it tries to be low latency. RTP might not re-transmit lost packets and might discard 'old' packets but otherwise might try to deliver packets in time sequence order for a speech application.

Implicit in the end-to-end and universal connectivity assumption is essentially free flow of data across geo-political borders. That assumption is vital, for example, for the implementation of multi-national 'cloud' computing systems in which data centres exchange data freely for purposes of replication to prevent loss of data. Various forms of fragmentation occur when this free flow is impeded, blocked, or filtered in some fashion. It is also important to recognize that the freedom of interchange can be eroded at different layers in the architecture. For example, a country might require that certain domain names be blocked by interfering with domain name lookups in the Domain Name System. Internet users in China cannot reach the domain www.google.com because the lookups return 'no such host'. The Chinese government can implement this effect by controlling the behaviour of the in-country domain name 'resolvers'. Attempts to bypass this control using 'virtual private networks' may work but can be detected and blocked.

Fragmentation of the Internet can occur at other layers in the system. Indeed, some countries require that search engines such as Google and Bing must not show responses for certain queries. In Germany and France, for example, it is illegal to facilitate any pecuniary benefit from the sale of Nazi war memorabilia from World War II. The European 'Right to be Forgotten' requires that search engines maintain a list of name-based lookups, the response to which must be discarded or blocked. Most countries require that Internet providers or application providers block the transport of child pornography or other child-based exploitation content. There can be harsh penalties for failure to meet these standards. Intellectual property violations (usually, copyright) can also engender serious fines and penalties which vary from country to country.

The general point is that discovery, retrieval, and transport of certain kinds or sources of information or data are prohibited in various ways across the global Internet. All of this adds up to varying degrees of interference with the free flow of information in the Internet. In many cases, such constraints are broadly agreed among most countries that house portions of the Internet. But there is also disagreement with some restrictions on the grounds that they violate universal rights of speech, access to information, ability to assemble (if virtually), and so on.

In this book, the authors select four possible representative futures for the Internet's evolution, depending on geo-political and policy frames that affect the otherwise free flow of information in the network. In reality, there already are and will be nuanced demands made by governments of the Internet access and application service providers and some of these demands will have extraterritorial character. The European Right to be Forgotten and the General Data Protection Regulation have already manifested outside of the European Union. The notion of 'Data Sovereignty' is becoming a popular meme, attempting to mirror in cyberspace the concepts captured in the 1648 Peace of Westphalia that countenanced sovereignty within geo-political boundaries. I am unpersuaded that this notion is beneficial, particularly in the context of distributed cloud computing which benefits everyone through the replication of data at multiple data centres to reduce latency of access (e.g. Content Distribution Networks) or to protect against data loss.

The arrival of social networking in the form of Facebook, Instagram, YouTube, Twitter, TikTok, WeChat, among many other applications, has ushered in new hazards to the free flow of information in the Internet. Of course, the issues here are misinformation, disinformation, hate speech, bullying, fake news, and a bevy of other speech-related concerns, to say nothing of the apparent feedback reward mechanisms that appear to exacerbate extreme expression for the purpose of gaining attention and potentially income from shared advertising revenues. To this we can also add the general problems of malware including denial of service attacks, hacking, ransomware, identity theft, webpage defacement, and other harmful or disruptive behaviours. That these can pose serious threats to infrastructure such as the power generation and distribution systems, healthcare systems, communication systems, and transportation control systems underlines the gravity of responses necessary. Whether such attacks rise to the level of national security and even military response is a conundrum for our twenty-first century. All of these potential hazards drive countries to adopt policies in response which may not be compatible in bilateral or multilateral terms. Indeed, these issues have elicited lengthy and unresolved debates over how they should be resolved and whether they can be treated through multilateral conventions and treaties akin to the Law of the Sea or agreements as to the peaceful uses of space.

In the long term, I hold the view that the Internet's benefits are well-established but that there are risks inherent in its abuse. Our task is to understand and articulate the various potential paths forward and to do our best to assess their implications, as Wendy Hall and Kieron O'Hara have attempted here.

8 November 2020
Vinton G. Cerf
Vice President and Chief Internet Evangelist
Google, LLC

PREFACE

The Internet appears a fixed part of modern reality. Its roots date back over fifty years, and by the first quarter of the twenty-first century it has become the pre-eminent means of distributing information. To those in their early twenties, it will have been a permanent, if mutable, background to their lives. It seems unquestionable, like electricity and roads. Its design was intended to make it tolerant of disruption and faults, and it is pretty robust and resilient. We can go further: it is surely evident by now (this book was completed in lockdown during the 2020 COVID-19 pandemic) that it has become a piece of critical infrastructure, and needs to be protected as such.

Yet it is surprisingly delicate all the same, a gossamer arrangement of different types of hardware, protocols to describe how systems communicate with each other, and methods of social coordination, ranging from regulations to contracts to what amount to little more than gentlemen's (and ladies') agreements. The Internet is not a monolithic technological creation, patented and run by a single company or government, but a congeries of systems, protocols, standards, hardware, and organizations. Some of these organizations have national standing, some have global reach, and others have international standing. Some are public bodies, some private companies, and some non-profit organizations. The Internet is one of the few institutions where the people round the table are as likely to be in corporate suits and Christian Louboutins, as black t-shirts with hoodies and Air Monarchs, or even (still, just about) tie-dyed denim and bare feet.[1]

Furthermore, the system is truly sociotechnical—we cannot hive the technology off from the people who use it in their everyday lives. Every design decision reflects, and imposes (perhaps unconsciously), a balance of power, while cultural, economic, and political tensions play out across collective-action problems. Neither computer science nor the social sciences are individually sufficient to encompass all the study required to understand the most complex piece of technology ever created, the structure of which is driven by the people who upload, download, and link content. The authors of this book have long argued that concentrated interdisciplinary research, encompassing social and technical studies, is required both to understand it and to engineer it.[2]

The Internet evolves so quickly that there is no good time to write about it. The year 2020 was peculiarly inopportune, it appears to us (now we have done it). The uncertainties were immense, and prediction seemed hopeless. We were privileged to be asked to write a short piece for a collection of prognostications for the future published in December 2019 called *The Wired World in 2020*. Not a single author predicted that we would spend most of the year sitting indoors while over a million people died, and the world economy tanked.

The future of the Internet depends on answers to many questions (some of which will by now be evident to the reader). Most obviously, the COVID-19 pandemic has completely reshaped our relationships with the Internet, and with the wider world. What will the new normal be?

There are political questions, of which the elephant in the room during the time of writing was the outcome of the 2020 US presidential election. President Trump's success or failure in 2020 would have massive influence over the Internet's future, and that of the technology industry generally. President Biden will certainly govern in a different style, but there may well be aspects of his predecessor's agenda that he preserves. Other unresolved issues concern the extent to which China will challenge the United States for global leadership (it currently heads four of the UN's fifteen specialized agencies, including the International Telecommunication Union), and how the European Union will work through Brexit, and the post-Merkel era.

The Internet is a co-creation of its users, and every year it adds in excess of a hundred million new co-creators. These people will change the Internet in unpredictable ways. Our study of India shows some of the different directions these changes may take.

Finally, there is the technology. The Internet creates data, the fuel for artificial intelligence and smart cities, which many see as the future for humankind. Will they produce utopia, or dystopia, or are they merely hype? Other important technological trends we had to ignore or skate over for reasons of space are blockchain, automatic face recognition, virtual or augmented reality, undetectable deepfake technology, quantum computing, ubiquitous wireless broadband, and medical wearables. Any one of these could have a massive effect on our privacy, public life, and well-being.

Our research, as we describe in Chapter 1, is structured by three basic ideas about the Internet as a network, the Internet as a producer of data, and the Internet as the key technology for digital modernity.

• The different networks connected by Internet protocols are governed by subtly different principles, which may, over time, make it harder to get data across the Internet as a whole, and therefore may increase the pressures to fragment.

- These different principles have a strong connection with attitudes towards data, which is the chief source of power on the Internet.
- The visions and models of the Internet we discuss in this book are all, in their way, responses to the prime imperatives of digital modernity.

We hope to weave the narratives of networks, data, and modernity into an understanding of how different cultures and ideologies see value in the Internet, and how it might be possible to keep it together, while respecting difference and diversity. The key, we claim, is how the Internet is governed.

The book is divided into three parts. In Part I, we introduce the question of Internet governance, and how it reflects values. We set out the original Internet vision, the ultimate techie ambition of an open, unmanaged, free information space.

In Part II, we consider some of the problems with this vision, and then look at the alternatives that have evolved through time. We focus on three that have become highly influential; these, plus the original open vision, give us the four Internets of the book's title. These aren't the only visions that are available— hence our title is *Four Internets*, not *The Four Internets*; a definite article would be misleading. Other Internets could be imagined, if the appropriate ethical vision found a technological realization and sufficiently powerful institutional backing. We will also look at another ideological model of how the Internet can be used as an instrument of policy—not one that comes with its own positive vision, but a spoiler that might undermine the integrity of the Internet and thereby (perhaps accidentally) contribute to fragmentation.

Part III of the book sets out some of the implications of the ideological centrifugal force. This isn't a Jeremiad, but it seems clear that the more closely the diversity of Internet governance tracks the diversity of the world it spans, the easier it will be to contain this force. There are radically different views of how communications should be managed, and these need to be reflected and respected in governance structures—even if engineering imperatives are compromised as a result.

Each geopolitical entity we describe is at the centre of many policy wrangles. To illustrate some of the choices and trade-offs involved in these, each of the six geopolitical chapters is succeeded by an unresolved 'policy question', giving us a deeper dive into how politics, technology, and regulation converge and diverge.

ACKNOWLEDGEMENTS

Conversations with a great many colleagues have contributed to the work you have before you, and our debts are immense. For direct help with this research, many thanks are due to Paul Smart for many ideas, and in particular his research into the Chinese AI and data protection scene. Thanks also to Les Carr for managing relevant projects and many illuminating discussions. Special thanks to Anni Rowland-Campbell for brave conversations, comments, and references. Our colleagues past and present at the University of Southampton Web Science Institute, drawn from across the university's various faculties, have been a constant source of inspiration, reminding us of the sheer range of perspectives from which one can view the Internet. The Web Science students we have taught over the years have—as is always the case—taught us at least as much in return.

We are particularly grateful to those brave and patient souls who read the whole thing and commented copiously: Peter Kingsley, Carolyn Nguyen, Srinath Srinivasa, Phil Tetlow, Bill Thompson. Thanks in particular to Vint Cerf, who not only commented, but kindly agreed to write our Foreword. Thanks also to anonymous reviewers at Oxford University Press, both at proposal and submission stage, and to Sarah Humphreville and the team at OUP who piloted us through the process. The feedback we received was extremely helpful, and it goes without saying—though we will now say it—that any errors that remain are our responsibility solely.

We are grateful to Mark Schueler and Jie Tang for their diagrams depicting the growth of the Web.

The ideas first saw the light of day as we collaborated to write a paper for the Centre for International Governance Innovation. Our gratitude goes to them for the opportunity, and also all the help of Fen Hampson and their excellent team in refining the argument, and presenting the paper so that we started to get feedback from a range of communities and disciplines. The full set of papers by us in which the broad argument has been presented (all authored by O'Hara & Hall, except where stated) is:

- *Four Internets: The Geopolitics of Digital Governance*, CIGI paper no. 206, https://www.cigionline.org/publications/four-internets-geopolitics-digital-governance
- Wendy Hall, 'Four Internets require geopolitical balancing act', *Financial Times*, https://www.cigionline.org/articles/four-internets-require-geopolitical-balancing-act
- 'There are now four competing visions of the internet. How should they be governed?' World Economic Forum Agenda blog, https://www.weforum.org/agenda/2019/03/there-are-now-four-competing-visions-of-the-internet/, re-published in *Global Policy*, https://www.globalpolicyjournal.com/blog/14/03/2019/there-are-now-four-competing-visions-internet-how-should-they-be-governed
- 'The dream of a global internet is edging towards destruction', *The Wired World in 2020*, https://www.wired.co.uk/article/internet-fragmentation
- 'Four Internets', *Communications of the ACM*, 63(3), 28–30, https://doi.org/10.1145/3341722

Thanks to audiences to which the argument has been presented, in particular the techies at the Our People-Centered Digital Future Conference in San Jose, California, an enthusiastic audience of young Chevening Scholars at the University of Southampton, a somewhat more mature audience at the University of Luxembourg's 2019 Rentrée Académique, and a mix of Parliamentarians and industrial technologists at the 2020 Parliament and Internet conference in Westminster.

Thanks also to journalists who have aired the arguments and given us a sense of how they may be received, including Martin Sandbu of the *Financial Times*, Jordi Peréz Colomé of *El País*, and Amol Rajan of the BBC.

CHAPTER 1

Preliminary Concepts

Networks and Data

The Internet is a technical system, but not purely a technical system. That it is a technical system brings with it a vital invariant that can never be neglected: *it has to work*. If it does not actually perform its function, then the question of governance may be of academic interest but is hardly pressing. But because the Internet is more than just a technical system, then it will inevitably be measured against other values concerning its role in society. The point of governance is to ensure that the system functions, while respecting other values too.

Evaluating that respect depends on many aspects that have become more complex as the Internet has grown. It is a global resource, used for commerce, politics, entertainment, health and well-being, socializing, scientific research, and education. It sustains the most advanced economies, and at the same time is a tool for development. It is a voice for the excluded, and a megaphone for the powerful. It is also a cog in many complex systems, delivering government services, hosting cryptocurrencies, coordinating defence and weapons systems, and enabling emergency services. It generates a record of our activities that can be used to personalize the services we receive, or that can be held against us in the future. It is the *sine qua non* for so many valuable things that hard choices, dilemmas, and trade-offs seem inevitable.

It is a global Internet. This means, in our ineffably plural world, that many different points of view must be taken with respect to its governance. What seems self-evident to a professor of computer science and fan of the Grateful Dead in San Francisco might be somewhat less obvious to a businessperson who relies on it to coordinate a complex supply chain across East Asia that

Four Internets. Kieron O'Hara and Wendy Hall, Oxford University Press. © Oxford University Press 2021.
DOI: 10.1093/oso/9780197523681.003.0001

employs thousands of people, and positively counterintuitive to a law enforcement officer in a combustible part of the world whose main job is containing the threat of inter-community violence. Different people have to cooperate, and agree to differ. As economist Jonathan Cave puts it:

> There is broad support among experts and laymen alike for a regulatory system based on common and attractive architectural and policy principles and values, many of which are endorsed throughout . . . currently-dominant developed nations. But they are not universally supported in the developing world and do not in any case receive the same ranking.
>
> If 'our' future internet differs widely from the global internet or the internets of other global powers, we may lose purchase or find ourselves bypassed. Expressing our values and reaching our objectives may be frustrated or excessively costly.[1]

In this book, our aim is to explore some of these issues, and to consider some of the value-sets that have emerged, with a boost from powerful geopolitical actors. We will not—cannot—decide how the Internet could, should, or must be. We, the authors, are as embedded in particular value systems as anyone else, and consequently as biased. We will try to take a dispassionate view of the range of perspectives, and think about the pressures they create. We will survey the powerful emerging visions of the Internet, show how they are implemented, and discover what happens when they clash. We will try to understand how new and exciting innovations in Internet technology may be shaped, depending on which of these visions gains a no doubt temporary upper hand. And ultimately, as these ideological conflicts are here to stay, we want to understand how Internet governance can best accommodate these heterogeneous views, while keeping the show on the road.

Perhaps most importantly, at some point in 2019, the proportion of people connected to the Internet exceeded 50 percent. This is an amazing feat, for which the Web, social networking, gaming, and streaming services must take a lot of the credit; it is not long since it was customary to point out that half the world's population had never even made a phone call, and there have long been claims that Internet growth would reach a ceiling. Three and a half billion people are now connected, and the number is only likely to grow. The question then is how the next three and a half billion will change the Internet, for change it they surely will.[2]

One study based on World Bank data from 2016 found the following percentages; at the time, global penetration was 46 percent, so note how the South Asian and sub-Saharan African regions pulled down the average (Table 1.1).

Growth will not be from the rich world; the United States has a surprisingly low rate of Internet penetration, but no other rich democracy has further

Table 1.1. INTERNET PENETRATION IN DIFFERENT REGIONS AND SELECTED COUNTRIES (2016)

Region	Percentage	Highs (%)	Lows (%)	Large Population Centres (%)
North America	78	Bermuda (98), Canada (90)	United States (76)	United States (76)
Europe and Central Asia	73	Iceland (98), Luxembourg (98)	Romania, Bulgaria (60; lowest in EU), Bosnia and Herzegovina (55; lowest in Continental Europe), Turkmenistan (18)	United Kingdom (95), Germany (90), France (86)
Latin America and Caribbean	57	Argentina (71), Chile (66)	El Salvador (29), Haiti (12)	Brazil (61)
East Asia and Pacific	53	South Korea (93), Japan (93)	Papua New Guinea (10), North Korea (<1)	Australia (88), China (53)
Middle East and North Africa	48	Qatar (94), United Arab Emirates (91)	Libya (20), Djibouti (13)	Iran (53), Egypt (41)
South Asia	26	Maldives (59), Bhutan (42)	Pakistan (16), Afghanistan (11)	India (30)
Sub-Saharan Africa	20	South Africa (54), Gabon (48)	Somalia (2), Eritrea (1)	Nigeria (26), Ethiopia (16)

Source: Max Roser, Hannah Ritchie, & Esteban Ortiz-Ospina, 'Internet', *Our World in Data*, https://ourworldindata.org/internet, except Bermuda figure from https://www.statista.com/statistics/731257/bermuda-internet-penetration/.

room. The new users are therefore going to be in sub-Saharan Africa, India, rural China, and other parts of South and East Asia. The people in these regions are not so different from everyone else; we must expect that they will be interested in news, sport, entertainment, pornography, dating, and networking,[3] but the balance of ideologies will change, and so will the pressures on Internet governance. We can't predict the exact nature of those pressures, but we can at least prepare for them.

To begin at the beginning, the Internet is a *network* of computers, connected for instance by copper or fibre-optic cable, which can carry *data*.[4] 'Internet' is short for 'Internetwork', and implies a network of connected computer networks. What makes it the Internet, as opposed to any old computer network, is the use of two particular sets of communication rules: the *Transmission Control Protocol* (TCP), and the *Internet Protocol* (IP), which together are known as the *Internet Protocol Suite* (TCP/IP). IP defines how computers can exchange data with each other, while TCP governs the connections between computers to exchange data using IP. A system of *IP addresses* identifies individual computers in such a way as to (a) locate each computer in a specific network, and then (b) identify a route through that network to the computer itself using IP. Between them, these protocols provide an end-to-end specification of how data gets transferred across the Internet. We will describe these protocols (without getting too technical), and their evolution, in Chapter 2.

The Internet is, then, a network of computer networks connected by TCP/IP, on which data can get from anywhere on the Internet to anywhere else pretty well instantaneously. This is what makes it so valuable—data becomes abundant, and can be reused by many people, sometimes in unanticipated and propitious circumstances. Part of the cleverness of the design lies in the fact that the Internet infrastructure is *simultaneously* a means of building a network designed to pass data between the nodes, *and* a means of stitching together pre-existing or independent networks, even when they operate on very different principles from each other.

Our investigations in this book therefore have two parallel foci. The first is the connectivity and size of the network. How are the nodes of the network connected, and how easy is it to get data from one part to another? The second is what is moved through the network facilitated by the connections. The ability to amalgamate data into larger aggregations, and then process it en masse, is the source of great technological potency. This can be done by bringing increasingly large quantities of data together at single points in the network, or by clever techniques using the network to bring inferential power to query data at its various different locations, thereby creating a large *virtual* dataset.

The value of the Internet lies in its status as a network, and as a data infrastructure. The job of this chapter, therefore, is to sketch the sometimes surprising properties of networks and data, before we proceed to the Internet itself. In particular, in terms of value and power, we will differentiate networks and hierarchies, and in terms of expressive power we will contrast data with information. The effects of the existence of an efficient, global, data-carrying network have upended a great deal of political, economic, and social thought; as our final introductory task, we will also describe the corresponding narrative of *digital modernity* as essential background. Where networks provide accessible means by which data can be collected and consumed at scale, many new technological affordances, such as artificial intelligence and smart cities, are created. These affordances, which are at the heart of digital modernity, will be discussed in Part III of this book.

NETWORKS AND THEIR VALUE

A network can be described using a set of points or nodes, with connections or edges between them, to create a *graph*. An edge connects a pair of nodes, but not every pair of nodes needs to be connected. The connections are usually defined in a particular way—for instance, in a network of human acquaintances, two nodes (people) would be connected if they knew each other, and the edge between them would symbolize their acquaintance. In a network of holding companies, two nodes (companies) would be connected if one of them was the legal owner of shares in the other. In a family tree, which is a type of network, two people would be connected if one was the parent of the other, and the edge would symbolize ancestry. Some connections have a direction (like ownership and parenthood), others (like acquaintance) don't. If the connections of the network are directed, this is a directed network; if not, it is undirected.

If two nodes are not directly connected, there may still be a route between them in the network. For instance, A and C may not be connected, but A is connected to B and B to C. What does this mean? In the case of parenthood, it means that A is C's grandparent. If we follow the edges following their correct direction, we will discover all cases of direct ancestry. If we look to see whether two nodes are indirectly connected without bothering about the actual direction of the edges concerned, we discover all cases of blood relation. In the case of acquaintance, it means that A and C have a chain of mutual acquaintances, but they themselves need not know each other at all. A network is *connected* if any node in the network is reachable from any other, even if by a circuitous route. A *hierarchy*, such as a family tree, is a special type of network where all the edges have a direction, and there are no cycles, so the whole network has a direction, and we can consider nodes to be 'above' or 'below' others (see Figure 1.1).

A network is more valuable when there is a relatively high number of connections between nodes. If we have several such networks, they might also be connected to each other to create a bigger network (a network of sub-networks is itself a network). The connections between sub-networks might be relatively few in number (rather as there are lots of roads within cities and towns, but only one or two highways connecting them), but only one or two between pairs of networks are needed to create a connected network of networks. There is a branch of mathematics that quantifies network concepts, enabling us to work out when networks are more or less connected, which

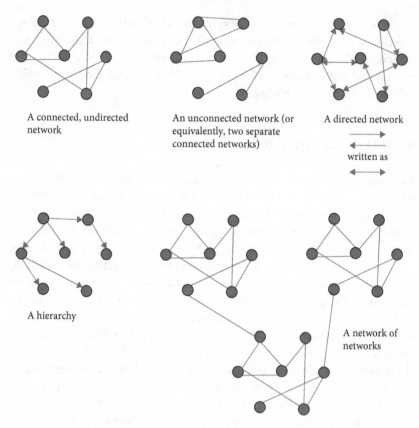

A connected, undirected network

An unconnected network (or equivalently, two separate connected networks)

A directed network

$\longrightarrow$
$\longleftarrow$

written as

$\longleftrightarrow$

A hierarchy

A network of networks

Figure 1.1. Different types of networks.

nodes in the network are more or less important in various different ways, but we will not pursue this type of analysis in this book.[5]

Metcalfe's Law, named after Robert Metcalfe, a co-inventor of the Ethernet networking technology which helps carry the Internet, states that as the number of nodes in the network grows, the value of the network to the nodes in it grows exponentially (in practice, this is hard to sustain as the network gets very large, because it is unlikely that everything is connected to everything else, but the growth rate is still greater than linear).[6] On the basis of Metcalfe's Law, we should expect more people to get more value from the Internet as it expands, since each node on the network (a computer) is serving at least one person or organization. This disproportionate increase in value is called a *network effect*. Network effects also create a virtuous circle: as the network becomes more valuable, so more outsiders wish to join it. The network produces what are known as *positive externalities*; outsiders join in order to benefit themselves, but because of network effects they also benefit everyone else in the network without intending to.

POWER: NETWORKS VERSUS HIERARCHIES

Historian Niall Ferguson brings out the potency of networks in his book *The Square and the Tower*, using the image of a medieval city-state such as Siena, where the rulers sat in a tower exercising their power, and the people—merchants, artisans, peasants, artists, beggars—mingled in the main square below (open source software pioneer Eric Raymond makes a similar comparison between the industrial division of labour and the networks of the Internet, as the Cathedral and the Bazaar).[7] The tower hosted a hierarchy, a top-down structure like a family tree; the square contained a network, a flatter structure with no restrictions on who is connected to whom. The rulers mainly interacted with their lieutenants, who passed on information about the conditions in the city, and who, given their orders, carried them out. While the arrangement has a certain parsimony, and for the rulers may be a rather nice deal, as a means of regulating the city it may be less than ideal. In particular, the amount of information received by the rulers is restricted by the number of lieutenants, and so their decisions may not be well-informed (especially as the lieutenants may themselves have interests that influence what they pass on). Put another way, knowledge of the state of the city can't be gathered effectively by the relatively small number of people at the top of the hierarchy.[8]

Meanwhile, on the square, the rest of the city's population mingled within a fruitful, innovative network structure. Artificial social distinctions may still count for something, but in principle anyone might bump into anyone else. Social problems, such as unemployment, crime, or widespread poverty, were evident to all. Information travelled quickly through the horizontal connections via gossip. Collective action happened through mutual support and reciprocity, not administrative fiat. And when the rulers failed to discern the mood in the square, and legislated inappropriately, a revolutionary situation might develop. Misunderstood patterns of behaviour in the networked square may then simply overwhelm the powers of the hierarchy to control them. This is not simply a medieval problem: the (hierarchical) French government has recently found it much easier to negotiate with the (hierarchical) trade unions than with the (networked) *gilets jaunes*.[9]

Hierarchies and centralization do have advantages. They provide a single point of control and order, so the city is more cohesive with a more defined identity and its government can move to a purpose (it is interesting that of Plato's ideal cities in *The Republic*, the simpler versions are decentralized, but he has to introduce the hierarchy of Guardians and Auxiliaries to support both complexity and sustainability).[10] The behaviour of a network is generally *emergent*—it has properties which the nodes in the network do not have, and did not deliberately create—and so is hard to steer in a desirable direction, or away from the undesirable.[11] Hierarchies are more easily planned, and can behave more strategically and consistently through time, following policies through and pursuing goals (the COVID-19 pandemic spread through decentralized networks, and was battled by hierarchies). The ideal arrangement for many places no doubt is a hierarchy with a light touch, encouraging pluralism, markets, civil society, and spontaneous order, while ensuring that defensive measures such as healthcare systems, infrastructure, and military and police forces are maintained.

The balance, though, may be hard to achieve, and as the city grows, or becomes richer, or as the royal family tree produces more princelings who need a job, the constitutional arrangements may not scale. At that point, the square will take over, in effect by swamping the tower with information with which it will not be able to cope. The spreading of communications and trade will tend to build networks and leave the hierarchies behind, as has been argued happened in a globalizing world in the seventeenth century;[12] hierarchies hit back through imperialism.

The Internet supports horizontal connections between networked individuals, and so gives them extra power relative to governmental and other hierarchies. This interplay between technology and social organization is a major socioeconomic change. 'A steel mill could operate regardless of whether it was running under Nazism, under Stalinist socialism or under liberal democracy.'[13] This is no longer the case, thanks to network technologies. Given the digital structures they have facilitated, the knowledge economy will function more smoothly under decentralized democratic structures than centralized ones. As one of the current authors argued elsewhere,[14] this poses an authoritarian nation like China serious problems—the effective solution adopted by China, as we will discover later, was to co-opt and reshape the Internet in its own image, to the extent possible. This has meant changes to Chinese society, and relations between government and governed, as much as to Internet engineering itself.

FRAGMENTATION

Governments will struggle to regulate the Internet. When they desire, or wish to prevent, some kinds of outcome, they are tempted to legislate for (or against) those outcomes, in terms of incentives, prohibitions, enforcement, or targets. Yet there is no one to respond to the incentives on offer. The individuals in the network may not even be aware of the phenomena emerging from their individual behaviours, or may not feel responsible, just as drivers don't feel responsible for traffic jams. A more intelligent type of engagement involves smarter regulation that influences the individuals rather than the network.[15] However, this is not always an immediately more attractive approach for a government anxious to achieve a definite outcome, because it takes a lot of thought and isn't guaranteed to work. Because the problem is emergent, it may not be obvious how the individuals cause it;[16] you may want to get rid of traffic jams, but equally you don't want to stop everyone driving.

In particular, because it is a network of networks—i.e. sets of highly connected nodes with relatively sparse connections between them—badly designed legislation may make the Internet vulnerable to *fragmentation*, meaning that the connected network becomes unconnected. The fragmentation of the Internet is often discussed using terms such as the 'Splinternet' or the 'Balkanization' of the Internet. The virtuous circle that Metcalfe's Law describes would become vicious, as users begin to drop off. Why would anyone break the Internet in two or more pieces? Governments might want to do it deliberately—some, like those of Iran and Russia, have toyed with the idea of having a national Internet (see Chapter 14). North Korea basically runs one, called the Kwangmyong.[17]

Suppose some scientists created an alternative version of TCP/IP that was incompatible with the old version—that might have the effect of Balkanizing the Internet. And this is not an empty worry—we will discuss later how certain nations and groups of nations have tried to alter the fundamental technological standards upon which the Internet sits. These basic standards have, so far, held, and this is a key factor in the Internet's longevity and value. Part of the reason for this is that its positive network effects are so powerful.[18]

There has been much recent talk of the possibility of the Internet falling into Eastern and Western halves, the former run by China and the latter by the United States. Eric Schmidt, no less, the former CEO of Google, has predicted that this will happen.[19] Different regulations would apply in the two halves, and—even if there were connections across the rift—it would still be complex, difficult, and slow to transfer data. Two completely separate information ecosystems might develop. There are some symptoms of this malaise appearing already; many Western sites are blocked in China, for instance, while Western suspicions of Huawei (see Chapter 12) could result in competing 5G standards.

In this book, we will explore the roots of this fear, which, unlike Schmidt, we believe to be unlikely. There are three reasons for this. Firstly, the situation is somewhat more complex than this—there are more than two significant views of how the Internet can be run. The world is not just America and China, although it may look that way from America and China. Secondly, the history and structure of the Internet shows that differing views can coexist simultaneously, and that there is room for different views, as long as we are prepared to accept diversity and cultural preferences. Pluralism is not out of reach on the Internet.

And thirdly, the notion of 'fragmentation' is not terribly well-defined. It looks relatively simple to fragment a network of networks. In Figure 1.1, the network of networks can be fragmented by removing one or two connections, but of course the Internet is far better connected than that. This means that, as Internet governance expert Milton Mueller puts it, 'the network effects and economic benefits of global compatibility are so powerful that they have consistently defeated, and will continue to defeat, any systematic deterioration of the global technical compatibility that the public Internet created'.[20] But it may be that the technical difficulty of breaking the Internet, rather than the benefits it brings, explains its survival, especially as the latter are somewhat intangible: the benefits don't guarantee its survival, any more than the undoubted benefits of the global trading system guarantee *its* survival.

Mueller is certainly correct to put the term 'fragmentation' under the microscope. Concerns about privacy, hate speech, and intellectual property, among other things, all suggest that connections can be and routinely are unpicked without threatening the integrity of the Internet. The Internet is already clustered in enclaves, strongly connected within but more sparsely connected outside (most obviously, it clusters around different languages).[21] Furthermore, many kinds of interruption to data flow are accidental, and so not really part of the fragmentation narrative. No one worries about the Splinternet when the router at home cuts out for a few hours.

Mueller's own definition of 'fragmentation' brings out these limitations. He focuses not on the collapse of the Internet or severing connections, but rather on significant obstruction.

> There has to be an *intentional* defection from the global Internet, led by a group of actors capable of taking with them a *substantial segment of the world's population*; this defection must succeed in establishing effective *technical incompatibilities* between their part of the Internet and the other part(s); and these incompatibilities must be *sustainable* over a significant period of time and able to *obstruct communications among parties that are willing to communicate*.[22]

This definition is excellent about the effects and the scope of fragmentation.[23] We ought, though, to think hard about the word 'intentional'. Varying views of the opportunities and threats that the Internet provides might lead to pressures to act (e.g. to legislate, or to approve standards, or to implement security measures) in incompatible ways, and a de facto fragmentation could then happen accidentally, if they made communication between different bits of the Internet impractically hard. We need to be prepared.

MANY INTERNETS IN ONE?

In 2002, there was talk of an 'Axis of Evil'. Today, we can discern a somewhat more potent *Axis of Incivility*, of nation-states jostling for advantage, with a view of international and economic relations as zero sum. Unlike the

Axis of Evil, which reflected US foreign policy concerns and had little significance otherwise, the Axis of Incivility has at its foundations all three major superpowers—the United States, China, and Russia—each of which in its different ways at the time of writing pursues aggressive nationalist policy goals while showing impatience with due process both internally and internationally.[24] Many other nations, including Brazil, Egypt, Hungary, India, Iran, Israel, the Philippines, Poland, Saudi Arabia, Turkey, and some might argue the United Kingdom, are following this lead.

Many of the members of the Axis of Incivility—the United States, Russia, China, India, and Turkey at least, as well possibly as Iran and Saudi Arabia—may qualify as *civilizational states*,[25] states that culturally transcend the nation-state, integrating ideological and political functions with a cultural identity which they try to project onto other nations and other civilizations and use as a diplomatic vehicle. Indeed, if we spread the civilizational state net wider than the term's originator intended, beyond nations that aim to undo the international order, we could also include less disruptive but no less assertive states. The European Union would arguably fall under this concept (as might France individually). Post-Brexit, the United Kingdom is likely to explore its hybrid identity, as simultaneously a European nation, the mother ship of the Anglosphere,[26] and a composite nation of nations. The entanglement of identity with nationality leads to a disregard of the rules of engagement and conflict management, and creates a sense of moral purpose and destiny that cannot always be negotiated or compromised away, even for clear win-wins. The growth of the civilizational state, and the associated 'total rejection of universalism',[27] is at least part of the explanation of the emergence of the Axis of Incivility. If geography is also taken into account, international relations analyst Robert Kaplan has argued that the old pattern of empires across Eurasia has propelled certain states, such as Russia, China, Iran (Persia), and Turkey, as well as the European Union, back into the limelight.[28]

In such a world, it is inconceivable that these countries will not include their competing visions of the Internet in their drive for international recognition, power, and coalition-building. The benefits of cooperation and connectedness, by which Mueller rightly sets great store, are unlikely to cut much ice, even with rational actors, if they display such a mindset.

In the context of the Axis of Incivility and the growth of the civilizational state, the binaries that Schmidt and others have detected (particularly US/China) are unrealistically Manichaean. Different nations have different views about the flow of information and how to balance the fecundity of international interaction against its disruptive influence. Different elements within government, civil society, business, political parties, the media, academe, expatriates, and other stakeholding groups—not least the technical community—will have their take. As Joseph Nye, political theorist of soft power, puts it:

> Everyone from hackers to large corporations is developing the code and norms of the Internet partly outside the control of formal political institutions. These private systems, such as corporate Intranets or worldwide newsgroups devoted to specific issues such as the environment, do not frontally challenge the governments of sovereign states; they simply add a layer of relations that sovereign states do not fully control.[29]

Everyone has their point of view, but not every point of view is efficacious. Those that prevail have both sufficient intellectual coherence and sufficient geopolitical support to make their mark, to influence both technical discussions and user expectations. Such geopolitical support requires the marshalling of institutions, some political and some technical, and communities. They meet opposition, which sometimes leads to creative compromises, but can also produce a breakdown of communication and trust, whereupon technical standards are likely to fail. A technical standard, however brilliant, is only as good as the number of people who agree to abide by it.

The first proposition we want to explore in this book is that the Internet may (and in fact has) become divergent in this sense: *the different networks connected by TCP/IP are governed by subtly different principles, which may, over time, make it harder to get data across the Internet as a whole, and therefore may increase the pressures to fragment*. Many of these principles derive from different attitudes towards data, a concept to which we now turn.

DATA VERSUS INFORMATION

The Internet is a network that transports data, and this is what drives the value of its network effects. Using the Internet generates data automatically, and the structure of the Internet (who is connected to whom, and what they have communicated) is itself of value. The data, which relates closely to people's interests and activities, is the raw material for online services, which become better tailored to users' requirements as the data gets richer. Better services mean more reason for people to use the Internet, and so more data, and so on. Hence the network effects have produced ever-increasing value, accounting for the Internet's extraordinary growth.

So far, in this book, we have talked about 'data', and occasionally about 'information'. The two are, in some sense, the same thing, but they have different connotations which affect our attitude towards them, both as engineers and as consumers of content. Different disciplines conceptualize data differently as well, but we will consider the understanding common among computer scientists of a distinct difference between data and information, as that will help explain the forces we describe.[30]

This may seem like pedantry: it isn't. Most disciplines need a word to discuss the input for their reasoning, and in most cases both 'data' and 'information' will do equally well, but in computer science we need *different* words to mark the distinction between what the computer manipulates, and what the human or the human/social system understands. The former is 'data', and the latter is 'information'.

We take a piece of data to be a string of uninterpreted symbols from a symbol system. The symbols that computers manipulate are binary digits (bits)—1s and 0s—but there are various conventions for using these to represent, for example, letters of the Roman alphabet. Data is manipulated by *programs*, which consider only its syntactic, structural aspects, not its meaning. Strictly speaking, it has no meaning, because it is uninterpreted.

Even this is a simplification. Data needs *some* interpretation—to be interpreted *as* a symbol. This is a basic type of mechanical comparison which is called *template matching*—in terms of similarity to members of the system. Template matching contrasts with more complex types of semantic interpretation which deal with the meanings or messages within data, and which require an observer. The computer 'does' template matching by dealing with certain voltages within its circuits as 1s, and others as 0s (and if the voltage is out of its expected range, it cannot manipulate it as a symbol at all). The actual 'representation' of 1s and 0s in the machine is a matter of a convention such as TTL (transistor-transistor logic), with whose details we need not concern ourselves here,[31] as long as we understand that computer data is an artefact of a physical system that is merely reacting to physical inputs and producing physical outputs. It can do the mechanical interpretation of an artefact as a symbol, because it has been designed to do it. It cannot reason about what the symbol may express. So we need to keep in mind the distinction between mechanical interpretation of an object as a symbol, and semantic interpretation of a symbol as having a particular meaning. Once the former process has been carried out, we have data, and once the latter has been done, we have information, as shown in Figure 1.2.

Data is usually intended to *represent* something. When someone creates data, they often write it out in mnemonic form. If they wanted a piece of data to represent, say, Mimi being the mother of Emmy, they might deliberately use the symbol string 'mother_of(mimi,emmy)', which makes its intended representation clear to an English-speaking human reader of the code, but this is not necessary for the computer. The computer could just as easily take 'x(y,z)', 'huey(dewey,louie)' or 'mejs(sjex,sjfjg)' to represent Mimi's relation to Emmy, or take 'mother_of(mimi,emmy)' to represent that Brussels is the capital of

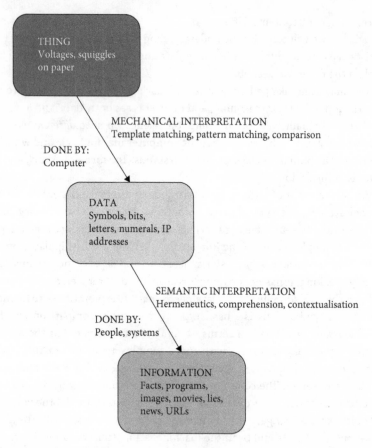

Figure 1.2. Mechanical and semantic interpretation.

Belgium. It just has to be consistent (so, in the latter case, would have to take 'mimi' to represent Brussels through the entire program). This mnemonic practice is common in computer science, where the aim is to render one's code readable by collaborating engineers, but not in mathematics or physics, where variables are often represented by a single letter, paradigmatically 'x'. Einstein could have written 'energy = mass times speed(light)^2', but being a physicist, he chose to write 'e = mc^2', rendering the formula a little more mysterious than it need be.

When we add context and interpretation to the data, we get *information*. When we interpret 'mother_of' as representing a particular relation, and 'mimi' and 'emmy' as two real-world entities, then we can say that the preceding data represents, contains, or means the information that the entities are connected by the relation, most probably in this case that Mimi is the mother of Emmy. Hence data and information are the same stuff, except information requires a semantic interpretation of the symbols which make it up. Computers do *not* do this interpretation; they deal only with uninterpreted data, and care not what it is all about. A parallel: the Post Office deals only with letters, and cares not what is in them. It must interpret something *as* a letter in order to deal with it, but its contents are not of interest to it, and it has no corporate capability for acting on them.

Note that the same set of symbols can be interpreted in a variety of ways, so the data does not tell you what information it carries. You have to bring the interpretation to it. For instance, take the string of bits '00100100'. One interpretation of this data might be the integer number expressed in binary, which in this case, re-expressed in decimal, would be 36. A second interpretation might be in terms of the American Standard Code for Information Interchange (ASCII), which is a standard for encoding text characters as strings of bits so they can be manipulated by computers. This particular string represents the dollar sign '$'. A third interpretation might be a series of answers to survey questions: 'no, no, yes, no, no, yes, no, no'. A fourth interpretation is the colour of an individual pixel on an 8-bit colour scheme. And so on—there is no limit to the number of ways we could interpret that piece of data to produce information, although only a tiny proportion would be useful.

We should also mention that not all interpretation is concerned with the message that the data is carrying. For instance, a signature does contain a message—a name—but its importance is not in the name particularly, which is often unreadable, but the two-dimensional form it takes, which needs to be similar enough to a specimen signature to authenticate it *as* a signature of a particular person. This type of interpretation is important in areas such as cybersecurity, but for the rest of this book we will make the simplifying assumption that the important thing about data is the message it carries, and that data + interpretation equals information, so any information stored in a computer is also data. Information is a relatively abstract concept, and when we want to draw attention to the medium of representation, then we will generally refer to data rather than information. But continue to bear in mind that even though we can often see that the data is 'about' something, a computer system cannot see that, and does not need to.

Information comes in many kinds. Some purports to be declarative information about the world, Mimi's being the mother of Emmy being an example. The information is true only in the case that Mimi is indeed the mother of Emmy, and false otherwise. Fake news, which is an important topic for us, is a false description of the world purporting to be a news item, and hence is data interpreted as declarative information.

Not all information is like this. We can take data and interpret it as other kinds of things. A *computer program* is data, which we interpret as a set of instructions. This interpretation goes quite deep; the computer is only able to deal with *machine code*, which directly manipulates bits. *Source code*, readable by humans but not computers, provides an interpretation of what the computer is able to do with the bits. The computer languages that we see written down are source code, and therefore information; having been written by humans, they are then *compiled* into data that can make the central processing unit perform a combination of its basic arithmetical, logical, and control tasks. A program is a special case of a set of *instructions*, or a *plan*, which cannot be true or false. Though these are not true or false, they can still be malign. A program designed to cause harm is called *malware*.

Other examples of information are images in JPEG, audio files in MP3, representing sounds, or video files in MP4. These can also be misleading, once they are semantically interpreted in a certain way. As an example, a video of violent aggression may be informative if understood properly (e.g. as a segment of a fictional movie, or as a piece of evidence in a courtroom), and misleading if mislabelled. We may also distinguish between images, audio and video that are captured by cameras and microphones, and those that are created or doctored using digital equipment (such as so-called *deepfakes*). Even then, the distinction isn't always clear or relevant. Disney's *Frozen* is in one sense a deepfake video, created entirely by animators, but hardly misleading. A scene from a live action film such as *The Shawshank Redemption* clearly happened, as the actors moved and spoke as they appear on the film, but it's not the same as documentary footage, where people also move and speak as they appear to do, but not to a script. However, these differences in genre have nothing to do with the technology used to capture them.

Interpretation, then, may come in two stages. First of all, a software program mechanically interprets the data as a set of symbols and produces some output, which may be a piece of text, an image, a video, or whatever. Typically, the data is deliberately structured to be readable by the program—if you try to open an image file with a word processor, you will see gibberish. Then there is a second, semantic layer of interpretation by a human being, or some social process, that perceives the output of the software as *meaning* something. A misleading image or a deepfake video depends on the *machine* interpretation integrating with the semantic *human* or *social* one to produce the malign effect. This may be far more complex than we suggest here; one discussion distinguishes between content's nature (what it depicts), intent (the effect its consumption is meant to have), unintended consequences (what else it does beyond the first-order intent), and meaning (relative to specific contexts and cultures).[32]

Data *qua* data isn't the sort of stuff that can be true or false, but a complex piece of data may only have one plausible or intended mechanical interpretation. In that case, we do say as shorthand that the data is true/false/misleading, meaning really that *the associated information is true/false/misleading*. 'mother_of(mimi,emmy)' is simple enough to have myriad interpretations, but the data in a 100-megabyte MP4 file will realistically only represent one movie. This particularly matters when we consider data from devices such as sensors. A sensor comes with a transfer function that models its output for each possible input, which is used as the basis for its semantic interpretation. If the output of the sensor is X, then we read backwards through the function to what input(s) might have caused it, and then interpret (at the semantic level) the data as *meaning* or *signalling* that the environment had whatever properties the sensor was designed to detect (say, the ambient temperature, or a movement within a particular location). Errors may creep into sensor performance, which mean that we constantly need to recalibrate them, but the design of the sensor as expressed by the transfer function gives us a straightforward and usually uncontroversial interpretation of the data. Hence we talk of the sensor 'gathering data' about its environment (we mean that the data it gathers has a ready interpretation, in terms defined by the transfer function, as information about the environment).

When such a sensor is connected to an actuator, the data it produces can act directly upon its environment. For instance, if a sensor in a dam senses a high water level, then it could actuate a valve which is designed to release some water harmlessly. Here the data is not interpreted (at the semantic level) before being acted upon, but the design of the total sensor + valve system does require a global interpretation of the transfer function of the sensor with respect to the inputs it receives. Similarly, the actuator does no interpretation, but performs a relatively mechanical action that will require semantic interpretation from an observer in terms of its effects in a real-world context. For instance, an actuator might simply cause a valve to open, which in the real-world context is interpretable by human observers as, say, draining the reservoir if the pressure on the dam is dangerously high. The sensor knows nothing of the dam, and the actuator knows nothing of the reservoir.[33] When we connect a sensor directly to an actuator, we need to be sure that the data that the sensor collects does, when interpreted, produce a description of reality that legitimizes the action that the actuator performs, for we are in effect taking the human out of the loop (perhaps for perfectly good reasons of speed, efficiency, or accuracy).

As another example, consider the record of an online transaction. When one buys something on an e-commerce site, the site will generally gather as much data as is feasible about the transaction, including data that will enable it to link the transaction to others, for example from cookies. The stored data will be maintained by the site with a ready-made interpretation, based on its own data storage and representation practices. As with other online data-gathering exercises, such as storing clickstreams, the data only has one realistic semantic interpretation thanks to the design of the system, but we should maintain the conceptual distinction between the data and the associated information.

Consequently, we can talk about, for example, location data (data gathered by devices which is informative about the device's, and therefore its owner's, location at a time), search data (data gathered by search engines about search terms from a computer), or biometric data (data gathered through a process of measuring someone's unique personal characteristics). All these kinds of data are also information when given the appropriate or conventional interpretation, but common usage and our concern with the computational context sometimes make it more intuitive and familiar to write about them as data. Storage and transfer will concern us, as least as much as interpretation.

POWER: DATA

In many cases, the terms 'data' and 'information' can be used interchangeably with philosophical impropriety but without much harm. All information in a computational context is represented by a piece of data, and furthermore, if data is being moved around a system, the usual reason is that it is held to be information—no point moving garbage around. This is where we should emphasize that the distinction between *uninterpreted data* and *interpreted information* is important, if often overlooked. When we talk of engineering the flow around a digital system, we are usually referring to the *flow of data*, because to the system hardware, any meaning that attaches to the 1s and 0s is irrelevant. It doesn't matter to the system whether they can be interpreted as meaning 'President Trump addressed a rally in North Carolina', or 'sjfcnfuess3', or 'President Obama is not a natural-born citizen of the United States'. Hence the hardware is focused entirely on getting the data from A to B as effectively as possible, independently of whether its interpretation produces truth, nonsense, or conspiratorial falsehood.

In terms of value, this matters. It is certainly meaningful to talk about the delivery of bits over the Internet in terms of efficiency, speed, reliability, and so on. The quicker, safer, and more efficient the transport, the better the system. But when we *interpret* the data so that we are concerned with the flow of meaningful *information*, the system doesn't necessarily work better just because it travels quickly. In particular, you might want *reliable* information to travel more efficiently than the unreliable sort. Whereas, on the contrary, it has been argued that Twitter furnishes its users more quickly with dross than with gold[34] (*pace* optimists who once dubbed it a 'truth machine').[35] One is reminded of Hannah Arendt's concept of the banality of evil, in which issues with great moral depth are treated as technical problems and solved as such.[36]

In our dealings with data/information, we need to consider its *quality*, which goes beyond mere truth of the information carried.[37] For example, we need to guard against a *closed world assumption* that the information completely describes a situation. There is probably more relevant information about the situation that is not represented in the database, and we certainly don't want to act as though 'if you're not represented in the data, you don't exist'. Second, we cannot expect total *consistency* between datasets and certainly not between the information that comes with their interpretation. Different methodologies, schemas, and techniques for gathering data will lead to differences of point of view, and we need to be careful about informational consistency, especially with data from heterogeneous sources. Third, we need to be aware of the uncertainty at any stage about decisions taken, and to guard against *hindsight*. And fourthly, we do not need to use all the data we collect. Informational *dignity* and *self-determination* are also important values that may require restricting our use of available data, or reducing the amount of data we collect. There are levels of precision, concision, and unambiguity. We might also look at the context of information, and think of its relevance, timeliness, and completeness. We would also want it to be easily interpretable. With respect to data, it is important that it be reliable, and that its interpretation is straightforward (even if the information that results is not so straightforward). Is it correctly formatted, and presented in an accessible way? Is it presented with useful metadata, so that we can contextualize it?[38]

Assuming the appropriate quality, data has a number of curious economic properties. It is *non-rivalrous*, which means that just because one person is using it, it doesn't mean that others can't too (unlike a physical good, like a chair, where one person sitting in it excludes everybody else). But it is also *excludable*, which means that others can be prevented from using it, for example by firewalls or encryption.[39] This means that it could be a private good, a new 'asset class' (as the World Economic Forum suggested personal data might become),[40] or something providing public value (a 'national asset').[41]

The massive growth of data creation in the last few years has been largely fuelled by the Internet, either because certain types of behaviour have migrated online, and can therefore be tracked and remembered (the spread of the smartphone has been a big part of that), or because new hardware has enabled the generation of data via Internet connections. For instance, autonomous vehicles will be able to effectively gather and transmit information about their journeys in real time, and to share the underlying data with other vehicles to anticipate congestion or other problems. Furthermore, the processing of very large quantities of data, whether produced on the Internet or not, may realistically need the Internet via cloud computing, because standalone technology will not have the capacity.

The potential surrounding the amalgamation of data from various sources has led to a great deal of hype about what is best called *data science*,[42] but is also often termed *machine learning* (ML)[43] or *artificial intelligence* (AI). AI is the term that has caught on, so we will use that. The idea is that very large quantities of data, ideally from a variety of heterogeneous sources, will produce a rich picture of the world—perhaps even a *digital twin*—and processing this data using ML or AI techniques can bring enormous insight.[44] Such giant and diverse datasets are often termed *big data*, sometimes characterized by three

Vs—a large *volume* of data, from a wide *variety* of sources, created and processed with great *velocity*.[45]

Data therefore gives access to a type of *power*, a means to survey and regulate a context, what social theorist Michel Foucault called *power/knowledge*.[46] As the nineteenth-century anarchist Proudhon wrote, not without justification, with his characteristic understatement:

> To be governed is to be watched, inspected, spied upon, directed, law-driven, numbered, regulated, enrolled, indoctrinated, preached at, controlled, checked, estimated, valued, censured, commanded, by creatures who have neither the right nor the wisdom nor the virtue to do so. To be governed is to be at every operation, at every transaction noted, registered, counted, taxed, stamped, measured, numbered, assessed, licensed, authorized, admonished, prevented, forbidden, reformed, corrected, punished. It is, under pretext of public utility, and in the name of the general interest, to be placed under contribution, drilled, fleeced, exploited, monopolized, extorted from, squeezed, hoaxed, robbed; then, at the slightest resistance, the first word of complaint, to be repressed, fined, vilified, harassed, hunted down, abused, clubbed, disarmed, bound, choked, imprisoned, judged, condemned, shot, deported, sacrificed, sold, betrayed; and to crown all, mocked, ridiculed, derided, outraged, dishonoured. That is government; that is its justice; that is its morality.[47]

The purpose of data-gathering is still as reflected in this Victorian complaint, to make a population legible, understandable, readable to those collecting the data.[48] In Proudhon's era, this would have been the state, but in the twenty-first century, we find private actors in the same game—who are often rather more effective.[49] Making a population legible to authorities need not work to their disadvantage, despite Proudhon's complaints—it may support government and welfare services, green technologies, or medical research. Our point is only that it gives power to whoever holds the data.

This leads us to a second proposition we wish to explore, which is that **the different principles respecting the Internet have a strong connection with attitudes towards data, which is the chief source of power on the Internet**.

THE INTERNET'S SOCIAL INFLUENCE: DIGITAL MODERNITY

The Internet is an ideological battleground, as it is an agent of social change that links civilizations and cultures, spreading information, and suppressing parochialism. It is the key driver in the development of modernity, from what we might call a twentieth-century *analogue* modernity, based on Enlightenment values, rationalism, and individualism, to a technologically inspired *digital modernity*.[50] Modernity has always been expressed variously across cultures, [51] and the battle for the Internet is a battle to drive digital modernity in certain directions, to resist it, or to resist aspects of it. The philosophies, ideologies, and cultures that have a view on the Internet's development identify a 'pure' digital modernity as an instrumental extension of Western values embodied in technology. In Part II of this book, we will explore this value/technology nexus, which is focused on *openness*, *networks*, and *data*.

Modernity, and the process of modernization, can appear in *descriptive*, *teleological*, and *normative* form.[52] *Descriptively*, we often say that greater uptake of technology, alongside other developments, such as an increase in the urban population, internationalization of culture, and the development of abstract, rational, professional, and expert systems, can be summarized in the simple statement that a place is *modernizing*. *Teleologically*, modernization is often experienced as a natural, unstoppable *process* that unfolds inexorably (the pre-eminent theorist of modernity Anthony Giddens uses the image of the juggernaut).[53] Viewed *normatively*, governments, companies, and even individuals *should* work to modernize their society or economy. The Internet has a particularly powerful role to play in this, facilitating globalization and expert systems, undermining traditional practices and hierarchies, and disintermediating existing practices.

Our aim here is not to critique these descriptive, teleological, and normative narratives (this has been attempted elsewhere);[54] they are set out here as important context for the politics we describe in this book. There is nothing inevitable about them, and the Internet and networked technology can provide many goods, such as justice, without manifesting themselves in digital modernity.[55] The truth or falsity of the digital modernization narrative is less to the point than that policymakers and organizations subscribe to it.[56] As the Thomas theorem has it: 'if men define situations as real, they are real in their consequences'.[57]

With that in mind, the language of modernization has driven many developments in Silicon Valley and the technology industry, where the implementation of modern ideas, processes, and technologies is often seen as an unalloyed good (political theorist Francis Fukuyama writes that 'the desire to live in a modern—that is, technologically advanced and prosperous—society' is 'universal').[58] Governments the world over have also signed up to these ideas, working to implement digital government, and where possible courting major figures from the technology industry. Many have represented these developments as leading to new societies, or discontinuities in human history, in which the technology actively reshapes the lives of people and the futures of nations and businesses. Digital modernity is therefore perceived and presented as a much more singular and revolutionary state than modernity in general.[59]

Modernity is a relative term—a society or culture is *more* modern than another, which could be another society or an earlier stage of the same society (a) where tradition and geography are stronger influences than rationalism and abstraction, (b) which are exclusive rather than inclusive, and (c) where social structures are constraining, imposed hierarchies, as opposed to contractual, transactional networks. Modernization narratives typically contrast *backward* societies and *advanced* ones on a single dimension, implying that if the backward society ceases to stubbornly resist progress, it will eventually evolve to become advanced. It is also possible for advanced societies to, as the revealing saying goes, slip back into backwardness or even barbarism, following failure of technology, natural calamity, social unrest, or rejection of advanced political wisdom.[60]

An important and often-noted effect of digital technology is to compress time, as increasingly many events or actions can take place within a given interval.[61] Automation of response means that entire processes involving the complex interaction of several agents can be carried out in a barely perceptible interval. Even processes that necessarily include humans in the loop can be disintermediated to focus on the efficiency of the basic input-output. Romance, which used to be the subject of nineteenth-century novels of hundreds of pages narrating the events of decades, can now be short-circuited from discovery to consummation in an evening using a dating app such as Tinder.[62]

On this narrative, it is the nature of digital technology to disintermediate and disrupt existing processes, where technologists look to create innovation. The ability of the advanced society to innovate at will distinguishes it from the backward one, and a highly advanced society would be expected to innovate routinely. If innovation is as disruptive as claimed,[63] the digitally modern society will be super-disruptive, a world of startups where disruption is routine, and where institutions and entrepreneurs would be expected to adapt constantly to new pressures:[64] Schumpeter's world of creative destruction come to fruition.[65]

Taken to the limit, this is a world in which to be advanced is to be a disruptor, and therefore it follows immediately that *to exist is to be backward*. Once a system is implemented, or a product produced, it is ripe for disruption from radical innovators.[66] The classic cases are Airbnb[67] and Uber,[68] each of which has not only disrupted an industry (of tourist accommodation and taxis, respectively), but also challenged regulatory systems across the globe. Even before the COVID-19 pandemic, which has forced them both to adapt, they were already the targets of new disruptive competitors.

Depending on one's view of digital modernity, the ability of the Internet to spread ideas, or to be the locus of innovation, may be seen as something to be nurtured, or to be managed and controlled, or even to be rejected. Networks tend to be more disruptive than hierarchies, partly because ideas travel quickly through connected networks and less so across vertical hierarchies, and partly because a centralized hierarchy might plan and take measures to prevent disruption, whereas a decentralized network is less likely to have such a brake.

This leads us to a third proposition around which we will structure our enquiry: *the visions and models of the Internet we discuss in this book are all, in their way, responses to the prime imperatives of digital modernity* that existence is backward and disruption should be routine.

In particular, we will argue that four visions of the Internet have gained prominence, partly because of the coherence of the viewpoints, partly because they have backing from major geopolitical actors, and partly because there is a sociotechnical infrastructure ready to implement them. Because of the political element, there is overlap between Mueller's argument about alignment of the Internet with national jurisdictions and our own. Where ours differs is that these are visions for the *Internet*, and so are meant to determine how the Internet functions *globally*; they are not the simple desire to restrict the function of the Internet within a particular jurisdiction. They may have effects in common; for instance, an entity may want to allow a particular type of censorship within its borders, which may require making common cause with nations who may also wish to have the power of censorship. However, some entities also see the Internet as a potential tool of foreign policy, which goes far beyond the internal control of communications.

We begin our exploration in Part I with a survey of the development of the Internet along the lines of the original open vision, which in many senses has powered the 'pure' idea of digital modernity. Part II will look at the responses to this idea. Part III will plot potential developments and future pressure points, in particular looking at those technologies where the confluence of networks and data is likely to influence the evolution of digital modernity itself.

PART I

The First Internet

The Silicon Valley Open Internet

The Internet has always been a focus of ideals of communication and free flow of information. This was partly because of a broadly libertarian prejudice on the part of the pioneers who built it, but also because of engineering imperatives. The free and efficient flow of bits that make up the data requires decentralization (to prevent bottlenecks occurring at choke points as the system scales), open standards (to allow interoperability and therefore the indefinite extension and scaling up of the network), and IP addresses (to identify destinations correctly). Connecting everything to everything worked since it was being designed as a platform for military command and control. Everything in the system was to collaborate to produce the desired effect.[1] We take this system for granted, but one doesn't need a very long memory to recall a time when IT was dominated by proprietary protocols like AppleTalk or DECnet, and when one couldn't easily send an email from AOL to Prodigy. Yet the Internet hasn't simply improved magically: it has evolved into an open system as a result of philosophical and political decisions, as well as technical ones.

Governance is the set of arrangements that enable decisions to be taken and enforced about a particular problem, institution, system, or set of objects. These arrangements coordinate interaction and decision-making that support the continued existence or reproduction of whatever is governed. They are in some sense authoritative, in that the arrangements will be followed by, constrain, or influence participants. Governance may involve coercion, incentives, or simply coordination. Sometimes it invokes moral considerations, but not always; when they are in play, ethical questions can be about what is governed (does the governance prevent bad behaviour? does it treat everyone fairly and equally?), or about the governance itself (are the right people making the decisions?). The Internet got where it is with minimal help from 'hard' law and regulation, recalling Internet pioneer David Clark's legendary motto that 'we reject kings, presidents and voting. We believe in rough consensus and running code.'[2] In the case of the Internet, technical considerations are also important inputs into governance. A technical innovation may influence or restrict the behaviour of millions or even billions of people.

For these reasons, in this book we prefer to refer to governance in the wider sense. Internet governance, as with most valued social systems, has grown up in an ad hoc manner, with measures and institutions adopted opportunistically to solve specific problems of coordination that have emerged over time. It is not a designed or streamlined system, but a constantly evolving, even emergent, ecosystem of constraints, norms, roles, rules, sanctions, standards, ideals, and protocols, implemented or challenged by international organizations, states, companies, non-profits, collectives, engineers, activists, criminals, social networks, social movements, visionaries, and lawyers.[3]

In Part I of this book, we will explore some of the philosophical and political decisions taken by this motley crew, and how they led to a particular 'purist' view of the Internet as an open information system, the first of our Four Internets—the first, not only because it was the earliest vision of the Internet to take on form and coherence, but also because in many ways it is conceptually prior to alternative visions, which will be the focus of Part II.

CHAPTER 2

How the Internet Developed

The development of the Internet has been a contingent matter, under constraints of technology, human resources, budgets, politics, the Cold War, business needs, and philosophical fashion. Many histories of the Internet focus on the individuals that made a difference, and, for ease of making the narrative, this book will often succumb to that temptation. However, it is important to understand that most innovations require groups of people working together, and don't appear from nowhere; the role of women in particular tends to get airbrushed from the histories.[1]

THE INTERNET'S PREHISTORY

The Internet's development began as an attempt to improve on batch processing for early stand-alone computers, whose operating systems (OSs) ran a 'batch' of programs in order, so that at any time a single program had control of the machine. This seemed wasteful for many purposes (not least because as computers sped up, the time taken to make the transition from one program to the next in the batch became a higher percentage of computer time), prompting research into parallel running of programs, and ultimately remote access via individual workstations, so that each 'computer' became in effect a very small network centred around a processing hub that did the computational work on demand. From here, the idea of linking computers themselves, using the pre-existing telephone network, was a fairly natural suggestion. J. C. R. Licklider, in a position of some power as director of the Information Processing Techniques Office at the Advanced Research Projects Agency (ARPA) in the US Department of Defense in the early 1960s, was able to fund research into the idea that ultimately one could connect all computers

Four Internets. Kieron O'Hara and Wendy Hall, Oxford University Press. © Oxford University Press 2021.
DOI: 10.1093/oso/9780197523681.003.0002

in such a way, to create the ARPANET network, which eventually went live in 1969, with an initial link between terminals at Doug Engelbart's laboratory at the Stanford Research Institute (now SRI International) and Len Kleinrock's at the University of California, Los Angeles.[2]

Its key technology was *packet switching*, an efficient and robust means for transferring data across a network. The sender initiates it by chopping the data into packets of uniform size, and attaching metadata to the packets about how to reassemble them, and giving their destination in a computer network. The sender pushes the packets into a network of connected computers, which, upon receiving a packet, check its metadata and forward it to another computer nearer its destination. Packets would not necessarily take the same route across the network, and as the network became more complex they would all take different routes. At the destination node, when all the packets were received, the receiving computer would use the metadata to reassemble the original data. The ARPANET connected geographically clustered networks via their host computers (e.g. at a particular university), using the telephone network, and so its ambitions at this stage were as a purely national proof of concept. The Network Information Center (NIC), run by Elizabeth Feinler, was required to keep track of addresses and coordinate ARPANET's operation as it grew.[3]

Packet switching produced a communication network that was robust to attack—remove one or more nodes from the network, and the network would still operate, as long as it remained connected (note that this implies redundancy in the network—there should be several routes from A to B), ensuring that communication could continue even if military strikes took out some communications hubs. Packet switching was not proprietary to the ARPANET. It was also promoted by scientists in the United Kingdom, who were impressed by its efficiency; if particular connections become congested, packets can easily be routed around them, thereby allowing speedy and resilient commercial use of data. Sadly, reliant on the government-run monopoly communications infrastructure, the British suggestion foundered. One interesting aspect of the development of the Internet is the reluctance of telecommunications monopolies such as the UK General Post Office and AT&T to engage with it in its formative years. Britain's telecoms network was split off in 1980, and became a private company in 1984; it is intriguing to imagine how the Internet might have developed differently had a commercial motive been introduced in the United Kingdom at this stage. Europe was finally connected to the ARPANET in 1973.[4]

Using packet switching across a network established three important ideas of how information could best be transferred. First, the nodes would take as little interest as possible in the packets, ignoring their contents entirely and examining only their metadata. Second, when a network joined others, it would commit to forwarding packets appropriately on behalf of other networks, and thereby doing some *pro bono* work. And third, perhaps most important, an *end-to-end* principle was established, whereby the bulk of the data processing happened at the sending and receiving nodes, minimizing the processing required en route. This really was innovative; other commonly used networks, such as the telephone network, do relatively little work at the ends (the telephones, in this case), so that the networks themselves perform at least some vital functions. The end-to-end principle improves efficiency by reducing congestion at bottlenecks.

It is important to remember that other networks flourished alongside the ARPANET, many but not all in the United States. Licklider's global vision was hamstrung by the incompatible protocols of these networks, which therefore led separate and parallel existences. Although the contents of the packets are irrelevant to a packet-switching network, the metadata needs to be understood across the network, interpreted and acted upon consistently. Hence each networked computer needs compatible protocols to express the metadata, and the appropriate actions that follow its interpretation.

THE INTERNET ARRIVES

The work of Vinton Cerf and Robert Kahn for the now-renamed DARPA got around the lack of standards by defining a protocol that would work on heterogeneous networks, thus being compatible with as many other protocols as possible, exploiting the end-to-end property of the networks by ignoring as far as possible their idiosyncrasies. The result of their work was TCP/IP, finalized in 1978, which became the approved ARPANET protocol in 1983, and subsequently was adopted by most of the leading networks. All ARPANET hosts were running TCP/IP by the end of 1983, and that year is often taken as the beginning of the Internet, when TCP/IP became the means to connect ARPANET with other packet-switching networks such as the Packet Radio Network and the Packet Satellite Network (although DARPA continued to fund the creation of TCP/IP implementations of important OSs such as UNIX, to the tune of tens of millions of dollars, so we shouldn't think of the Internet even at that stage as a done deal).[5]

The beauty of TCP/IP is thus that it connects networks without constraining them, so it acts as a *lingua franca*, which we take as the defining aspect of what we call 'the Internet'. The network is not controlled by anyone, so any network or computer able to follow TCP/IP could join; in other words, it is a *permissionless* system. By the end of the 1980s, Europe was firmly integrated, with the help of research groups such as that of Cerf's collaborator Peter Kirstein of University College, London, which connected to the ARPANET in 1973 and adopted TCP/IP early, in 1982.[6] The ARPANET was decommissioned in 1990, leaving the Internet as a worldwide, self-standing network of networks. Cerf and Kahn anticipated the importance of their innovation with a newly minted term: 'Internet', signifying the *Internetwork* as a network of networks, and *internetworking* as the practice of joining networks together.[7]

The US government still played an important part, as the National Science Foundation's NSFNET acted as the skeleton of the newly minted Internet (other important backbones sponsored by the government included the Department of Energy's ESNET and NASA's NSINET).[8] The voluntary open standards defining the Internet, particularly TCP/IP, were developed by the Internet Engineering Task Force (IETF), also originally set up by the US government in 1986. Government involvement made commercial innovation difficult, for both legal and political reasons, and so the NSF pushed the Internet into the private sector (the IETF was handed over to the non-profit Internet Society [ISOC] in 1993). Privatization was a key decision, and the future of the Internet was influenced by the way it happened. It might simply have been transferred to a major company like AT&T or IBM, but the decision was taken to open it up to what became known as *Internet Service Providers* (ISPs).[9]

The role of ISPs in addressing illustrates the delicate balancing acts in Internet governance, and the way that technical issues require institutional implementation as well as technological solutions. For example, let's consider how data gets to its final destination. The main identifier introduced by IP is the numerical IP address, which specifies a single—but not necessarily permanent—destination for data; most addresses are assigned dynamically to computers, so they are more akin to a piece of rental property than a permanent address. A single IP address is typically occupied by different computers over time, but by only a single one at a time, and hence is always unique. The assignment is done by *registries* that allocate them in batches to ISPs, and by the ISPs that go on to assign smaller groups to networks of computers which have paid for the service. Dynamic addressing leads to greater efficiency, preventing a scarcity of available addresses while many stand vacant. You only use as many addresses as needed at any particular time.

It also sets a few puzzles. Firstly, the management of IP addresses by senders and receivers of data in the network is only straightforward as long as they stay constant in between a request for information and its receipt. When combined with the mechanism of packet switching, a coordination problem will arise, as sending a packet through the network depends on knowing where all the addresses are, and crucially that they haven't changed, during its journey. Imagine posting a letter without knowing for sure that your correspondent will remain at the address long enough to receive it. The Internet gets round this by assigning part of the address to a sub-network, and having devices called routers which use these for deciding where to send packets. Routers and address registries must constantly inform each other about changes to assignments, so that means a lot of extra information having to flow around the network to maintain packet-switching schedules, so that the 'dumb' network with its end-to-end principle has to do a bit of work after all, keeping track of which computer is referred to by which IP address.

Secondly, the ability of the network to do this constrains its ability to scale. One aim of the decentralized Internet architecture is to allow new people to join the network easily, but there is an obvious problem if there aren't enough IP addresses to go round. This was an issue with earlier versions, and a difficult (and not yet complete) upgrade was required from Internet Protocol version 4 (IPv4), whose addresses are 32 bits in length (i.e. there are 2^{32} of them, about four and a quarter billion), to IPv6, 128 bits long, which became a draft IETF standard as long ago as 1998. We will return to this issue later.

A third issue is that if the amount of information that routers have to process for packet switching increases too quickly, they will not be able to plan routes efficiently enough. Technologically, this problem is under control, but the cost of the solution is that organizations can't take their blocks of IP addresses with them if they change their ISPs, and unused IP address blocks can't be traded. These mean that addressing can't be as efficient as it could be, as the cost of efficient addressing would be inefficiency of packet switching.[10]

ISPs jointly cooperate on a gateway to exchange data between them, to give users a seamless experience of the Internet—a system known as *peering*, located at physical structures known as *Internet Exchange Points*, or IXPs. The exchange of data at IXPs is largely free, their upkeep paid for by charging the ISPs for access, which pay from the revenue they receive from their customers. This turns out to be essential for the free movement of data round the network; had the IXPs demanded payment per bit of data exchanged, that would have had the effect of putting a meter on the dataflow, and ISPs would have tried to save money by inhibiting the flow of data through IXPs. Furthermore, routing decisions for data would have had to take the number of exchanges into account, making them more complex, and requiring even more intelligence in the network. As peering is effectively charged at a flat rate, there are no economic disincentives for rich dataflow.[11]

The story is not exclusively technical. The early steps of the Internet were taken in response to uses and demands of relatively small but influential groups of people. Most obviously, engineers in universities, companies, and government agencies shaped the network, but not only through the designs they created, protocols they wrote, and funding decisions they made. The Internet was woven into this research culture at an early stage, and the researchers used it to send messages, converse, and pass on insights, papers, and code, and this usage also informed the design; researchers designed the network to do what they wanted it to do, which is what they were already using it to do. Bulletin Boards allowed like-minded groups, interested in topics such as *Star Trek*, Buddhism, or feminism, as well as the mechanics of programming themselves, to get together, chat, and play. Early businesses also chipped in.[12]

Thus the medium became a space where a reasonably *simpático* set of well-behaved and culturally aligned people congregated, even if separated by geography, and the Internet gradually came to signify both a technically linked net of machines and a socially linked network of people. Such people collaborated in designing and developing the new space, and a principle of consensus emerged, exemplified by the RFC (Request For Comments), which would be placed in the documentation for a new program or specification, inviting positive and negative feedback. An RFC is not a formal constraint, but invites discussion, amendment, and improvement, and is a means of demonstrating consensus among a wide group. And because they were like-minded, culturally similar, often government-funded, and generally acting in good faith, security and censorship hardly seemed pressing (John Gilmore, one of the founders of the Electronic Frontier Foundation, pointed out in 1993 that 'the Net interprets censorship as damage and routes around it'.).[13] Bad behaviour took relatively asinine and apparently harmless forms, such as flaming, where a discussion would degenerate into argument and insult, often written in capital letters with lots of exclamation marks. But as the Internet grew, new populations supplanted the small group of engineers, behaviour deteriorated, and bad faith (or simply different interests) needed to be factored in. With commerce would come cybercrime; with e-government would come spying and cyberwarfare.[14]

The Internet is often conceived using immaterial metaphors—'cloud', 'cyberspace', 'Web', 'virtual'—or liminal ones—'surfing', 'superhighway', 'portal'. But it is very much a real-world phenomenon with important political, social, and economic effects. We can sketch its basic principles, and see how they led to the extraordinary technology in place today. In this section we have looked at some technical matters, some institutional matters, and the social factors involved in its creation. The Internet Architecture Board Network Working Group asserted in 1996 that 'the community believes that the goal is connectivity, the tool is the Internet Protocol, and the intelligence is end to end rather than hidden in the network'.[15] We might add the importance of decentralization, the ease of joining the network, and the technology of packet switching.

APPLICATIONS ON THE INTERNET

Because no permission is needed, it is relatively straightforward to create an application to which access is gained via the Internet; the application *sits on* the Internet, as it were, using it to transfer data. Some applications have grown to such size and pervasiveness that they are often mistaken for the Internet, and for many might be the only access to it. Examples include the World Wide Web and Facebook; the former was the main vector for the massive growth of the Internet in the early 1990s, while the latter certainly would like to be the gateway to the Internet in parts of the developing world (see Chapter 9). Yet we mustn't confuse the application with the delivery method, like confusing the train with the track. The Internet delivers the application, and its lightweight design has meant that it has been able to scale up, and deliver ever more data to ever more users, continuing to support these applications, even while it grows. The current scale of the Internet must be beyond the wildest of dreams of all but the most visionary of its pioneers.

The Web was the brainchild of physicist Tim Berners-Lee, who wanted an application to enable scientists to see each other's papers and data and collaborate, using the Internet protocols. The basic technology, *hypertext*, had already been widely theorized by thinkers such as Ted Nelson; a non-linear conception of text whereby links in the text could take the reader to an arbitrary text or graphic elsewhere in the document, in a different version of the document, or even in a different document altogether.[16] Berners-Lee's idea was not only to put the hypertext system on the Internet to facilitate access and use, but also to make it an open, permissionless, system describable with open and transparent standards, and requiring neither licence nor fee to exploit the intellectual property of the protocols. The key protocols were the Hypertext Transfer Protocol (HTTP) that governs how hypertext documents get transferred across the Web, the Hypertext Markup Language (HTML), which describes the structure and layout of those documents, and the notion of a Uniform Resource Identifier (URI) or Locator (URL), that identifies a Web resource unambiguously, and also gives an indication of where the resource is held (commonly called a Web address).[17] A link created in one document to a second document utilizes the Web address of the second document, and clicking on the blue hyperlink in the first causes the Web browser to resolve (seek out) the destination address, and to present the resource it found there.

Ultimately, the Web evolved into a giant platform on which many further applications have been created—its openness supporting the spectacular growth of networks that would be inhibited in a closed or proprietary system. Its open standards are coordinated by a non-profit organization called the World Wide Web Consortium (W3C).

The growth of the Web was facilitated not only by W3C standards-setters, but also by people innovating on it, using W3C standards, to increase its utility. Mosaic was the first browser to display the hypertext documents on the Web as single entities, including the graphics, and so became the first commonly used access point. A browser turns the Web into a seamless experience, as if all the documents it displays were stored on one's own hard drive. Mosaic facilitated the growth of the Web, and inspired other browsers, including Netscape Navigator, Internet Explorer, Google Chrome, Firefox, and Safari.

The growth of the Web resulted in a wider user base, outgrowing the culture of academics and scientists sharing static documents, exposing its limitations.

Users wanted to personalize Web resources, conduct conversations, interact commercially (e-commerce), remember where they had been online, collaborate with others. So-called Web 2.0 arrived, with the development of *HTTPS* (a securely encrypted version of HTTP), *cookies* (which allowed websites to store current and previous states of their interactions with users, *JavaScript* (a programming language for webpages), browsers which were adaptable by *plugins* (for example, introducing audio and video), *RSS* (which kept readers updated about changes to websites), *APIs* (application programming interfaces, which allowed other websites and organizations access to a site's data), *wikis* (sites whose content could be modified collaboratively by users), and so on. None of these, and certainly not their combination, was planned from the top down; they may have been developed by specialized standards groups, but they were all responses to demand. Nevertheless, these technologies opened up the Web to innovations such as e-commerce, blogs, and complex games, and none of them required permission to develop; Web technology patent rates soared.[18] Web 2.0 is a heterogeneous set of tools and ideas, but between them they created a read-write Web sitting on top of a read-only Web 1.0 of static documents, which itself sits on top of the Internet transport network.[19]

Openness meant that collective intelligence could be realized by the artful aggregation of data, like a market arriving at a price through the balance of supply and demand. Peer review systems in e-commerce, such as eBay's seller ratings and Amazon's product reviews, allowed the bootstrapping of reputational trust for would-be purchasers, while other sites enabled the aggregation of lots of small chunks of information into, say, an encyclopaedia (such as Wikipedia) or a database of movie credits and reviews (such as IMDb, the Internet Movie Database).[20] Most spectacularly, Google's PageRank algorithm aggregated the information about which documents are linked on the Web. No single link creator need consider anything more than where it would be helpful to send a reader, but aggregation of all these decisions by PageRank resulted in the Google search engine, which became the market leader (partly through its brilliant algorithm, and partly because of the large quantity of data it generates about search, thanks to its popularity).[21]

One more development of the Web has been a move from linking documents (rendered as webpages), to linking data, via languages such as the Resource Description Framework (RDF), which uses URIs to describe and link objects and the relationships between them. In its more ambitious form, this ideal was called the *Semantic Web*, while the less ambitious desire merely to create links between pieces of data gives us the *Linked Data Web*.[22] The original Web linked entire documents, but the original vision was always meant to be extended to connect multimedia data, with 'the evolution of objects from being principally human-readable documents to contain more machine-oriented semantic information, allowing more sophisticated processing'.[23] The Linked Data Web now allows individual pieces of data to be linked, so, for example, it is possible to automate the extraction of all the data about a particular object (via its URI) expressed in RDF from a large series of documents (or, put another way, RDF enables someone to turn data distributed over the Web into a structure analogous to a single spreadsheet). This concept enables a number of important applications, such as Google's *knowledge graph*, a giant database of entities, concepts, and links that populates the 'infoboxes' positioned to the right of Google search pages.

Another important application is the cloud. Cloud computing is the pooling of data storage and processing capabilities, maintained by cloud providers such as Apple, Microsoft, and Amazon, accessible to users from any Internet-connected device. Data centres make data available to users as they need it; the data might be private data (such as photographs or audio files), software, or computing infrastructure. The arrangement means that programs and data storage no longer represent up-front costs for a user, but are delivered as services, allowing economies of scale while users pay only for the computing power they use. The cloud is made possible by high-speed, high-reliability networks, and can be public, private, commercial, or in-house (so one organization can run a cloud for all its computing needs). It raises interesting issues of jurisdiction (the data centres which make up the cloud hold data in a particular nation—does its government get access to the data?), security (how should the data be protected?), privacy (what data is legal to keep?), and liability (who is responsible if it goes missing?).

The cloud was in turn important for the revolution of mobile computing via smartphones. Mobile devices, including larger tablet computers, as well as the sensors that are crucial for the so-called Internet of Things, have the potential to attract billions more to the Internet, as they do not require the hefty investment in hardware or reliable electricity supplies needed for desktop computing. Mobile devices can access programs and data (input and output) in a cloud when needed, giving them impressive functionality, despite being small with limited power supplies.

All of these developments have cumulatively made the way for what for many is the ultimate application of the Internet. *Social media*, linked in particular to social networking sites (SNSs) such as Facebook[24] and Instagram,[25] as well as former SNSs such as Friendster and MySpace, and special-purpose ones like LinkedIn, have turned out to be extremely important applications. They allow users to construct profiles of themselves which act as points of contact, avatars of the real-world individual, to connect their profiles with those of others, and to communicate, interact, and share (often user-generated) content.[26] 'Classic' SNSs share features with other types of sites, such as gaming, microblogging, and media-sharing sites, where networks of contacts and friends also help determine the user experience.[27] The graphs of these social networks are valuable to users, to SNSs, and to third parties (such as advertisers), as are the data trails that interactions leave behind.[28]

CHAPTER 3

Governing the Internet

Internet governance emerged as the technology blossomed, but in general has been reactive to developments both within and without the Internet. Many structures and institutions are post hoc rationalizations of improvisations that made sense in a particular milieu populated by a not-too-diverse set of actors whose good faith could more or less be assumed, on an Internet that was less pervasive and used for fewer purposes than it is now. The question of Internet governance as a whole has generated a whole skeleton-worth of bones of contention, as it has outgrown this homogeneous community to include billions of people across the globe. In this chapter, we will consider how it is governed, but first we look at who might have the right to govern it at all.

LEGITIMACY AND MULTISTAKEHOLDERISM

Who gets to govern the Internet is hard to describe, with its complex mélange of states, public sector bodies, private companies, and non-profits, seasoned by the occasional guru. The history of the Internet is part of the explanation for its Heath Robinson (for US readers: Rube Goldberg) nature. The other part is the requirements dictated by the nature of the system. Legal relationships and top-down control, whether by contract or statute,[1] cannot be the whole story, because much of the behaviour is extra-legal and implicit within a community.[2] For instance, the IETF cannot mandate or police the usage of its standards, but merely asks that those who say they are using a standard do in fact use it (and properly). As such communities have been involved in the development of the Internet from the beginning quite successfully, and as this coincided with a general decrease in faith in top-down *dirigisme*, the legitimacy of private and informal means of regulating the Internet was accepted on the

Four Internets. Kieron O'Hara and Wendy Hall, Oxford University Press. © Oxford University Press 2021.
DOI: 10.1093/oso/9780197523681.003.0003

grounds of their success in practical innovation, their democratic ethos, and their compatibility with the growing anti-statist *Zeitgeist*.[3]

The United States began the Internet, and many of the important innovations were developed there; it retains an outsized influence. International bodies have called for responsibility for the Internet to be transferred to more international arenas; for example, the Working Group on Internet Governance under the auspices of the International Telecommunication Union (ITU) recommended in 2005 that the United States relinquish oversight of the system, ideally to be replaced by a UN body.[4] This was perhaps the first time that Internet governance emerged blinking from nerdy penumbra into the glaring spotlight of the geopolitical arena (although Russia had been pressing its case to detach Internet governance from the US at the ITU since the 1990s).[5] Although the pressures leading to the 2005 debate had existed before, the debate and the role of the United Nations and the ITU were crystallized at this point. Attempting to extend the ITU's mandate to cover the Internet became a focal point for dissenters such as China and Russia, as we will see, while the United Nations as a whole also staked its own claim, reinterpreting the Internet in the context of its wider social programmes (as for example with the High Level Panel for Digital Cooperation in 2019, which we mention briefly in the final chapter).[6]

The aim of such measures is to replace ad hoc, decentralized, distributed governance with a system of greater formality, on the ground that it would have greater global legitimacy.[7] The danger is that such a system would be centralized and sclerotic, focused on government power rather than the inclusion of, for example, civil society or industry voices.[8] Such proposals have therefore struggled to find support, especially as few doubt that the United States' motherly concern has on the whole been a benign influence, and has nurtured it as few others could or would.[9] Could the ITU or the squabbling United Nations (which at the time of writing has elected representatives from Sudan, Venezuela, Libya, Eritrea, and Poland sitting on its Human Rights Council) manage it better?[10]

In any case, the United States can't just turn out the lights and leave the keys under the mat for the ITU. The Internet is not a state. It has no powers of compulsion, no monopoly of violence, and few means of enforcement. Standards are open, and innovation is permissionless. Its administrators can persuade or cajole. It thrives on network effects, and so it needs participants. This means it must be easy to join, and the value it provides must be evident. Virtually all of the ITU's activities, in contrast, have been defined by treaties and legislation.[11]

It is common to link legitimacy with a social contract, accountability with democracy, and some political theories even float the idea of a 'general will', the settled decision or choice of 'the people' as a whole. Yet what could the social contract be online? Can democracy work given that the Internet is a highly technical zone whose operation is over the heads of the vast majority of its users? How can the general will be determined given the utter impracticality of holding elections or canvassing opinion across the Internet? The actual content of democratic governance over the Internet has to be left flexible to the point of vagueness, as there is no way to consult users or stakeholders. Yet stakeholders have an influence: simply by using the technology, they affect it and bend it to particular uses; each click, each link made is a vote. So to enhance legitimacy by a 'democratic' system looks rather redundant. If sufficient people were concerned by a failure of legitimacy or accountability, then the Internet would be threatened by non-use, or simply by someone else setting up a parallel system—there would be nothing to stop them.

The means by which these circles are squared is the doctrine of *multistakeholderism*—not the most elegant of words, but it suggests that all stakeholders should have a voice in its governance where this is appropriate and feasible. There is a constantly shifting mix of governments (serving their citizens), supranational organizations (serving the states that make them up), companies (serving their customers and clients), civil society groups (serving their constituencies), and engineers (who keep an eye on the Internet's function). Legitimacy is established via transparent decision-making by consensus.[12]

Multistakeholderism has its critics. After all, it is one thing to say that stakeholders should have a voice, and quite another to determine how loud. Some dismiss it as 'a rhetorical exercise aimed at naturalizing criticism rather than a truly unique participatory mechanism for governing a global resource',[13] or agree that it is 'a slogan and a last-minute concern rather than an integrated element in decision-making'.[14] But if the legitimacy of the *procedures* of an institution is in question, another type of legitimacy that could be invoked is that of the *outcomes* it produces. Bear with us, says this approach, because we will all benefit in the end. That means that multistakeholder institutions have to deliver, and keep delivering.

HOW IS THE INTERNET GOVERNED?

We cannot understand multistakeholderism without considering the complex and untidy interactions of government, private-sector companies (sometimes very large ones), political and civil society groups, international agencies, and the masses of individual users that go into the mix. Systems relevant to Internet governance include (but are not limited to) such items as the system for allocating domain names, information intermediaries, security systems, exchange points, autonomous systems, ISPs, registers, databases, and standards bodies. It may well extend beyond these in future.[15]

The Domain Name System (DNS) is an intriguing part, in that it has relatively little direct influence on the Internet's running *qua* system, yet is a major political battleground, and so is a convenient introduction to the complexities and indeterminacies. The naming system's function is to give a device a constant identity, what we might call a technical persona, on the Internet. As we have noted, identifiers have to be globally unique and universally accepted for the Internet to function as a global space. IP addresses are managed by the Internet Assigned Numbers Authority (IANA), and often are dynamically assigned. Added to the fact that they are 128 bits in IPv6 (requiring up to 39 numerals in decimal notation), they are impossible to use in the absence of databases of address assignments held by ISPs. The DNS gives memorable, constant domain names (at least, memorable for the 70 percent of the world's population who use the Latin alphabet) to online entities. These names have no Internet presence until they are assigned IP addresses, and the assignments are maintained by a hierarchically federated database curated by the DNS, which provides the means of translating between them and the IP address which is the key identifier.[16]

The DNS needs to coordinate several tasks in real time and at scale in order that unique naming be preserved. Domain names need to be assigned, and to be resolvable into IP addresses via the database; the database needs to be edited and maintained; the naming hierarchy needs to be curated (e.g. authorizing new top-level domains on a par with .com or .org); the servers containing this material need to be operated and housed (and paid for); new language scripts beyond the Latin alphabet need to be authorized and integrated; disputes need to be resolved in a timely and legitimate fashion; and not least, the system needs to be secured from malicious attack (the DNS root servers receive billions of queries each per day, any one of which might smuggle in some malware).

For many years, this extraordinarily complex task was largely administered by a single individual, Jon Postel, at the University of Southern California, with the aid of the NIC—his sudden death in 1998 at the age of fifty-five underlined the need for dedicated institutional support. The Internet Corporation for Assigned Names and Numbers (ICANN) is the body that has managed the DNS for IANA since it was founded in 1998 under Esther Dyson.[17] For a long period it was under the direct oversight of the US Department of Commerce (DOC), which finally relinquished control in 2016.[18]

Nevertheless, the United States retains a good deal of soft power with respect to ICANN—it is headquartered in Los Angeles and incorporated under California law—and there have been many calls to internationalize it (not only from enemies of the US, but also from the EU, France especially, and Japan). One of the main reasons for the United States giving up its formal unilateral power over ICANN was to avert the powerful challenge to its control from other states, the endgame of which would likely have been some sort of international power-sharing arrangement. Better no countries in charge than dictatorships like Russia or China (who might press policies such as preventing ISPs from allowing anonymous users). As a matter of fact, the United States' outsized influence prior to 2016 was better expressed as a reluctance to interfere; it rarely made interventions designed to steer ICANN in a particular direction, leaving its decisions to be made on engineering rather than political grounds (although many have criticized ICANN's transparency and accountability, and still do).[19] To fend off accusations of partiality, ICANN hosts a Government Advisory Committee (GAC) which contains the representatives of over a hundred states (including all members of the UN General Assembly) which, though not a decision-making body, does feed into decision-making with a direct channel to ICANN's board (there are other advisory committees also representing various technical interests).[20]

The dilemma for ICANN is how it can govern the DNS without 'taking sides' in some highly controversial debates, which have flourished since that 2005 ITU working group. For instance, it has sometimes been argued that it should demand good behaviour from its registrants, such as suppressing hate speech, protecting intellectual property, or assisting law enforcement, but this caused one American commentator to worry that 'Down the road, one can imagine demands from Brussels that ICANN cooperate with EU efforts to tax commercial sales negotiated over the Internet.'[21] In 2012, Russia attempted to table a proposal at the ITU to take over the DNS in terms that would allow national censorship; despite initial interest, the proposal collapsed in the face of determined Western opposition.[22] ICANN tries to avoid arbitrating definitions of bad online behaviour; it does have a dispute-resolution policy designed to inhibit cybersquatting (where someone registers a domain name likely to be of value to someone else, and then demands a fee to relinquish the name), but this is a special case of a harm actually created by the DNS itself. In other cases, though copyright breaches or hate speech are undeniably contraventions of rights facilitated by the Internet, they are not problems *caused* by the DNS, and so far, ICANN has shown no inclination to address them.[23]

The nature of ICANN's power is intangible at best. The DNS connects domain names with IP addresses, and hence a query for a particular domain name works its way through a series of databases holding the details of each part of the domain. ICANN is responsible for the root zone, where the top-level domains (i.e. the final part of a name, such as .com or a country code) are stored, and assigned to particular registries. The first part of the query to be addressed goes to the root zone. This means that ICANN's power is apparently very large—it can make a domain visible to Internet users, or alternatively conceal it, for example by re-delegating a top-level domain to another registry. Or it could limit or expand the number of top-level domains. Yet this power has its limits; if ICANN started demanding high rents, or required that registries police their users in certain ways, then it would risk a significant number of nations walking away and setting up their own naming system. We do not have to look far for examples of such alternative naming systems; social networks often use an internal and independent system for their members, inaccessible to outsiders. There aren't so many registries that they couldn't band together in the event that ICANN tried to prevent them getting access to IP addresses. Indeed, the registries themselves, which as well as being coordinating institutions act as gatekeepers to the address space, have it in their own power to bring down the Internet by facilitating conflicts between IP addresses (e.g. giving the same address to more than one recipient), which would undermine the uniqueness principle. Similarly, even if registries continued to respect the principle, the ISPs to which registries allocate IP addresses also have the ability to undermine it within their own jurisdiction (often national, and therefore within the influence of national governments). Much of the behaviour here is conventional and 'understood'; the system works because organizations within it play their parts. Certainly much of it is governed by contract with ICANN, but the parties are often distributed across jurisdictions (many of which have their own regulations governing their national top-level domain), and so contract can only be part of the governance story.[24]

Domain names are, broadly speaking, mnemonic in function. The key thing is the unique IP address; no IP address, no existence on the Internet. Without a domain name, but with an IP address, you would be hard for a human to find, but you would be on the Internet nonetheless, whatever the DNS said about it. Furthermore, access to Internet sites is increasingly via bookmarks, search engines, or social networks using a different naming system. Each of these other queries resolves into an IP address, but none depends on a handy domain name. As these types become relatively more important, so will the power of the DNS diminish (which is not to say it will disappear).

We have discussed ICANN in a little detail to show some of the issues and complexities that arise. Table 3.1 briefly describes some of the other components of this ever-evolving system. When governments or other powerful organizations want to adjust, temper, or nudge the Internet for some reason, each of these types of organization represents one more lever for them to pull.

We have written so far about the Internet as a system designed to transport data. It underlies many operations, as we are all aware, but so far we don't have an explanation of why it is controversial. Like engineered artefacts generally, it should not be taken on its own terms; it is a co-creation of people and technologists, companies and governments, being reproduced in different circumstances by local resources, labour, consumption, and policies, helped and hindered by entrepreneurialism, poverty, and language, and as such it incorporates both social and engineering values. These values are often contested.[25]

In particular, *openness* is a key value built into the Internet's design, and if this is to be preserved, all the preceding components of the governance system need to buy into it. But nothing guarantees that they will. The next section

Table 3.1. COMPONENTS OF THE INTERNET GOVERNANCE SUITE

Component	Description
Registries	Registries associated with top-level domains (TLDs) maintain databases of domain names and associated IP addresses for each domain name within its TLD.
Root zone	The database of servers for TLDs, perhaps the apex of the Internet, is the root zone file.
Regional Internet Registries (RIRs)	Five non-profit registries (covering respectively Africa, Asia/Pacific, North America, Latin America/Caribbean, and Europe/Middle East/Central Asia) which receive reserves of IP addresses from IANA and distribute them to autonomous systems within their geographical region
Autonomous systems	The networks administering IP addresses in those network domains, or in other domains which pay the autonomous systems to connect to the Internet
IXPs	Physical infrastructure where autonomous systems meet so that data can be transferred from one to another, usually run by non-profit organizations
ISPs	Organizations connecting Internet users to the Internet, for example by providing access via cable or wireless, providing email services, or hosting Web resources
Computer Security Incident Response Teams (CSIRTs)	Expert groups that work together and separately to coordinate responses to global Internet security problems, such as a fast-spreading virus or worm
Certificate authorities	Trusted third parties that vouch for digital certificates, used to authenticate websites
Standards bodies	Institutions which define protocols, usually by an inclusive, drawn-out process of design and consensus involving representatives of many sectors
Information intermediaries	These are typically private companies that control much of the information flow over the Internet, and therefore are a vital part of its public face.

[a] Giblin 2014; Petersen & Riis 2016; Jougleux & Synodinou 2016.
[b] Durumeric et al. 2013; Kasten et al. 2013; Berkowsky & Hayajneh 2017.
[c] Scheitle et al. 2017.
Source: See DeNardis 2014a.

Notes

TLDs are of two types, generic TLDs, which we often know by their suffixes, like .com, .org, .edu, and .gov, and country code TLDs (ccTLDs), such as .uk, .fr, and .br. Different kinds of organizations operate registries, often non-profits, government agencies, or academic institutes (see Chapter 9 for controversy over the .org domain).

It is administered by ICANN, and US company Verisign manages it on a day-to-day basis. The US DOC relinquished oversight in 2016.

Despite the name, RIRs are not registries in the sense of the first row of this table.

Each has an Autonomous System Number provided by an RIR. They have a consistent routing policy, and use protocols to route packets to the correct destination. They use their own protocols for routing within the system, and Border Gateway Protocol (BGP) when packets have to be sent to another autonomous system. Typical autonomous systems include ISPs, large institutions that operate networks, and large content providers.

Discussion on p. 31

Because the relationship with their users creates a durable bottleneck, and because most ISPs are located within a particular jurisdiction, they are often co-opted by governments to police the Internet or put it under surveillance, despite being usually privately owned, and generally do so quite effectively. They are often required to store months or even years of data (e.g. traffic data, subscriber data, and downloaded content, as well as having access to identities) about their users, for government access at a later date, and sometimes are required to block access. This creates a *prima facie* conflict with ISPs' role as trusted intermediaries.[a]

Most nations run a CSIRT, and most of these are members of the international Forum of Incident Response and Security Teams (FIRST). The US Department of Homeland Security runs US-CERT, while CERT/CC is an academic effort run by Carnegie Mellon University. China has the CNCERT/CC, the United Kingdom has the National Cyber Security Centre (NCSC), and Singapore SingCERT. Russia, for some reason, has several, but only one is a member of FIRST.

There is an enormous range of such authorities, which some consider to be a serious vulnerability.[b] In response, the DNS proposed a recording system (Certification Authority Authorization; CAA) whereby domain name holders could specify which authorities could vouch for their certificates.[c]

Membership of many bodies is unpaid, and usually open. Most coordinate subgroups that look at specific protocols, while also ensuring the wider group of protocols is an integrated set. As the definition of a protocol is central to how and which interactions can occur, it is a powerful position to hold.

Examples include the IETF, which develops the Internet protocol, the W3C, for the Web, and the Institute of Electrical and Electronics Engineers (IEEE), which organizes standards for hardware (such as WiFi), networking, and even ethics. Some international standards bodies bring together national representatives, such as the ITU for telecommunications protocols, and the International Organization for Standardization (ISO), which coordinates a range of standards used in industry, including standards for industrial processes.

The information that a user is able to receive will depend on what information intermediaries are prepared to provide—and the affordances of the Internet will depend on what they are prepared to gather, store, and analyse. Prominent types of intermediary include search engines, SNSs, content aggregation platforms, financial intermediaries, blogging and microblogging platforms, online marketplaces and advertising platforms.

will discuss how value is expressed in systems generally, and the Internet in particular.

THE LAYERS OF THE INTERNET

The governance task is complicated by the different levels of abstraction at which various protocols are situated (commonly called the *protocol stack*). Protocols influence each other, from basic ones governing hardware to highly abstract ones governing applications such as SNSs, and they collectively underlie the content which we see and consume. Actions taken at one level of the protocol stack may affect what goes on at other layers unpredictably, and so decisions by one governance body aren't independent of those of others.

One way of modelling this is by the layers of the Open Systems Interconnection (OSI) model (Figure 3.1). Each layer represents a specific set of functions, which can be used by functions defined at higher layers, while the details of the lower-layer functions are shielded from the higher layers (rather as one can employ an electrician to rewire the house without knowing or caring how it is done). They are characterized by agreed standards, which assume the existence and reliability of functions and protocols defined at lower layers. Each layer, therefore, is dependent on agreement and consensus not only in itself, but also across those layers below it.

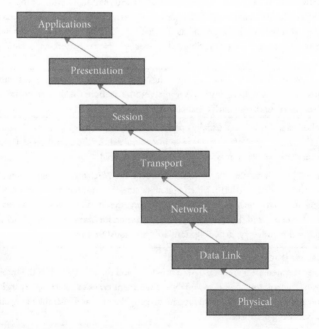

Figure 3.1. The OSI layers model of the Internet.

The layers are as follows, from the bottom up:[26]

- **Physical layer**: transmission and reception of the raw bits of data between a device and a physical transmission medium. This gets down to issues such as voltages and cable specifications where the physical medium is a wire, or frequencies for wireless transmission standards such as Bluetooth.
- **Data link layer**: effective and reliable transfer of data between two devices with a physical connection.
- **Network layer**: structure and management of a network of nodes. This will include addresses within the network so individual nodes can be identified, and packets of data can be routed through the network to specified addresses. IP lives at this layer.
- **Transport layer**: transfer of packets reliably through a network, including means to acknowledge arrival at destination, and to detect and correct errors. TCP lives at this layer.
- **Session layer**: communications between computers to manage their interactions.
- **Presentation layer**: translation of data formats to make data transferable across networks for specific applications. This can include compressing or encrypting the data.
- **Applications layer**: interactions with specific applications or pieces of software, to enable them to be run across the network. The applications themselves run on top of the Internet, and therefore are not modelled within it.

Vinton Cerf has argued that there is a fundamental division between these layers of the Internet, which together function to keep the open Internet flowing, and what he called the 'virtual political layer', sitting even higher in the virtual stack, or perhaps to one side of it, where content (information, or interpreted data) is consumed and judged. At the lower levels, protocols such as TCP and HTTP ignore content, using only metadata such as payload types, timestamps, and email formats. Cerf worries that constraints or censorship imposed on information at the upper levels will have effects on data further down the stack.[27]

We concur with that assessment, but we must beware of concluding that values are only relevant above the architecture where the social effects of processing information become evident, while down below, all the Internet's plumbing just gets collections of bits to the right place in the right order as efficiently as possible. Aiming for seamless interoperability is certainly important, but that in itself is not value neutral.[28] Each level brings its own set of values with it, not least engineering values such as efficiency, elegance, accuracy, openness, independence (i.e. not requiring oversight or intervention), and reliability. Consider these five assumptions:

- IP addresses should be neither regulated nor subject to market forces.[29]
- The institutions that administer the Internet are a mix of governmental, private, and non-profit, whose stewardship ethos is preferable to devolving entirely to government or supranational agencies.[30]
- The openness of open standards means open *access* to the standards, as opposed to, say, the development of the standards by an open community.
- We can meaningfully evaluate the efficiency of dataflow independently of its content.
- In the design of IPv6, abundance of IP addresses is more important than backwards-compatibility with IPv4.[31]

None of these is silly, but each is a value-laden idea which might have been different and which has ramifications. IP addresses could be sold or rented, which would have delayed, if not solved, the problem of address exhaustion. The Internet could be entirely run by governments or supranational agencies, and many governments and supranational agencies have suggested exactly that. The standards which govern Internet protocols might have been developed using open source methods, and so by an open *community*, rather than simply being accessible to all. And as we have already discussed, we might drop the interest in efficient dataflow in order to factor in the value of the information that the data expresses, or to make it easier to copyright content or to censor offensive content. This will be a constant theme when we discuss our other Internets in Part II.

As a detailed example, let's consider the switch from IPv4 to IPv6, briefly introduced in Chapter 2. There is a crisis at the network layer because the IPv4 address space is relatively small (although many of its addresses are allocated but unused because their holders no longer need or use them, and have not handed them back, which has exacerbated the scarcity problem IPv6 was meant to solve). That problem in turn is compounded by the lack of backwards-compatibility, because any network that switched exclusively to IPv6 would be cut off from the majority of the Internet that continues to use IPv4. It was assumed by the IETF that people would run both versions in parallel and gradually wind down their IPv4 operations, but the costs of doing so, combined with the lack of incentives, meant that didn't happen. There are certainly benefits from running IPv6, including better security and ability to deal with mobile communications, but the network effects mean that the benefits are dwarfed by the costs of leaving the IPv4 network. Hence compatibility is managed by running both protocols, or by improvising a translation, both costly and ad hoc solutions. The result is a kind of tragedy of the commons, where there are no incentives for early adopters of IPv6, because the network effects that would result from its widespread use are absent, because there are no incentives for early adopters, and so on. After a two-decade-long soap opera, still by 2018 only a quarter of networks were advertising IPv6 connectivity. The original fault was with the IPv4 design, which doesn't enable it to deal with addresses that are not 32-bit; hence one can kludge a translation backwards from IPv6 to IPv4, but there is no *forwards*-compatibility from IPv4 to anything (and will IPv6 be forwards-compatible with a putative IPv7?). But we are where we are.[32]

Is this a values issue? Arguably, yes. First of all, there was clearly an assumption of forwards movement, progress, and growth—IPv6 was the future, IPv4 the past, and the former is better than the latter. Secondly, when the inadequacy of IPv4 was becoming apparent, there was a case to use an existing variable-length ISO addressing standard, which was argued by the Internet Architecture Board (IAB), which at the time (1992) ran the IETF. Having a proper ISO standard seemed neater to many, especially to governments, and it would have enabled addresses to have a variable length, thereby avoiding IPv4's compatibility problem. However, the very formality of the standard counted against it. 'Everyone actually running the Internet, or developing new protocols for it . . . didn't like the fact that the IAB was purporting to make a major technical decision about the future of the Internet, while the engineers in the IETF were still analysing the problem and debating the alternatives.' The IAB lost control of the IETF, which 'became what it is today—a self-defined, self-governing group of engineers' working to 'make the Internet work better'.[33] The newly empowered IETF rejected the ISO standard and instead developed its own from the bottom up, and variable-length addresses died their death. What is clear is how much this decision was influenced, not by the content of the decision (by most accounts, the ISO standard was adequate), but by a decision about how decisions should be made—informally, by consensus, by engineers. Furthermore, the ISO standard was independent of the Internet, and adopting it would have made the Internet rather less special and unique.[34] The breakaway of the IETF from the IAB confirmed the exceptional status of *Internet* engineers and users as those who would decide the properties of the platform.

The lesson is that values are encoded both in technical standards, and in the means of developing them. Or, put another way, the values in engineering may have a moral or political aspect, but they are also implicated in the imperative to produce a functioning artefact. Simple technical solutions aren't always the way forward. Cerf's point also holds good; if the lower layers of the protocol stack hold, then the chances of connectivity holding are so much the better. The transport layer is key, since transport is what the network is there to do.

The role of Internet governance, then, is to balance the demands of value and function. The strategy employed by the Internet pioneers was to focus on a single value to bind the others. *Openness* within a system at the transport layer can be characterized as decentralized control, making it possible to join the system and mark out space with one's own rules. The system is not designed for exclusion, and in the ideal, exclusion is frowned upon. Openness enables the lower layers to send packets with as few impedances as possible.

The adoption of openness brings with it further imperatives across other layers. It implies *transparency*, so that actors can see what standards are used to define systems, and can therefore adopt them, and crucially can easily collaborate to pursue joint goals. Hence such a system is inherently favourable to the cooperation that produces *bottom-up* or *user-driven innovation*, not determined from the top down by hierarchical authorities. It will evolve, therefore, in accordance with the behaviour, needs, and desires of the users, and, to that extent, will favour *network* structures, and will work against hierarchies. It will also be *democratic*, in the sense that no one will be in charge, and decision-making will have to be consultatory. The network is *permissionless*; anyone with an innovation that requires data input can build their system, join the Internet, and use it to receive the data and disseminate the innovation more widely.

The *end-to-end principle* abrogates responsibility for processing within the network, so that the network's primary function against which its performance will be measured is the transmission of data. This applies to the transport layer, but has implications at the presentation layer, in that it rules out discriminating between packets from different applications. The end-to-end principle implies that *efficiency* of data transport is the most important metric of the successful function of the Internet.

The network has to be *resilient*, because it will always be at risk from permissionless innovation (which for instance allows the development and dissemination of viruses and malware). To be resilient, the network has to contain a lot of *redundancy*—this is already clear from the principle of packet switching, but also it follows from the ideals we discuss here. If the functionality that the network provides is offered by many sources, there will be fewer bottlenecks.

Permissionless innovation ought also to allow for *interoperability*—that is, new entrants are not shut out of participation in large, valuable, existing networks, and transparent and open standards allow them to produce compatible technologies. In an interoperable utopia, software environments would be interchangeable, and code, once written, could run everywhere.

Network effects are powerful, and so we should expect a successful network to grow. Resilience includes withstanding the pressures that come with growth, i.e. it should be *scalable*. It should work as well for a million users as a thousand, and as well for a billion as a million. In that, it has to be said, it has succeeded extraordinarily well over the years. In that respect it is one of the major engineering feats of our time; from a communications network used by a few hundred *cognoscenti* with a few dozen nodes to the ubiquitous resource we have today, the system has remained utterly robust.

Because we only interact with it as individuals, aware of our own experience but not of the totality, it is easy to miss this incredible development (see Figure 3.2 for its growth). Compare it with a football stadium, which can take a hundred people, a thousand, ten thousand. But it will struggle to accommodate a hundred thousand, and a million is out of the question. Compare it with the road network, which can accommodate a certain number of cars, but will succumb to congestion eventually. One could expensively increase the capacity of the roads, but this is as likely to make congestion worse than better.[35] All the layers of the Internet need to combine to meet the requirements of scalability. It is no good having a scalable transport layer if the network layer will struggle to provide names for all the nodes on the network.

Another value that has been applied to the Internet infrastructure retrospectively is *generativity*. This suggests that the value of the Internet, as an infrastructure with the capacity to host new services, developed unprompted by large and uncoordinated bodies of users, resides in its ability to be applied to new (and unforeseen) tasks and problems. Generative technologies, argues Internet law professor Jonathan Zittrain, can be characterized by:

- **Leverage**: they enable a wide range of accomplishments that would otherwise be very difficult to achieve.
- **Adaptability**: they offer many different kinds of use.
- **Ease of mastery**: they can be both adopted and adapted easily by broad groups of users.
- **Accessibility**: they are openly available, with few barriers to adoption.
- **Recursively generative**: given the preceding four criteria, they can be purposed by new innovators to generate new products and services that themselves are sources of further innovation.[36]

Most of this is occasioned by the *desiderata* of permissionless innovation and openness upon which the Internet and Web pioneers laid emphasis.

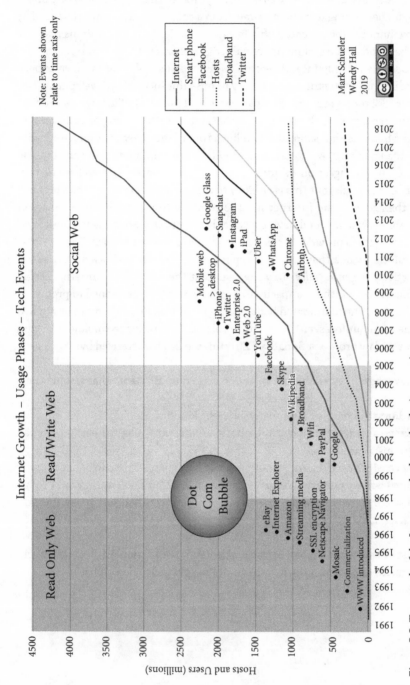

Figure 3.2. The growth of the Internet and other technologies over time.

Source: Thanks to Mark Schueler for this diagram.

CHAPTER 4

The Vision of the Open Internet

The adoption of the openness principle, particularly at the transport layer, ripples out to other values, and up and down the protocol stack. The apparently technical decision to get packets from A to B as efficiently as possible has many repercussions, which are the background to (and the cause of) the debates featured in the rest of the book. The philosophy of openness suggested to many of the Internet pioneers a vision covering the totality, and we can call this the *Silicon Valley Open Internet*, the first of our four Internets in two senses. To begin with, it was, historically, the first vision of the Internet to be articulated *and implemented* in a real-world setting. It therefore has first-mover advantage. But it is also *conceptually* prior to the other visions, in the sense that those we will discuss in Part II are responses to problems posed by the first vision.

Admiration of the technical brilliance of the Internet design combines with an idealistic view of its affordances to prompt an exceptionalist view of the Internet as a *sui generis* domain, subject to its own imperatives.[1] The speed and efficiency with which data can travel from A to B resonate with a general approval of unimpeded speech, free association, and other aspects of individual liberty. On this view, the brilliant and elegant design complements the excitement of the freedom it offers, and each becomes normative—the Internet *should* be free, because its design frees people to develop authentically and autonomously. 'The best technological network is also the most open political network. The best network is not only simple, low-cost, robust, and innovation-friendly, it is also best at promoting a free, democratic, pluralistic, participatory society; a society in which people with new business ideas are free to fail and free to succeed in the marketplace.'[2] Access to the Internet is not, of course, free, but many have argued that it ought to be, and some that

Four Internets. Kieron O'Hara and Wendy Hall, Oxford University Press. © Oxford University Press 2021.
DOI: 10.1093/oso/9780197523681.003.0004

access itself is a 'moral human right . . . which should be publicly provided free of charge for those unable to afford it'.[3]

The most famous statement of this philosophy is John Perry Barlow's *Declaration of the Independence of Cyberspace*, which rejects the idea that cyberspace can cause real-world problems that will not succumb to a technical solution, and argues that:

> Cyberspace consists of transactions, relationships, and thought itself, arrayed like a standing wave in the web of our communications. Ours is a world that is both everywhere and nowhere, but it is not where bodies live.
>
> We are creating a world that all may enter without privilege or prejudice accorded by race, economic power, military force, or station of birth.
>
> We are creating a world where anyone, anywhere may express his or her beliefs, no matter how singular, without fear of being coerced into silence or conformity.
>
> Your legal concepts of property, expression, identity, movement, and context do not apply to us. They are all based on matter, and there is no matter here.
>
> . . . The only law that all our constituent cultures would generally recognize is the Golden Rule.[4]

Legal scholar Yochai Benkler argues that 'the emergence of less capital-dependent forms of productive social organization offers the possibility that the emergence of the networked information economy will open up opportunities for improvement in economic justice, on scales both global and local'.[5] It was certainly a gospel that resonated.[6] Open network architectures supporting interoperable systems became a European standard as well as an American one, 'a rare early example of full technical harmonization which allowed the Internet to flourish across borders without being stymied by preexisting telephony regulation'.[7]

Internet governance bodies are reflexively open. The IETF is highly participatory and transparent. Participation is not restricted by credentials, and its documentation and records are open and freely available, allowing oversight and accountability. It prefers to approve standards that do not rest on intellectual property and patents; where these do exist, it prefers royalty-free licensing. The W3C has a similar policy, with open standards and opposition to royalties, although it has a membership model and accepts institutions of any kind as members.

The United States is a natural home for an open technology. The history of its competition policy generally shows bias towards open standards as the main means for solving problems of monopoly that stem from network effects. Lawyers Dolmans and Piana characterize openness as comprising six principles:[8]

- Access to decision-making
- Transparent procedures
- Published pro-competition goals
- Published objective criteria for technology selection
- No overstandardization
- Access to the standard.

Open standards do not mean software has to be free, but the Internet pioneers were not enthusiastic about licensing and pricing. One of the most famous early controversies over openness took place over the UNIX OS, developed at Bell Labs in AT&T in the 1970s.[9] UNIX was an important technology, addressing many of the problems which prompted Licklider's alternative vision, by supporting multitasking and portability across different machines. It brought with it its own aesthetic and set of values, based around minimalism, modularity, and reusability of software.[10] It was a proprietary system, designed for use within AT&T, although it was so handy that it was often licensed to other organizations, which led to the UNIX philosophy spreading. The lack of openness led to frustrations, as engineers found themselves having to pay for licences in order to code on the system. Unhappy with this, Richard Stallman and colleagues formed the Free Software Foundation, and began to develop a UNIX variant, GNU (standing for 'GNU's Not UNIX'), under a new type of open licence. In 1991 in Helsinki, Linus Torvalds released the source code for his own OS based on earlier work on GNU, allowing a community of programmers to develop the system, called Linux, further. It became one of the earliest important pieces of *open source* software, recognizably UNIX-like, with its advantages, but built by a relatively decentralized cooperative community. Open source software does not mean that 'anything goes'—the Mozilla community, which develops and supports basic software such as the Firefox Web browser and the Thunderbird email client, is underpinned by a foundation which maintains a system of rules and roles for the community—but the model of open and collaborative peer production has proved important both for innovation and for the development of sustainable communities. By the early 2000s, the open source model was a common inspiration for those seeking new models for the digital economy, and a regular feature in airport business bestseller stands (people bought books in those far-off days).[11]

The Silicon Valley ideal, then, is for an open network with decentralized control, together with an additional exhortation that openness be preserved by controllers in the areas of the network they do control. In other words, where one has control, one should not exploit it by excluding others from it, but rather should encourage the same interoperability and user-based innovation as is expected across the network. That exhortation is not a neutral addition. Decentralization of control can be self-undermining, in that it clearly implies the possibility of marking out, controlling, and policing one's own space within a wider open environment, and the full possibilities of that were not worked out until major commercial exploitation of the Internet—most obviously with social media.

This has always been a fight that the Silicon Valley vision of the Open Internet has been willing to take on. Tim Berners-Lee's original idea of the Web was focused around openness, and CERN's announcement in 1993 that the Web technology that Berners-Lee had pioneered as a member of its staff could be accessed and used by anyone, without a need for a licence or royalties, was key to its rapid spread out of the laboratory and into spare bedrooms across the globe. Even then, it was a surprise to many that quality information ended up on the Web, and in such quantities that search was needed. To many, such as CompuServe or America Online (AOL), this was an opportunity to provide services for fees or subscriptions; but as the Web scaled, these services did not. This gave Google its opportunity to provide scalable search via crawlers collecting copies of sites and caching them on Google's own servers. On a smallish Web, a provider like AOL, with access restrictions, simple services, and a centralized environment, could tempt subscribers into its 'walled garden', but gradually the Web outside AOL began to look more exciting even to the most conservative users, and the walls, at least in this early phase of the Internet's development, came tumbling down.

Google, which has tempered its philosophy as it has become a more commercial operation, has always argued that its mission is 'to organize the world's information and make it universally accessible and useful', which implies a degree of openness, and still defends this position. Search results, YouTube, maps, and other services are free and openly available. Google also benefits from openness, as most obviously a search engine needs access for its crawlers to as much of the Web as possible; indeed, as its search engine is its loss leader, a decline in quality of search could be extremely damaging. It was fortunate as it began its services that few Webmasters took advantage of the robots.txt standard, which signals to a crawler that (parts of) a website should not be scanned, therefore giving Google wide access. In its early days, it was conveniently opposed to the king of proprietary software, Microsoft, and more recently was also able to contrast itself with the new prince, Facebook. However, openness is not in and of itself a means of paying for the services it offers, and the immense hardware and R&D required to create them; Google's commitment to openness has therefore been somewhat ambivalent, and ultimately, as it has adopted a business model based on advertising, its ideals have moved closer to Facebook's than Benkler's.[12]

Facebook also has a foot in both camps; its CEO Mark Zuckerberg defended free speech in 2019: 'more people across the spectrum believe that achieving the political outcomes they think matter is more important than every person having a voice. I think that's dangerous.'[13] A solid defence, but although it can be represented as defending free speech against political ideologues, there are at least two outcomes that Facebook is committed to engineering, at whatever cost to openness—growth of its network, and profits. Free speech, and openness generally, cannot be dependent on achieving or avoiding specific outcomes, except in very clear and agreed direct cases of harm (one cannot shout 'fire!' in a crowded theatre). In a business context, the defence of openness is conditional, and therefore not thoroughgoing.

An Open Internet supports arguments about the spread of knowledge promoting the public good, but creates problems for attempts to extract value using traditional market mechanisms, particularly where intellectual property is concerned. The Open Internet changes economic relationships with data and information. Most sustainable economic models are built around scarcity, in which producers manipulate supply (dial scarcity up or down) in response to what would-be consumers are prepared to exchange. Data, on the other hand, is hardly scarce, and with the Internet—and the Web in particular, built around copying and distribution—it is abundant.[14] On many levels, this is an opportunity for disseminating useful knowledge, fulfilling the dream of the eighteenth-century *philosophe* Diderot, who criticized the 'narrow minds, deformed souls' who asked:

> What is the good of divulging the knowledge a nation possesses, its private transactions, its inventions, its industrial processes, its resources, its trade secrets, its enlightenment, its arts, and all its wisdom? Are not these the things to which it owes a part of its superiority over the rival nations that surround it? This is what they say; and this is what they might add: would it not be desirable if, instead of enlightening the foreigner, we could spread darkness over him or even plunge all the rest of the world into barbarism so that we could dominate more securely over everyone? These people do not realize that they occupy only a single point on our globe and that they will endure only a moment of its existence. To this point and to this moment they would sacrifice the happiness of future ages and that of the entire human race.[15]

Part of the philosophy of openness, therefore, includes the idea of opening data for use, and sharing it with others.[16] There will always be limits to open data, where concerns about privacy, intellectual property, or commercial confidentiality restrict flows, but open data has been an ideological focus.[17] It has developed in tandem with the idea of rights to information and data protection rights.[18] Rights to information include Freedom of Information (FoI) legislation; the difference between this and open data is that FoI gives rights to citizens to demand information of particular defined kinds, whereas open data envisages the automatic publication of data, whether or not there is demand or the widespread ability to use it.[19] Governments in particular are being pushed in the direction of greater transparency as a means to accountability, as well as causing their data to be more widely available in the public interest.[20] Data protection gives rights to people to see and correct information held about them; formally, data protection is the regulation of what is called *personal data*. Personal data is defined as data from which a person can be identified, and the identifiable person is then called the data subject. In our terms, identification *from* data requires interpretation *of* data, so personal data is better thought of as a class of information (in the US it is called, less misleadingly, personally identifying information, or PII). In countries with such regimes, data can only be as open as is consistent with data protection. The period 2005–2010 was a period of progress in the direction of openness, as governments and international agencies worldwide began to promote these ideas.[21]

At the level of the individual, this vision pushes back against privacy as a blocker to innovation and social sharing;[22] a recent fictional invocation of this mindset is Dave Eggers's *The Circle*.[23] The strongest version of this position is exemplified by WikiLeaks,[24] a non-profit organization whose guiding light is Julian Assange, with a radical philosophy of openness, and of fighting corruption through transparency. Its mission is to publish inconvenient information released by whistleblowers anonymously, without editing or questioning their motives, and it has certainly produced some *coups de théâtre* in its time, notably revealing a manual for US operations in its prison in Guantánamo Bay, US State Department diplomatic cables, a chapter of the draft Trans-Pacific Partnership trade deal, and emails from the Democratic Party during the 2016 presidential election campaign.

The vision of the Silicon Valley Open Internet has also absorbed the assumption that it is a thoroughly Good Thing, and we should all have it, and if we don't want it we should have it anyway. Google never asked whether we wanted the world's information organized in the first place. The decision to map the entire globe was taken unilaterally by John Hanke, founder of geospatial visualization firm Keyhole, and executive in charge of Google Earth, Google Maps, and Google Street View; he didn't ask whether you wanted your house photographed or your street mapped. Elon Musk's company SpaceX, whose mission is to facilitate interplanetary travel, has begun to create a constellation of small satellites called Starlink,[25] which when complete will consist of thousands of standardized communications satellites in low-level Earth orbit to provide (among other paying services) global broadband Internet, especially for parts of the world which are currently underserved. It will also, if SpaceX's mission succeeds, provide Internet access to spacecraft or colonies on the Moon or even Mars. The decision to provide broadband everywhere is Musk's, no one else's, whether you want it in your idyllic rural retreat or your sacred burial ground or not, never mind the dangers of debris from his satellites when they fail or their impedance of astronomical observations. This is permissionless innovation all right, moving fast and breaking things, but in the real world, not just in the constructed world of the Internet. Innovation, on the Silicon Valley view, is too important to wait for permission.

Ardour for permissionlessness often expresses itself as libertarianism, or opposition to regulation. The pared-down end-to-end view of the network in the Silicon Valley Open Internet brings an implicit commitment to efficiency as a key value, which suggests that if we try to oversee or gerrymander certain outcomes, efficiency might be compromised. But regulation is not necessarily bad, if it is needed to *ensure* the unfettered flow of information. The Open Network Architecture, for example, was an early regulatory requirement placed on US telecom firms in the 1980s by the Federal Communications Commission (FCC). Common carriers were safeguarded to allow computer networks to flourish, and competitive markets were encouraged to be interoperable, while also segregated from non-competitive markets.[26]

Net neutrality is a signature policy of the Silicon Valley Open Internet. It is the principle that Internet providers should not discriminate between different types of packets of data transmitted over the Internet, to give preferential treatment to some types rather than others. Discrimination might happen for engineering reasons (certain information-heavy and time-sensitive uses, such as video or game streaming, might clog up the network), economic reasons (a mobile operator might not wish to provide the infrastructure for free Internet telephony or VOIP services that will undermine its business model), or ideological reasons (an operator might wish to discriminate against child pornography, say, or the messaging of an opposition political party).[27]

Net neutrality has more of an impact on the last mile of Internet delivery, than on global governance. In countries with sufficient competition between providers, anyone who objected to such discrimination could simply switch to a provider that respected net neutrality. As an issue, it looms largest in the United States, where competition is relatively thin, and where free speech is a highly prominent shared and constitutionally enshrined value. In contrast, European telecoms regulators tend to have a more economic remit, and so are less well equipped to consider rights-based issues. Public interest has consequently been far higher in the United States; consultations on the topic by the European Commission and the United Kingdom's Ofcom pulled in about 400 responses between them in 2010, whereas an American inquiry at the same time attracted 30,000 responses and a petition in favour of neutrality received two million signatures. Emerging economies are more concerned with problems of capacity and politically motivated censorship, rather than discriminatory pricing.[28]

Engineers, including Cerf and Berners-Lee, have tended to favour net neutrality because of its positive effects on the network's efficiency, and its facilitation of permissionless innovation. Other supporters have been motivated by business reasons; Google, Amazon, and eBay want as much access to their popular sites as possible, while companies that offer VOIP services (such as

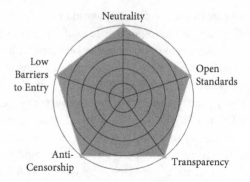

Figure 4.1. The ideals of the Silicon Valley Open Internet.
Source: Thanks to Paul Smart, who conceived and created this diagram via Highcharts.

Microsoft, which owns Teams), and streaming companies such as Netflix need to avoid their content being throttled or slowed down.

The Silicon Valley Open Internet, therefore, combines values such as decentralization, efficient flow of data and net neutrality, open standards and freedom of speech into a satisfying whole where the engineering vision supports and is supported by political ideals, giving us the promise of technological solutions to problems, the end-to-end principle, interoperability and the 'move fast and break things' approach to innovation. We can summarize the Open Internet in the diagram in Figure 4.1, focusing on five ideals: net neutrality, open standards, open data and transparency, opposition to censorship, and low barriers to entry.

CHAPTER 5

Policy Question

How Can Quality Be Ensured in an Open System
Like Wikipedia?

B ut if you have an open Internet, how do you know that what is on it will be any good? Won't you just get all the world's crazies posting content? To round off this opening part of the book, we will briefly examine one of the most well-known products of the open world, the online encyclopaedia Wikipedia.[1] It surely needs no introduction—as a simple means for discovering information it is peerless, and it receives about half a billion pageviews per day.[2] Its appeal was described by Michael Scott from the sitcom *The Office*: 'Wikipedia is the best thing ever. Anyone in the world can write anything they want about any subject. So you know that you are getting the best possible information.'[3] Its coverage may not reflect the ultimate importance of a topic, so that, for example, Trevor Philips, protagonist of *Grand Theft Auto V*, receives greater coverage than Elisabeth Lutyens, the modernist, pioneer of serialism, and rare example of a female composer (greater coverage even if we discount the 55 scholarly references that the fictional character merits).[4] No doubt it might be argued that 'importance' doesn't have to be given an elitist meaning, and it is better measured by counting clicks. No need to resolve that big question here, but let's flag it: it will crop up again in Part II.

The initial growth of the Internet would not have been possible had it remained a proprietary system, and certain common resources have provided immense value to the many Internet users. Wikipedia is an example of an information commons, and is a symbol of the potential of the Open Internet; North Korean defectors in the South send balloons carrying flash drives loaded with Wikipedia pages (alongside non-digital chocolate biscuits) over

Four Internets. Kieron O'Hara and Wendy Hall, Oxford University Press. © Oxford University Press 2021.
DOI: 10.1093/oso/9780197523681.003.0005

the border to remind their countrymen and women what a free society can provide.[5] It was recently lauded as 'the last best place on the Internet'.

> It is the only not-for-profit site in the top 10, and one of only a handful in the top 100. It does not plaster itself with advertising, intrude on privacy, or provide a breeding ground for neo-Nazi trolling. Like Instagram, Twitter, and Facebook, it broadcasts user-generated content. Unlike them, it makes its product de-personified, collaborative, and for the general good. More than an encyclopedia, Wikipedia has become a community, a library, a constitution, an experiment, a political manifesto—the closest thing there is to an online public square. It is one of the few remaining places that retains the faintly utopian glow of the early World Wide Web. A free encyclopedia encompassing the whole of human knowledge, written almost entirely by unpaid volunteers: Can you believe *that* was the one that worked?[6]

HTTPS://EN.WIKIPEDIA.ORG/WIKI/GARDEN_OF_EDEN

The failed experiment that precipitated Wikipedia was Nupedia, an attempt by Internet entrepreneur Jimmy Wales to produce a free online encyclopaedia along relatively traditional lines—its articles would be free to access, and could be submitted by anyone, but they would be reviewed by a committee of experts to verify their contribution. This model failed because the net-worked elements of the project were subservient to the hierarchical ones, so as the scarce and busy experts struggled to review the articles, they became a bottleneck and Nupedia couldn't grow. It was put out of its misery in early 2001 when its editor-in-chief Larry Sanger was introduced to the concept of a *wiki*, a website accessible through a Web browser that allows collaborative authoring of documents. It eases hierarchy out of the system by relinquishing the idea of central control or a privileged editor.

The original aim was to use a wiki to speed up article generation, but Nupedia's editors, perhaps sensing a potential land grab, resisted, and in January 2001 Wikipedia was born as a separate entity. Article generation was open, transparent, and decentralized, because no one decided who did what, or when. The decision was made, wisely, to keep all the logs of changes made, and to make these open too, in the sense of open data, so that anyone could understand the provenance of an article and how it evolved—allowing the process of content creation to be studied academically. Sanger worked out four principles governing the writing of Wikipedia articles: no original research (i.e. only report existing work), verifiability (i.e. cite reputable sources for claims), neutral point of view (i.e. don't take sides in a debate), and ignore all rules (i.e. be alert to wider issues than mere obedience).[7]

Despite scepticism, even from Wales, who feared it would produce 'complete rubbish',[8] the networked Wikipedia outgrew hierarchical Nupedia, which eventually died, within days. It now presents in 300 languages, and just in English has of the order of 50 million pages. It is relatively cheap to run, especially given its enormous size. It was quickly discovered to be pretty good in terms of accuracy, if less good than specialist reference works.[9] An influential study in 2005 found that although Wikipedia science articles contained more inaccuracies than those in the *Encyclopaedia Britannica*, the difference wasn't colossal, and after all Wikipedia had wider coverage, and was more accessible to very many people across the world, not least because it is available in a range of languages.[10] Furthermore, the collaborative wiki structure means that when an inaccuracy is discovered, it is not an onerous task to correct it speedily.[11]

It is not surprising therefore that Wikipedia quickly became a poster child for collaborative methods of aggregating and extracting the wisdom of crowds. It also helped the development of the Web by demonstrating the value of hypertext as an accessible means of non-linear presentation of information, and demolishing the suspicion that the Web would host low-quality content. The Web of Linked Data was boosted by the use of DBpedia,[12] a project to make structured information from Wikipedia available on the Web for querying and linking to other datasets, whose text is often used to train ML systems because there is enough of it to make a large training set. DBpedia's data is rich enough to make it a hub that can connect and help translate between other online databases, and it is an important source of ontological and conceptual information for AI systems.[13]

The continuation and reproduction of Wikipedia's culture depends not only on the network of collaborators, but also on a hierarchical meritocratic management system, moderated by an administrative bureaucracy armed with technology. At the bottom of this hierarchy are anonymous users. Contributions are overseen progressively up the scale. Procedures and protocols organize and orchestrate human collaborations. In particular, a number of edits and corrections are made by non-human bots (software that performs repetitive tasks at scale over the Internet), which are treated as more reliable (they have more permissions) than registered users. Bots are a vital part of the Wikipedia ecosystem, performing administrative tasks like detecting spam, copyright violation, and vandalism, blocking banned users, spellchecking, and linking articles upwards to categories, sideways to similar articles, and downwards to more focused pieces. Some tools semi-automatically generate content, for instance pulling material from public databases. The development of Wikipedia in languages that are less commonly spoken is largely dependent on bots.[14]

It would be foolish to dismiss Wikipedia as anything other than a triumph, albeit a counter-intuitive one—who would have predicted in advance, other than a small group of converts, that you could create a giant and pretty good, if not foolproof, encyclopaedia by crowdsourcing content from non-expert communities, without payment or external incentive (rewards for Wikipedians tend to be the granting of more permissions to do more work for the encyclopaedia, rather than anything useful outside the website)? Since Wikipedia there have been other examples, such as IMDb, so it is not a one-off flash in the pan, although it is still a rare achievement. In terms of disruption, it has been going for a couple of decades, during which it has seen off the challenge of the traditional multi-volume paper-based encyclopaedia.

But it has not all been plain sailing, and the need for its hierarchical bureaucracy is itself of interest. In the next section, we will briefly look at some of the problems that Wikipedia has encountered along the way, and how they illustrate both the power and the limitations of openness.

HTTPS://EN.WIKIPEDIA.ORG/WIKI/SERPENTS_IN_THE_ BIBLE#EDEN

The optimistic view of Wikipedia as a technology-mediated collaboration was soon to be challenged. In particular, we should not assume that all contributors, despite offering their services for free, are motivated by good faith. Wikipedia has its fair share of vandals, who add (often quite amusing) misinformation to articles; where this is clearly absurd, it is unlikely to be harmful, and will be picked up pretty quickly by other editors. For example, after the French footballer Thierry Henry blatantly cheated with a handball to eliminate Ireland from the football World Cup, his Wikipedia page was changed (possibly by an Irishman, maybe?) so that every one of the very many references to Henry himself was replaced with an obscene noun.[15] More serious cases can be damaging; an article about a journalist and member of the Kennedy administration asserted falsely that he had been suspected of complicity in the assassinations of both John F. and Robert Kennedy, and remained uncorrected for four months in 2005. The article was actually posted by a man who did not know the journalist, but wanted to play a prank on a friend who did. He did not believe that the piece would be taken seriously or remain live for a significant period of time.[16]

Some of the more convincing hoaxes have been surprisingly influential. A piece about Jar'Edo Wens, an entirely fictitious Australian Aboriginal deity, which went unchallenged for nearly a decade, led to a reference to him in a serious book on religion. Others have been transmitted virally from other collaborative sites, such as a Wikipedia article about a non-existent 1900 silent film called *Another Demonstration of the Cliff-Guibert Fire Hose Reel*, which was written up, apparently in good faith, using a hoax article on IMDb as its source.[17] A study of hoax articles detected a few tell-tale giveaways. Successful hoaxes tend to be longer than legitimate articles, but differ from genuine articles in structural ways, such as use of templates or links. New genuine articles are often preceded by a large number of mentions of the concept in other articles, foreshadowing a need for a stand-alone article, whereas this, unsurprisingly, doesn't typically happen with hoax concepts. Most hoaxers are newly registered, whereas genuine articles are far more likely to be written by authors with a long and respectable Wikipedia pedigree. These hidden structural factors mean that machine learning techniques tend to outperform human hoax-hunters, who are more likely to be led astray by good formatting, and are also more likely to erroneously label genuine but badly formatted articles as hoaxes.[18]

Larry Sanger, who had originally proposed the use of wikis, quickly grew disillusioned by the lack of order and reliability, but while he was berating the Wikipedia team because 'the notion that there would be anyone in authority . . . was just completely anathema to them', a bureaucracy had been created to police reliability. Wikipedia's relationship to its ecosystem was complex. In the words of one commentator, 'the systematic disavowal of its own authority is central to the way Wikipedia is conceived and organized'.[19] Sanger's view was that this reverse Wizard-of-Oz trick worked when Wikipedia was small and virtually all Wikipedians shared the founders' values and acted in good faith, but that he and Wales 'failed to realize . . . that our initial anarchy would be taken by the next wave of contributors as the very essence of the project'.[20]

Would more experts help? Sanger's attempt to revisit the Nupedia concept with another crowdsourced but expert-moderated encyclopaedia called Citizendium had its own problems. For instance, when practitioners of alternative medicine were certified as experts on their specialist topic, they proceeded to approve positive articles about the benefits of homeopathy and the like, while ruthlessly censoring critiques of these activities by medically trained scientists.[21] The Wikipedia solution both to the expert problem and the danger that anonymous users would abuse the system intentionally or otherwise was to make external citation the gold standard. This has the odd side effect that one cannot correct mistakes in one's own Wikipedia biography, because one cannot demonstrate the right credentials without publishing a memoir or autobiography.

A *sine qua non* of crowd wisdom is the diversity which prevents groupthink from taking root, but openness to all does not reliably produce diversity, especially in the nerdy digital world where disproportionate numbers of users are young white males. Where young males congregate, we might expect certain types of language to prevail, and possibly a certain level of competitiveness and aggression, which women may find off-putting; one study of Wikipedia argues that 'soft deletion' and the ability to flag up harassing behaviour might help, but that many aspects of the culture repel women, while another suggests that women tend to be less confident in their own competence. Death threats have been reported during edit wars. Wikipedia runs special editathons deliberately to attract more women. Figures are hard to get hold of, especially given the anonymity policy of Wikipedia, but according to the Wikimedia Foundation, the non-profit that runs it, women make up about one Wikipedian in six, and several concerted attempts to increase that proportion have been unsuccessful. There are four times as many articles about men as about women.[22]

Wikipedia's public image sometimes trades on its anarchic and argumentative culture, with every contributor telling combat stories of flaming and edit wars; Wales downplays his own role as its public face, and that of the bureaucrats and administrators who ensure a unified product. Yet we know nevertheless that a Wikipedia article does present a consensus (without taking sides, if necessary by providing metalevel descriptions of ongoing debates), and it has been hypothesized that the means to force consensus are particularly off-putting to women. Yet while the radical crowdsourcing of content has been emphasized by most commentators, the role of technology, especially the various bots used to craft the Wikipedia style, in hiding the lengthy and sometimes vicious debates between contributors, is less prominent in commentaries. One particular controversy erupted in 2014–2015 following the Gamergate harassment campaign against certain feminist game developers and critics. A Wikipedia article devoted to the topic became controversial in its own right, as some editors believed it was misogynist, while others that it was feminist (therefore in each case breaking the neutral point of view principle). Editors on both sides were banned for violating conduct guidelines, but the possibility of Wikipedia's *bureaucracy* being able to maintain a neutral point of view (in its own statement, 'The Arbitration Committee does not and cannot take a stance on the content of articles, nor on broader issues such as the Gamergate controversy itself'),[23] given its gender balance, was questioned by some commentators.[24] Such controversies are not presented in the articles themselves, and so expertise is rejected as a means of enforcing consensus; technology or bureaucracy does the job instead invisibly. The system is open, so this is observable, but it is not evident from the front end of the product, and lines of accountability are not clear.[25]

Meanwhile, in specific areas of importance, Wikipedia is almost returning to the safety of expertise. For example, one section of Wikipedia is called WikiProject Medicine, a group of 35,000 articles on medical topics which are edited with almost academic rigour by a corps of editors many of whom have a relevant postgraduate degree, insisting on higher standards for their 'reliable sources' by limiting them to peer-reviewed papers. The result is that its articles on matters medical are impressive, and—unlike in SNSs—misinformation about COVID-19 is pretty well absent. But to reach this authoritative position, it appears to be moving away from its stated aim of reworking its procedures to be more inclusive. A 2020 interview with a female doctor about WikiProject Medicine and its COVID-19 coverage reiterated many of the familiar complaints about Wikipedia's aggressive culture; she had stopped being open about her identity, the rigorous culture was 'intimidating'. Editorial scrutiny of medical articles was conducted with 'exceptional ferocity'; all this, in the context of widespread misinformation about the pandemic, was perceived to be in the service of epistemological quality.[26] In other words, it appears that, to achieve a standard of reliability in a particularly sensitive area, Wikipedia, along with other tech giants,[27] has had to compromise its stated aims of democracy and inclusivity, and to revisit unfashionable models of hierarchy, rigidity, exclusion, and intolerance.

Openness is a tempting ideal, but delivering it consistently is not quite as unproblematic as its proponents claim. A successful site may not necessarily have to be a safe space for all its participants, as evinced by 4chan and others, but a successful *inclusive* site does. Wikipedia hasn't mastered how to do that as an open anonymous site.[28] In the second part of this book, we move on from the vision of an Open Internet to consider how others have reacted to the effects that openness can have on technology, discourse, and wider society.

PART II

Alternatives to Openness

The Silicon Valley Open Internet is an ideal, rather than a reality, but it has both political and engineering arguments in its favour, as we have seen. However, not everyone supports the political ideal, and very many people have been concerned about the unintended consequences of the unimpeded flow of information. Opposition to the Silicon Valley Open Internet has crystallized around alternative views of how the Internet should function, in terms both of serving its users and of its effects on wider society.

In Part II, we will explore these alternatives. Three are alternative visions of the Internet—hence these three, plus the Silicon Valley Open Internet, give us the Four Internets of the book's title. Another alternative is not a vision for the Internet, but a model for its exploitation. Their relationship is shown in Figure II.1. We will meet each of them, together with a policy question they raise, in the next few chapters.

We precede Part II with a health warning. Each of the models is named after a geopolitical entity which has devoted the most effort and resource to implement the model. The Silicon Valley Open Internet is an example—it references an ideal, the openness of the Internet, and associates it with a place, Silicon Valley, where it happened to originate and where much of its support resides. The other models will also be associated with places—Brussels, Washington DC, Beijing, and Moscow—where the most powerful geopolitical support for the model can be found. These geopolitical labels are suggestive enough to give an immediate sense of how the model is intended to operate.

This does not mean that we subscribe to any kind of cultural or technological determinism, whereby the future of the Internet, or of any corner of it, can be predicted with any degree of accuracy from cultural, geopolitical, or technological facts (or vice versa). In fact, we think the exact opposite. The key *desideratum* of governance policy and strategy is to be prepared, and we believe that our particular narrative is helpful for anticipating squalls ahead.

Neither do we want to say that governments dictate everything. Internet governance is also affected by companies, supranational organizations, and so

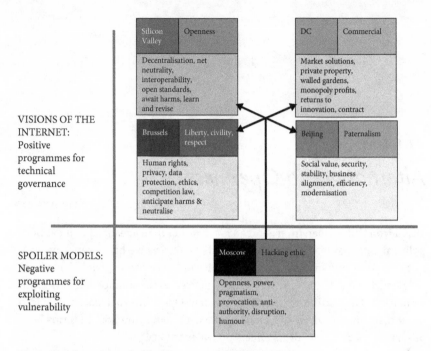

Figure II.1. Four visions for the Internet and a spoiler.

on. Not every aspect of the Chinese Internet is dictated by its government—we also need to look to Tencent, Ant Financial, Huawei, and, not least, the Chinese people. Indeed, not everything in the Chinese Internet conforms to our 'Beijing' model, and conversely other nations, including democracies as will become clear, are attracted to the Beijing model in at least some contexts, and will employ it in their own tailored way.[1] Even when we do focus on government, we should not make the elementary mistake of assuming that governments are single actors with an indivisible corporate view. Within any particular government, the finance, health, defence, interior, telecommunications, and education ministries may all adopt wildly differing views about how the Internet should best be governed and how it might serve their own purposes. Many of them play conflicting roles in Internet governance; for instance, trade ministries sit on ICANN's GAC where they feed into decision-making with a direct channel to ICANN's board, while telecommunications ministries in the ITU plot ICANN's destruction.[2] It will be obvious anyway that our schema is not centred around national governments, and this is a deliberate decision. As Internet policy experts Ian Brown and Christopher Marsden argue, 'It is not possible to map Internet regulation as a patchwork of national networks where international regulatory discussion centers on areas with overlapping jurisdictions or unclear jurisdiction. This comparison of Internet regulation with the Law of the Sea or medieval mercantile law . . . is untenable in practice.'[3]

In short, when reading these chapters, don't focus on the geopolitical exemplar, but on the *adjective*: open, bourgeois, commercial, paternal. These adjectival aims can be adopted by anyone, at any time, permanently or temporarily, for principled reasons or opportunistic ones.

The labels are labels, suggestive but not destiny. Other models are possible, and indeed exist, and other narratives than ours could no doubt be generated. We have attempted to construct abstract, hypothetical visions, stressing some aspects of ideological engagement with the Internet, with the aim of interpreting actions and policies and making sense of debates. Think of them as Weberian ideal types (perhaps even World Wide Weberian ideal types), placing (an) order on the complexity of experience. We believe that these Four Internets are a useful clustering of attitudes towards the Internet, indicative of likely future directions, controversies, tensions, and risks.

CHAPTER 6

Openness and Its Discontents

Until recently, it was assumed by many that the philosophy of openness and liberty would carry all before it, but many of the challenges facing authoritarian opponents of openness ten years ago have been overcome.[1] The warm approval of commentators like Yochai Benkler or John Perry Barlow is not the only possible reflection on the design of the Internet, especially when we think of it as a sociotechnical construct, rather than a set of elegant technical protocols.[2] Most obviously, the very idea of openness—in trade, migration, capital movements, and so on—is under threat across the globe following the financial crisis of 2007–2009, the growth of the Axis of Incivility, and the COVID-19 pandemic, and the Open Internet has been a key enabler of globalization. Furthermore, openness does not always guarantee equitable outcomes—Silicon Valley has been called 'a monoculture of white male nerds'[3] in which companies founded by women received 2 percent of venture capital funding in 2017.[4]

Brown and Marsden demand regulation of the Internet on the basis of five types of market failure they call 'hard cases': *data protection*, where data subjects' rights and awareness campaigns have not translated into meaningful protection of privacy; *copyright*, where protection measures have been disproportionate so that new means of creativity have struggled, and minor artists have less protection than the corporates;[5] *censorship*, where the input of civil society groups has been marginalized, limiting freedom of expression; *social networks*, which exploit users;[6] and *net neutrality*. They argue that these and other failures have rendered 'Anglo-Saxon Internet libertarianism' (i.e. the Silicon Valley Open Internet) a 'straw man'.[7]

The world, in other words, has moved on. There are, broadly, three potentially problematic effects of openness. First, because anyone can join an open network, it is hard to ensure cohesion and to keep out bad actors, even if it

Four Internets. Kieron O'Hara and Wendy Hall, Oxford University Press. © Oxford University Press 2021.
DOI: 10.1093/oso/9780197523681.003.0006

grows from homogeneous roots. The good faith shown by the small community of scientists in the early years has not been preserved, but many component technologies were designed on the assumption of such a community.

Second, if it is desirable to get a representative, diverse, and inclusive network, it may not be possible in an open system, because although anyone can join it, (a) people may not join in representative proportions (the digital divide problem), and (b) the network may be made unfriendly to outsiders. This is the problem we have seen with Wikipedia over gender issues.

Third, as a network grows, we are likely to see collective action problems, such as free-riding, tragedies of the commons, and negative externalities. In the Internet, for example, where so many issues are decided by counting clicks, 'clickbait' and sensationalism appear higher in search results than more sober analyses.

Openness may no longer be the only game in town. Many of the inefficiencies that were addressed by the end-to-end principle now have far better technological solutions that allow the network to scale.[8] Technologies such as Deep Packet Inspection and techniques such as differential pricing are far more feasible and smooth. VOIP and video are far more dependent on the timely arrival of packets than email or images, and the growing use of the Internet for streaming audio and video content means that there is far more data flowing around the system. At the beginning of the COVID-19 pandemic, locked down and isolated populations began working from home with video-conferencing, and then (or instead) streaming videos for entertainment, resulting in a 50 percent increase in global Internet traffic. The European Union was forced to appeal to streaming companies to lower the definition of their content (although there is no evidence this was needed in the end).[9]

There is little agreement about exactly what to do to remedy these issues, because concerns about openness tend to come from different perspectives: worries about *privacy* and *human rights*; thoughts about a *business model*; enforcing *social goals*, most notably security and policing; and *mischief*. In Part II, we argue that each of these responses to the Internet's design, architecture, and governance underpins a particular model of how it should be run, competing with the original purist libertarian vision.

THE DARK ARTS

The models we sketch are not the only responses to the Silicon Valley vision of openness, but they are important in the 2020s, as they all have powerful institutional backing and sociotechnical realizations. While much of the Internet revolves around standards, and an accountable, open, and transparent standard-setting process, this does not mean that governments are not under pressure to intervene, either as regulators, or developers, or via procurement.

Many nations, at least when going through idealistic and optimistic periods (often coinciding with economic growth), have supported open standards, as for example India and Brazil in recent years.[10] However, many social effects of the Internet, including the spread of social media, perceived threats to individuals' (especially children's) psychological well-being, cybercrime, cyberwar, and a coarsening of public debate, have led some governments to step in more assertively. The perception that the Internet is of necessity a disseminator of liberal and democratic ideals has also caused pushback.[11] Certain types of issues, such as net neutrality, or the extent of liability of information intermediaries for the information they carry, fall directly within governments' remit to legislate.[12]

Governments therefore do have power to shape the Internet and to reconfigure the trust relationships on it, using what Laura DeNardis calls the 'dark arts' of Internet governance (in Ferguson's terms, the tower fights back against the square).[13] For example, accessing websites depends on the maintenance by Web browsers of lists of trusted certifying and authenticating authorities; this system is only as secure as its least common denominator. A government could compel a browser-trusted authority to certify an imposter mail server, for instance, to support surveillance of its citizens or residents in its territory.[14] As another example, routing systems often assume trustworthiness and good faith, but in 2008, the Pakistani government took down YouTube in Pakistan by compelling Pakistan Telecom to redirect YouTube's IP addresses.[15] The technology community responds to trust deficits with improvements in security, but any technical solution is only part of a sociotechnical whole that is much harder to predict or control than the technological component.

There are certain types of content which most governments try to curb, such as child pornography or pirated intellectual property. There are other areas, such as political discussion, Holocaust denial, or blasphemy, where (a) only some governments wish to intervene, and (b) typically they do not agree on what to censor. This does not mean that they will not try. An important means for governments to control or censor the content distributed on the Internet is to intervene in the protocols, the systems, or the technology, as with the Pakistani take-down of YouTube. Such censorship is not unavoidable—the so-called Dark Web (i.e. that part of the Web that uses customized, often peer-to-peer, protocols to make access and tracing hard) often provides technologies to circumvent such interventions—but it is pretty effective in stopping messages being disseminated through audiences whose interest is more casual. It also raises issues of security and resilience of the network; the Pakistani operation could not be confined to Pakistan itself, and instead affected ISPs around the world, leading to the global disappearance of YouTube for an hour (which was not the Pakistani government's intention).

These powers, however limited, mean that governments' actions implement different conceptions of what the Internet should be. Certain national governments have even tried to go it alone completely, to insulate the national borders from the global Internet entirely. Mueller draws the important distinction between trying to align Internet governance with territorial sovereignty, which he calls *alignment*, and a genuine severing of connection with the wider Internet, with replacement of foreign-run services (such as search, email, or media) with local alternatives.[16] This more drastic thinking has gone furthest in Iran,[17] Russia,[18] and North Korea;[19] we discuss Russia and Iran in Chapter 14.

It is not only dictators who worry. As well as viewing openness as a technical aspiration, many also see it as a worrying source of uncertainty and risk. As Zittrain puts it, 'The most plausible path along which the Internet might develop is one that finds greater stability by imposing greater constraint on, if not outright elimination of, the capacity of upstart innovators to demonstrate and deploy their genius to large audiences. Financial transactions over such an Internet will be more trustworthy, but the range of its users' business models will be narrow. This Internet's attached consumer hardware will be easier to understand and will be easier to use for purposes that the hardware manufacturers preconceive, but it will be off limits to amateur tinkering.'[20] As we will see in China, such centralization of many functions on messaging apps like WeChat has accelerated the Internet's growth there.

SOME SPECIFIC COMPLAINTS ABOUT OPENNESS

Openness is both an engineering and a sociopolitical ideal, so the challenges it poses range across this spectrum. Whether their interests lie in the tech or in the agora, most people will find something to concern them. In this section, we will briefly canvass a few of the most-aired complaints about the Silicon Valley vision of the Open Internet.

These impact on various aspects of the engineering, but if we refer to the layered OSI diagram of the Internet's protocol stack (Figure 3.1), they are arranged roughly from bottom to top. In other words, the earlier the complaint appears in the list below, the lower down the stack its effects will be felt. Depending on which problems concern the observer, it may be sufficient to address issues at the higher layers, and leave the lower, more technical layers relatively unscathed. Although the effects of interference at any layer ripple up and down the stack, probably the key layers for connectivity are the lower layers, specifically the network and transport layers.

- **Demands of different media ignored**: As noted earlier, some media are more time-sensitive than others, so that streaming video and VOIP need to arrive in a more timely fashion than email or a downloaded website. Making this happen also provides a handy revenue stream for ISPs to exploit, which the pure Open Internet frowns upon. To manage traffic more effectively, we need to challenge the ideals of both the end-to-end principle, so that data packets can be inspected to see what kind of data they contain, and net neutrality, so that different types of packets can be treated differently.[21]

- **Assumptions of good faith not borne out at scale**: A number of Internet and Web technologies are designed with the good-faith user in mind, and methods to maintain security or prevent subversion once a system is scaled up are afterthoughts.[22] A classic example is Tay, a Microsoft chatbot for 'young people', which within a day had been turned into a racist by the crowd.[23] Arguments about the value of big data similarly often ignore the probability that those with access to big data might have interests of their own.[24]

- **Interoperability increases the threat surface**: Interoperable systems are vulnerable to attack and infiltration. Because they are designed to work and interface with other systems, they have entry points which can be exploited by malware or hackers. As systems become more embedded in everyday life, as for example with the Internet of Things (IoT) or any kind of so-called smart technology, connections between devices will spawn threats, partly because strong security would be socially unacceptable (imagine having to remember a complex password every time you wanted to turn the kettle on).[25]

- **Data is uninterpreted by the network**: Each packet is treated as equivalent to any other, and even if not, the network is to do as little as possible. This means that the data is treated as uninterpreted, rather than meaningful information. It can therefore not be identified as spam, malware, or fake news. The need for greater trust and reliability in data transfer led almost immediately to dilution of the end-to-end principle, as trusted agents (often ISPs, or automatic systems such as spam filters and security firewalls) were integrated.[26]

- **Generating data through interaction**: When an interaction of any kind takes place online, data is passed between the interlocutors. If the Internet is open, then there is nothing stopping this data from being saved, either by the interlocutors or by the carriers of the data. Because this data is informative and can relatively easily be resolved to an individual device, this has serious privacy implications, which is important because privacy is argued by many to be a prerequisite for the autonomy of the individual, as well as for the smooth functioning of democracy. Some commentators have also argued that culture and human dignity are compromised by the persistent surveillance.[27]

- **Anonymity**: It is widely held that some of the most boorish and anti-social behaviour online, such as trolling, death threats, misogyny, and vandalism, is rendered possible by anonymity.[28] If we are to hold people accountable for their online behaviour, then there has to be a means of associating people with that behaviour in the first place.[29]

- **Humans removed from the loop**: One of the supposed economic benefits of digital technology and digital modernity is *disintermediation*, where a complex process can be reduced to its essentials. However, sometimes a human in the loop is important, for example for helping make the process more legible, or more just, for those taking part.[30]
- **Biased data not challenged**: The Silicon Valley Open Internet tends to treat data processing as a procedure performed on a resource. Analysis and learning bring out *only* the information contained within a dataset (such as the matrix of page links on the Web that the PageRank algorithm crunches). Furthermore, if we make the further closed world assumption that 'to be is to be in the dataset', so that the dataset tells the whole story, then the algorithm may continue to conceal, rather than reveal. For example, if the dataset results from historic behaviour of, say, disproportionately recruiting men into senior jobs, or sentencing black felons more harshly, then the best AI will inevitably find sexist and racist rules within the data.[31]
- **Innovations deployed at scale**: What seems like a good idea between a small group might have deleterious social effects at scale (independently of the preceding good faith complaint). The Facebook, the online version of Harvard's student directory, was harmless; when it has grown to billions of users, we have a different story.[32] The Starlink satellite network provides the Internet to everyone, whether they want it or not, but brings its own problems for other satellites, and for astronomers.[33]
- **Lack of diversity without positive measures to support it**: Diversity among technology developers is not high, although we should be careful not to airbrush the contribution of women and various ethnic groups from history. This means that products very often suit white men (or other ethnicities dominant in the industry), and not others. Virtual reality headsets are more likely to make women feel sick than men,[34] while in a famous example a soap dispenser would dispense soap to white people, while failing to do so for black people, because its optic sensor was better tuned to lighter skin tones.[35]

In all these cases, the Silicon Valley Open Internet falls short of the ideal. Detractors will typically be moved by a subset of these problems, and certain sets of issues group together quite naturally, with a focus on problems with human rights, or revenue streams, or the public good. The governance methods on offer to remedy them encompass both hard and soft power, deploying both virtual and physical means, and have effects both in cyberspace and in the physical world.[36] In the rest of Part II, we will describe and motivate the alternative models that are significant at the beginning of the 2020s.

CHAPTER 7

The Second Internet

The Brussels Bourgeois Internet

The first alternative take on the effects of the Silicon Valley Open Internet descends from the liberal settlement underpinning mainstream modern thought about politics and citizenship in wealthy democracies. Liberalism is the philosophy of pluralism, individualism, restrictions of power, human progress, reason, and civic respect,[1] and the measures urged in this vision include protections for the individual's autonomy and authenticity, in particular using human rights and privacy protections against supposedly unrestricted invasions of the personal realm by open technologies.

THE IDEAL

There is little consensus in our ideologically fragmented times, but there is no doubt that liberty is taken by large groups of people, especially in the richer parts of the world, to be a social good, all things being equal. The Silicon Valley Open Internet is premised on libertarian ideas. Yet 'liberty', as Isaiah Berlin established many years ago, is an ambiguous term. It can signify the *freedom to* do things unhindered by governments or public opinion, or *freedom from* certain types of oppression or interference.[2] In Berlin's terms, positive liberty is a type of self-mastery or control of one's own environment, exemplified by Aristotle's view of a citizen exercising his free will in the public sphere. Negative liberty, expressed by more recent political philosophers from Hobbes to Mill, says that one is unrestrained, a slave to no one, implying many ideas characteristic of modernity, such as freedom of movement, speech, religion,

Four Internets. Kieron O'Hara and Wendy Hall, Oxford University Press. © Oxford University Press 2021.
DOI: 10.1093/oso/9780197523681.003.0007

and association. Hence, for example, we might say that a drug addict has negative liberty, in that no one prevents certain behaviour, but not positive liberty, because the addiction means he or she is unable to make mature, considered decisions. We might argue that women's positive liberty is hindered by structural obstacles to the exercise of their agency, via sexism or gendered social norms, even if their negative liberty has grown in recent years with the removal of laws and regulations that had curtailed their activities.

This leads to the observation that the Silicon Valley Open Internet provides negative liberty, with its decentralized system lacking a central editing bottleneck, allowing anyone to post or link. Negative liberty can, though, interpose on positive liberty, because few actions are so private that they don't impinge on others. In R.H. Tawney's words, quoted by Berlin, 'freedom for the pike is death to the minnows'.[3] In particular, the Internet amplifies interference in its users' negative liberty in two ways. First of all, it provides connectivity within the telecommunications network, so that online activity is directly connected to other people's online space. Secondly, many formerly real-world interactions and activities have migrated online, so that activity on the Internet now intrudes directly into the offline world. To take one obvious example, negative liberty allows someone to spread a rumour that they may wrongly believe to be true, or that they feel it would be amusing to spread. Such rumours may cause others to form incorrect opinions, and act in a way that they wouldn't—possibly, as with the case of prevalent misinformation about COVID-19 or other diseases, with directly deleterious results. Other examples include trolling, spam, and astroturfing, the practice of publishing messages under a false identity, to make it appear that the messages are more credible or disinterested than they actually are.

In particular, many of the institutions that protect liberty, including democracy, a free press, and a free economy, depend on the existence, maintenance, and sustainability of a space where the public can meet, run independently of government, for ideas to be debated—Jürgen Habermas is perhaps the foremost theorist of the idea of the public sphere, but many others have defended the importance of such spaces, such as legal scholar Cass Sunstein, who contrasts (negative) freedom of speech with the (positive) right of access to places and other people allowing for unplanned encounters, and the pioneer of Internet Studies William Dutton, who sees the Internet as a 'fifth estate', a new source of accountability. Such public fora require a baseline of decent behaviour and respect for others. Certain digital spaces could in principle provide the infrastructure for a functioning public sphere.[4]

The exact form and desirability of the public sphere has been debated at length without reaching consensus. A certain pattern of behaviour and social organization underpins policymaking in this space, and Habermas locates it in his history of the development of the public sphere during the Enlightenment.

The bourgeois public sphere may be conceived above all as the sphere of private people come together as a public; they soon claimed the public sphere regulated from above against the public authorities themselves, to engage them in a debate over the general rules governing relations in the basically privatized but publicly relevant sphere of commodity exchange and social labour.[5]

Habermas chronicled the original impetus towards a public sphere in the growing (in numbers, wealth, and political influence) bourgeois society of the eighteenth century. The bourgeoisie has had a bad press over the years, from aristocrats, academics, Marxists, and snobs (many people are, regrettably, all four).[6] Sociologically, the concept has been defined thus:

City dweller practising an honored profession or owning a business or functioning at a managerial level in someone else's enterprise, including governmental and non-profit enterprises.[7]

Morally, we can circumscribe the ethical world of such a person.

Such a person faces a particular set of ethical problems. He has the anxious ethical task of learning how to be a counselor yet self-prudent, a salesman yet other-loving, a boss yet just, a bureaucrat yet courageous, a scientist yet faithful.[8]

Bourgeois society is self-interested, but stable, and the suburbs, where it flourishes, are safe, cautious, and quiet; they tend not to host pogroms, protection rackets, or riots. They produce neither great art nor great violence. They are neither 'edgy' nor 'hip'. The bourgeoisie may be fairly criticized for being boring or hypocritical, but however much we prefer the idea of rock stars or pirates, most writers and readers of books like this one live calm, hard-working, stoical sorts of lives, as chronicled by John Betjeman in Britain and John Cheever in the United States, and are the object of contempt from teenagers and all sorts of self-identifying 'free spirits'.

The value of liberty depends on how far underlying order allows one to benefit from it, as Edmund Burke reminded us, while musing in 1790 upon the murderous carnage into which the French Revolution was about to descend.

Is it because liberty in the abstract may be classed amongst the blessings of mankind, that I am seriously to felicitate a madman, who has escaped from the protecting restraint and wholesome darkness of his cell, on his restoration to the enjoyment of light and liberty? Am I to congratulate an highwayman and murderer, who has broke prison, upon the recovery of his natural rights?[9]

The bourgeois world is ordered, respectful, polite, decent, well-behaved, well-mannered, and considerate, and because of this foundation, liberty within it is meaningful and valuable, a positive liberty. The second vision we will discuss in this book wishes to project this foundation onto the Internet. We can characterize the bourgeois vision as the conjunction of two principles:

- The preservation of human rights and human dignity
- A precautionary ideal of anticipating harms and neutralizing them in advance.

Each of these diverges from the Silicon Valley Open Internet. For the first principle, the Open Internet focuses on those rights of negative liberty, particularly freedoms of speech and association, rather than the fuller range of rights—which notably includes privacy and the ability to make authentic and informed democratic choices. The second principle clearly goes against the Silicon Valley ideal of moving fast and breaking things. The bourgeois vision instead implicitly balances the innovation that this makes possible against the disruption it may cause.

THE EXEMPLAR

Europe's political attitudes often differ from those of the United States, whose political and public space are defined by a liberal creed and common law. The Continental European tradition is descended from Roman Law and the Napoleonic Code, which tend to favour centralization, and whose main role is to define and bolster the coordinating and protective role of the state, as opposed to the common law, whose function is to defend the interests of the citizen as he or she sees them. The bourgeois world rests upon virtuous behaviour, civility, and prudence, and Western European governments by and large work within the European Union to secure this world. Their economies tend towards corporatism and incremental development, with firms drawing upon non-market resources to implement strategy and construct core competencies in coordinated market economies.[10] European thinking on ethics and privacy focuses on dignity, where the American tradition looks towards liberty,[11] so it is not surprising to find an EU Ethics Advisory Group worrying about the relationship between personhood and personal data, the risks of discrimination as a result of data processing, and the risks of undermining the foundations of democracy—all areas where a parochial and distinctively European ethical view is threatened by the Silicon Valley Open Internet.[12] Legal scholar Anu Bradford argues that the European Union generally favours 'precautionary regulatory action . . . even in the absence of absolute, quantifiable certainty of the risk'.[13]

In Europe, history is never far away. Nation-states have learned, through incessant and often brutal war, to focus on peace, prosperity, and cohesion. The European Union was originally posited as an end point to these integrative processes, and, in cyberspace, it has taken it upon itself to defend a civilized public space against incivility, for example taking action against disruptors such as Airbnb, which is blamed for swamping beautiful cities with tourists.[14] It is instinctively sceptical towards openness and negative liberty, which are perceived as disruptive, increasing transaction costs, and sometimes as producing an incoherent or inefficient Internet where private gain crowds out public good. In 2017, the EU's then-Competition Commissioner Margrethe Vestager launched an antitrust blast against American tech giants on the ground that they might swallow rivals or force them out of business, leaving consumers with a poorer standard of service. Her work was highly commended, and her clout within the European Union evidenced by her unusual promotion to the position of executive vice president in the new commission of 2019.[15] Since then, she has argued that 'China has the data, the US has the money, and we have the purpose', and that the European Union should retain its 'willingness to protect the fundamental values' that had 'made us one of the most attractive places to live on the planet ever'.[16]

Several institutional actors combine to adapt the Internet to the bourgeois vision of the European Union. The European Commission makes strategic decisions on the scope of treaties, where and when to regulate, and also administers regulation, so that, for instance, it decides whether a non-member state has 'adequate' privacy protection for data sharing. The European Parliament is increasingly active, for example in shaping the General Data Protection Regulation (GDPR). Many individual states of the European Union, notably Germany, have strong traditions of resisting state or business arguments for more information about or greater interference in private life. France, geopolitically ambitious, pushed ahead in 2020 with a 3 percent tax on the annual revenues of technology companies providing services to French consumers, wherever they book their profits, despite threats from the Trump administration to retaliate.[17] Regulators work across national and international levels, including for example the joint groups of data-protection regulators, the Article 29 Working Party, which became (in 2018) the European Data Protection Board. A lively set of advocacy and civil society groups provides policy input, while multinational businesses keen to operate in European markets usually pursue the strategy of adopting the European Union's stringent regulations across worldwide operations. The Commission of 2019, under Ursula von der Leyen, has geopolitical ambitions too, but at the time of writing it is not clear how these will translate into policy, especially post-pandemic.[18] Some European consulates in San Francisco are major players in technological diplomacy,[19] and the European Union's detailed approach to privacy is recognized as a gold standard.[20]

The European Union deploys a number of administrative means and 'soft law' to protect European citizens, passing enforcement responsibilities to ISPs and search engines, and looking at models of civic responsibility and self-regulation.[21] Meanwhile, European courts are regulating the Internet increasingly aggressively. National courts, the Court of Justice of the European Union (CJEU), and the European Court of Human Rights (ECHR) have interpreted human rights in the technological context, preventing states from building large databases of information about citizens, and supporting rights to be de-indexed from online searches. In the latter example, discussed in detail later in the chapter, the original decision was welcomed by many commentators (including the present authors) as allowing the European Union to police its own jurisdiction, with the search engine involved administering the process. However, since the judgement, the French data-protection regulator CNIL has upped the ante by pushing back against searches for EU citizens in *any* jurisdiction, and the GDPR of 2018 has enshrined that universalism into EU law, switching the emphasis from contextual delisting to permanent erasure.[22]

Privacy has become central to the European Union's self-image as a value-based organization,[23] and is prominent in the EU policy toolbox,[24] so we will focus on it in this chapter, but it is not the only tool. For instance, its update of its copyright laws attracted opprobrium because of its aggressive stance on copyright breaches.[25] Characteristic of the European Union's attitude towards technology firms is its default assumption that complaints about regulation are exaggerated. Article 13 of the new copyright law compels Internet firms to work closely with copyright holders to bring down copyright materials as soon as possible, which (given the imprecise nature of copyright identification algorithms) is likely to result in over-zealous policing. Article 11 requires aggregators to obtain a licence from publishers if they display excerpts from content. A similar rule introduced in Spain in 2014 led Google to withdraw its aggregation service from there; the bet underlying Article 11 is that Google could not afford to do the same across the whole of Europe.

The European mindset is that cooperative behaviour is unlikely (if not impossible) in the absence of rules: one study for the European Union about the interconnection of the Internet's autonomous systems concluded: 'A recurrent theme in the discussion of IP interconnection is whether network operators will be motivated to interconnect (on reasonable terms) in the absence of a regulatory obligation'.[26] This is an old theme—as Tocqueville wrote in 1856 about the conditions in pre-Revolutionary France, 'No one could imagine succeeding in any important project unless the state became involved'!²⁷

We suggest that the Internet as envisaged by the European Commission, and by most if not all of the governments of the member states of the European Union, can stand as representative of the bourgeois vision, and so we call our second Internet the *Brussels Bourgeois Internet*. We find that the Brussels Internet values open standards, neutrality, and transparency highly,

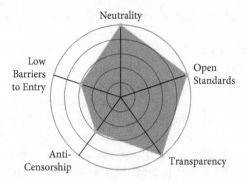

Figure 7.1. The ideals of the Brussels Bourgeois Internet.
Source: Thanks to Paul Smart, who conceived and created this diagram via Highcharts.

because it is concerned with inclusion and liberty, as long as human rights and good behaviour are secured in advance. It is therefore less supportive than the Silicon Valley Internet of low barriers to entry, in that disruptive actors are to be repelled if possible, and somewhat happier with censorship, preventing or deterring trolling or fake news, or at least holding their perpetrators to account. Mapped onto the OSI layers of Chapter 3, the Brussels Bourgeois Internet tries to preserve openness in the network layer and downwards, to preserve the benefits of connectivity, but higher up openness is conditional on the preservation of civility and respect (Figure 7.1).[28]

THE EU PRIVACY WARS

Privacy has long been seen in Europe as a key democratic value, a necessary condition for the autonomy of the citizen,[29] and as such it has been supported by most of the major political institutions in the European Union. The bourgeois ideal is not paternalistic—the aim is not to suggest particular outcomes or values, but to allow the independent citizen the space to pursue his or her own ideals. Democracy depends on reasonable privacy for individuals to consume news, political speech, or other cultural artefacts, to associate without surveillance, and to organize action. But although it might be possible to address the issue using open standards, such as the Platform for Privacy Preferences (P3P)[30] and 'Do Not Track',[31] to assert the claims of privacy and tailor the use of information to one's preferences, these have not caught on as well as blunter instruments like encryption standards, behind which both the innocent and guilty can shelter. The problem is that they make individuals set their own privacy preferences by hand, which in economists' terms increases the transaction costs (in lay terms, it's a pain in the backside and what kind of schmuck has the time?). Hence, on the bourgeois account, government must step in.

There is a debate over whether the United States, where privacy protection is based on different principles, reaches EU standards.[32] The US approach is sectoral—i.e. the extent of protection depends on what kind of information we are talking about. Financial or health information receives more protection than, say, commercial information, whereas in the European Union, personal data of any kind has the same coverage, whether it refers to the data subject's health or hobbies. The US approach suggests that certain types of information have the proven potential to cause more harms, and they therefore get more legal protection consistent with its common law system, where privacy is treated as a tort.[33] A frequent response from those who prefer universal coverage is that, in a world where identification of data subjects tends to happen as a result of piecing together clues from several pieces of data, it is impossible to say which types of information are more or less harmful, because it is impossible to predict which will be the final piece of the jigsaw in an identification.[34]

The European Commission has had the expansion of global influence of its privacy standards (which it contentiously calls 'universal principles')[35] as a policy aim at least since 2010, and long before that, data protection was touted as a 'successful . . . example of the EU creating a global standard that reflects its values'.[36] The ECHR, the CJEU, and several national constitutional courts have extended privacy protection in line with the privacy rights in the European Convention on Human Rights, while the European Parliament has become increasingly assertive internationally. The GDPR, now the cornerstone of EU data-protection law, has given the European Union apparent powers to be the world's 'privacy cop'. GDPR rests largely on two ideas, that individuals' views about where and how information about them gets used should be given weight, and that those handling such information are accountable for keeping it safe. It is intended to crack down upon unauthorized, concealed, or automated decision-making, as well as insecure data handling. The size of Europe's markets in the aggregate, if not as large or growing so quickly as the United States' or China's, is hardly peanuts. A multinational company wishing to transfer data across borders is faced with the choice of expensively crafting different rules and practices for data processing for the jurisdictions involved, or taking the simpler option of universally respecting the most stringent rules, which in general will be GDPR. Hence there should be a 'race to the top'.[37]

As one might perhaps expect, those nations, such as Germany, which have greater concerns about privacy have pressed harder to strengthen EU standards than others. The United Kingdom (a common law jurisdiction, with much in common with the US) has a more laissez faire attitude towards privacy and data protection, as evinced by its looser implementation of the 1995

Data Protection Directive, but it was unable to dilute the GDPR, which as a regulation applied equally to all EU and European Economic Area (EEA) nations. When GDPR was bogged down in the EU legislative process with 3,999 amendments, the Snowden revelations of massive surveillance by the US government functioned as what Commissioner Viviane Reding called a 'wake-up call'[38] and lubricated its progress—almost certainly not unconnected with the publication by WikiLeaks of US National Security Agency intercepts of Chancellor Angela Merkel's telephone conversations.[39]

In the remainder of this chapter, we will delve further into detail about the European Union's projections of soft power in the privacy sphere, first with the original 1995 Data Protection Directive (DPD), and then with the revised GDPR, which came into force in 2018. Each of these carefully crafted pieces of regulation was somewhat behind the technological curve. The DPD was developed for a world of stand-alone databases, just as the Web came along to connect them and complicate the picture. GDPR filled in some of the DPD's lacunae, but itself is somewhat behind the technology curve of networks and data we described in Chapter 1, and hence is in tension with the narrative of big data and digital modernity. Nevertheless, despite the strains inherent in both DPD and GDPR, they have each been able to exert a strong influence on the use of technology, as we will describe.

DATA PROTECTION UNDER THE DATA PROTECTION DIRECTIVE

Part of the European Union's privacy apparatus includes regulation of the transfer of personal data across the borders of nation states, which is only legal when the receivers of the data have adequate privacy protection. In practice, the definition of 'adequacy' is strongly connected to EU data-protection rules—i.e. if a third country's privacy protection is broadly of a piece with the European Union's (and certified as such by the European Commission), then cross-border sharing is legal. If not, it is not. From 2000, the transfer of personal data to the United States, essential to trade in goods and services, was governed by the Safe Harbor compromise, by which US companies storing European personal data could self-certify that they adhered to a series of data-protection principles.[40] Over 4,000 organizations self-certified; few officials bothered to check compliance.

Safe Harbor was overturned by the CJEU in 2015, following a complaint by campaigner Max Schrems that the Snowden revelations showed that his Facebook data was not safe from public surveillance in the United States.[41] One American law professor thundered 'An improvident, but final and unreviewable, decision by the European Union's highest court has invalidated EU approval for one of the most popular legal bases . . . for transferring personal data from the EU to the USA.'[42] The decision in Schrems meant a severe problem for businesses needing to process data on both sides of the Atlantic (and processing data may mean simply copying it), which had to cease this practice immediately.[43] After the disruption, there was a scramble to set up an alternative, beefed-up version called the EU-US Privacy Shield. That came under immediate pressure,[44] and was struck down by the CJEU in 2020.[45]

Other cases at the same time showed the CJEU flexing its muscles. Most famously, the Google Spain case demonstrated that a right to be forgotten was implicit in the DPD (enforcement of such a right had been an aspiration of the European Commission since 2010).[46] A Spanish newspaper's digital archive preserved an old story related to the plaintiff's past financial diffi- culties, and Googling his name would reliably resurface the story. The man asked the newspaper to take down the piece, and Google Spain to de-list it, on the data-protection grounds that the information was irrelevant (a past story about difficulties that had been overcome) and excessive (it was prejudicial to him and his business to keep the information easily available). The Spanish data-protection authority, the AEPD, decided in his favour against Google Spain, which then appealed to the CJEU. In a decision which was a shock at the time (the AEPD was supported by neither its fellow European data- protection authorities, nor the CJEU's special advisor, the Advocate General), the CJEU rejected Google's appeal in 2014 (even extending the AEPD's ori- ginal judgement).[47]

This was a step in the process to extend EU privacy law beyond the accepted jurisdiction of the European Union and the European Economic Area, to in- crease the reach of the Bourgeois Internet. Google Spain made a number of arguments to the CJEU, of which two concern us. Their initial argument was that indexing search results was not data processing at all, because it only in- volved locating, indexing, and perhaps storing data *qua* data. In other words, the data was not treated as interpreted, i.e. as information, but was genuinely uninterpreted, subject only to syntactic processes such as searching for and matching uninterpreted symbol strings. If the initial argument was rejected and the court judged that indexing *was* processing data, Google Spain's second argument was that the processing was done in the United States by Google Inc., an American company distinct from Google Spain, and therefore outside EU jurisdiction, as neither a European company nor a European server was involved.

All Google's arguments were rejected. Of these two, the initial one was re- jected on the grounds that data *was* being processed. Google's case relied on the computer science data/information distinction which we have assumed in this book, and so argued that personal data is *information*, and therefore interpreted, and conversely that uninterpreted data are 'about' nothing. The CJEU followed the DPD and rejected this distinction, so that data had merely to be *interpretable* (and therefore could be used to identify people in some circumstances), even if the operations carried out on it did not require its interpretation. Interestingly, the Advocate General sided with Google on this and not the court, drawing the same distinction between 'processing of personal data, that is "information relating to an identified or identifiable natural person" in some semantically relevant way and . . . mere computer code'.[48] As we have argued, there is a confusion between uninterpreted data and interpreted information, and so-called personal data would be better labelled 'personal information', as it is in the United States.

The court also squashed Google Spain's arguments that if personal data was being processed, Google Inc. was doing it. First, the court noted that Spanish law applied to Google Spain since it was established in the European Union. It then argued that the processing (admittedly in the US) was carried out in the context of the activities of Google Spain on the territory of the member state Spain, to aid its Spanish advertising business, which both financed and provided the raison d'être for the search engine. Hence the location of the data processing is irrelevant because its purpose is to support business activities taking place in the European Union (an EU company running a business in the EU and using data about EU citizens). It refused to accept that Google Spain could move its data-protection liability offshore. It also added to both these arguments that as the DPD was meant to cover the rights of EU citizens within the European Union, the court was bound to interpret the various concepts widely rather than narrowly.

Hence, even before the GDPR, the Google Spain decision established the European Union's sway over data processing in the United States to protect EU citizens in the European Union. This was not an unreasonable decision by the CJEU, either in terms of its interpretation of the DPD, or of the position of Google Spain as ultimately responsible for the processing. It was also proportionate; the decision did not demand the removal of any information (assuming it true) from the Internet. The possibility of creating an overview of an individual is the privacy breach; the information objected to should only be de-listed in the judgement if the search's keywords are the individual's name. Privacy is contravened far more seriously by someone searching for a named individual, than when they search for something else and find the name among the results, because in the former case they're clearly interested in the individual personally and would receive a dossier about them via the search engine, whereas in the latter case they would have other purposes and no means of getting an overview of any individual.

The court also left loopholes in case the individual involved was a public figure, whose private life may be of legitimate public interest even after the (true) information has become outdated. On the other hand, someone wanting to be de-indexed would have to show that the information committed one of the data-protection sins of being excessive, outdated, or otherwise misleading. Even then, that argument could still be countermanded by better reasons (such as the public interest in knowing about it).

The decision, strongly attacked at the time, had much to commend it. The information would simply be de-indexed; it would remain online and discoverable by Google search, unless it was a targeted search for the individual. History wouldn't be changed, and there was no Orwellian control of the past. The only free speech curtailed was that of a search engine to say that a certain webpage was the nth most relevant page about an individual. It recognized that Google is a starting point for inquiry, not the whole truth; casual fishing expeditions might be undermined, but a serious journalist on an important story would still be able to dig out the information. The judgement applied to Google's presence in national domains within the European Union, google.es, google.fr, and so on, and not to international domains like .com. It was an obstacle for frivolous and speculative searches, without hindering serious inquiry. It was not perfect privacy protection, but neither did it force European standards of privacy onto different cultures and societies.

The judgement wasn't perfect in other ways, not least because it made Google the (initial) judge of whether a request for de-indexing was justified (subject to appeal to one's national data-protection authority), so in effect partially privatizing the roles of arbiter and censor, a perennial problem with content moderation, as we shall see. But perhaps the real significance of the decision was the suggestion of future direction, following a consistent trend of interpreting data-protection rules widely against tech giants.

THE LONG SHADOW OF GDPR

The DPD had become a powerful tool, and GDPR amplified this effect via swingeing sanctions of up to 4 percent of a company's worldwide revenue, or €20m, whichever is greater. It is explicitly intended to cover, not only EU citizens' data originating in the European Union, but the data of EU citizens held or processed anywhere in the world (the first enforcement notice under GDPR was sent to a Canadian firm).[49] Furthermore, the GDPR has extended the scope, as well as the reach, of many of the rights. The right to be forgotten has now gone beyond the limited right to de-indexation that was discovered by the Google Spain judgement, to a full-fledged right of erasure of inappropriate information, under certain circumstances.

The major multinational tech firms have generally fallen in with GDPR, despite earlier grumbles. Zuckerberg has called for greater regulation, and cynics were quick to spot that onerous regulations may bring costs to the tech giants, but were handy barriers to market entry, because of the enormous potential costs of breaches, and the very large concrete costs of compliance, for smaller companies.[50] One response to the cynics is that it is not the job of privacy regulators to angst over the fates of small and medium-sized enterprises. If protecting privacy in an age of big data is expensive, then that is one of the costs of being in the business.

It is also worth pointing out that GDPR is likely to be supplemented by an ePrivacy regulation, currently (2020) a European Commission proposal to even up privacy coverage fragmented across the European Union by different national laws to implement the ePrivacy Directive of 2002. The regulation will beef up the 2002 directive, applying directly to metadata, producing simpler rules for cookies (intended to get rid of the plethora of consent requests that GDPR has spawned in Europe every time one visits a website) and more effective protection against spam.[51] It too has extra-territorial scope, for example applying to anyone placing cookies on the devices of individuals in the European Union (it will not become part of UK law as a result of Brexit, but will still apply to UK companies marketing in the EU).

Even before GDPR, US lawyers Jack Goldsmith and Tim Wu had set out the basis of the European Union's hegemony in this area: it has unilaterally developed its own concept of privacy law based on its own unusual concern for citizens' privacy; it is a major market (and component of supply chains) of great technological sophistication from which multinationals cannot withdraw easily; it would be expensive to treat European data differently from data about non-EU citizens originating elsewhere.[52] Bradford draws attention to the effect of multinationals, coerced into conformity with EU law, lobbying their home governments to even up the legal playing field by enacting EU-style privacy laws, thereby helping spread the principles globally through hard law.[53]

Bradford adds further factors: the European Union, consistent with its bourgeois propensities and civil law system, typically favours precautionary measures over regulations informed by empirical evaluation of actual risk; it targets less mobile consumer markets over markets in more mobile commodities, such as capital; it is also harder to separate out and treat data differently in different markets, compared to more separable factors such as labour. The net result is that the European Union has developed global reach via the size of its single market, which is hard for large companies to ignore. It is unsurprising that the EU data-protection regime has proven adaptable across the globe, as historically it was developed as a means of harmonizing different data-protection regimes, and the European Union also has great experience in helping nations adapt to its regime following the accession of thirteen new members since the enactment of the DPD.[54] In a 2019 survey, Australian law professor Graham Greenleaf found that 132 countries have now enacted 'EU-style' data privacy laws, with another 28 attempting to enact bills, and that 'the move toward stronger standards within [new privacy] laws is reflected not only by the GDPR adherence of EU member states, but also in the constant inclusion of many GDPR-like principles in both new and revised laws outside the EU'.[55]

Finally, the European Union has developed, since the enactment of the DPD, extraordinary regulatory capacity and expertise in data protection. Each member state has its own regulator, which can be proactive and aggressive. At EU level, each division of the civil service has a major focus on data protection. The European Parliament, especially via its influential civil liberties committee, has played an important role in framing regulation, such as the GDPR and the ill-fated EU-US Privacy Shield. And the European Union has its own Data Protection Supervisor, as well as an advisory committee of national regulators. Such depth of expertise (and appetite for a scrap) is not found elsewhere.

As a comparator, consider the Cross-Border Privacy Rules (CBPR) system, developed in 2011 by Asia-Pacific Economic Cooperation (APEC) members to facilitate privacy-respecting cross-border dataflows. Unlike GDPR, it functions rather like Safe Harbor, in that it is a voluntary principles-based framework that requires opting in, and it is based on weaker data-protection principles. Hence, fewer than half of APEC's members have adopted CBPR, even after almost a decade. Despite its sceptical view of cross-border trade, the Trump administration endorsed CBPR, and even incorporated it into the United States-Mexico-Canada Agreement (USMCA, the trade deal which replaced NAFTA in 2019). So far, no company has ever lost its CBPR certification. Four thousand US companies registered to join the EU-US Privacy Shield, whereas a mere twenty-three have registered with CBPR, which is several years older. China, a key APEC member, hasn't bothered to join.[56]

However, the story of the European Union's global reach via GDPR is not as simple as this tale of hegemony implies, as illustrated by case studies developed by information law scholar Paul M. Schwartz.[57] In each case, the European Union has been prepared to negotiate, from a strong position but with an adaptable legal model that seems acceptable to many businesses and governments. Japan chose to upgrade its data-protection regulation during negotiations. Meanwhile, the history of engagement with the United States shows the European Union at first in a weak position in negotiating Safe Harbor, which was relatively toothless and poorly enforced. But that was negotiated before many US firms had experience of the European regime, while the Privacy Shield, which would have been far more favourable to the European Union, received support from both the US government and the private sector. It is also worth noting that the European Union has been prepared to learn from other jurisdictions how to ratchet the regime in a tighter direction; for instance, the idea of compulsory notification of a data breach was an innovation from California in 2000,[58] while that of data protection-by-design was adapted from the Ontario Privacy Commissioner's concept of privacy-by-design.[59]

There are also costs to the occupation of the moral high ground. Europe's tech companies are rarely as large or as innovative as those of the United States (or China, for that matter). The business software company SAP is the only European company in the largest twenty internationally; Wirecard, a German payment processor, was thought to be a rare European success story, until it turned out that €1.9bn on its balance sheet had been invented.[60] Perhaps strong regulation curbs innovation and keeps European firms small—or perhaps it is the other way around. Might we think that the European Union is keener to regulate Facebook or Google than it would be if they were French or Italian companies? We can say that the 'Brussels effect' amplifying its regulations may help spread the bourgeois vision across the Internet, but it hasn't always helped European companies.[61] Profits and taxes go elsewhere. The Europeans may struggle to keep up in AI, and be out-competed by less ethically rigorous firms, and it may lose out in data-heavy industries like ad-tech.[62] The regulatory race to the top that the European Union currently presides over may not be sustained when technologies like 3-D printing make it easier to tailor different products to different markets.

There are a lot of 'maybes' and 'perhapses' in the previous paragraph; it is not our purpose to argue that GDPR will necessarily handicap the European economy, only that we should not blithely assume that it will be economically neutral. Yet the GDPR remains a source of advantage for the European Union, and is also a totemic symbol of the ambitious bourgeois vision: 'This new data protection ecosystem stems from the strong roots of another kind of ecosystem: the European project itself, that of unifying the values drawn from a shared historical experience with a process of industrial, political, economic and social integration of States, in order to sustain peace, collaboration, social welfare and economic development'.[63]

CHAPTER 8

Policy Question

When Is Surveillance Justified?

On the Brussels Bourgeois vision, human rights and civil respect are pre-eminent. Privacy in particular has been elevated to prime status, what one academic has called 'the EU's First Amendment'.[1] This does raise questions about when it is reasonable to take advantage of the data that flows around the system. There is an economic value to the data, which we may discount against human rights aspects, but sometimes there is a social value to using the data for the purpose of surveillance of the population.

In the physical world, surveillance requires a physical presence, either of a watcher or an artefact (e.g. a CCTV camera or loyalty card). But as any process on the Internet involves the movement of data from A to B, all that is needed online is for the transaction to be logged, and there will be more opportunity as more processes and interactions are 'datafied'. Datafication refers to the progressive increase in the gathering of data, facilitated by shifting processes online, and by instrumenting the environment to extract information. If one reads a book, or listens to a CD, no one knows about it, except perhaps an unfortunate neighbour in the latter case. If one uses an e-reader or music-streaming service, data is created which is informative not only about what one reads or listens to, but how the content is consumed, in small or larger chunks, which words are looked up most often, which tracks are skipped. Suddenly the provider knows way more about one's reading or listening habits than even the most assiduous librarian of the analogue age. Many worry about private companies having access to this data; others worry about governments. This book is not about surveillance or privacy, but they bear on our question of the kind of Internet being created.[2]

Four Internets. Kieron O'Hara and Wendy Hall, Oxford University Press. © Oxford University Press 2021.
DOI: 10.1093/oso/9780197523681.003.0008

Online surveillance records what was until recently unrecorded and unrecordable, giving the state unprecedented access to its citizens, and turning fleeting behaviour into a permanent record that can be exchanged in a market.[3] Polanyi noted how transformation of a phenomenon into a tradable resource had earlier happened with human labour, land, and other factors of production.[4] As we move into digital modernity, the individual is now rendered as the data about him or her, and policy is made by reasoning about their avatar or digital twin.[5]

Surveillance can also play a political role as well as an economic one. To govern the networked square, the hierarchical tower needs information, and surveillance provides it. Whereas democracies and free economies provide mechanisms to signal problems, autocracies often don't have access to the same kind of mechanisms (because they have been suppressed). In that case:

> Surveillance powered by artificial intelligence . . . allows despots to automate the monitoring and tracking of their opposition in ways that are far less intrusive than traditional surveillance. Not only do these digital tools enable authoritarian regimes to cast a wider net than with human-dependent methods; they can do so using far fewer resources: no one has to pay a software program to monitor people's text messages, read their social media posts, or track their movements. And once citizens learn to assume that all those things are happening, they alter their behavior without the regime having to resort to physical repression.[6]

Meanwhile, the citizenry, if it is inclined to resistance, will need to coordinate its responses, which requires knowledge about what benefits the autocracy is providing, what other people or groups are likely to do, and how strong their commitment is to revolt. Hence another requirement of the autocrat is the control and even manipulation of the information space to suppress or prevent self-calibration amongst the population.[7] This is why, as we will see later, social media have been seen by some as supporting democracy by their very nature. Conversely, it has been argued that more efficient coverage by security services in dictatorships is associated with decreases in violence and repression.[8] Surveillance, therefore, can be the key to enabling a dictatorship to function effectively without collapsing into chaos or barbarism.

Smartphones have revolutionized deep online surveillance. Data collected by the apps on the device finds its way back to parent companies (one study found that Alphabet-owned trackers had a presence in over 73 percent of apps in their dataset, an extraordinary monopoly), and thence to other subsidiaries or even third parties.[9] Users may be tracked across devices. Privacy policies—where they exist—can be permissive, or misleading, or even on occasion ignored. They are generally long, complex, and unreadable—one suspects by design.[10] The data-brokering industry holds instantaneous auctions, enabling the data to be used in real time to coordinate marketing or behavioural prediction. There are many legitimate purposes for gathering such data, including sending crash reports, analytics, A/B testing, integrating with other services, and for billing purposes, but there is little transparency, or what human-computer interaction expert m. c. schraefel and her colleagues call *apparency*, i.e. providing understandable cues to the user in the moment.[11]

Jurisdictions try to regulate these markets (for example, via GDPR, while in the US children's data is regulated by the Children's Online Privacy Protection Act), but the brokers operate so quickly and at such scale that this is easier said than done. In her critique of surveillance capitalism (see Chapter 9), social psychologist Shoshanna Zuboff argues that Google has shrugged off legal and social protests in relation to the digitization of books, Street View, capturing of voice communications, bypassing privacy settings, manipulation of search results, extensive retention of search data, tracking smartphone location data, wearable technologies and face-recognition abilities, collecting student data for commercial purposes, and consolidating user profiles across Google's services and devices.[12]

The next revolution is likely to be face-recognition technology, as it enables identification without cooperation or awareness, supported by a *prima facie* argument that it doesn't break privacy norms (as faces are usually on show in public spaces).[13] Vestager has argued to the contrary that automated face recognition without consent breaches GDPR, since biometric identifying data is sensitive personal data, and courts elsewhere are alert to the technology.[14] Facebook, for example, was charged in the state of Illinois with using 'face templates' to produce suggestions for tags for images on its site without consent; it settled a class action for $550 million.[15]

SURVEILLANCE: ALL BAD?

Surveillance gets a bad press. We can define it as the monitoring of behaviour in order to manage or direct it, thus implying that surveillance connects to intervention strategies of some sort. Sometimes these are immediate, as when one constantly watches over a toddler, ready to intervene when it encounters danger. But more usually, and particularly online, surveillance involves the gathering and storage of information for use in the future to prevent, adjust, or profit from behaviour.

The dialectic of surveillance has tended towards a trade-off. The developments of digital modernity described in Chapter 1 provide benefits that require the rendering of individuals and organizations as data, which inevitably supports surveillance. Surveillance is a price we pay, and if digital modernity is seen as a teleological inevitability, or even a normative imperative, then it is a price we will *have* to pay.[16] Surveillance is most obviously a breach of privacy, but it is also often and quite generally seen as symptomatic of a lack of trust in the person under surveillance, likely to produce chilling effects where people refrain from doing what they might wish to do, asymmetries of power between those under surveillance and those doing it, systematic errors of false positives and presumptions of guilt, and social discrimination where people of particular characteristics fall under greater suspicion.[17] It is therefore unsurprising that surveillance is rarely welcomed in the abstract, but it has positive aspects, and, it has been argued, is essential in the modern world.

There are three reasons for this. Firstly, the numbers of people and sociotechnical systems that need to be coordinated in order to achieve expected social functions has been growing for decades. An apparently simple process, such as getting meat to the table, used to involve a farmer and maybe a butcher, and a ride into the village to make a purchase, whereas now any supermarket involves the organization of thousands of employees, experts, safety systems, food provenance systems, technicians, logistical services, traffic and parking management services, accountants, marketing services, and legal services, all working to an ever-expanding rulebook in the glare of scrutiny from the mass media, political entities, animal rights and environmental activists, international investors, and millions of consumers with changing tastes and incompatible desires for quality and bargains. The routine production of goods and services by business and others in a modern economy is an extraordinary achievement, way beyond what would have been conceivable even a few decades ago, and requires an immense amount of knowledge about people and their lives. Government and business must be able to understand the milieux in which they hope to operate, and to receive feedback about the services they provide. For that, people must be rendered visible to, and legible by, the systems which provide for them.[18]

Secondly, a characteristic feature of modernity is what Giddens calls *reflexivity*, the ability and desire to reflect on and adapt one's circumstances. Individuality is expressed via *choice*: democracy, free markets, freedom of association, freedom of religion, and so on, which all require space for such reflection.[19] As modernity evolves into digital modernity, reflexivity is outsourced to data gatherers, using machine learning and AI. Individuality under digital modernity is expressed via *personalization*: rather than the world being presented to you so that you can select the bits of it that interest you, increased data allows the world to be moulded around your tastes and preferences. Surveillance is therefore even more important. In the world of analogue modernity described by Giddens, privacy is essential, a space into which one can withdraw in order to make authentic, autonomous choices, and so surveillance is a trade-off. Under digital modernity, privacy rather gets in the way, because the quality of a personalized service depends crucially on information; the more that is known about the recipient, the better the service will be.

Hence, surveillance is a means of negotiating the complexity of the choices we are faced with in digital modernity.[20]

Thirdly, surveillance is often thought of, following Foucault, in terms of *control*. It is also clear that surveillance may also be a means of *care*, for the elderly or infirm, for instance, or for the complex ecosystems in the natural environment.[21] The promise of personalized medicine depends on understanding one's genome, and genomic databases are as revealing as it is possible to be, not only about the people represented in them, but also their blood relations. Surveillance also clearly has an important role in guaranteeing security and enforcing the law, which present even greater ethical challenges.[22] Deterrence (e.g. speed cameras) may require surveillance of the innocent. In a liberal society, the acceptability of this kind of surveillance depends on independent oversight of decision-making, and a distinction (made in the US Bill of Rights) between reasonable and unreasonable searches.[23] Welfare systems require surveillance, but they can be conflicted. Is it to ensure that the people who need help are detected and effectively supported, or to intrusively deter free-riding and fraud?[24] There are tests that can be applied, at least in democracies, to balance the harm of intrusion against the public good—if regulation can keep pace with the development of surveillance technology.[25]

To take one example, the problem of carbon emissions is often framed as one of negative economic externalities. The carbon emitted by production of a good is not factored into its price, and so the cost of dealing with it lies with neither producer nor consumer, but with society as a whole. As carbon accounting gains regulatory support and becomes more accurate, there will be imperatives to capture and price our carbon footprints.[26] The Internet will be key. Supply-chain management and e-commerce platforms could easily provide the means to gather information about the carbon footprints of particular goods, and particular consumers; smartphones and the IoT must surely also be central to such a system. Some of China's advantages in the surveillance industry (discussed in Chapter 11) are seen as advantages in its growing environmentalism.[27] It is likely that any scheme to reduce carbon emissions at anything like the scale needed to make serious inroads into the current trajectory of global warming will depend on extensive and thoroughgoing surveillance.

As a further small example of how worries about surveillance, combined with the Bourgeois preference for anticipating and neutralizing harms, can result in a lack of flexibility, consider the travails of Germany's Christian Democratic Union (CDU), the party of Angela Merkel. After electoral reverses in 2018, Merkel promised not to seek a record fifth term as German chancellor in 2021. She relinquished the leadership of the CDU, but her replacement was disappointing and in turn had to resign in 2020. That meant the CDU needed to elect a new leader prior to the next federal election in 2021, as its candidate to replace Chancellor Merkel.

The unanticipated problem was the pandemic. The Germans, unsurprisingly given their traumatic history, are intensely nervous about surveillance, especially in political matters. Political parties are not treated as common law associations, but are regulated by the constitution, the *Grundgesetz* or Basic Law, according to which elections of representatives must be 'general, direct, free, equal and secret'. 'Secret' here means, among other things, that there can be no possibility of connecting voter and vote (unlike, say, in the UK, where ballot papers have serial numbers to make them theoretically traceable back to voters), and it follows from this that online can never be secret, since traceability (at least back to a device) will always be possible. Rather, in an election it would be essential, because any remote vote must be auditable (to ensure that only the entitled voted), which demands traceability. Only a direct physical measure, such as restricting voting to a particular location and time, allows integrity without auditability.

But when the COVID pandemic struck, a new leader couldn't be elected at all, because party members could not be gathered together for a special conference, such as that in Hamburg where Mrs. Merkel had been replaced in 2018, so offline and online (and postal) were arguably all ruled out. The elections had to be delayed over and again while the legalities of the situation were explored, and the candidates squabbled.[28] Were secrecy and privacy such overriding rights that they couldn't have been waived in the very special conditions of 2020? After all, the likelihood of a delegate being persecuted for supporting one CDU bigwig over another would be relatively low, even if the general principle of secret ballots is held to be paramount. Fraud and security would be serious issues to negotiate, but the numbers of voters in the case of the CDU leadership would surely be tractable (the 2018 leadership election drew 999 votes).

The European Union's promotion of privacy as a pre-eminent value is a top-down, elite-driven project. In general, it is supported by its citizens, but this may be at least partly because the costs of promoting privacy have largely been borne by the business sector. Would public support for the data protection and privacy regime be as strong if citizens themselves bore the direct costs? And should privacy warriors clutch their pearls if surveillance can save lives or the planet? That question looks more urgent following the pandemic.

SURVEILLANCE IN A PANDEMIC

The 2020 COVID-19 pandemic was hardly good news for anyone, but the tech companies were well-placed to provide necessary services. Family gatherings, yoga lessons, and university lectures were facilitated by videoconferencing platforms like Zoom and Microsoft Teams, concerts went out over YouTube, and art galleries went virtual. Trips to the shop and restaurant were replaced by Amazon and Deliveroo, while Netflix and the Kindle provided the entertainment. A further function was also promised by the Internet infrastructure: tracing and managing the progress of the virus.

Information technology had already had a couple of goes at this, during the SARS epidemic of 2002–2003 and H1N1 in 2009–2010. During SARS, the Singaporean government, a world leader in e-government, set up a system for monitoring the crisis, tracing contacts, and enforcing quarantine. The Defence Science and Technology Agency (DSTA) realized that the Ministry of Health's unstructured, sometimes paper-based, information-processing operations wouldn't scale up, even with an injection of new technology. The DSTA built a case management system in two weeks flat, with a complex architecture covering contact tracing, epidemiology, disease control, front-line operations, quarantine, and provision of leave of absence from work. Nearly 200 different data formats needed to be resolved. The portal needed to be usable by novices and experts alike, and responsive to unanticipated demands. It was an impressive effort—being an illiberal one-party state helped—and the outbreak was contained.[29]

Fast forward to 2020, and the situation was very different. In 2003, the difficulty was developing an online interface with an integrated back end for efficient processing. The SARS epidemic actually helped speed up online social networking in some countries, especially in East Asia, where people were locked down. By 2020, not only were the information flows already in place, but the data itself was provided by existing infrastructure. The surveillance so often deplored by commentators now looked like a saviour.

The surveillance infrastructure suggests a number of applications in a pandemic. The simplest is gathering data that enables governments to understand how it is developing, and whether measures taken are adequate. In the case of COVID-19, aggregated non-identifying data could be used from smartphone locations or via the resources of social networks to develop models of social movement, and therefore ideas of how well lockdowns were working and how quickly the virus might spread. Increased access to previously unavailable populations and information about mobility would help with the situational awareness problem of identifying trends and geographic distribution. The consequences of implementing different measures could be mapped, to establish which variables made a difference and whether they might cause further problems. Data about mobility and population would help predict the course of the pandemic. And the impact of interventions and the obstacles hampering the achievement of certain objectives could be measured. Particularly valuable data types include origin-destination matrices (i.e. journeys people were making), hotspots (places where many people congregated), amount of time spent at particular locations, particularly work and home, and proximity matrices of when people are close.[30]

A second use of the infrastructure is to enforce lockdowns. If someone is quarantined, then their devices can be used to verify that they remain out of circulation. South Korea developed an app to alert the authorities if people broke their quarantine, and by March about 5,000 quarantined people (half the total) used the apps. In Taiwan, people's own smartphone's location data was used to track them. Conversely, there were also apps developed that could be used to prove that one was immune from the virus, by providing an e-certificate that one was allowed to roam.[31]

Thirdly, the infrastructure might be used for contact tracing. This is, of course, highly sensitive, especially as it has uses beyond managing pandemics, but a number of countries attempted it.[32] Israel's security service Shin Bet used the phone and credit card data of people known to be infected to re-trace their steps and find those they had been in close proximity to; within a few days it claimed to have identified 500 new people who were found to have been infected by the virus.[33] The Singaporean government developed an app, TraceTogether, that noted other phones within two metres with the app, and recorded encounters that lasted longer than half an hour (timestamps were collected, but location data not). Someone infected, or who had been close to someone infected, had to donate their data to the Ministry of Health, which could decrypt it and contact other parties. Downloading the app was not compulsory (although it was an offence to fail to hand over the data if one had downloaded it), and within a couple of weeks it had a million downloads. The app was made open source, so that others could continue development or could customize it for their own context.[34] Despite the publicity surrounding such contact-tracing apps, it wasn't obvious that they would be downloaded and used by a sufficient number of people to enable the quick suppression of the virus (as opposed to providing useful data to policymakers, which even small levels of use of the app would achieve). Even the Singaporean app was not downloaded enough.[35] In Israel, a reported surfeit of false positives meant that the Shin Bet app failed to gain traction, despite a strong push from the government, and many Israelis were reported to be leaving their smartphones at home when possible, in order to avoid being tracked.[36]

Rollout and, despite the experience with SARS, development worldwide were relatively slow, even though data was far more abundant in 2020 than in 2003. An international group of distinguished data scientists identified five reasons why smartphone data was not used routinely by governments during complex pandemics such as COVID-19. First, public authorities often lack the capacity to understand the problem, and bring together the necessary multidisciplinary teams. Some decision-makers are simply not aware of the possibilities. Second, there are problems with access to data. Phone companies can be reluctant to share, sometimes for data-protection reasons, sometimes because of worries about commercial confidentiality. Third, data scientists and domain experts tend to see research from their own perspective and communicate in their own silos, failing to see broader benefits. Fourth, governments don't have the procedures and protocols in place for immediate emergency action. The fifth reason they identified is directly concerned with the problems of surveillance and privacy.[37]

It is possible that even very privacy-sensitive populations would get used to these levels of intrusion if the public health outcomes were sufficiently positive, but resistance is always possible, with several ethical minefields to negotiate.[38] Because of such worries, a COVID-19 digital rights tracker was set up by one activist to document new measures.[39] Apple and Google worked together to produce in quick time an interoperable API to exchange Bluetooth signals, allowing iPhones and Android devices to gather data about close proximity between phones of either type and store it on the phones, without interfering with normal phone function or battery life. If someone tested positive, then the users of smartphones that had been in their proximity could then be alerted. During the 2020 pandemic, it was generally mobile phone data that was sought, but some researchers argued that SNS data was more fine-grained and predictive, at least in the early stages.[40]

Technological contact tracing appeared to be at best part of a strategy; some of the more grandiose claims were clearly overblown, and although at the time of writing we lack proper evaluations, it appears that contact tracing is better done by human beings using traditional measures and repurposing existing facilities such as call centres. Mobile apps do add important functions and gather data, for example supplementing the memories of patients who may already be feeling ill, and finding contacts unknown to the patient (for instance, on public transport).[41] Whatever happens, apps need to be integrated into offline systems that can handle the potential combinatorial explosion of cases, and the definition of 'close contact' needs to be calibrated so as not to overwhelm them with false positives.[42]

Three interesting issues emerged during the scramble to put apps in place. First, there was the question of centralization versus decentralization. A centralized system gathers information, for example location data from smartphones, and holds it in one place for querying and monitoring. Such a system can be used for contact tracing and mapping the course of the pandemic, and is therefore helpful for developing and adjusting policy, such as deciding whether to relax or tighten lockdown. The centralized body of data can also be used to spot patterns of fraud and misuse. There is a danger from cross-referring and linking people, especially as location data is pretty identifying when matched up with information about addresses or places of work. There is also a security problem raised, where a centralized database is a single point of vulnerability. The alternative is a decentralized system, where data is kept on individual smartphones, as with the Apple/Google system. This avoids both the security vulnerability and most possibilities of identification, although if someone does test positive for the virus, there would have to be a way of getting from the encrypted information about which phones had been in the vicinity to the contact details of those people (which in European law is personal data, putting such apps under the shadow of GDPR). However, there is far less useful data made available for guiding policy.

Second, not very many apps emerged in Europe. The United Kingdom, like many European countries, wanted a centralized app to inform pandemic policy, but whereas most nations eventually went down the decentralized route because of the functionality provided by Apple/Google, the United Kingdom's NHSX agency built and tested its own app. This proved hopelessly flawed, partly because it did not have the insight of the Apple/Google engineers who understood their own devices, and so did not take into account, for example, that Apple phones go to sleep if not used for a short while, and would therefore go unrecognized by the app.[43] Other apps were developed in the United Kingdom independently which had wide take-up and were able to provide some sort of real-time sample of the current state of play. The government focus on not confusing the public, and therefore not publicizing the independent apps, meant that when its own scheme collapsed, it had missed the opportunity to exploit the new tracing app ecosystem, which might have been aggregated into a reasonable source of data.[44] In a similar glitch, a Norwegian app had to be closed down because so few people used it, in a small population, in which the virus was not prevalent, that the national data protection agency demanded it be removed, as the breach of privacy was disproportionate to the benefits of its use.[45] The approved Dutch CoronaMelder app was created but not deployed for several weeks as the government struggled to pass enabling legislation.[46]

Third, so dominant are Apple and Google in the smartphone market that their API quickly became the standard for contact-tracing apps. This put extra pressure on those governments that wanted to centralize information for pandemic management, because their apps would not be interoperable with those of neighbouring countries that did use the Apple/Google system—an important factor in Europe, where borders are porous. The Apple/Google system did support privacy, which was also important in Europe, where trust in the corporate tech giants is not traditionally high. But many European governments pointed out that these American companies were in effect deciding European epidemic control policy directly by their design decisions. An advisor to the Latvian government complained:

> Acknowledging the intrusive power of the tool, and the potential for malicious abuse of it, Apple and Google have set preconditions for accessing its contact-tracing framework. The companies will allow only one app per country, approved by its government or its national health authority, but they will not allow a country's disease-control authority to connect the dots that are critical for analysing

data. Manually Latvia's disease-control authority will call a coronavirus-positive patient, query their contacts to determine the potential exposure, inform those people of a risk, follow up on further developments and build 'the tree' of virus spread. The Google-Apple approach will not allow the sole and official 'national app' to establish the connection between contacts and carrier.[47]

Centralization/intrusion and decentralization/privacy was a false dichotomy, she argued, because the key thing that a responsible government like her own wished to do was not to centralize everything, but rather have the ability to bring information to the centre if it proved necessary (e.g. only when someone tested positive).

GDPR puts limits on the flow of personal data. On the other hand, the COVID-19 saga shows us how sometimes we want that data to flow. The work-arounds that scientists and policymakers have to use to extract information from personal data are complex and extensive (see Chapter 18 for examples). Yet privacy involves more than personal data—if personal data is aggregated or sufficiently anonymized, the result is data that does not identify, but can still be used to profile and influence.[48] The practice of profiling (constructing artificial representations of segments of a population based on correlations and behaviour patterns) doesn't involve personal data at all, but can still be highly influential on behaviour. By making it harder to query data in an emergency, but providing less regulation for anonymous profiles, GDPR cannot be the ultimate solution to the online privacy problem.

Surveillance, though not pleasant, does have social uses, even if not a panacea. Yet the interaction between private-sector technologies and public defences of security, privacy, and rights is not always easy. Our next vision of the Internet focuses on the direct social benefits of commercial exploitation. It could be argued that Apple and Google were central to the contact-tracing effort precisely because they are successful businesses, not governmental or philanthropic agencies, and had they been given free rein with respect to the use of data from their devices, contact tracing would have been much more straightforward. To that end, we now move on to a more commercial vision of the Internet.

CHAPTER 9

The Third Internet

The DC Commercial Internet

Reflection about the *business models* that the Internet has ushered in leads us to our third Internet, in which firms are encouraged to exploit its *commercial* potential. The identity infrastructure that underpins the Internet provides the foundation of a targeted advertising model that finances free (at the point of consumption) online services ranging from search to social media to email to news to user-provided content. This model has driven extraordinary innovation online, and has created high-value network effects, with a strong correlation between rates of patenting of Web technology and levels of the tech-heavy NASDAQ composite stock index.[1] Privacy may be a good, but most people appear to be willing to trade it away, and so, on this vision, why should they be prevented from so doing?

THE IDEAL

In the previous chapter, we discussed the importance of surveillance in coordinating the complex systems that support prosperity and well-being. Not all such systems require centralized gathering of feedback and management. A free market is a network of buyers and sellers with low epistemological requirements—all a consumer need know is whether he is willing to buy at the price offered, and all a producer need know is whether she is prepared to invest to supply at a particular price, and eventually an optimal price will emerge. To enable this to happen, the sphere of the state and its *dirigiste* solutions should ideally be constrained, and private individuals should possess the

Four Internets. Kieron O'Hara and Wendy Hall, Oxford University Press. © Oxford University Press 2021.
DOI: 10.1093/oso/9780197523681.003.0009

rights and tools to defend their own interests as they see them. A vital part of this is the institution of private property, the ability to secure, control, and exchange objects both physical and abstract, and to deny others the use of them. Thus economic liberty is an important aspect of liberty in general, central to enabling individuals to protect their well-being and security and that of others for whom they provide.[2]

This kind of spontaneous order is harder to generate as complexity becomes greater, because more coordination is needed. As economist Ronald Coase argued, at some point the transaction costs of seeking out all the information required in order to coordinate the large numbers of operators to put meat on a supermarket shelf will outweigh the flexibility of the free market, creating an opportunity for the command-and-control structure of a firm to make savings.[3] In our terms, when transaction costs rise because of the complexity of the network, a hierarchy may be needed to create optimal outcomes. One hierarchical structure is a firm, and when the networks administered by such firms become very large, we see the formation and sustenance of large corporations such as the tech giants.

Markets have *externalities*, effects on parties external to a transaction that are not covered by the exchange or the economic activity. Much of the literature focuses on negative externalities, the costs imposed on a community by activities that are not borne by the participants. Common examples include environmental pollution caused by an industrial process that is not paid for by either producer or consumer, but rather by wider society, of which carbon emissions are perhaps the most pressing current example. Many exchanges also provide *positive externalities*, where wider society benefits—for instance, the existence of a factory in a town may result in positive spillover effects on other businesses which benefit from the wages paid to the workers. It has been argued that positive externalities—in particular, the innovations that capitalism has produced, whose benefits cannot be restricted to the direct parties to transactions—are responsible for many of the social and economic advances of Western societies since the eighteenth century.[4]

Networks have externalities thanks to the connections they make. Ideas and knowledge travel through them efficiently, as we have seen[5]—and so can misinformation, meaning the externalities can be positive or negative. The negative externalities of the Open Internet are the subject matter of Chapter 6. Network effects are examples of positive externalities within the network. A person joins a network to gain value for him- or herself; by increasing the network's size by one, he or she also inadvertently increases the value of the network for all the other participants.[6]

This is the basis of the third vision of the Internet, a *commercial* vision in which Internet resources are treated as property, which can be managed as the owner or rights-holder determines. Innovation and service provision are incentivized by the possibility of profit, and market solutions can be found for resource allocation, conflict resolution, and regulation. The bet of this vision is that the positive effects of private networks, which may be closed or restrict the flow of data, will exceed those of the open networks envisaged by the Silicon Valley Open Internet. Even if many benefits of networks are creamed off by firms, there will still be more positive externalities than would have occurred in the absence of the incentives provided by the profit motive.

THE EXEMPLAR

It will come as no surprise that this commercial ideal is most closely associated with the United States. The idea of Internet-as-property has commonly been defended by US governments, particularly but not exclusively of the Republican Party, and cases to determine the extent of property rights have received fairly consistent support from the Supreme Court in Washington, DC. Hence, we call this third Internet the *DC Commercial Internet*.

The DC Commercial Internet is marked by closed networks, legitimate (i.e. not illegal, ideally contractual) barriers to market entry and network exit, and conditional tolerance of monopoly. Regulation, where possible, should be replaced by contract. Owners of sites should have control, so need not respect interoperability if it does not support their business model, making the Internet a more fragmented experience. The justification for such non-interoperable 'walled gardens' is the innovation they foster. If the controller of a walled garden can monetize the innovations they produce, then the revenue shows that value is being created.

In terms of the values diagram (Figure 9.1), the DC Commercial Internet has the following shape, with opposition to censorship (at least by external authorities; private entities have the right to censor content on their own resources), lukewarm support for open standards (there should be open

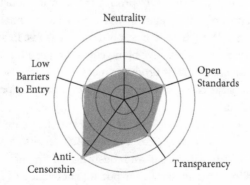

Figure 9.1. The ideals of the DC Commercial Internet.
Source: Thanks to Paul Smart, who conceived and created this diagram via Highcharts.

standards for the Web and Internet, but not necessarily inside walled gardens) and transparency (private entities need to reveal sufficient information to allow rational investment decisions, and satisfy the informational demands of stock exchanges if they are publicly quoted—and many important tech companies are privately owned—but don't have to explain their situation or reasons for action), mild concern for open markets, and not much support at all for net neutrality.

The Silicon Valley Open Internet and the DC Commercial Internet obviously stem from the same nation, one from its libertarian West Coast, and the other from the suits in the East. This not unnaturally leads to some convergence. Common law is a central factor, stemming from English law whose principles are founded on precedent, and which has tended to favour separation of politics and law, respect for negative liberties, custom, contracts, absolute property rights, trusts, and covenants, which means that nations who still use common law in their legal systems (which broadly covers what is sometimes called the Anglosphere) are relatively tolerant of the disruptive practices of the technology giants. The associated economy tends to be a liberal market economy, characterized by exchange of goods and services in a context of competition, contract, and price signals.[7] The contrasts to the somewhat more controlling characteristics of civil law and coordinated market economies as exemplified in the Brussels Bourgeois Internet.

For instance, whereas the Brussels approach to Internet governance is to try to engineer the right sort of behaviour—for example, taking the lead in the implementation of privacy-by-design—the US government has usually preferred to resort to self-regulation and the policing of deception—for instance, failure to adhere to privacy policies as contracts with users. We can boil US privacy policy down to six words, 'tell the truth, do no harm' (i.e. follow your privacy policy, and be prepared to be sued if you cause someone financial loss or physical hurt), consistent with the view of privacy breaches as tortious, and it is the job of the national consumer protection agency, the Federal Trade Commission (FTC), to prosecute if privacy policies are ignored. Self-regulation appears equally appropriate from a commercial perspective as in an open setting, although perhaps for different reasons. In an open regime, regulation is seen as bad, all things being equal, because it limits behaviour, whereas in a commercial one, it produces red tape and imposes costs on producers (even if only the costs of compliance). Either way it is perceived as suppressing innovation.

From this perspective, GDPR is a red rag to the corporate bull. As noted, large global firms can absorb the costs of compliance, but smaller companies make common cause with legal and business commentators to deplore European meddling, and as one paper put it, 'thousands of online entities, both in the EU and abroad, have proactively shuttered their European operations for fear of getting caught in the regulatory crosshairs'.[8] A number of US companies, not only tech ones, refuse to risk taking customer details and have closed their websites in Europe (including in 2020, for example, furnishings chain Pottery Barn).[9] It's not as if privacy is not protected 'on the ground' in the United States, because the potential costs of litigation mean that companies can't afford to not be respectful of the concept.[10] However, many companies support a federal US privacy law, as it would be likely to be weak and compromised, and better than the complex patchwork of data protection legislation at US state level.

OH, EAST IS EAST AND WEST IS WEST, AND NEVER THE TWAIN . . . ?

The Silicon Valley Open Internet and the DC Commercial Internet have three sets of common roots. First, they are opposite coasts of the same nation, and so share a common federal legal regime. Second, their basic legal traditions descend from English common law. And third, there is a great deal of intermingling of the relevant personnel; for example, Internet pioneer Vinton Cerf is an 'Internet Evangelist' at commercial giant Google. Several major commercial operations, including Alphabet/Google and Facebook, are based in Silicon Valley, and many of them benefit to a large extent from openness. The intermingling may have reached a natural limit; the tech giants are so keen to buy upstart startups that they are threatening the culture for which Silicon Valley is famous.[11]

Broadly speaking, although both major political parties in the United States are supportive of their tech industries, the Republicans are less ideologically committed to openness as a first-order ideal. The Democrats do share the DC Commercial vision, but also have commitments to openness which they make a greater effort to balance. The Obama administration in particular hosted a number of present and former technologists,[12] and it has been argued that Obama and the European Commission under José Manuel Barroso (2004–2013) 'institutionalized a somewhat more consensual transatlantic (if not trans-Pacific) basis for Internet regulation'.[13] Meanwhile, although the Republican Party's libertarian wing was pretty prominent until the Trump era, the Trump administration veered, as in so many matters, from Obama-era policy.

It has been argued that open standards protect fundamental rights more effectively than proprietary ones, and so technologies such as Linux, Android, and Firefox are 'better' than their protected competitors.[14] But the relation between commercial property interests and consumer rights is particularly contested in the United States, where corporations have a more substantial legal personality than elsewhere, thanks to the common law inheritance.[15] Hence the consumer (and other) rights of individuals face a stronger challenge from corporate private property rights than in other jurisdictions.[16] For example, the use of cookies to pass information between servers and clients raised privacy concerns almost immediately after their invention, and in 1996 the FTC was suggesting that control of cookies should default to users. Advertisers pushed back strongly, but even at the turn of the century cookies were still banned from US federal government websites. In the event, the discovery by Google and others of how to monetize the surveillant possibilities of the digital infrastructure turned the argument away from user empowerment.[17]

More widely, this property-based model threatens the Internet's, and subsequently the Web's, interoperability. Berners-Lee, in his 2018 Turing Lecture, argued that the universality of identifiers for online resources underpinned the added-value of the Web, and if walled gardens included unique, non-interoperable identification schemes this value would be diminished.[18] In the years since Zittrain described non-generative models of the Internet, which created walled gardens and undermined innovation, the extraordinary growth of social networking has only built the walls still higher, while arguably making the gardens prettier and more habitable.[19]

In particular, SNSs bypass some of the Internet's interoperability mechanisms.[20] They don't support cross-platform compatibility (so interacting between two SNSs is not as simple as, say, sending an email from Gmail to a .edu address). Personal data is not portable between sites, although GDPR is attempting to change this. Search is restricted. Resources are not identified or located by universal formalisms. As Berners-Lee put it, 'connections among data exist only within a site. So the more you enter, the more you become locked in. Your [SNS] becomes . . . a closed silo of content. . . . The more this kind of architecture gains widespread use, the more the Web becomes fragmented, and the less we enjoy a single, universal information space'.[21] The DC Commercial response is that SNSs provide services that people actually wish to access, in large numbers, and the only responsibilities their owners have are to their customers, assuming that they do not interfere with the running of the Internet as a whole. On this view, just as someone who wishes to build a wall around their garden should be allowed to do so as long as they cause no harms elsewhere, Internet resource owners should be the best judges of the value to be obtained from their property. Attempts to provide interoperable functionality for SNSs via common OpenSocial APIs did not succeed, as demand was not sufficient. Facebook's proprietary platform enabled it to gain market share at the expense of the OpenSocial Alliance.[22]

Perhaps the most fraught issue between the two visions is net neutrality. The early text-based applications in the Internet didn't really cause much of a problem because packets' arrivals were not time-critical. Now, more information is being created and shared, and the Internet is used for synchronous communication and other time-sensitive applications, so there are limits to acceptable levels of latency beyond which the quality of service suffers, and certain media, such as video, consume scarce bandwidth. Inevitably, the partly technical question of whether the net should be neutral has become a victim of US political partisanship.

Net neutrality has been something of a political football at least since the term was coined in 2003.[23] The FCC made a commitment to net neutrality under the Obama administration in 2015, but under Trump voted in December 2017 by 3–2 to repeal it. The *Star Wars* actor Mark Hamill criticized the FCC for siding with large corporations against the individual; Senator Ted Cruz replied that Darth Vader is the kind of guy who would have regulated the Internet. The head of the FCC, Ajit Pai (appointed by President Obama, but elevated to its Chair by President Trump), claims to support net neutrality, but argues that federal regulation will suppress innovation, and this ought to be a contractual matter between ISPs and their customers, dealt with in terms and conditions.[24] In general, the American courts, all the way up to the Supreme Court, have tended to protect the claims of property: 'all too often in recent years, when courts have perceived a conflict between intellectual property rights and free speech rights, property has trumped speech'.[25]

Net neutrality is not a binary. Pure Silicon Valley (no discrimination, absolutely neutral between packets) and pure DC (no regulation, any discrimination allowed, fee charging allowed, including the exclusion of content providers from the network) are endpoints on a scale. In the middle, one could imagine combinations of congestion charging with 'common carriage', i.e. the service provider guarantees to carry whatever it is asked to carry (rather like a national postal service, as opposed to a courier which can be selective about what it takes on). This might allow discrimination to improve quality of service, but not on the basis of price (so the network might speed up VOIP or video, but would not charge those content providers more, or offer discounts to those on slower speeds). Or one could imagine allowing price discrimination with a multi-tier price structure (higher fees guarantee greater minimum speeds), in tandem with a basic free service guaranteeing universal access. Or there may be something closer to the DC model, where providers could be excluded from the network if they didn't pay the fee, but could not be excluded if they were willing to pay (so that, for example, a network operator which also provided a sports channel could not exclude rival sports channels simply because they were competitors, though it could charge them the going rate). Preferential treatment might be in terms of speed, volume, or both. Content providers or content consumers, or both, could be charged for heavy use. As we move from Silicon Valley to DC, the end-to-end principle is decreasingly respected, reducing efficiency, but engineering efficiency is not the only relevant metric. For example, allowing monetization of network speed might provide incentives for innovation.[26]

Most economists appear to view the judgement between alternatives as dependent on the detail of the conditions imposed on network operators, but they broadly agree that the ability to discriminate on price will improve service, all things being equal, and that regulation should ideally be *post hoc* following empirical evaluation of the costs and benefits of a particular arrangement, using competition or consumer protection law to address harms as they emerge.[27] Up to 2020, it seems that rule changes on net neutrality in the United States haven't caused detectable upheaval,[28] or had a great deal of effect on investment,[29] somewhat undermining both the pure Silicon Valley and pure DC positions.

Using the market to solve issues of latency and bandwidth implies not only the development of property rights to allow infrastructure owners to make managerial decisions to hold up or speed up traffic, but also the technology to determine what needs to be speeded up. Under the end-to-end principle, all that is needed is to view the metadata of each packet (which gives information about its journey, but nothing about its content); a more fine-grained treatment requires intrusive technology to peer into each packet and determine what is in it. This technology is called Deep Packet Inspection (DPI), and has many legitimate uses, particularly in security.

The large telecom companies generally oppose net neutrality, preferring differential charging both to increase revenue, and to improve service, sensitive to clients' required latency levels. This is an investment and planning issue for them—if they are not allowed to invest in DPI technology, then they will have to produce far greater bandwidth.

The debate is exacerbated by its American epicentre, where the extent and limits of free speech are of major constitutional interest. The First Amendment forbids the state to curb free speech, but there are divergent interpretations of this. Does the state have a positive duty to make sure speech is promoted, even on private property, or does the First Amendment's scope only cover publicly administered spaces so that private property owners' rights are unaffected by it? The first interpretation, which held sway during much of the twentieth century, holds that the state is *justified* in intervening in public spaces for expression (even ones that are privately owned, such as telecommunications networks) to support the societal goal of facilitating expression of a multiplicity of viewpoints, and restricting the rights of the owners to censor or limit the messages they carry. The second interpretation implies that the First Amendment *forbids* the state from intervening in such spaces, as to do so will restrict the free speech rights of the owners to determine what voices are heard in their spaces; this negative interpretation has been the majority view of the Supreme Court since the 1980s. The positive interpretation favours net neutrality and Silicon Valley openness, while the negative interpretation favours private property interests. It is a parochial argument to many of the rest of us, but the way it plays out will affect the Internet as a whole.[30]

PRIVATIZING GOVERNANCE

The roots of the Silicon Valley/DC split lie in the collective action problem that affects Internet operators. They compete with each other for customers, but on the other hand their cooperation in connecting their networks using standard protocols and handling their competitors' traffic makes the Internet the Internet, rather than a series of disconnected or weakly connected islands. This creates a tension between what we might think of as the public good of a seamless Internet, and the private interests of these operators.[31]

Hence supporters of the DC Commercial Internet typically do benefit from openness, and so will often join in coalition with more unconditional defenders of openness against more broadly commercial interests. One such flashpoint has been on intellectual property and digital rights management (DRM). The Stop Online Piracy Act (SOPA) of 2012 was introduced to give US law enforcement agencies greater powers to address a bag of issues, including the online sale of counterfeit goods, especially drugs, and copyright infringement; powers included the ability to target websites deemed to be infringing these rules by preventing search engines from linking to them and financial service companies from handling their payments. ISPs, search engines, domain name registrars, financial services companies, and advertisers would all have come under its sway. In the bill's original form (later modified), the integrity of the DNS was also compromised, as DNS servers in the United States would not be allowed to transfer browser requests to the associated IP address—with the concomitant possibility of DNS requests from within the United States shifting to offshore servers.

SOPA was meant to defend private property, but went too far for those companies which benefit from openness, which allowed an effective and coherent Silicon Valley/DC coalition to form. Yahoo!, Facebook, Twitter, and Google were joined by Wikipedia, civil society groups such as Reporters Without Borders, companies such as Kaspersky Lab, activists such as Anonymous, policy wonks, and many users and consumers. When President Obama voiced disapproval, the bill died in the Senate, causing traditional media tycoon and News International chairman Rupert Murdoch to fume that 'Obama has thrown in his lot with Silicon Valley paymasters who threaten all software creators with piracy, plain thievery'. The campaign also deterred the European Union, which had signed the 2012 Anti-Counterfeiting Trade Agreement that would have set up a new international body to govern counterfeiting and copyright issues, but following the collapse of SOPA, many arms of the European Union then worked to prevent its member states ratifying it.[32]

SOPA rejected the Silicon Valley Open vision, but also did not fully respect the DC Commercial vision; as Murdoch's interjection suggested, it was really an attempt by pre-Internet businesses to shackle the Internet. Proponents of the DC Commercial Internet have a more focused agenda in making the

Internet, and preferably their particular firm, the default communication infrastructure. For example, Mark Zuckerberg has spoken of his aspiration to bring Internet access 'to every person in the world', and argued that Facebook's social network will 'be a better map of how you navigate the web than the traditional link structure'.[33] If Google's search engine can be superseded by the view from *within* Facebook, why would one leave Facebook at all? Still, Zuckerberg can also overreach; the proposal that Facebook implement a cryptocurrency called Libra resulted in a spectacular backlash, given its poor reputation for privacy, the potential for money laundering by disconnecting currency from the banking system, and the unknown consequences of allowing a powerful private monopoly into the financial sector.[34]

With regard to the growth of the Internet into new parts of the world, the DC agenda is particularly plausible. Zuckerberg, claiming that connectivity is a human right, announced that he would support free mobile data for those who couldn't afford plans.[35] So-called *zero-rating* looks interesting in the development context as a way of helping the poor leverage value from smartphones, which are fast becoming the go-to development technology for every ill. The practicalities of this kind of offer depend on the flow of data—how is it to be monetized? Will there be a basic package of free services, and better ones for those who can afford them? In which case, how would the distinction be made? What services would be denied those with zero-rated connectivity—healthcare services, access to markets, educational sites, or news outlets?[36] Facebook's offering, jointly managed with other networking and hardware giants, is called Free Basics.[37]

The distance from the Silicon Valley Open Internet is evident by now—there would have to be some manipulation of the dataflow, and therefore net neutrality would be a casualty of Zuckerberg's human right to connectivity. The free services would mark out a basic walled garden—or public park. Yet the park would still be privately provided (in Zuckerberg's vision, by Facebook). Private operators could gain data via surveillance of the poor—by definition a new constituency which has not been online before, and therefore a potential source of value.

Technology can surely help, but is there a danger that it will crowd out less flashy infrastructure? Drones might help poorly governed or remote regions which have inadequate transport and medical infrastructure, but those regions still need roads—to get people to hospitals or to help them escape conflict zones, or just to get food to market before it rots in the cart. E-health is great, but people still need nurses and clinics for primary care. Smartphones can be a part of education, but they won't replace schools. A 2017 report into Free Basics concluded that it failed to meet linguistic, content, and privacy needs of its users, and that 'Free Basics' architectural and content limitations are largely artificial and exist primarily as a mechanism for collecting profitable data from users'.[38] As Linnet Taylor, a researcher into data justice, puts it:

The leapfrogging vision, like the efficiency-as-development vision, both work fine for specific cases when presented to gatherings of development economists. However, when you try to imagine your own world with no computer hardware, no Internet search functionality, no doctors, no hospitals, and no roads, it pretty soon becomes apparent that (to put it mildly) these solutions might create more problems than they solve.[39]

It is disingenuous to see zero-rating as a contribution to human rights. It appears not only to apply pressure to net neutrality and the end-to-end principle, but also to mark out a particular online territory that looks like a biased version of what people really need. Wikipedia is a splendid thing, but given the choice between it and paid-for, professional educational technology, the latter might be of rather more use, especially for people too poor to pay for it (and decent schools might be of even greater value). The 'right to connectivity' looks rather more like an opportunity to bring more people to the Internet on terms dictated by whoever builds the walled gardens.

The merits of the DC Commercial Internet do not mean we should not think hard about the provision of public goods. We have already seen concerns about how Google has been given a vital role in administering the right to be forgotten, and similar remarks might be made about censorship of pornography, hateful content, or copyright material by platforms like Facebook and YouTube. Sarah Roberts, a researcher into content moderation, has argued that 'any discussion of the nature of the contemporary internet is fundamentally incomplete if it does not address the processes by which certain content created by users is allowed to remain visible and other content is removed, who makes these decisions, how they are made, and whom they benefit'.[40]

But commercial instincts are particularly concerning in the actual governance processes of parts of the Internet, many of which are privately administered. For example, a furore erupted in 2019 about the running of the .org top-level domain of Internet names; .org, the domain for addresses generally if not exclusively used by non-profit organizations, has been run by the Public Interest Registry (PIR), owned by the Internet Society (ISOC), since 2003. ISOC is a non-profit, and was awarded the rights to run .org for free (it also is the home of the IETF). This sort of rather messy, contingent but generally *pro bono* arrangement, as we have seen, is typical of the governance of the Internet. Users of .org addresses, which include many well-meaning organizations, are charged a relatively small amount annually, but as there are ten million of them, they are also a potentially lucrative monopoly. ISOC trousers not far off $100 million every year.

So the proposed sale by ISOC of the PIR to a private equity firm, with the airy but ultimately meaningless name of Ethos, for a cool billion dollars, a substantial chunk of which was financed through debt, did not go unnoticed. The PIR discarded its non-profit status. Price controls were lifted. Former ICANN executives apparently helped broker the deal. Ethos promised not to milk the cash cow it aimed to appropriate, but a price tag of $1 billion implied they anticipated a significant return. ICANN appeared conflicted, possibly because any attempt to use its public interest remit to stymie the bid might have ended up in the courts.[41]

The whole imbroglio was ultimately resolved against the sale, as ICANN blocked the transfer of PIR,[42] but this flare-up between West Coast libertarians and East Coast commercial types is a highly experimental departure for the Internet's plumbing, whose public service ethos would have been replaced by, well, Ethos. This could have serious repercussions. As we have seen, a top-level domain only really functions through the goodwill of the ISPs who connect organizations to the Internet using its nomenclature. The whole issue remains in abeyance, as ISOC's actions in 2019 make it clear it does not want the responsibility for .org as a non-profit public service domain.

But however it is ultimately resolved, the .org affair, which involved competing American ideologies, and American companies operating under American law, and which may yet be decided in American courts, will have global repercussions. It will seriously undermine the United States' claims of legitimacy, which chafe with many other nations. A billion dollars admittedly sing very loudly, but this would have been one of the more tone deaf sales in history.

SURVEILLANCE CAPITALISM

The way that the DC Commercial Internet has played out has not been to everyone's taste. One influential recent polemic has been Zuboff's *Surveillance Capitalism*, in which she redescribes datafication and the commercialization of new sources of data as exploitation, and an assault on human dignity. 'Terms whose meanings we take to be positive or at least banal—"the open internet," "interoperability," and "connectivity"—have been quietly harnessed to a market process in which individuals are definitively cast as the means to others' market ends.'[43] Another who has made similar points is Evgeny Morozov, in a series of pugnacious attacks on 'solutionism': 'we have let digital platforms and telecom operators treat our entire digital universe as their fiefdom. . . . They run it with just one goal in mind: keep the micro-targeting going, and micro-payments flowing. As a result, little thought has gone into building digital technologies that would produce macro-level anonymous insights about collective behaviour of non-consumers. The digital platforms of today are the sites of individualized consumption, not of mutual assistance and solidarity.'[44] Morozov is critical of Zuboff's view, which he sees as failing to understand the continuities between 'traditional' capitalism and surveillance capitalism; on his view, the shift from a money economy to a data economy is exaggerated in many respects.[45]

On Zuboff's account, Google was a leader in the crafting of surveillance capitalism. At its inception, it was a fully paid-up member of the Silicon Valley fraternity, with a mission to organize the world's information and make it universally accessible and useful. This, though hegemonic, pretty arrogant, and arguably megalomaniacal, did not in itself make any property claims or rights grabs, although neither did it specify a business model. There was no product. It provided the best search in the world at the turn of the century, so had lots of users, who provided it with data, which improved the search, but with no monetizable product—the searches were free, the small amount of advertising was bolted on and not very sophisticated. Apple's smart-looking hardware, in contrast, provided an income stream, so users would provide data and feedback to Apple, who could use it to improve its products and develop new ones, which would sustain and expand the current user base, therefore providing more feedback in a virtuous commercial circle.

The key discovery for Google was *data exhaust*, a waste product which could be interpreted to provide information about behavioural indicators such as dwell times, locations, clickthrough patterns, spelling and punctuation, and phrasing, and so could be turned into gold by being mined to find out not just about the search, but about the searcher, and aggregated to make discoveries about populations. This could be used to provide more services for the searcher, such as spellchecking or translation, but now could also fuel new services to third parties, initially advertising, but afterwards many types of behavioural observations, predictions, or interventions.[46] This development coincided with the arrival of Eric Schmidt in 2002, and marks the point at which Google definitively switched from the Silicon Valley to the DC vision. The vast quantities of data that were made available allowed extraordinarily accurate predictions of behaviour, at least in the aggregate, to be made. Google's AdSense product targeted adverts to users based on content, and was extraordinarily successful. Executive Sheryl Sandberg led the growth of its advertising model from a sideline to its main product, and later, took these insights into the aggressive gathering and mining of data to Facebook as chief operating officer, leading them into profit too.[47] Google was even able to challenge Apple directly on smartphones; whereas Apple smartphones retailed on the basis of their cool design, Google competed with its Android OS, which was designed instead to proliferate apps and capture information (and so was open source and licensed for free). Facebook's 'like' button turned out to be extraordinarily informative about behaviour and preferences.[48] Users were quite often willing to provide their own labour and information to improve products, for example in the games sector, or via gig economy platforms such as Mechanical Turk.[49]

Once data exhaust was monetized and turned into property, Google's Silicon Valley passion for openness evaporated, and it became one of the more secretive global outfits, partly to preserve commercial advantage no doubt, but also to diminish the likelihood of consumer or civil society backlash. Zuboff calls the monetized data 'behavioural surplus', and notes that hunger for it was an important driver for big tech's acquisitive strategies.[50]

The Facebook/Google defence is that their services and walled gardens provide a large quantity of public good, and the proofs of this are the number of people who use their services, and the profits they make. If they provided no benefits, then they would not be profitable, never mind the largest firms in the world. If there is another measure of the public good than that, then (as Zuckerberg said in 2020), let the democratic West provide it, before someone else (i.e. China) does.[51] In its absence, it is self-defeating to allow suspicion of their motives to get in the way of the services they provide. Reflect for a moment on how much more substantial a logistic and practical problem the COVID-19 lockdown of 2020 would have been without the tech giants and SNSs.

One response to this is that, without exit and voice, consumers are not in a position to argue. The tech giants are serving the population, but only after manipulating their preferences in the first place. For instance, an SNS provides hits which can prove seductive, even addictive; can one behave autonomously and authentically in such an environment? Can one break an addiction to something without giving it up (there is surely no prospect of ditching the Internet)?[52] Eggers's *The Circle* has been lauded as the literary depiction of the tech giants, but its narrative of the allure of and mania for transparency is only a light satire of the Silicon Valley Open Internet, without broaching the topic of darker and more acquisitive motives behind the transparency drive. The literary voice of the DC Commercial Internet may well be a famous novel that preceded the triumph of digital technology, Aldous Huxley's *Brave New World* of 1932.[53]

This debate leaves us with three possible reactions. We can celebrate the range of innovation and services that the tech giants' use of data has provided us with, or (Zuboff's response) work towards a Commercial Internet that still allowed monetization of Internet resources as property, but rejected the exploitation of data exhaust, and instead restored a more traditional exchange/money-based capitalism, or (Morozov's response) reject the notion that capitalism and private property can work towards the public good at all.

Capitalism and free markets are two separate things, but one interpretation of Zuboff's polemic is that we should reconnect them, so that one of the key disciplines of free markets, competition, is restored as a brake on the actions of the tech giants. This has typically been the response of policymakers in the United States and the European Union, and we will consider the prospects of using antitrust regulation to reshape the DC Commercial Internet in the next chapter.

CHAPTER 10

Policy Question

How Can Competition against the Tech Giants
Be Fostered?

The DC Commercial Internet and the Brussels Bourgeois Internet share some features, in particular the use of competition policy to regulate the tech world. But although competition law doesn't differ by much across the Atlantic, 'soft law' and pragmatics do. In particular, the European Union is generally suspicious of powerful operators within markets, and works to prevent competitors being either bought up or driven out by bigger rivals.[1] In the United States, where the memory of Schumpeter flourishes, a regulator would ask whether dominance was a result of innovation and providing what consumers want, whether large monopoly profits help drive further innovation (or provide incentives for competitors), and whether the actual practices of monopolies and oligopolies can be shown empirically to harm consumers.[2] Furthermore, the burden of proof lies with the plaintiff, who has to prove that consumers are harmed. Experienced technology executive Kai-Fu Lee adds that the increasing use of AI technology will tend to concentrate market power, so innovative companies will become *more* monopolistic.[3]

Competition issues are regulated by antitrust law, which aims to penalize anti-competitive practices, and use the state of a market (e.g. how many suppliers are within it, and how many provide the lion's share of goods and services) as evidence. Recent economic work has tended to show that markets in a number of sectors, including tech, are becoming more concentrated.[4] This concentration has been additionally blamed for low levels of investment.[5] One important issue with respect to the Internet is that most competition law is nationally based (the EU being an exception), but that the Internet is

Four Internets. Kieron O'Hara and Wendy Hall, Oxford University Press. © Oxford University Press 2021.
DOI: 10.1093/oso/9780197523681.003.0010

global. One may look like a monopoly supplier from the perspective of a single nation-state, but rather a small player on the global scene. Globalization tends to create superstar firms.[6]

The situation is complicated further by some of the major tech companies being platforms—in other words, market-makers which bring together two separate sets of customers who benefit from being in touch—drivers and those needing transport, retailers and consumers, consumers and advertisers, people wanting to date. Such platforms in particular gain from network effects, and economists have shown that many platforms thrive by allowing in one side, and making their money from the other.[7] For instance, Google and Facebook provide free services to individuals, while fleecing advertisers who want access to them. Some platform-owners, such as Amazon, are also players on the platform, and it is non-trivial to determine when the platform rules are unfairly rigged. Hence the application of antitrust law is not always obvious or straightforward. Broadly speaking, proponents of the Open Internet prefer to support small start-ups against the large behemoths, while supporters of the Commercial Internet would defend the market power of the giants, at least up to a point, as benefiting consumers and promoting innovation.

In the battle between regulators and companies, the playing field in the United States is tilted towards the companies, at least compared to the European Union. The European Commission is judge and jury over antitrust cases, and companies can only appeal decisions, whereas in the United States the prosecutor has to prove an antitrust case in court initially. American states are relatively powerless to pursue antitrust cases, although they can and do combine to do so, whereas both national governments and the European Commission can apply European antitrust law. Finally, in Europe GDPR and competition law are seen as complementary attacks on the market power of the tech giants, whereas the US view is that they should be separate: 'if the problem is one of market power, then antitrust is the solution, not data protection regulation'. Proponents of the DC vision complain darkly of a coalition between Europeans and 'hipster' antitrust Silicon Valley types that argues 'that the evidentiary consumer welfare standard, long a transatlantic touchstone, should be abandoned in favour of the public interest, a German ordoliberal concept that the state should intervene in the market to produce a normative outcome'.[8]

BREAKING UP IS HARD TO DO

Antitrust measures usually take the form of fines or compensating those who have lost out through anticompetitive behaviour. One problem with the tech industry is the sheer size of its firms. For the record, the combined stock market value of Alphabet, Amazon, Apple, Facebook, and Microsoft was, at the beginning of 2020, well in excess of $4 trillion. How damaging could fines be to such goldmines? A second measure—the obvious one—is to demand that the uncompetitive practice cease. The problem there is that the law moves so slowly, and the tech industry so quickly, that the damage is done by the time the judgement arrives (for instance, the antitrust case brought against Microsoft's bundling its Internet Explorer Web browser in with its Windows OS ended in late 2001, after its competitors in the browser market had already gone out of business).[9] But there is a third option (that was considered in the Microsoft case): breakup.

The classic examples of antitrust judgements, both from the United States, are Standard Oil and AT&T, each of which was broken up into many smaller firms, releasing a great deal of value from the confines of the behemoths. The nascent Internet, as we have seen, was a bystander in the latter case: AT&T's horizontal and vertical integration left it uninterested in innovative technologies that might disrupt its own business, and, despite developing the influential UNIX OS, it failed to get into the Internet on the ground floor.

How could a breakup work in the tech industry? There are several different potential strategies. One would be to prevent new anticompetitive mergers, and by extension to force the giants to divest companies they had swallowed in order to suppress competition. Deals such as the purchase by Facebook of WhatsApp and Instagram may come under that rubric, because ownership of these two, combined with its original Messenger service, gave Facebook an enormous slice of the messaging market. A second idea would be to try to ring-fence the giants into particular sectors; Amazon's purchase of the health food supermarket chain Whole Foods Market might be an example of the type of acquisition that would be prevented on this strategy.

A third, more significant, move would be to look at companies which both operate and operate on platforms. Apple hosts its App Store for iOS apps, hosting 1.8 million apps as of the fourth quarter of 2019, including some of its own.[10] In 2020, complaints from music-streaming firm Spotify, game developers Epic, and others about Apple charging 30% for every app sale, and every sale within every app, on the App Store, prompted an EU antitrust investigation.[11] Amazon hosts an e-commerce platform on which it also sells products. With such a set-up, as noted earlier, there is potential to use the platform to favour one's own products by, for example, making them prominent in search results—as Standard Oil discriminated against rival oil producers in access to its own pipelines. Platforms over a certain size (Amazon's generated $123 billion in 2018)[12] could be regulated in order to prevent price-gouging or favouritism, exactly as, for example, financial advisors are prevented from favouring their own products to clients without transparency.

A fourth possibility is actually to break up the giants—for example, splitting Amazon into its e-commerce platform, its physical stores, Amazon Web Services, and the advertising business. Alphabet might be split into the advertising and search business, Google Cloud, YouTube, and its app store Play. Apple is largely built around designer hardware, but the App Store and Apple Music might go. Facebook could say cheerio to Instagram and Messenger.[13]

The scale of network effects makes it difficult to calculate what the different cross-subsidizing parts of a tech giant's networks might be worth if hived off. For example, Alphabet's advertising marketplace might be separated off from services operating on it, as proposed by Elizabeth Warren in her failed bid for the Democratic nomination in the 2020 US presidential election, but putting numbers on those revenue streams is hard; harder still as Alphabet does not volunteer them; and even harder given that it is difficult to predict how two or more separate companies might partition the commercial value of the marketplace. A poor working relationship post-breakup might end up destroying value by undermining synergies, and making what are currently highly integrated offerings far more complex for consumers and other businesses.

These virtual systems create value in data, and one particular question that regulators must address is exactly how the data generated by transactions should be divided between platform and service. How much of a description of an interaction should belong to the platform and how much to the provider? A social network doesn't have much value if its members cannot contact their friends, but does that mean a messaging service is part of the networking platform, or a necessary if separable service? What about a service to tag photos with the names of the people in them, if the data required to do that was generated by the network—can the naming service be separated, or alternatively is it necessarily part of the platform, as the data upon which it runs can only be generated by the platform (not the service)? What if a rival image-tagging service came along? Could it legally demand the data from the SNS? And what should happen while the dispute was dragging for years through the courts?

The matter is complicated further by the different kinds of power for trustbusters to counter. Amazon, Apple, and Microsoft wield market power in relatively well-understood domains, of retail commerce, stylish hardware and software, and OSs, respectively. Google and Facebook set a different exam question, because the services these companies provide affect the nature of an individual's presence and activity online and offline. And other types of Internet governance organizations, such as ICANN, although not the specific targets of either the United States or the European Union, have powers whose extent is similarly hard to pin down.[14] Furthermore, competition seems to be thriving in some areas of the tech industry, especially those where network effects are less salient, such as video streaming and cloud computing.

The giants' defence against the regulators rests on innovation and service. They have been extraordinarily creative by any standards—arguably the twenty-first century has been the most innovative in human business history. Digital modernity is built around the notion of disruption of existing patterns of behaviour and markets, and the tech giants have developed a social system with an entirely new set of previously unsuspected and certainly unarticulated needs and desires, which furthermore has delivered immense social value during the COVID-19 emergency. The returns to innovation have been large, but—on the Commercial view—deserved. A crucial aspect of this is the unprecedentedly large networks built up on their platforms.

It has become textbook strategy in the tech industry to build your network aggressively—'blitzscaling'. Newcomers disrupt existing industries initially by disintermediating—removing intermediary stages and sabotaging the business models of go-betweens and market-makers—and thereby lowering the price of the final service or product. Cost reduction spurs growth, and the current willingness of investors in many industries to support unprofitable firms allows platforms to build up large and therefore valuable networks, even before they have worked out a way to monetize them. Most of the tech giants went through a long period of failing to make money, and the current wave of would-be giants, such as Uber and Airbnb, is also spending to grow. It is common to find very large networks looking like monopolies or oligopolies which do not actually provide monopoly profits, or indeed any profits at all.

There is a lot of scepticism at the time of writing, for example, about Uber's ability to make money on the back of the valuable platform it has created to connect drivers and ride-seekers. Uncertainty about autonomous vehicles brings the whiff of a future business model, but Uber's strategy is fundamentally risky. It is restricted by geography—a ride-seeker in Nairobi has no use for a car in New York—and is not exclusive—registering on Uber does not prevent one from working on competing platforms, such as Lyft. Hence the mere fact that a tech company maintains a large network does not in and of itself suggest a harmful monopoly.

Valuation data may flatter; many companies have achieved large valuations by masquerading as tech companies. WeWork, an office space rental company whose founder believed it could change the world, managed to sustain a delusional valuation with its visionary techy new-agey vibe (and correspondingly flaky metrics, such as 'community-adjusted earnings before interest, taxes, depreciation and amortisation', which turned accounting losses into apparent profits) until it tried to go public and sell shares on an open exchange, at which point it found out what they were really worth.[15] Zume, which at one point was valued at well over $2 billion, used robots to make the pizzas it delivered, predictive algorithms to anticipate choices, and ovens equipped with GPS in its vans. This did not make it a tech company; it remained fundamentally a pizza company whose pizzas weren't terribly nice. It had to stop making them. If you are not selling communication, then you will struggle to achieve network effects. What value do I gain from your office or your pizza? As Nicholas Negroponte, pioneer and founder of the MIT Media Lab, argued in the 1990s, bits have very different properties from atoms.[16]

On the other hand, so quickly does the tech move, it will always be hard to spot the moment when technological innovation and entrepreneurialism disrupt large tech firms. The giants seem part of the scenery at the moment, but upstarts can suddenly emerge; there have been casualties, most obviously MySpace, Yahoo!, and AOL, and new opportunities will doubtless materialize in the future.[17] But fundamental change has to dissipate the combination of network effects and lock-in that allows the growth. Without that, a breakup may not solve the problem of market concentration, and may even make it worse. Suppose a large network is broken up into smaller, less valuable constituents. Who is to say that one of those Baby Googles or Mini Facebooks, or a new start-up that would in the old days have been gobbled up for a giant's breakfast, won't take advantage of the same network effects that the original company exploited, and expand to the size and influence of the previous monopoly?

THE AMERICAN POLITICS OF ANTITRUST

The tide may be turning against the tech companies, as US lawmakers were assembling legal restraints in 2019 and 2020. Much of this is a tentative phoney war, and much, we suspect, will depend on what agenda President Biden adopts. The tech companies find themselves out of kilter with US politics at the moment. Their visceral liberal (and green) preferences are more likely to be shared with Democrats, while their economic aim of treating their data as a monetizable asset appeals more to Republican thinking. For some time, this mismatch enabled them to ride both tigers at once, gaining support across the aisle. However, as tech and privacy scandals accumulated, and as US politics descended into hyper-partisan self-harm, in which the friend of my enemy is my enemy, lawmakers grew less forgiving. While the tech companies themselves are inevitably becoming more cautious and nuanced in their deployment of technologies, both US parties, sensing voter discontent, are beginning to put them under more pressure.

A perception spread among Republicans that the industry was biased against them.[18] Google pulled out of Project Maven, an AI project to analyse defence drone video, after thousands of its employees signed a petition against it, while many have accused Facebook algorithms of anti-conservative bias. That helped undermine Republican defences of its commercial freedom. Foreign policy hawks turned against them.[19] Meanwhile the Democrats focused on embarrassing issues such as the amount of tax the tech giants pay, the political power they wield, the invasions of privacy they facilitate, and the way they were allegedly used by non-Americans to influence the 2016 presidential election. As a result of this shift in the political climate round about 2018–2019, a number of bipartisan bills with idiotic acronyms appeared in the

Senate, including the Social Media Addiction Reduction Technology (SMART) Act, the Designing Accounting Safeguards to Help Broaden Oversight And Regulations on Data (DASHBOARD) Act, and the *pièce de résistance*, the Stop Bad Employers by Zeroing Out Subsidies (Stop BEZOS) Act (geddit?), this last introduced by Bernie Sanders.[20] Republican Senator Josh Hawley of Missouri, from the 2019 intake, has speedily made his mark as a would-be hi-tech dragon-slayer.

Breakup is a serious challenge, but the tech companies often welcome regulation, which can usually be gamed; the companies themselves would provide plenty of lobbying and advice to help shape the law in the first place, and badly (or cleverly) designed regulations can act as barriers to entry to new competitors. In October 2019, a recording emerged of Zuckerberg describing Elizabeth Warren's breakup plans as an existential threat;[21] compare that with his earlier request to lawmakers for more regulation 'in four areas: harmful content, election integrity, privacy and data portability'.[22] The need to schmooze governments more effectively was taken on board by the tech companies. Facebook employed a former Eurocrat and deputy prime minister of the United Kingdom, Sir Nick Clegg, to handle its diplomacy and PR.[23] Alphabet was more concerned by the change of mood in the Republican Party, and appointed a former chief of staff to Republican Senator Rob Portman as its top lobbyist. It also began funding right-wing small-government groups.[24]

National US agencies have been looking to existing law to probe anticompetitive behaviour. The Department of Justice began a broad antitrust review in July 2019, while fifty states attorneys-general launched an antitrust investigation into Alphabet's search and advertising businesses in September. Meanwhile, Facebook had to announce that it was the target of an FTC probe in June of the same year, and by September the attorneys-general of eight states and DC were looking at whether Facebook 'endangered consumer data, reduced the quality of consumers' choices, or increased the price of advertising'. Sen. Hawley, it is worth noting, began to be noticed in this area when he was attorney-general of Missouri; even if the states can't launch official antitrust actions, that doesn't mean they don't have some resources to improvise with.[25]

An authoritative Congressional Committee report appeared in October 2020, accusing the tech companies of violating antitrust law in a number of respects, especially in the acquisition of competing start-ups and bullying those on their platforms. Despite the predictable failure of representatives of the two parties to agree on the way forward, they certainly agreed on what was wrong. The report called for a lowering of the bar for antitrust violations (to protect entrepreneurs, free markets, and democracy, as well as consumers), and a raising of the bar for acquisitions. The Republican minority on the committee released a minority report that aired some of its own concerns, such as the alleged anti-conservative bias, and dissented from some of the Democratic majority's ideas about intervening in the market.[26]

The forces ranged against the tech giants look formidable. Facebook's myriad defensive acquisitions, combined with its cavalier attitude to privacy, its alleged role in spreading misinformation, and the global perception that it is not paying its way in tax, made it seem the most vulnerable to regulatory attack. But the first company in the sights of William Barr's Department of Justice, immediately prior to the 2020 presidential election, was Google (despite the fact that an EU fine against Google's uncompetitive practices in 2018 had been met by a tweet from President Trump saying, 'The European Union just slapped a Five Billion Dollar fine on one of our great companies, Google. They truly have taken advantage of the US, but not for long!').[27] The lawsuit, which is unlikely to be resolved for years (unless it is withdrawn), accused Google of abusing its position as a gatekeeper to the Internet to maintain an illegal monopoly of search and search advertising.[28]

Why wait till 2020 to litigate? It was an election year, when legislators and the administration want to be able to demonstrate progress in certain areas. The campaign, especially the Democratic primaries, revealed that attacking the tech companies was a positive strategy for the politicians, and a rare area of bipartisan agreement. This was perhaps an unexpected revival of the ideals of the Silicon Valley Open Internet, as the Congressional Committee metaphorically shed their suits and donned 1960s tie-dye.

The tech companies pushed back, with classic statements of the DC Commercial ethos. Facebook argued that 'Facebook is an American success story. We compete with a wide variety of services with millions, even billions, of people using them. Acquisitions are part of every industry, and just one way we innovate new technologies to deliver more value to people. Instagram and WhatsApp have reached new heights of success because Facebook has invested billions in those businesses. A strongly competitive landscape existed at the time of both acquisitions and exists today. Regulators thoroughly reviewed each deal and rightly did not see any reason to stop them at the time.'[29] We will have to wait to discover whether the new-found appetite for openness on Capitol Hill will survive the frenzy and peculiar dynamics of an election year, or whether the tech giants' formidable lobbying power will allow them to vacate the naughty step. Even if the Google case is not followed by others, it is clear that the Department of Justice will have to devote several years to its pursuit, probably under more than one attorney-general. Will the US government have greater staying power than Google itself?[30]

CHAPTER 11
The Fourth Internet

The Beijing Paternal Internet

Another response to the problems of openness is to welcome an *op-portunity* to use the Internet's powers of surveillance for social good, including to counteract the difficulties discussed in Chapter 6 that openness presents. Security and law enforcement loom large in the responsibilities of government, and the use of the Internet as a communication medium gives the prospect of learning about criminal and terrorist networks that threaten public security. Furthermore, the patterns of interaction might also allow interventions to use the data generated to optimize certain social functions. The increasing prevalence of mobile devices and the Internet of Things (IoT) will extend the reach of such governance, facilitating interventions in, say, improving healthcare and well-being, addressing climate change, and reducing transport congestion.

The fact that an IP address is essential for existence on the Internet presents the opportunity for governments to take more control. Collecting errant IP addresses can, for example, help copyright holders trace peer-to-peer (P2P) file-sharing transgressions, governments block subversive, pornographic, hate-filled, or racist content, and global law enforcement agencies look for organized and cyber-criminals. All this has created a constituency of actors who (for legitimate reasons) are interested in getting ISPs to reveal the location and ideally identity of occupants of particular IP addresses. This is one reason why many governments are keen to remove ICANN and the RIRs and to replace them with a multinational agency such as the ITU to allocate IP addresses directly to national authorities, under direct state control.[1]

Four Internets. Kieron O'Hara and Wendy Hall, Oxford University Press. © Oxford University Press 2021.
DOI: 10.1093/oso/9780197523681.003.0011

The Brussels Bourgeois Internet is an attempt to ensure a standard of decent behaviour online upon which freedom of action can rest. 'Decent', of course, can be defined in a number of ways, and the exercise of power may be needed to determine and apply standards of decency. Paternalism is an authoritarian policy that defines 'decent' in a top-down manner, limiting freedom and autonomy in order to promote the good of individuals, on the tacit assumption that the authority has both a greater appreciation of where their interests really lie, and the legitimacy to take action.

A Paternal Internet sees the Internet as continuous with and integrated within the offline world, and asserts that Internet engineering and governance should be subordinate to centrally defined beneficial outcomes. In contrast to the Burkean idea that meaningful liberty must rest upon constraint, the paternal view is that liberty, if meaningful, is a perpetual threat to the beneficial order. Therefore the authority does not need the consent of individuals to act, *as long as it acts for their welfare, and not for a self-interested reason*, so it is important that we do not confuse the Paternal ideal with the mere manipulation of the Internet by an autocrat to remain in power or to silence the opposition (although the paternalist's plan may include such suppression).

Although 'paternalism' is usually a pejorative term nowadays in the West, we should not automatically assume that the paternalist is morally wrong; it is a 'salient cultural characteristic' in Pacific Asian, Middle Eastern, and Latin American cultures.[2] Many paternal relationships are healthy and genuinely intended for the good of the individual. As the name suggests, the archetypal paternalistic relationship is between parents and their children, while others include doctor–patient, lawyer–client, religious leader–worshipper, agricultural scientist–peasant farmer, mentor–protégé. Political leaders as different as Gladstone and Lenin have been in the paternalistic camp, but not all cultures in which paternalism thrives will accept it from the state.[3]

For paternalism to flourish and be implemented, there must be an authority with widely accepted legitimacy and an inclination to define what 'beneficial' means. Those in the square must accept the legitimacy of the tower, because resistance will put legitimacy in question, and will make the paternalistic relationship extremely problematic. The hierarchy also needs to ensure that its legitimacy isn't damaged by epistemological failings that mean it screws up too often.[4] Finally, it must have the ability to get things done.

We should be sure to distinguish the bourgeois approach and the paternal approach. The bourgeois view is that the conditions for freedom need to be created and maintained, and once they have been secured, individuals can pursue their own idea of the good. The paternal view, rather, aims to secure particular outcomes or values. So individuals cannot be left free, because if they were, those outcomes may not obtain. Free persons might work, deliberately or accidently, to stymie them. Paternalism sees human autonomy as at best one value among others. The bourgeois approach, on the other hand, forbears to insist on any outcome as more proper than another, as long as dignity is respected. The bourgeois view is that it is better that people make their own mistakes, as long as they are not hoodwinked or coerced, and as long as they do not undermine the social order by their behaviour; the paternal view is that beneficial outcomes are better than costly ones, even if people prefer the costly ones.

The distinction between the Commercial Internet and the Paternal Internet is easier to see. Let us return to Zuckerberg's attack, quoted in Chapter 4, on 'people across the spectrum [who] believe that achieving the political outcomes they think matter is more important than every person having a voice'.[5] Zuckerberg's description of the enemy in terms of their adherence to particular political and social outcomes clearly evokes the supporters of the Paternal Internet.

In this category, the Chinese state, backed by the Communist Party and (at the time of writing) helmed by the fiercely nationalistic President Xi Jinping, is the chief geopolitical entity that fits the bill. Hence we call our fourth Internet the *Beijing Paternal Internet*, although, as we shall see, many nations are attracted by paternalism. In a society whose Confucian underpinnings remain powerful, despite frequent attempts through history (not least by the Communist Party itself) to deny them, acceptance of national goals determined by the party and the state is conditioned by almost universal acceptance of their legitimacy and authority.

THE EXEMPLAR

China includes about 18 percent of the world's population, on about 6 percent of its land mass. It is not an insignificant place, therefore, and its geopolitical eclipse between its defeat in the Opium Wars and the incompetent chaos of the Mao era is best seen, historically, as a blip. After Deng Xiaoping restored effective government and liberalized the economy, it is neither surprising nor disturbing that China has pushed to regain superpower status.

That said, China is a different proposition, historically and culturally, from other influential geopolitical entities discussed earlier. Its history goes back several millennia, and it was effectively unified in 221 BC by the first Qin emperor's conquest of his six rivals. His victory was made possible by earlier administrative reforms in the Qin kingdom—replacing the nobility with a meritocratic bureaucracy, which was able to provide effective taxation, an up-to-date army, widespread education, and social mobility—which enabled it to outperform the competition. These basic characteristics of good governance have remained central to Chinese identity through the very many ups and downs of Chinese history, including the rise of the Communist Party. China is a paradigm case of a civilizational state.[6]

In the terms of our analysis, it is very hierarchical, at least partly thanks to its Confucian heritage. Confucius's philosophy of social ordering (ancestors above descendants, elder above younger, men above women, emperor above all) means that in effect all families and clans are self-governing reflections of the political order (or, put another way, the political order and the social order are two sides of the same coin). The system wasn't completely deterministic, with tensions baked into it (women were answerable both to their husbands and their own birth families, sons revered but did not necessarily have affection for their fathers, and a good education could raise anyone in the social hierarchy), but these ambiguities provided the flexibility to roll with social change over the millennia. The needs of the hierarchy dominated law; as with European civil law, traditional Chinese law contains much to do with the criminal code and the administration of the state, and far less to do with the dispute resolution and defences of individual liberty that provide the main thrust of the common law tradition.

It differs from its civilizational peers in another respect. The Anglosphere and Europe have consistently tried (often successfully) to impose their proselytizing religions, political systems, and universalized conceptions of human rights onto weaker nations. China, in contrast, has tended not to project itself culturally, although it has always reserved the right to govern unconditionally within its own borders, and has taken an expansive view of where its writ might extend (for example, with respect to Hong Kong, Tibet, Xinjiang, and the South China Sea). When it trades, it does not force its (or any) values on its partners, so it will not be scolding dictators about their human rights records any time soon. It will make deals conditional on a *quid pro quo* (such as not recognizing Taiwan diplomatically).

A key Confucian concept is *li*, which can be translated as 'conventions', but covers ritual, practice, etiquette, manners, or propriety.[7] *Li* is definitive in Confucian culture; for instance, Confucius himself never questioned or criticized it (compare Socrates, his near contemporary, who was always ready to critique particular customs). *Li* therefore is not only descriptive but normative. As Joseph Needham, doyen of Western experts on China, put it:

> In China there was always a struggle between systematic law and the law that the officials administered paternalistically, where every case was considered on its merits and in accordance with *li*. The full force of the meaning of *li* was profound, and could not be divorced from the customs, usages and ceremonies which epitomised it. The significance of these was deep, lying not merely in the fact that they had arisen because they agreed with the instinctive feeling of rightness experienced by the Chinese, but also in the conviction that they accorded with

the 'will of heaven', with the structure of the whole universe. Hence the basic disquiet aroused in the Chinese mind by crimes, or even by disputes, since these were felt to be disturbances in the Order of Nature.[8]

From that cultural perspective, how threatening the rambunctious Silicon Valley Open Internet seems.

China's importance not only to the world economy, but also to the Internet, has grown remarkably in recent years, so that over half the country is connected to the Internet, and a quarter of Internet users are in China. Furthermore, the Chinese Internet mainly grew on mobile devices, and so its entire ecosystem is well adapted to the smartphone.[9] According to President Xi in 2016, the Internet is the 'common spiritual home' for hundreds of millions of people, and he has also spoken of his ambition that China should be a 'cyber super-power'.[10] The Communist Party and the Chinese state are well placed to set national goals, which unite Confucianism about society with nationalism about history and geopolitics.

- The first goal speaks to the Confucian imperative: **social stability**. China wants to avoid social upheaval, and its attitude to disruption—the keystone of digital modernity—is disapproval, which marks it out from the other visionaries of the Internet.
- The second goal is the **preservation of the Communist Party's position** as sole governing entity of the Chinese state. The Chinese learned from the collapse of the Soviet Union that openness (*glasnost*) often leads to disruption and reconstruction (*perestroika*)—and where is Mikhail Gorbachev now?
- The third goal is to restore China to where it considers it should stand as **a regional and world superpower**, after a couple of centuries of loss of influence and humiliating submission to Western powers.

Trying to balance these goals produces an awkward hybrid, in which legitimacy rests upon two distinct pillars.

- The first is a claim of **technocratic efficiency** based on engineering expertise managed by collective party decisions; against this, the cacophony from the West of free speech, social media, free press, anti-authoritarianism, multiparty elections, and populist revolt are taken as evidence of the chaos wrought by unmanaged discourse.
- The second is a claim about the **unique capabilities of the Communist Party** to manage the technocratic government (in the traditional position of the emperor atop the hierarchy), which in recent years has morphed into a personality cult around President Xi and **'Xi Jinping Thought'**.

Given this understanding of legitimacy, Chinese Internet policy rests broadly on four strategic aims:

- direction of the online environment (if not direct control);
- cybersecurity;
- national autonomy, where possible, in technological provision (if not full self-sufficiency); and
- influence, via outreach.

As a result, particularly of the first strategic aim, the Chinese Internet has been monitored closely throughout its growth. Censorship and monitoring have always been in place, to counter the disruptive effects extolled by its Western creators. Technology, for example, is used to monitor populations such as the Uighurs of Xinjiang province, as part of a drive to erase distinctive cultural identities (alongside more physical oppression, including the use of 're-education' camps in Xinjiang).[11] Famously, the Chinese put the 'Great Firewall' in place at an early stage, involving low-tech measures such as using informers, intensive surveillance, well-publicized arrests, bureaucratic red tape, physical shutdowns of the Internet, and labour-intensive censorship of websites, email, and search, as well as DPI, automatic monitoring, filtering, and blocking.[12] China's hacking skills have remained powerful and effective throughout.[13] The Great Firewall really did function like a firewall, only allowing selected content through. It is structured with bottlenecks at exchanges which make cutting off geographical regions (such as Xinjiang or Tibet) relatively straightforward. Many tools, such as onion routing and virtual private networks (VPNs), have always been used to get round it,[14] but the Chinese Internet now contains plenty of interesting content (while under-representing the interests of minorities), and American companies have largely been beaten off by local rivals (with more than a little help from the government),[15] so the need to go abroad for content for all but the most committed is relatively low. Exceptions have been made when the Firewall was magically opened, not least during the Beijing Olympics of 2008, and more recently for students studying abroad who were stranded in China during the COVID-19 pandemic.[16] We can see how the Chinese Internet has grown in Figure 11.1.

The Beijing Paternal Internet therefore shares few values with the models we have covered so far, as our value diagram shows. The only value of importance is open technical standards, as it still needs to be possible for people to join and flourish on the Internet. Otherwise, control is the order of the day (Figure 11.2).

As party and state more or less coincide, it is well placed to push favoured technologies. Its 'Made in China 2025' policy, intended to bring together innovative and smart technologies to make China a centre for cutting-edge advanced manufacturing, was a particular target of ire from the Trump

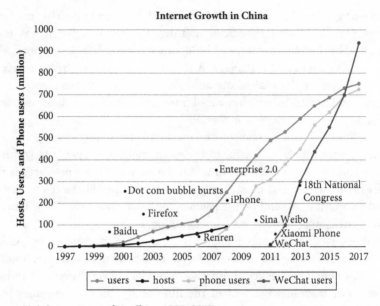

Figure 11.1. Internet growth in China 1997–2017.
Source: Thanks to Jie Tang and the China Internet Network Information Center.

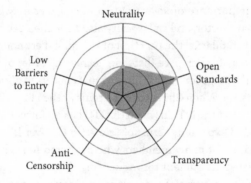

Figure 11.2. The ideals of the Beijing Paternal Internet.
Source: Thanks to Paul Smart, who conceived and created this diagram via Highcharts.

administration.[17] Although, as an industrial policy, it owes a good deal to Germany's Industry 4.0 initiative of 2013,[18] the scale of its ambition is remarkable, attempting to tool China up in key infrastructure such as robotics, sensors, the IoT, chip-making, smartphones, renewable energy, 3D-printing, and not least, AI, throwing eye-watering sums of money at these industries, while creating barriers to market access and obstacles to business models for overseas competitors and inward investors.[19]

Exogenous events, particularly coronaviruses, have also had major and unpredictable effects in the Chinese information ecosystem. The 2020 COVID-19 pandemic gave a substantial boost to many information industries, not least surveillance, but also telemedicine and digital payments. But it was foreshadowed by the SARS outbreak of 2003, which, although far less serious, also affected economies and commerce. A risk-averse population began to adopt online services and social media at scale. Several e-commerce enterprises began, notably JD.com, which changed from bricks to clicks in direct response to the SARS-related decrease in footfall.[20]

The Chinese vision is premised on a vanguard of privately owned tech companies, astonishingly successful in their own right, but operating within a tightly controlled environment in which the ruling Communist Party is the referee. The largest and most successful of these are Alibaba (e-commerce, cloud computing, AI, and online payments), Baidu (search and AI), Tencent (games, streaming content, social networking, online payments, AI, and the ubiquitous WeChat messaging app), and Sina Weibo (microblogging). China also has an increasing presence on international bodies; for instance, heading the ITU, where it pushes for alternative technological standards that will aid government micromanagement of the Internet.[21] Chinese companies have dominated submissions to the ITU of surveillance technology standards.[22] China also engages with ICANN, mainly via the advisory GAC. It supports a kind of hierarchical multistakeholderism in which government predominates because of the importance of sovereignty and cybersecurity, but where academics, the private sector, and civil society also have their say on the topics of engineering and standards, the function of the digital economy, and the conduct and freedoms of cyberspace (listed in decreasing order of importance).[23]

The ITU was the stage for one of China's most concerted efforts to influence Internet governance. When China took the reins at the ITU in 2015, it set up a study group to look at the IoT (in which the ITU has no formal role), which consistently pushed to expand its terms of reference to cover IP-related matters, against the instincts of many members who preferred to stick to the original remit. Its suggested instrument for influencing the IoT was an old formalism for managing digital information, developed by Internet pioneer Robert Kahn in the 1990s, called the Digital Object Architecture (DOA)—a classic example of how technologies can be repurposed from their intended use.

The DOA was originally an attempt to shift the Internet's emphasis from the transport of data around the network (which is expressed with TCP/IP), to thinking in terms of digital 'information objects' that would persist online. If you wanted to access an object via a device, a DOA system would identify both the device and the object, and authenticate the access (or not, if you were not authorized). In order to do this, unique names (called *handles*) would be needed that would last as long as the objects themselves (which may be decades); these handles are simultaneously names and addresses, since they both identify and provide a means of accessing the digital objects. There was some interest in this in a few sectors, notably academic publishing, where the

Digital Object Identifier system (DOI), standardized by the ISO, allows persistent reference to articles, videos, and datasets (you can see many DOIs in the reference section of this book). The complexities and structures of DOA are not dissimilar to the DNS.[24]

DOA was originally a DARPA project, but in 2015 the top-level registry of handles passed to the DONA Foundation, created by the ITU. It has not gone out of its way to foster trust; it is not particularly transparent in process or open in policy development, does not seem to have the cybersecurity capabilities to cope with the responsibility of an important system, or the infrastructure to scale up to the size of the IoT, and via the ITU is cosier with governments rather than other stakeholders.

It is not, therefore, a particularly promising organization for Internet governance, but DOA was still put forward as a potential standard for the IoT, and ideally for a wider set of digital resources. China, supported by Russia and Saudi Arabia, among others, liked the idea of a basic Internet protocol which identified both parties to an interaction (and indeed all connected devices on the network), and gave a central authority the power to prevent them accessing each other. Inserted into the IoT, it would allow all connected items to be identified and tracked. If it was extended to all devices, one's handle would function as an IP address, but unlike the latter would be persistent, and one would have to register one in order to join the Internet.

The 2016 attempt to put DOA at the centre of the Internet was resisted. Some thought it a power grab, others that it couldn't impose its own standard in a system of open standards, and so the threat was overblown.[25] Network effects mean that the threat is not trivial, even if the latter point is true. The advantages of keeping the Internet connected are so strong that even a flawed and intrusive system could gather a critical mass of users.

The lesson of this move, just one year after China took over leadership of the ITU, is that its involvement in standards-setting organizations is not simply for prestige or to carry on business as usual. China has an agenda, which with respect to the Internet is strongly connected to its Paternal vision. The existence of a persistent naming standard was a means for turning the Internet from a network in which one could hide, to one in which one was permanently visible and identifiable. Shifting the Internet in this direction will remain an imperative for the Chinese government. In 2020, a database of information, built by a Chinese data company with links to the state, about millions of overseas citizens from publicly available sources such as social media, came to light. It is no doubt not the only example of its kind.[26]

The state owns much of the 'private' sector in the Chinese economy, but not the most innovative companies. Instead, it provides large amounts of funding of technology, and has a plethora of indirect methods of influence or control to hand, creating what Rogier Creemers, a researcher into Chinese Internet law, calls a 'strategic public-private nexus', though with 'public' in the box seat.[27] It can absorb risk, divert cheap finance, underwrite infrastructure, and squelch noisy civil society opposition. For firms listed on foreign stock exchanges, it ensures that audits are conducted in China, and makes them hard for foreigners to inspect.[28] Its impressive hacking capabilities are used in the service of Chinese businesses.[29] It has a large pool of cheap labour, which has been strategically important at various points in the history of the Chinese Internet, from manning the Great Firewall to marking up data for machine learning. It is a giant and growing unified market, which has developed rapidly from primitive beginnings (for example, a cashless economy has risen from nowhere, using smartphone payments on apps run by the major firms).

The state is immune to public opinion, at least in the short term, and in total command of geography; if it felt that a technology such as autonomous vehicles should be promoted, it could easily clear and redesign neighbourhoods to provide testing grounds, and if it wanted to furnish a research cluster, it could evict businesses and transfer others in.[30] It insists that inward investment from abroad provides not only capital but also knowledge transfer—aided by an Intellectual Property regime that was loose and ineffective when China was a copying nation (Baidu displaced Google in China because it could be used to locate pirated MP3 files), and is policed rather better now that it has become an innovator. All these put it in a strong position with respect to maintaining the Beijing Paternal Internet, subservient to the three major goals outlined earlier, and any other intermediate targets which the state specifies. The private sector, even very large companies such as Alibaba, Tencent, and Baidu, has powerful incentives to align themselves with these goals. A Mercator Institute paper argues that one key element of Chinese digital strategy is 'the explicit goal of spreading China's homegrown cyber norms and standards by leveraging the strength of its IT sector'.[31]

On the thorny issue of data protection, its foundation, the Personal Information Security Specification of 2018, is modelled in many respects on GDPR. It has wider scope in its definition of sensitive personal information, demands data subjects' consent as the only ground for data sharing (GDPR has six grounds for sharing, so plenty of alternatives to consent), and is more rigorous in other ways, which have been extended further by a 2020 update.[32]

The main way in which the Specification exceeds GDPR is in the demands it makes with respect to data security. This reflects Chinese understanding of data protection as a national security issue, which is absent from GDPR; the

Specification is not a law in its own right, but part of a wider cybersecurity law. Personal data and sensitive data generated by operations within China must be stored in China. Furthermore, although the Specification appears more powerful than GDPR, its aims are aligned with the need for companies to have rationales for data-sharing, rather than to protect individuals, and is intended to allow access to large datasets to help grow the AI industry. Given the informal but close relationships between companies and government, and the need to store Chinese data on Chinese servers, data will generally be within the reach and protection of the government. Data protection here means protection of data, and Chinese data interests, from foreign interference. It is easy to overestimate the convergence between Chinese and European concerns.[33]

At home and abroad, China invests heavily in technology using venture capital models.[34] Alibaba and Tencent are among the largest of China's venture capital investors, and are shaping the domestic start-up world.[35] National and local government promote certain industries with 'guiding funds'.[36] Chinese companies have invested billions of dollars in Western start-ups, despite pushback from the Trump administration and the European Union.[37] Much of this activity is helped by the nimbleness with which its firms adapt to the Chinese business environment, characterized by shaky rule of law, massive consumer scale, extremely changeable demand, cut-throat competition, and proximity to an efficient low-cost manufacturing base, which results in them displaying highly opportunistic behaviour, expanding quickly into new markets. Some of this adaptability is necessary simply to avoid disaster when the government abruptly changes course; Tencent's business model was upended in 2018 by a sudden state crackdown on gaming addiction, for instance,[38] while the Initial Public Offering of the Ant Group in 2020, which would have been the largest in the world, was suspended on two days' notice after founder Jack Ma made some unwisely critical comments about Chinese regulators.[39] US firms, in contrast, have developed to take advantage of their own more stable and business-friendly environment, with high breadth of ownership and relatively transparent management. Lee has argued that Chinese companies are hungrier, less complacent, more vigorous, more eager for competition, and less constrained by pious mission statements and 'core values' than their American counterparts.[40]

NEITHER TOP-DOWN NOR BOTTOM-UP

The Beijing Paternal Internet was originally supposed to be strictly administered by orders trickling down from the governmental hierarchy, and many commentators, including one of the present authors, believed this would cause it classic square-and-tower problems.[41] It resolved these ultimately by relinquishing direct control, because its population, which respects the governing hierarchy and contains many enthusiastic supporters, is generally willing to engage with the Internet on its terms to minimize threats to social stability.[42] The elite Chinese academics and Internet policymakers interviewed by Gianluigi Negro, while pragmatic, are all behind their government's attempts to challenge American dominance of Internet governance.[43] Popular tolerance of online dissent often disappears if there is any hint of choreography by outsiders. For instance, at the beginning of the COVID-19 epidemic, Fang Fang's bleak diary of life in Wuhan during lockdown was extraordinarily popular, but when news broke that it would be translated and published in Germany and the United States, public opinion turned on her viciously.[44]

The means of steering networks are openly discussed, in terms of value rather than power, as described by two Chinese academics:

> In order to build the network propaganda field of socialist core values, we must first 'seize' the network to . . . increase the network dissemination and quantity of socialist core values in various forms. . . . The media and other emerging network media are used to educate socialist core values. Using various media such as Weibo, WeChat, public account, and other media is [sic] to expand the scope and speed of the spread of socialist core values on the network platform.[45]

In 2019, the *Provisions on the Governance of the Online Information Content Ecosystem* appeared, a leaden attempt to improve public discourse, in accordance with the ideal. Content is divided into three types: encouraged, negative (legal, but watch out), and illegal (see Table 11.1).[46]

The state may set the parameters for censorship, and it strong-arms private companies into identifying problematic material, but the task attracts individual volunteers too. Officials have harnessed popular enthusiasm in some schemes, outsourcing the policing of content, while organizations such as the Communist Youth League favour zealous amateur censors, but liberals should not let their own suspicion of censorship blind them to the fact that much of this activity is simply an expression of solidarity from the bottom up. It is no surprise that citizens in a Confucian culture should be concerned by pseudoscience, rumour, fake news, and porn, and want to play their part in eradicating them.[47]

As the overlapping hierarchies of classical Confucianism suggest, it does not contain the same legacy of a fundamental distinction between a public and a private sphere, such as we find in, say, Aristotle.[48] Convergence is not apparent, and we need to avoid optimistic, Western-centric, and culturally insensitive assumptions that 'some ethical safeguards, constraints and desiderata are universal and are universally accepted and cherished, such as the nature and scope of human rights'.[49]

Table 11.1. THREE TYPES OF CONTENT IN THE CHINESE PROVISIONS (2019)

Encouraged	Illegal	Negative
Spreading and explaining Party doctrine	Content opposing the basic principles set forth in the Constitution	Sensationalizing headlines
Spreading Party action	Content endangering national security, divulging State secrets, subverting	Excessive celebrity intrigue and gossip
Spreading economic and social achievement	the national regime, and destroying national unity	Improper comments on tragedies
Spreading the Core Socialist Values	Content harming the nation's honour and interests	Sexual innuendo, suggestion, or enticement
Guidance to the public on social concerns	Content demeaning or denying the deeds and spirit of heroes and martyrs	Gore and horror
Increasing international influence	Content promoting terrorism or extremism	Incitement of discrimination
Other positive and wholesome content	Content inciting ethnic hatred or ethnic discrimination, or destroying ethnic unity	Coarse or vulgar language and behaviour
	Content undermining the nation's policy on religions, promoting cults and superstitions	Bad habits or dangerous activity that might be imitated by minors
	Dissemination of rumours, disrupting economic or social order	Other content with a negative impact to the online information ecosystem
	Obscenity, erotica, gambling, violence, murder, terror, or instigating crime	
	Content insulting or defaming others, infringing other persons' honour, privacy, or other lawful rights and interests	
	Other content prohibited by laws or administrative regulations	
Article 5	Article 6	Article 7

Source: *Governing the E-cosystem 2*, China Law Translate, 1 March 2020, https://www.chinalawtranslate.com/en/governing-the-e-cosystem-2/.

That is not to say that the Chinese population always acquiesces in invasions of privacy. An interesting case emerged in 2019 around a legal academic in Hangzhou who objected to the use of facial scans by his local safari park in order to speed up service.[50] A pandemic-related issue arose when home-schooling for children proved harder than ideal because of the requirement to submit lesson plans for review by censors.[51] But the surveillance has also produced expectations that are sometimes unmet. Most Chinese people accept that they live in an all-powerful surveillance state, and so many were amazed that the authorities struggled to police the lockdown of the city of Wuhan and the state of Hubei during the COVID-19 epidemic. One Weibo user asked indignantly why all the passengers of flights and trains that had left Wuhan couldn't be traced: 'aren't we all 2020-big-data-high-tech now'?[52]

Social media are tolerated in China, and they have created a lively public space (as one example, students quickly found a wheeze whereby they gave teaching apps 1-star ratings on app stores to get them removed, which also didn't help the home-schooling effort). Political comment on Sina Weibo is more prevalent than on Twitter, and a higher proportion of that content is produced by 'ordinary' users, rather than established opinion formers.[53] Attacking state agencies or organizing resistance is risky. Conversation is shut down quickly if it becomes critical, so it tends to police itself.[54] Nevertheless, microblogging is also an important source of information for the government about when things are going wrong, whether they be illegal land appropriations by local government, corruption, or high levels of pollution.[55] Local chiefs have few incentives to pass bad news upwards (the perennial epistemological problem of hierarchies). If social media complaints exceed a threshold, the government will take it upon itself to sort things out.

The cost of this partial acceptance of the informative power of social media is cynicism and a lack of trust.[56] The beginning of the COVID-19 pandemic was marked by the widely publicized punishment of eight 'spreaders of rumours', who turned out to be doctors alerting colleagues on a WeChat group to the emergence of a new virus in Wuhan; following the death of one of those doctors, censors continued to mute online debate about China's response, and to make it harder to get onto VPNs capable of getting round the Great Firewall.[57]

China's response to COVID-19 was a characteristic joint mobilization of vast numbers of people abetted by surveillance technology. Large cohorts of people were sent to test temperatures, man checkpoints, and do door-to-door checks on populations. Meanwhile, part of the pandemic infrastructure they were administering was also delivered through apps, often developed by cities, which might flag up potential carriers, leading to restrictions on their movements, or might trace contacts in the event of a positive test. But the overall response relied on the effective combination of human labour and digital wizardry, in a context of popular acceptance of high levels of intrusion.[58]

The infrastructure that delivered this surveillance was largely supplied by the private sector and used voluntarily by those overseen. In 2020, the most popular app in China was Tencent's WeChat, a messaging app which also allows electronic payments, videoconferencing, gaming, location sharing, business-to-consumer services, social networking and updates about friends, human resources functions, e-commerce, and news feeds.[59] Whereas on the DC Commercial Internet companies approach universality by growing larger networks, on the Beijing Paternal Internet companies try to provide blanket coverage of the services people need and deliver them by smartphone, so that each person need never leave the app. WeChat gathers information from both online and offline worlds, whereas the DC Commercial Internet focuses on online behaviour such as searches and likes; WeChat's approach thereby facilitated COVID-19 self-assessment and contact-tracing apps being bundled in with the main app. China's Internet ecosystem gives it the scope to make significant interventions in contact tracing, rather as its control of cities allows them to be reshaped for autonomous vehicles.[60]

Alibaba's affiliate company Ant Financial, which runs a similarly giant (1 billion users) payment app called Alipay, also provided specific pandemic-related apps. Between them, payment apps are squeezing the use of cash and credit cards and creating a cashless economy. The ecosystem produces enormous quantities of data, providing information about minute aspects of their users' lives; thanks to its permissive environment for data sharing and trading, China has been called the 'Saudi Arabia' of data. Most obviously, payment apps show where economic activity is taking place; transport apps suggest how populations are moving; social networking and messaging apps allow data about acquaintances to be connected. Using face recognition as an identification method in immersive environments is convenient for the user, and handy for the snoop.[61] The result is a highly detailed understanding of quotidian lives, both for individuals and in the aggregate. Although the information is held in private hands, in general it will prove easier to use this evidence for the state's purposes during an emergency like the pandemic (for instance, contact-tracing apps used data from, and returned data to, various ministries and government agencies) than in 'normal' times. Integrating such data for general use, rather than for a specific purpose, like suppressing COVID-19 in Wuhan or Islamic devotion in Xinjiang, is harder. This is one of the reasons behind the Chinese government's introduction of a digital currency, the e-RMB, to allow it to monitor cash flow without the complexities of retrieving and integrating transaction data from different payment schemes.[62]

The complexities of integrating data on this scale are illustrated by the *social credit* system, which has caught the attention of Western commentators. Social credit is an extension of ideas such as (financial) credit scoring in two directions: first, it scores performance in more areas of life than those concerned with money, including social media activity; second, it also incorporates the idea of crowdsourcing scores from wider publics, as with Amazon or eBay ratings, than just government or companies. The idea is to provide a method of determining how trustworthy a citizen is, which simultaneously demonstrates the government's ability to regulate personal conduct without bias (because data-driven) and provides guidelines for citizens' self-regulation and self-censorship. The idea is rooted in Confucian principles ('sincerity in government affairs, commercial sincerity, social sincerity, and judicial credibility', as the State Council put it in 2014), and aims to counter problems stemming from lack of respect, such as tax evasion, plagiarism, counterfeiting, corruption, or free-riding on the efforts of others. Rewards can be given through social credit for altruistic behaviour, such as donating blood.[63]

The social credit score would therefore be used to rank or score the population, and then to dole out rewards or punishments (such as preventing people from travelling on high-speed trains, or even borrowing books from libraries). Depending what data was integrated into the system, it could become very intrusive—for instance, sites that allow commenting would have to keep blacklists of those making defamatory statements. Punishments may become more effective if expertise in face recognition were integrated, e.g. to prevent travel.

This idea is certainly disturbing for Western democrats, and it suits all sides to talk up the social credit system—in the West as a means of criticizing or demonizing China, and in China to give the impression that the government is in control. However, we should never underestimate the difficulty of seamlessly integrating data from heterogeneous sources, especially in a nation like China where government has many faces (many agencies, ministries, and companies are run as personal fiefdoms and power centres) and where standardization (and Silicon Valley values such as interoperability) is not always pursued vigorously. There has been little discussion and no consensus on exactly how to calculate a social credit score: how many blood donations should remove the stigma of having criticized a senior Politburo member? Calculations of negative behaviour tend to be more transparent than those of positive behaviour.[64] The evidence of the social credit 'system' is that there is no system at all, only a few local experiments, of which many citizens are unaware. They are often commercially, rather than politically, focused—news coverage of social credit tends to emphasize commercial benefits—and as often as not, serve as enforcement mechanisms for pre-existing social conduct norms and ideals, as opposed to completely novel constraints.[65]

Conversely, similar systems operate in a number of democracies. For instance, predictive analytics are used in the United States to generate no-fly lists, and democratic local governments are not above a little snooping, for instance to see if people are recycling their rubbish correctly,[66] so the Chinese initiative is more of an outlier, in terms of its ambition, than a radical departure.

China is ambitious for superpower status, but is more concerned with sovereignty within its own borders than interfering elsewhere. Furthermore, its ruinous one-child policy, ended in 2015, will hobble its economy for decades to come, when it might have expected a demographic dividend. But it is a trading nation, and where there is demand, it is keen to export both its vision of the Beijing Paternal Internet and the technology to implement it.[67]

EXPORTING THE PATERNAL VISION

The Paternal Internet is not going to work everywhere. It is impossible to imagine it taking root in a highly polarized society, or one with low trust in government, or one in which independence is a strong individual value—all three of which apply to the United States, for example. Nevertheless, there is no shortage of global interest in its principles.

Authoritarian states routinely censor or block certain Internet outlets. Iran has banned Facebook, while Saudi Arabia restricts the flow of information about any topic that would be troubling to its hard-line brand of Islam, whether it be women's or gay rights, or Shia theology. Those nations which are relatively isolated, in terms of (a) having only a few exchange points between home-based ISPs and the global Internet, and (b) providing relatively little content that is consumed internationally, are particularly well-placed to censor. In the first place, the government can focus its technical efforts on the bottlenecks around exchange points or isolated cables connecting to the network. The second condition means that it is unlikely to disrupt home businesses, which might have a powerful political voice. In an extreme example, in 2019, the government of Kazakhstan began to intercept all HTTPS traffic within its borders. Local ISPs were ordered to direct their users to a government website from which they could download a certificate onto their machines, without which they could not access the Internet at all. The certificate allowed the government to decrypt HTTPS traffic to examine it, and then encrypt it again and send it on to its destination. The rationale was protection of the population from fraud and hacking.[68]

The focus of this chapter is not the manipulation of the Internet for authoritarian ends. Many governments other than China's, including both dictatorships and democracies, are genuinely concerned to ensure that the Internet does not cause harm. It can be hard to work out how much of an authoritarian policy is devoted to social value and how much to securing the government. Singapore's Protection from Online Falsehoods and Manipulation Act (2019) is intended to suppress fake news—not an unworthy object in a small and racially mixed nation where social harmony is prized—but its maximum fines of S$1 million (about $700,000) and jail sentences of 10 years send a remarkably strong message. An online falsehood is defined as a false or misleading statement of fact (not a parody or satire), whose publication is against the public interest—a concept whose definition includes interfering with public tranquillity and diminishing public confidence in the government's performance. Fifteen ministries found themselves with the power to define truth. The act became an important factor in suppressing false rumours about the 2020 COVID-19 pandemic, and the first punishments doled out were proportionate, demanding retractions and corrections. But the recipients of those punishments tended to be opposition figures and NGOs—often targets in practice of other justifiable Singaporean laws such as libel.[69]

Culturally, Singapore has Chinese links, and is democratic and not corrupt, but hardly liberal. But this sort of thinking is in evidence anywhere where governments take it upon themselves to intervene in citizens' lives to keep them healthy and safe.[70] The debate over harmful material began with obscenity and graduated to pornography, hate speech, and now covers material that is 'merely' undesirable. As one example, Britain's Health Minister Matt Hancock argued in March 2019 that anti-vaccination propaganda, a particularly dangerous type of conspiracy theory whose influence has grown alongside the spread of online forums, should be curbed by social media platforms—this after the United Kingdom had lost its measles-free status with the World Health Organization (WHO).[71] This was pointedly argued shortly after the United Kingdom brought out a white paper on 'Online Harms', suggesting a mandatory duty of care for platforms to take reasonable steps to protect users from a range of harms, such as bullying and exposure to sites promoting self-harm, suicide, or eating disorders. In other words, the UK government of the time was clearly moving beyond the suppression of illegal content such as child pornography or threatening behaviour, and towards suppressing that which, though undesirable, is hard to define.[72] Analogous debates have happened in Australia (following the live-streaming of a terrorist atrocity in 2019), India, and Germany.

Beijing-style paternalism as a result brings with it the potential to cause rifts in the Internet, because what is perceived as a negative externality, social problem, or abuse will vary across cultures. Most oppose child pornography, but only some are concerned about Holocaust denial, glorification of anorexia, blasphemy, or gay material. Hence monitoring and censorship of these can't easily be scaled.[73] AI will be able to help, but cannot solve the problem. With an automatic system, platforms would have to err on the side of caution and take down false positives, so legitimate users would find their content eliminated (as has happened with YouTube's ContentID system, aimed at curbing copyright infringements).[74] There is no reason to think that it will be accurate enough any time soon for this not to be a major problem. As Mark Zuckerberg, who ought to know, said in 2018, 'It's much easier to build an AI system that can detect a nipple than it is to determine what is linguistically hate speech'.[75] Content moderation will, for the foreseeable future, have to involve large-scale human labour; there are currently about 100,000 people worldwide employed in screening violence, pornography, and other inappropriate (and for the moderators, often distressing) content.[76]

Attempts to limit misleading or inflammatory political speech would certainly be controversial, particularly in the United States, where it is protected by the First Amendment—but wherever one is in the world, allowing private companies to determine which political claims are factual and which mendacious will surely be a very large can of worms. We already see aspects of this, with a number of services unavailable in China, and not always because they are blocked by the Chinese government. YouTube has blocked anti-Chinese content from non-Chinese contributors, possibly—but not definitely—because large numbers of Chinese citizens have flagged it as contentious. The fact that YouTube's owner Google couldn't locate the cause of the censorship indicates the complexity of content moderation.[77]

There is, therefore, demand for the Paternal vision of the Internet, even in the democratic world, and by happy coincidence, China is prepared to export it. In 2013, President Xi unveiled an infrastructure and trade initiative, entitled The Silk Road Economic Belt and the 21st Century Maritime Silk Road, often called by the shortened (though not short) name 'The Belt and Road Initiative' (BRI), or its original Chinese name 'One Belt, One Road'. This aims to link the Eurasian world with connective and cooperative ventures, as a route for future Chinese (and other) trade, with Chinese-financed infrastructure across Asia, Europe, and Africa. The Paternal Internet is likely to become part of this project, a 'digital silk road', comprising the technological areas where China sees advantage, including AI, big data, quantum computing, smart cities, and cloud storage.[78] Most of the BRI has until now been focused on construction and energy, but the digital element is growing. The Mercator Institute has made what it calls a conservative estimate of contributions of 'at least $7bn in loans and FDI for fiber-optic cable and telecommunication network projects completed since 2013, more than $10bn for e-commerce and mobile payment deals, [and] for smart and safe city-related projects, at least several hundred million USD',[79] while Freedom House documents the export of network equipment to at least 38 countries, surveillance technology such as face recognition to at least 18 countries, and training in data governance to at least 36 countries.[80] The Chinese company Aegis even exports a version of the Great Firewall.[81] Digital infrastructure projects will help standardize Chinese institutions and project Chinese power in wider spheres, while the widespread use of WeChat Pay and Alipay will position the yuan as a global currency for cross-border payments. Ant Financial, for example, is a major investor in bKash, a mobile money operator which accounts for over half of the $51 billion of financial transactions made by mobile phones in Bangladesh in 2019.[82] The city of Xi'an in Shaanxi province, a bastion of the original medieval Silk Road, has already positioned itself as a tech centre.

Such an Internet might easily be supported by poorer countries for which the Internet has proved problematic—for instance, Mauritania, Algeria, Uzbekistan, Iraq, Ethiopia, and others have been forced to turn the Internet off during school exams, because of the prevalence of cheating.[83] International companies increasingly take the BRI into account in planning; for example, Hewlett Packard has relocated its Chinese factories to the inland city of Chongqing, to take advantage of rail connections to the Netherlands and the port of Rotterdam via Kazakhstan.[84] China has a considerable financial stake in Africa, and will seek to influence the Internet there. While US firms tend to transplant their usual services into the new markets under their own names (often failing to adapt to local preferences; eBay even bought up a Chinese auction site and *deleted* its Chinese-specific interface in the name of integration, thereby muffing its chance to make a splash in what became an enormous market),[85] Chinese firms have a less overt strategy of buying stakes in promising start-ups—2017 saw $5 billion invested in Indian start-ups by Chinese tech firms.[86]

Security is an obvious area for China's expertise. For instance, Zimbabwe's government is reportedly interested in China's expertise in face recognition in general, and in particular its surveillance systems in Xinjiang (remembering that social media played a prominent role in undermining, if not ultimately removing, former president Robert Mugabe). CloudWalk Technology has proposed to build a database of faces, which would have the additional effect of giving a Chinese company a trove of valuable data about Southern African faces, and the BRI provides the mechanism for technology transfer, training, and finance.[87]

Having said that, the technology may mean that the BRI is less about projecting Chinese culture, and more about processing international data in China to enrich Chinese companies. For example, Chinese expertise and infrastructure have been used to build special economic zones across South East Asia; businesses investing can expect favourable tax, customs, and tariff treatment. China's economic heft tends to dominate in countries such as Cambodia and Laos. Not only do the businesses in these zones often import their raw materials from China, but Chinese businesses located there prefer Chinese employees who patronize Chinese-owned shops, restaurants, and hotels. The twist added by technology is that the majority of these workers will pay using apps like Alipay, so the money supposedly circulating in a different nation doesn't even leave China.[88]

CHAPTER 12

Policy Question

Is Huawei Infrastructure a Threat to Western National Security?

China's Paternal view of the Internet is clearly shared by many authoritarian states, and its more muscular approach to Internet governance and other international agreements has perhaps inevitably brought it into collision with the United States, just as the latter withdrew into an isolationist shell under President Trump. After some years of attempted American cooperation following China's accession to the World Trade Organization (WTO) in 2001, the Trump administration, which contained within it a number of China hawks, switched course, pushing back on grounds of trade rule violations and national security. China's own behaviour in its domestic political sphere, particularly in Xinjiang and Hong Kong, and its aggressive stance with respect to Taiwan, lost it friends in Washington. The Trump administration probably succeeded in shifting attitudes permanently across the political spectrum, but in its campaign against China, it has at times seemed to abandon any consistent principle of Internet governance, in favour of hitting where it might hurt most. The biggest flashpoint of many was a company called Huawei, which had developed a number of important technologies, and was a world-leading maker of equipment for what is called 5G networking.

First, the company: Huawei was founded in 1987 as a maker of telecommunications network hardware by Ren Zhengfei, a former research technologist with the People's Liberation Army (PLA) Research Unit. It gradually expanded into other aspects of networking, and is now one of the leading companies in the world providing hardware, software, and services in this area. It grew rapidly on the back of government contracts as China increased its network

Four Internets. Kieron O'Hara and Wendy Hall, Oxford University Press. © Oxford University Press 2021.
DOI: 10.1093/oso/9780197523681.003.0012

capacity, but the quality of its products enabled it to expand internationally, eventually overtaking rivals such as Ericsson, Nokia, and (in smartphone production) Samsung. It is one of the Chinese tech giants, central to the Made in China 2025 initiative. Strategically, its equipment is key to anticipated growth areas such as the IoT and smart cities (Chapter 19).[1]

'5G' stands for the fifth generation of cellular network technology standards. A cellular network divides land into regular units or *cells*, each of which is served by physical transceivers (the ubiquitous mobile phone masts) that provide wireless data communications. The network covers a geographical space, and can be used to transmit and receive data (including from the Internet) by mobile devices which can therefore roam about and still receive seamless service by connecting to different transceivers as the device is moved from cell to cell.

5G is the planned upgrade of the current 4G network, which is challenged by the growing volume of data-heavy smartphone use. It is therefore a big deal. Although not a major technical departure from 4G technology, the strategic purpose of 5G is to galvanize the IoT by supporting decentralized data processing by IoT devices (so-called *edge processing*). This would mean more data could be processed, for example, in an autonomous vehicle, which would then be able to communicate more sophisticated output to the wider network.

China has a massive interest in the rollout of 5G, after earlier failures to become a major player in mobile infrastructure. It has worked for several years, through its technology and industry ministries, academic institutions, and technical institutes, with private-sector giants including ZTE as well as Huawei, device makers such as Xiaomi, and mobile carriers such as China Mobile and China Telecom, to prepare the ground. It made itself prominent in international standard-setting for 5G, which features in Made in China 2025, and it wants to be a major player in determining how the digitally networked economy evolves. This is not necessarily an aggressive stance, but rather the desire by a growing superpower to make its own weather. The implementation challenge for a nation of China's size and stage of economic development is large; a 5G network can piggyback on existing 4G infrastructure, but a standalone 5G network will require far more fibre and antennae to facilitate low latency machine-to-machine (M2M) communication, a matter of hundreds of billions of dollars. Domestic success will no doubt support its export industry across the Belt and Road. It will also spur innovation in mobile devices—which means more lovely data![2]

Huawei is at the centre of these plans. It builds the handsets, chips that connect devices to the network, antennae, base stations, and data centres that together will implement the 5G network—pretty well the whole technology stack. It could implement a network on its own; no other company in the world can boast that level of dominance. It also makes good-quality equipment at competitive prices.

So where's the problem? 'Major Chinese Exporter Exports!' is hardly a shock headline. But some are concerned by the possibility of Chinese dominance in 5G. The data the IoT will produce promises to be the richest ever description of the interactions of individuals with and within their environment. Huawei's Mr Ren is a former PLA man, and many worry that the Communist Party and PLA still have influence on Huawei's direction. In particular, if Huawei becomes the chief provider of 5G kit internationally, will it be able to use the infrastructure to send that treasure trove of data to China? If so, then there are two worrying effects: first, the data would give a substantial boost to its AI industry; and second, it would become very well informed about its rivals and enemies.

As a matter of fact, there is no evidence that Huawei's equipment contains such back doors. Many have argued that such a claim 'is ridiculous. It only resonates with people who do not understand how software and equipment vulnerabilities play out'.[3] Funnelling of data at scale would probably be spotted, and could be addressed via encryption. More subtle threats include sabotage, or not disseminating security patches. But the United Kingdom's NCSC has run the Huawei Cyber Security Evaluation Centre (HCSEC) since 2010 'to mitigate any perceived risks arising from the involvement of Huawei in parts of the United Kingdom's critical national infrastructure', and in that time has not found any evidence of wrongdoing—although shoddy software engineering created vulnerabilities and risk of poor performance. Furthermore, as Huawei staffs the HSCEC under an oversight board, there is an issue as to how reliable its reports are.[4]

There is no evidence that Huawei is doing the bidding of the Chinese government, or that it intends to put backdoors into its 5G equipment, or that it will use the IoT to control objects or data outside China. Nevertheless, anyone building a critical 5G network should be careful. Huawei is a major player in the Beijing Paternal Internet, and will of necessity have to align its interests with those of the Chinese state. That does not mean it is always following orders from Beijing, but if such orders materialize, it has little choice but to fall into line.

Huawei was not the first Chinese company to be targeted. The Trump administration had surprised and perhaps even frightened itself by its first attack on a Chinese technology giant. In April 2018, the United States found that ZTE had not only failed to comply with an earlier punishment for sanctions-busting in North Korea and Iran, but also misled Congress about it. This asked for a stiff response, and got it: the United States revoked ZTE's export privileges, meaning that it could not use parts manufactured in the United States for its equipment. This turned out to be one of the most effective penalties ever seen in commercial law; ZTE, a giant company holding tens of thousands of patents, effectively went bust in a matter of weeks, and ceased trading. President Trump then baffled friends and enemies alike by reversing course, negotiating instead a $1 billion fine, a replacement board, and an embedded American compliance team within ZTE.[5]

The wider significance of the ZTE affair was its demonstration of the political power provided by American economic weight, and the consequent potency of sanctions as a policy tool. The administration seems not to have considered this nuclear option initially for Huawei (inconveniently, unlike ZTE, it had not been shown to have done anything wrong), but instead invoked its Export Administration Regulations, originally developed as a means of controlling the flow of weapons of mass destruction. Huawei was placed on the list of threats to US national security, which provided means to prevent it getting hold of American-made components.[6]

Sadly, the administration's grasp of US law was imperfect, and it turned out that this only prevented the transfer of the components from American soil, so proved fairly easy to work around. The long-term effect of preventing the use of US components would be that it would source components from elsewhere, boosting the economies of China and allies. To begin with, the effects of the US campaign on Huawei's bottom line were small, a dent in profits but strong growth, increased sales particularly in China and emerging markets, and even a small increase in its use of American inputs. In May 2020, the Americans retaliated with even stronger sanctions, forbidding suppliers to make Huawei's products using American-made equipment (so that a factory in Taiwan churning out Huawei silicon chips under contract could not use American tools, on pain of falling under sanctions itself).[7]

In August, the United States went even further, prohibiting anyone selling any chips to Huawei if they had been produced with American technology, without a licence from the Department of Commerce. This pretty well ruled out selling Huawei any chips at all, given the spread of US technology in the industry; a Chinese company could sell chips to Huawei, at risk of becoming the target of similar measures.[8] Huawei had already built up a stockpile of chips, so it could ride out the immediate storm; China complained about illegal restrictions on trade, and of course also has the option of taking on some of the United States' corporate presence in China in retaliation, notably Apple. The Department of Commerce's discretion to licence chip suppliers might also be leveraged by US trade negotiators. At the time of writing, Huawei's fate was uncertain; things were put on hold until the US elections of 2020, but the post-Trump American establishment appears generally more hostile to Chinese ambition than it was during the Obama years.

The United States also raised the diplomatic stakes, demanding the arrest of Huawei's chief financial officer, who happened to be the daughter of Mr Ren, in 2018 on sanctions-busting charges in Canada, which caused a flare-up between Canada and China. The United States also refused to use Huawei's kit as part of its infrastructure, and demanded that its allies followed suit; Australia and Japan did, while the United Kingdom, armed with HSCEC reports, and Germany sought compromise. The holdouts were in a tough spot, as there were anti-Huawei rebels in both Prime Minister Boris Johnson and Chancellor Angela Merkel's governing parties,[9] and the worse American sanctions got, the riskier a positive choice for Huawei would be. A problem that quickly came to light was that the United States couldn't really suggest a ready alternative to Huawei's products, which are both cheaper and superior than their competitors'. There was already a lot of Huawei equipment, for example, making up British Telecom's 4G network in the United Kingdom. But when Johnson eventually bowed to the pressure in 2020 and pledged to remove Huawei from UK mobile networks before 2027, he was still criticized from his own party for setting the deadline too far into the future.[10] In general, it seemed possible that Huawei would end up shut out of lucrative European markets, hitting its bottom line at a time in which it would need to invest in order to keep ahead of the 5G rollout curve, but that Western countries would equally be denied access to top-notch 5G hardware. Indeed, the risk may become international if the uncertainties interfere with global supply chains.[11]

Huawei does have other markets. Along with other private sector giants, it is an essential component of the BRI. The Australian government, a leading critic, got a scare when Huawei looked set to connect many Pacific islands to the Internet with undersea cabling, posing a threat to Australian security strategy, whose starting point is that it is the biggest fish in the South Pacific. In the end, the Australians themselves were driven to lay the cable, cutting Huawei out, while applying pressure to the island governments to reject offers for digital infrastructure involving Huawei. Such is the volume of activity badged 'BRI' that Western powers will need to be constantly vigilant to prevent intrusion into their bailiwicks, and will have to pay attention to places that have been diplomatically and strategically neglected in the past. Huawei is well placed to provide basic infrastructure within the Western sphere; it is central to a programme of improvements to Piraeus port near Athens in Greece, a member both of NATO and the European Union. It is a major provider of infrastructure in Africa as well, including filtering and censoring technology, and is reported to be helping governments in Uganda and Zambia to spy on political opponents. It is developing an international series of 'safe city' initiatives, aimed at providing integrated command lines to exploit data from surveillance technology.[12]

Huawei complained about American pressure and 'disinformation', but was not averse to applying a little force itself. It sent protective medical gear during the pandemic to countries which were deciding whether to allow it to bid for 5G contracts, such as Canada and the Netherlands. The Chinese Ambassadors to Germany, Poland, and the Czech Republic tried, counterproductively, to strongarm those countries; investigations later showed that

Huawei employees were giving evidence about their clients to the Chinese Embassy in Prague.[13]

Huawei is not the only Chinese company that gives the Americans sleepless nights. TikTok, developed by Chinese startup ByteDance, is a version of a Chinese app which serves up cheerful fifteen-second clips made by teenagers. It was the most downloaded app in the United States in October 2018, and by February 2019 had racked up a billion global downloads. US politicians fretted that TikTok gives the Beijing government access to data on American teenagers (although TikTok's servers are situated where it has markets, and not in China), and its clever recommendation engine might spread misinformation. India too has TikTok concerns (see Chapter 16).[14]

In 2020, President Trump signed an executive order banning TikTok unless it was sold by ByteDance to an American company, and after a short bidding war, database company Oracle stepped in.[15] The rationale for Oracle's bid caused some head-scratching (perhaps Oracle wanted a captive customer for its nascent cloud offering), but the deal was put on hold anyway as TikTok went to court. Meanwhile, the Chinese government prevented ByteDance selling some of TikTok's key technologies, including some of its AI, personalization technology, and data-analysis techniques, as being crucial for national security (read: Made in China 2025).[16] Both Chinese and American sides claimed to be in control of the new spinout company, TikTok Global (ByteDance retained the majority of the TikTok shares, but American venture capitalists own a large minority of ByteDance shares, and while the technology remained on Chinese servers, the new company had access to them). Ambiguity probably suited both sides.

An even more pungent case is that of Grindr, a dating app for gay, bi, trans, and queer people. Banned in many countries, and apparently used by law enforcement agencies to locate gay men in some countries where homosexuality is illegal, it was bought by a Chinese gaming company in 2016. No one seemed to mind, until the Huawei controversy blew up, whereupon the Committee for Foreign Investment in the United States revoked the permission to buy (three years late) on national security grounds, presumably on the basis of the app holding sensitive data about gay men's locations, HIV status, and sexual preferences. It was sold to a mysterious investment group 'wholly owned' by Americans, including James Lu, former software engineer at NASA, and marketing executive at Amazon—and former vice president of Baidu. The world may be a little too globalized to make fine distinctions these days.[17]

GEOPOLITICS, SECURITY, AND OPENNESS

Perhaps this is a tale of the unspeakable in pursuit of the uneatable. It is certainly not an edifying narrative. The DC Commercial vision focuses on success in business—this means that in different circumstances, it can veer towards the Silicon Valley Open vision, by promoting competition and openness, or towards the Beijing Paternal vision, by supporting incumbents and national champions. A commercial policy doesn't pin down the detail of who the winners and losers will be—this is why the Washington lobbying industry is worth $3.5 billion annually.[18] The Trump administration clearly focused on the Paternal, protectionist option (consistent with a long-term decline in competitiveness in a number of sectors of the US economy),[19] and so, despite the friction with China, its 5G policy turns out to be not so very different. It is, however, arguably a losing strategy, partly because China can easily mobilize resources and steer them more effectively than any democracy, and partly because Huawei has such a head start over the opposition. It also hobbles the United States' own tech industry by taking away one of its best customers, as so many of its companies are suppliers to Huawei.

The Trump administration was concerned not only about national security issues, but also with the whole concept of Chinese dominance of 5G. Attorney General William Barr was reported in 2020 as having argued that 'for the first time in history, the United States is not leading the next technological era', and that therefore 'we should mobilize to surmount China's drive to dominate 5G'. He also said that 'for China, success is a zero-sum game', and it is not apparent that he disagrees. Barr's speech floated the idea of the US government itself investing in Ericsson and Nokia. He pointed out that 'as a dictatorship, China can marshal an all-of-nation approach', and that 'if we are going to maintain our technological leadership, our economic strength, and ultimately our national security, we need the public and private sectors to work together and come shoulder to shoulder'. This looks remarkably like trying to marshal an all-of-nation approach.[20]

The United States has also taken to playing softball with some of its champions on hardware. Qualcomm, whose takeover by a Singaporean rival had already been blocked by the Trump administration in 2018, appealed against an FTC antitrust ruling in 2020, backed by the Department of Justice—that's right, the DoJ *supporting* an appellant against the FTC. Qualcomm had been accused of, and had admitted, using its dominant position in the chip industry to force handset makers to sign expensive patent licensing agreements. The appeals court questioned the FTC aggressively, with one judge asking, even if patent licensing 'helped Qualcomm make lots of money for a few years, is that in and of itself an antitrust violation, even if consumers paid higher prices for cell phones?' Another asked, 'Doesn't the Supreme Court say that patent holders have the right to price their patents? What would be anticompetitive about that?' The third claimed he was being asked to draw a line between anticompetitive behaviour (illegal) and hypercompetitive behaviour (legal). The DoJ's justification for supporting Qualcomm was that forcing it to renegotiate its licensing agreements would give it fewer monopoly profits, hindering its innovation programmes.[21]

All this began to congeal into a strategy. In August 2020, Secretary of State Mike Pompeo (possibly with half an eye on a run for the Presidency in 2024) announced a drive to create a 'clean' Internet—the Clean Network program to develop China-free secure 5G data networks, based on clean carriers, clean stores (no Chinese apps on US mobile app stores), clean apps (no US apps on Chinese mobile app stores—US companies 'should remove their apps from Huawei's app store to ensure they are not partnering with a human rights abuser'), a clean cloud without involvement of Alibaba, Baidu, and Tencent, and clean cable (unclear what this means except that US undersea cabling would not be 'subverted for intelligence gathering by the PRC [China] at hyper scale'). No doubt the aim was to prevent Chinese interference in US affairs, as opposed to preventing Americans getting access to alternative sources of information, but, that not insignificant detail aside, the outcome of such a programme would be the 'wall' that President Trump promised to build during his 2016 campaign—only a giant virtual firewall, rather than bricks and mortar.[22]

The technology industry thrives on competition within recognized standards. The danger is that Huawei will create 5G networking capacity without American involvement, which will not be allowed into the United States. There will be no obvious incentives for companies across the divide to agree on standards (a gruelling process that needs goodwill), and so we may easily end up with a fragmented 5G system, affecting smartphones, the IoT, telemedicine, and so on. This technological Iron Curtain will quickly infect all kinds of communications. It will also ramify, as other nations are forced to pick sides—China is actively exporting its technological vision via the BRI and so has a ready vector for disseminating its standard, whereas the United States, already behind in the 'race', has no such strategy in place. And recall China's use of the ITU to promote DOA in IoT protocols; the division of the IoT into a 'Splinternet of Things' would remove much of the opposition to that move.

Arguably a better way to pare back Huawei's lead in this field is to outinnovate it, and surely the way to do that is to promote competition rather than confirm existing oligopolies. If (say) Qualcomm or Nokia realize that they only have to achieve a certain acceptable standard in 5G kit to make sales in America, then why should they commit to the R&D to improve products and close the gap with Huawei if they know that it will be kept out of their most lucrative market? It will clearly be better for them to rest on lower-quality products with a guaranteed market while raking in the money. Away from the major players, interesting innovations can still be found which may shake up the field, such as Rakuten's and NEC's virtual cloud-based 5G plans.[23]

Any strategy for dealing with big Chinese companies needs to bear that fact in mind, and plan accordingly. But fragmenting the 5G space, hobbling the United States' own technology industry, and settling for second best in terms of standards is a very curious way to defend America's interests. However the battle against Huawei ends, or whether it peters out, the trend is clear. The more China feels directly under American attack, the greater the extent of self-sufficiency it will pursue, developing the 'dual circulation' strategy at the heart of its 2021–25 Five Year Plan. And American suspicion of Chinese technological ambitions is no longer restricted to China hawks at the top of the Republican Party. The danger of fragmented standards for portions of the Internet will probably not dissipate for some time.

CHAPTER 13

The Moscow Spoiler Model

A coda: the Internet requires design, standards, and cooperative behaviour. This implies one final response to the Internet, beyond the four positive visions of openness, bourgeois sensibilities, commerce, and paternalism which we have outlined in the preceding chapters. This negative response does not create anything, but rather attacks whatever is already in place. The response, which we tend to find as a human response to any elaborate system, is *subversion*. Plain vandalism is a comment on the complexity and elegance of the Internet, but subversion has an aesthetic of its own that is pleased to undermine the basic functions or promises of a system using those basic functions themselves to demonstrate its inconsistencies. The subversive aesthetic also drives a global position on the Internet, originally a dispersed and ad hoc response that manifested itself as cybercrime and hacking, but which in more recent years has attracted institutional backers at the level of the nation-state.

THE IDEAL

A hacking ethic has long been detectable in scientific and technological practice, celebrating the expertise of gifted programmers able to create innovative code with unexpected output using elegant means. It contrasts with the traditional work ethic, replacing its ideals of duty and service with joy, creativity and competitiveness. It subverts the values of capitalism, with the division of labour and the work ethic superseded by passion, freedom, and autonomy.[1]

The combination of joy, creativity, and competitiveness naturally leads to practical jokes: 'the hacker makes trouble for everyone, but this modern-day trickster has a powerful purpose: the realization of a mythic utopia locked up by our stagnating tendencies to freeze revolutionary technologies in the ice of

Four Internets. Kieron O'Hara and Wendy Hall, Oxford University Press. © Oxford University Press 2021.
DOI: 10.1093/oso/9780197523681.003.0013

outdated social patterns'.[2] This hacking philosophy took a subversive turn with the discovery of the ability to challenge projected norms of good behaviour by well-executed pieces of code that had deliberately bad effects (i.e. malware), or alternatively by dodging supposedly impenetrable security measures. The hacker's challenge was to outwit cybersecurity and leave a calling card, often an irritating or malicious one. It did not take long for this subversion to develop an ideology of its own, *hacktivism*, a method for challenging power in asymmetric contexts.

Political parties devoted to the principles of sharing knowledge for free sprang up, starting in 2006, becoming known as Pirate Parties, some of which gained Parliamentary representation at the national or EU level;[3] WikiLeaks also shares some of this piratical viewpoint.[4] Piracy has been seen by some as a means for reducing digital divides. Anthropologist Payal Arora, who highlights the importance of entertainment in the spread of the Internet, excoriates the Western media industry for 'privileging the interests of the haves', 'corporate profiteering', 'hypocritical moralizing' about piracy, 'classic colonial divide-and-rule practices', and operating 'a double standard', while piracy by contrast is 'rightful defiance', 'legitimizing the ingenuity of the poor in creating a marketplace for digital leisure through pirated goods'. She argues that 'it is time for the global media conglomerates to reform their business models to make their media available to people with scarce resources, instead of continuing to tighten the noose in enforcing regulations that make a majority of the world's people unable to access their products by legal means'.[5] Piratical ideology spawned what Harry Halpin, a radical Web scientist, called 'a new social force': Anonymous.[6]

Anonymous is a decentralized movement with no official leader or membership, which has disrupted the operations of organizations with greater material and financial resource. It began as a 4Chan group which attacked the Church of Scientology in 2008, following up with distributed denial of service (DDoS) attacks on various financial organizations in support of WikiLeaks, before apparently losing its mojo in the face of the even more subversive figure of President Trump.[7] In its pomp, it attracted breathless praise from armchair revolutionaries. It has been called a 'meme-complex',[8] while others preferred 'extraordinary bandits (e-bandits) that engage in the politics of no one via anonymizing Internet technologies . . . akin to Robin Hood'.[9] This e-Robin Hood was deliberately pitched as a collective; individuality was suppressed, and when Anonymous sympathizers occasionally gathered physically, they wore identical masks depicting Guy Fawkes (who for the record was a reactionary undemocratic would-be assassin) from *V for Vendetta*, a graphic novel and film. Their slogan was 'Knowledge is free. We are anonymous. We are legion. We do not forgive. Expect us', combining Silicon Valley ideals with a gothic comic-book focus on mischief, to demonstrate that the emperor has no clothes, security is a myth, and all the pretensions of the Internet are smoke and mirrors.[10]

Halpin conjectured whether Anonymous was 'the vanguard defending the Internet, the Internet not only *in-itself* but *for itself*', or 'the incarnation of the long-awaited altruistic invisible army of hackers needed by various social movements, as promised by science-fiction writers for the last decade', before settling on 'Anonymous is the *Stimmung*, the voice, of the Internet; not only a set of individual voices, but a collection of bodies that becomes organized and articulates a common voice . . . via massively scalable Web-collective organization, so commencing the long-awaited political-ontological transformation of our current social totality, long thought impossible'.[11] The direction of travel was the Internet becoming an agent in its own right, a collective subconscious that would assert its rights to freedom, justice, and opposition to oppression.

The problem with the subconscious, as Freud discovered, is that it is not always awfully well behaved. Be careful what you wish for.

The hacking ethic was amplified by a general erosion in academic support for epistemological authority. Ideas of scientific method, formal connections between theory and data, and the rational evaluation of theory against evidence all came under pressure from the 1960s on. The replacement view considers the production of knowledge as exclusively a social phenomenon, bolstered by power and inheriting all the complexities of social relationships (including fault lines over gender, ethnicity, and class). Science is correct only because influential people say it is correct. Some philosophers, Paul Feyerabend in particular, denounced scientific method and proclaimed epistemological anarchy. Both postmodernism and the strong programme in science and technology studies rejected truth or falsity as a relevant factor in a proposition's being believed, and preferred instead to look for social causes of credibility.[12]

When the idea of knowledge as dependent on social forces, rather than reason, met the hacking ethic that power could be manufactured and enjoyed, the Internet's subconscious grew wings, and concocted ideological discourses which lacked the history and enduring grassroots support that enables more venerable ideologies to balance intellectual content, imagination, and emotion. Claims such as climate change denial and anti-vaccination pseudo-science, causes that few of the original radical epistemologists would have espoused, flourished in the epistemological vacuum they had created. The newer discourse, as political philosopher Michael Freeden argued, is founded on 'immediacy of production and response', 'the very opposite of the deliberately measured style of public pronouncements that liberal-democracies are expected to cultivate, even if they do not'. The urgency that Twitter seems to demand has resulted in debate whose effects are stochastic in nature, which is 'redrawing . . . the map of what is ideologically permissible'.[13]

To repeat: be careful what you wish for.

Russia under President Vladimir Putin has reasserted the imperial Eurasian geography of the past to engineer an ideological space a long way from the pseudoscientific sub-Marxian certainty of the old Soviet Union.[14] This ideology is opposed to the West, based on a mystical *mélange* of nationalism and destiny, *ressentiment* and victimhood, power and calculation, cynicism and conspiracy theories, a defensive version of the belief in the unique spiritual capacity of the Russian people that can be found in Pushkin, Dostoyevsky, and beyond.[15] This exceptionalist picture can be traced through a number of Russian thinkers in the twentieth century, notably Ivan Ilyin (1883–1954), an exile from communism who saw Russia as a unity rather than a decadent collection of individuals ('evil begins where the person begins'),[16] facts as tawdry reflections of God's flawed and corrupt creation, and progress as illusory. Rather, 'true' seeing requires an act of faith, to see innocence, purity, righteousness, and perfection in Russia where it is invisible. Truth, on this vision, is not bolstered by evidence but rather undermined by it. Life in the Soviet Union, where many people were used to professing a faith in communism they had long since lost, familiarized many to a society of simulacra and simulations.[17]

Putin, it is not irrelevant to note, is a contemporary champion of Ilyin, even organizing his reburial in Russia in 2005. He evokes a special Russian ability to thrive in the midst of chaos, which suggests two important imperatives: (i) repress the rule of law at home, in order to allow the Russian genius to express itself, and (ii) undermine international rule-based norms to create a world where Russia can outperform its enemies in the West.[18] Rules and norms, on this account, are means of oppressing Russia; it feels no duty to objectivity or good faith. One of Putin's closest ideologues early in his presidency, Vladislav Surkov, was reported as advertising himself as 'the author of the new Russian system', characterized as 'a system of make-believe'.[19] Nationalist groups sympathetic to Russian exceptionalism are willing to play their part, such as the Night Wolves biker gang.[20] For those on this philosophical mission, the decentralized Internet, without institutionalized editing and fact-checking, has been an ally and an opportunity. For this reason, we call the use of technological prowess to undermine truth at scale the *Moscow Spoiler model*, naming it after its most adept practitioners. The polarization of politics in the West, particularly in the United States, provided an opening to infiltrate uncertainty and obfuscation by cheaply importing narratives, arguments, and conspiracies, using the power of bots. Much of this has been revealed by Robert Mueller's inquiry into Russian interference in the 2016 US presidential election.[21]

The Russians have certainly exercised the black arts, standard in democracies and dictatorships alike, of surveillance and also cyberwar, accompanying its invasion of Georgia in 2008, for example, and preceding its invasion of

Ukraine in 2014.[22] One important early run-out was the massive cyberattack on Estonia in 2007, following the removal of a Soviet-era statue from a prominent position in Tallinn, which prompted clashes between Estonian nationalists and ethnic Russians. The day after a fatal riot, a network of bots launched a massive DDoS attack on Estonian government facilities; this particularly mattered, as Estonia has always prided itself as a pioneer in e-government and the digitization of administration (one can apply to become an e-resident of the country). Responsibility for the attack was almost as distributed as the botnet, across various Russian nationalist 'hacker patriot' groups, especially youth group Nashi,[23] but the Russian government denies its own complicity. Such information campaigns soften up the enemy, and alter its perceptions and threat models, which then may open up new offensive vectors, but the attack did not deter the Estonians from their aim of becoming the world leader in e-government and digitally enabled institutions.[24] The 'facts of the matter' continued to be disputed, in arenas like Wikipedia (where the Estonian language article is short, about 1,800 words, emphasizing the riots and the common practice of removing Soviet-era statues; the English article is the same length, but with 70,000 words of discussion; while the Russian article is a much larger 7,500 words, emphasizing the statue's history and purpose, and quoting international condemnation of Estonia).[25]

The differences between Russian and other nations' approaches to cyberattacks have been summed up succinctly.

> The Kremlin's tactics were opposite of China's, where the regime directly oversees cyber attacks and it is possible to identify the chain of command. In Russia, all kinds of informal actors—from patriotic hackers, to Kremlin-funded youth movement activists, to employees of cybersecurity companies forced into cooperation by government officials—have been involved in operations targeting the Kremlin's enemies both within the country and in former Soviet states.
>
> This heterogeneous group had developed an impressively efficient set of tactics. In general there were three common features. The first was the use of rank-and-file hacktivists not directly connected to the state in order to help the Kremlin maintain plausible deniability. The second was guidance and protection from criminal prosecution, provided by the president's administration alongside the secret services. Finally, hacked information was published as *kompromat* (i.e. compromising materials) online as a way of smearing an opponent.[26]

Cyber espionage is not the focus of this book. All nations indulge in it, and although Russian distributed-cyberwar techniques are and always have been advanced, they are not the chief characteristic of the Moscow Spoiler model. But cyber espionage is given an interesting twist by the Moscow Spoiler. The Americans see espionage as an arm of military action and intelligence gathering (for example, with the deployment of the Stuxnet virus in Iran, and the surveillance revealed by Snowden). China has a more holistic, continuous view of the state and business, and so it blurs the distinction between state and industrial espionage. Russia *attacks the concept of truth itself*, using the Internet to disseminate falsehood, partisanship, misdirection, and conspiracies, and as a result *changing the Internet's very nature*.[27]

The tactic has been called *implausible deniability*,[28] which has no better illustration than the TV channel Russia Today's (RT) interview of two Russians suspected of carrying out the poisoning in the United Kingdom of a former Russian officer (a British agent) and his daughter. They claimed not to be Russian agents, but sports nutritionists who wanted to see Salisbury Cathedral, whose Wikipedia article they seemed to have memorized. So absurd was this story that not even they pretended to believe it, but it muddied the water sufficiently that the United Kingdom's opposition Labour Party demanded further proof of Russian involvement in the poisonings from the British government.[29]

Shortly before the Russian invasion of Ukraine (itself denied in the teeth of the evidence), intelligence sources spread false stories using fictitious personae about Ukrainian fascists committing atrocities. The cyber operation that accompanied the invasion cited spurious justifications for the war, while simultaneously denying it was happening, and rejecting the notion that there were Russian troops in Ukraine even as Crimea was annexed. As historian Timothy Snyder put it, 'no war was taking place, and it was thoroughly justified'. No one really tried to make anyone believe the idiotic story that there were no Russians in Ukraine, even as soldiers, unable to speak Ukrainian, were marching around in Russian uniforms minus their insignia. Rather, the aim was to undo the concept and the processes of factuality. This became substantially more serious when those apparently non-existent Russian troops almost certainly shot down Malaysia Airlines flight MH17, with the loss of 298 souls. The Russian 'explanations' of that disaster included contradictory claims that Ukrainian troops shot it down, that it was not a civilian aircraft but a Ukrainian air force plane, that it was a failed attempt to assassinate Vladimir Putin, that it was a setup as the people on the aeroplane were already dead. More serious evidence presented by the official Joint Investigation Team (JIT) was dismissed as fake; the JIT dismissed Russian counter-evidence as fake. In the middle of a social media storm, the relative reliability of the two organizations is lost, and all that is heard is mindless retaliation. The defences are implausible, but in the scrum the sense of a factual base goes missing.[30]

The fictitious personae apparently in Ukraine were actually dreamed up by an organization called the Internet Research Agency (IRA). The IRA, based in St Petersburg, uses nationalist rhetoric to smear opposition politicians as traitors or CIA agents. It can interfere by order, to spread confusion in the reporting of a specific event such as the downing of MH17, or the assassination of former deputy prime minister Boris Nemtsov in 2015.[31] Its activities abroad are designed to foster division; as a report for the European Council on Foreign Relations argued, 'Russia supports anti-establishment forces in Europe because it lacks friends among establishments', adding primly, 'Its use of unconventional methods is not a demonstration of creative strategy but an attempt to compensate for deficiencies.'[32]

It appears that there was Russian interference in the 2014 Scottish Independence Referendum (on the disruptive side of independence), and then, when the referendum was lost, further output questioning the result.[33] In 2016, 419 Twitter accounts located close to the IRA contributed to the debate in the United Kingdom's Brexit referendum; all of them later that year moved on to the US presidential election. In both of those cases, the more disruptive option won. Around a third of Brexit debate on Twitter was generated by automatic bots, of which less than 10 percent came from the United Kingdom itself.[34] The Mueller investigation found thousands of fake accounts and groups in the United States, creating fictitious persons ranging from gun-toting white supremacists supporting candidate Donald Trump, to black civil rights activists criticizing his Democratic opponent Hillary Clinton.

Many interventions appear strategically inexplicable, except as a means of sowing division and mistrust; journalist-turned-academic Gregory Asmolov has argued that one of the major purposes of disinformation is to sabotage horizontal connections and make it harder to sustain a network.[35] Health data researchers report that Russian bots and trolls regularly tweet about vaccination in divisive terms, linking the issues to controversies in American politics. The tweets are both pro- and anti-vaccination, but the purpose appears to be less to establish a position as to associate vaccination with the several other wedge issues in America's dysfunctional politics.[36] Freeden points out that whereas totalitarian lies are intended to protect the regime and are therefore predictable, these interventions point randomly in all directions, distorting public discourse to a greater extent.[37]

Conspiracy theories and misinformation about COVID-19 flourished online, and both the United States and the European Union accused Russia of being behind much of it.[38] Russian accounts run from Africa, discovered by Facebook in March 2020, included misinformation about COVID-19, bundled up with other controversial 'hot button' topics, including civil rights, police brutality, and sexual politics.[39] A report compiled for the European Union looked at eighty examples of disinformation in early 2020 which claimed that the virus was, variously, a Chinese, American, or British biological weapon, was brought by migrants, or was a hoax, and concluded, 'Pro-Kremlin media outlets have been prominent in spreading disinformation about the coronavirus, with the aim to aggravate the public health crisis in western countries, specifically by undermining public trust in national healthcare systems.'[40] The report argued that the Russians were not creating these stories, but rather were amplifying existing conspiracy theories.

Of course, polluting the debate and trolling elections are not a magic wand. There is no reason to think that these tactics actually swung any results or changed opinions (rather than entrenching existing views). In elections especially, all sides have used political advertising and so the combined efforts of, say, the Russians, Mr Trump, and Mrs Clinton (who spent heavily on Facebook) during 2016 may have cancelled each other out, and even if not, it would be very hard to prove that the Russians made the decisive difference.[41] It is in the interests of the online adtech industry to boost its own importance by exaggerating its potency.[42]

The unlikelihood of altering election results is less to the point than the general undermining of discourse, and especially the negative effects of abuse, hectoring, and bullying. Finnish journalist Jessikka Aro, for example, was trolled after exposing the work of the IRA; some of the pressure was old-fashioned thuggery, such as a phone call which included a gunshot, but much of the rest was misinformation or exaggeration. A narrative of her working for Western security forces and persecuting those of Russian origin was central. A (genuine) drug conviction was turned into an accusation of Western government-sponsored drug-dealing. Her mental health was impugned. As a final insult, she was informed she would receive one of the 2019 International Women of Courage Awards, but when it came to light she had been a vocal critic of President Trump, the award was rescinded.[43]

The Moscow Spoiler works on three separate levels. First of all, people may actually believe some of the stories they read. One can easily imagine those of Russian origin feeling targeted by a constant stream of anti-Russian stories (of which the present narrative is an example), and preferring alternative accounts, while in the partisan atmosphere of the United States, both sides may be abnormally disposed to believe divisive narratives. Secondly, there may be a chilling effect by which people will be nervous of speaking out if they feel they will be trolled.

The main effect, though, is that when trolling is commonplace, and implausible denials are treated apparently seriously, a narrative emerges that *everybody* trolls, that *all* news is fake, *everything* is opinion, and there is no truth to be found anywhere. Misinformation spread in non-journalistic outlets, such as YouTube, Russian SNS VKontakte, and Facebook, might be followed up by Russian state media companies, until the story becomes large enough to be covered widely. What appears to be in-depth analysis may be published in a blog with references to disinformation sites. Unmasking falsehoods or absurd conspiracy theories is not enough, because the aim is to delegitimate any epistemological authority, to show rationality to be a sham. So although denouncing nonsense is what all people committed to the truth

THE MOSCOW SPOILER MODEL [161]

should do, it is hard rhetorically to prevent debate descending into a tit-for-tat squabble. That is to play the misinformers' game.

> Getting caught is half the point, making it easier for the Kremlin to argue that all protests everywhere are just covert foreign influence operations. . . . This re-inforces the larger narrative the Russian (and Iranian and Chinese) media are trying to reinforce: that colour revolutions and the Arab Spring are not genuine but rather American-engineered 'regime changes'. Indeed, that there is actually no such thing as truly bottom-up, people-powered protest, a message that is only reinforced when the American government gets caught trying to use social media to covertly stir up anti-government sentiment abroad, as it has in Cuba.[44]

It took the Russians a while to develop this model. During the abortive Soviet coup of 1991, attempts to stifle the flow of information about and to Gorbachev were stymied by Russian pioneers of networked communications, out of commitment to the free flow of information, not for any political grand plan.[45] The early years of Putin's presidency were focused on attempts to exercise control over broadcast television, and for some years he missed the growing importance of digital information sources. As elsewhere, the shift from mass media to online (which was driven by Putin's own policies, as the public lost confidence in television) undermined the resources that supported quality journalism, and promoted opinion over objective investigation.[46] Eventually, the Russians learned that the Internet was a disruptor, and asked the Chinese for technical support.[47]

Censorship could be achieved by a combination of mislabelled rules and some cooperation from the Internet companies. As in several other countries, filtering techniques were announced as essential to protect children and to remove child pornography; terrorism was another pretext. An early, highly impractical, plan in 2012 to block websites at the level of IP address was abandoned when the IT industry agreed to cooperate in the use of DPI to compile more fine-grained blacklists.[48] Surveillance was outsourced; media regulator Roskomnadzor would generate the blacklist, but it was the responsibility of ISPs to implement it.[49] Even the big US social media have been forced to block individuals' accounts.[50] Loyal citizens volunteer to flag content themselves, via the ubiquitous youth organizations or the Cyberguards of the Safe Internet League.[51] A law of 2014 required bloggers with large audiences to register with the government, forfeit anonymity, retain records of posts, and otherwise provide the bureaucracy with the tools to hold them to account.[52]

The Russian establishment has always struggled to understand and leverage openness (its attempt to nurture its own Silicon Valley in Skolkovo has been mired in corruption charges without making much of a splash in the tech world).[53] It has had trouble accepting the democratic nature of crowdsourcing from the Internet and Web, and appreciating that algorithms to select content are genuinely based on aggregating input from users at scale.[54] For instance, it was caught on the hop when its denial of the invasion of Ukraine was contradicted by Russian soldiers posting about their exploits on VKontakte.[55] At the time of the invasion of Georgia, the government was unhappy with the news coverage it got on the main Russian search engine Yandex, unable to accept that the selection was made by machine, not organized by a human.[56] Russian suspicion was stoked by American valorization of the Internet and its threat to dictatorships, particularly during the Arab Spring (as exemplified by George W. Bush's advisor Mark Pfeifle nominating Twitter for the Nobel Peace Prize following the failed Iranian revolution).[57] Putin called the Internet a 'CIA project' as recently as 2014.[58]

Eventually, the potential to use the weight of the Internet against itself, as a means to induce enemies to undermine their own strengths with their own weaknesses, dawned. The key is to spot where the Internet itself supplies a weakness, where it subtly changes the rules of engagement.[59]

The idea of disinformation—both spreading it abroad and defending against it at home—was embedded in the Russian regulatory system from the electronic intelligence apparatus that descended from the old KGB. The Maidan protests in Ukraine in 2014 were countered by effective measures; at one point a threatening text message was sent via the three Kievan mobile operators to everyone present in Independence Square, the focus of the protests.[60] The cyberattack on Ukraine that preceded the invasions of the Donbas and Crimea showed that the Russians had moved on from their Estonian and Georgian methods; rather than DDoS and other recognizable attacks, the onslaught came via VKontakte (with 20 million users in Ukraine) and other social media, including the big American networks, and in the comments sections of major international news sites.[61] The Kremlin has mastered the art of sending different messages to different audiences (internationally it has used RT to woo far-right figures with anti-EU messages, left-wingers with anti-American, anti-war, and anti-imperialism messages, and religious fundamentalists with homophobia).[62]

VKontakte (now VK), and Yandex, as the largest social network and search engine, respectively, in the Russian-speaking world, together with news channel RT (the sixth largest YouTube news channel, with about 4 million followers), are central to Russian strategy.[63] VK's founder Pavel Durov was fired by the company, and claimed he was forced out by pro-Kremlin oligarchs.[64] Yandex also came under heavy pressure; in 2017 it had to deliver Ukrainian customers' data to Russia, and in 2019 it was ordered to hand over its encryption keys to the Russian FSB spy agency, although in the latter case it resisted.[65] Having said this, we should note that Russia tends not to act repressively to online criticism in the way that the Chinese or Turkish governments often do. Bloggers and media outlets may be intimidated into self-censorship, but few end up in prison.[66]

Not all *kompromat* is disinformation. The Russian establishment has a liking for WikiLeaks (Assange had a talk show on RT), whose mission to publish information while protecting its anonymous sources makes it a perfect conduit for *kompromat*.[67] The ideal information is something that is true but embarrassing for its creator or subject. One of WikiLeaks' greatest triumphs is the publication of material hacked from the Democratic National Committee's (DNC) servers, as well as the emails of Hillary Clinton's campaign chairman John Podesta, during the 2016 presidential election. The material was hacked by two groups, known as Cozy Bear and Fancy Bear, widely believed to be associated with Russian intelligence services. The information published wasn't false, but it embarrassed Clinton.[68]

WikiLeaks came to Russia's aid during a scandal concerning the Panama Papers, 11.5 million confidential financial and legal documents relating to thousands of offshore entities, ranging from the absolutely upright to the downright shady. These were leaked (not by WikiLeaks) to a consortium of professional investigative journalists, who uncovered information relating to a number of public figures, including Sergei Roldugin, a professional cellist and businessman who happened to be a long-standing friend of President Putin. It turned out that he had a number of multi-million-dollar accounts that surely exceeded his resources, and he was named by Russian journalists as the likely curator of some of Putin's own wealth. WikiLeaks—which appeared to have little skin in the game—suddenly launched into the journalism that led to the discovery, and claimed (baselessly) that it was funded by George Soros (a favourite Jewish target of conspiracy theorists) and USAID—blithely ignoring its own oft-repeated and self-justificatory claim that the motives for the release of information should be irrelevant. Putin himself, in perfect coordination, referenced WikiLeaks' attack when dismissing the furore as an American conspiracy.[69]

The relationship between the Russian government and WikiLeaks is surprisingly cosy. Whether or not there is a direct connection, it is arguable that WikiLeaks, via the hacking ethic outlined at the beginning of this chapter, is less a part of the Silicon Valley Open Internet, than a missing link between it and the Moscow Spoiler model.

FURTHER EXAMPLES

The Moscow Spoiler is not just a Russian tactic.[70] No doubt all nations with the technical capacity indulge in what was called disinformation, deliberately propagating falsehood (the term 'disinformation' was originally a Soviet one coined during the Stalin era, but many previous cultures in earlier eras have also worried about propaganda and truth—Orwell called the 1940s the 'Age of Lies').[71] It is a particularly potent weapon against the West, where speech is freer, ideas spread easily, and controlling the public sphere is frowned upon. A 2017 report from the Oxford Internet Institute argued that 'computational propaganda is now one of the most powerful tools against democracy', and found evidence that, for instance, 45 percent of Twitter activity in Russia was automated for the creation of disinformation, and that political debate in Germany, the United States, Poland, Brazil, Ukraine, and Taiwan was compromised.[72] Culprits there were several. In August 2018, Facebook and Twitter shut down hundreds of accounts accused of spreading disinformation, not only from Russia, but also from Iran.[73] A report by the Institute for the Future (IFTF) produced case studies from Azerbaijan, Bahrain, Ecuador, the Philippines, Turkey, the United States, and Venezuela.[74]

Another report outlined misinformation networks, 'industrial in [their] scope and organization', used in politics in the Philippines, which helped popu-list President Duterte to power in 2016, but routinely used by other parties as well. The structures uncovered had more or less the same hierarchy: well-heeled executives at advertisers and PR firms, together with social media in-fluencers working for fees, organizing the activities of poorly paid operators of fake social media accounts, each taking on dozens of personae to make friends and praise or criticize politicians to order.[75]

Where the state gets involved, the IFTF report found four types of inter-action where, as Arora puts it, 'countercultural spaces . . . become instru-ments of the state'.[76] State-funded groups, whether amateur or professional, might follow direct orders, sometimes for financial advantage, but also for political favours. President Duterte put many of his cyber-volunteers on the government payroll after election, while China's Fifty Cent Army gets paid small sums of money to promote positive news which drowns out controver-sies.[77] Vietnam's Force 47's 'reinformation' campaigns are supported by the Ministry of Public Security. Government-sponsored youth groups, such as Nashi in Russia, are one means for recruiting, while businesses wishing to ingratiate themselves with government might chip in funding too. A second strategy was for the government to coordinate but not execute cyberattacks (e.g. Venezuela, and Ecuador under the government of Rafael Correa). Thirdly, some cyber campaigns are incited but not executed by the state; examples can be found in Turkey, and in the United States via alt-right sites such as Breitbart, following signals from the Trump White House about certain jour-nalists or politicians. Fourthly, the state may simply welcome trolling cam-paigns, and use them as 'evidence' of public opinion, legitimizing state policies or positions; this kind of strategy has been used in China, by President Modi's Bharatiya Janata Party in India (which is supported by a volunteer army of trolls), and by President Bolsonaro's government in Brazil, for example.[78] It should also be said that anti-government protestors and campaigners against corruption have also been found to use networks of bots to spread their messages.[79]

Sex is an important vector for misinformation or *kompromat*. Women are often the target of sexist abuse, and politicians of both sexes have been humiliated by the release of sexual images of them, ranging from a series of senior (male) members of the Turkish opposition who quit en masse after secretly taken sex tapes of them in action were broadcast on a website,[80] to a (female) Democrat member of the US Congress who was forced to resign after (undenied) allegations of inappropriate behaviour with a staffer were published by a right-wing website, accompanied by a nude image of her circulated without her consent, allegedly by her estranged husband.[81]

These cases are at least genuine, even if their publication is brutal, distasteful, and dismaying for those of us who prefer democracies to be governed by reason. But many slurs are lies, backed up by deepfake technology.[82] Women candidates in the 2018 Iraqi election endured misogynist abuse from 'electronic armies',[83] including the circulation of sex tapes which their subjects claimed were fake. An Indian journalist who orchestrated a sting to reveal a cover-up about massacres of Muslims in Gujarat when Narendra Modi was the state's chief minister had her face grafted onto the body of a woman in a porn video.[84] An environmental activist and reformer was disqualified from her seat in the Iranian Parliament when a photo she claimed was fake showed her without her *hijab* in public.[85] Conversely, the wife of the information minister of Myanmar published a picture of then-opposition leader Aung San Suu Kyi doctored to show her wearing a *hijab*, in a nation where anti-Muslim prejudice is widespread.[86]

Of greatest moment at this particular point in history is the adoption of this philosophy by the 45th president of the United States, who demolished the protective wall of propriety carefully erected by the founding fathers around public office in that country, undermining legitimacy wherever it could be found. A key part of his campaign in 2015–2016, for example, was echoing doubt over the birthplace of President Obama (had Obama not been born in the United States, then he would not have been eligible to be president, a devastating blow but for the inconvenient circumstance of his birth in Hawaii). Trump certainly benefited from the WikiLeaks publication of the DNC material, and his advisor Roger Stone, later convicted of a number of criminal offences, had links with Julian Assange and appeared to many to have prior knowledge of the *kompromat* leaks.[87]

That murky case is unproven and hardly a smoking gun. More to the point was Trump's masterly use of Twitter to dominate the agenda, at least until the final days of his presidency, fostering the impression of a rough-hewn but successful businessman with the common touch and the right instincts (Silvio Berlusconi was a pioneer of this genre). If he oversteps the line, well, hey, give the guy a break, y'know? He doesn't pretend to be a saint, and—this is straight out of the Russian playbook—you can trust him because at least he is honest about not being honest. All the other guys pretend to be honest, and are therefore entirely untrustworthy. This inversion has always been a populist tactic but it is facilitated by the radically decentralized Internet. Snyder argues that 'Trump was the payload of a cyberweapon, meant to create chaos and weakness, as in fact he has done'.[88] This goes too far; the Russians clearly welcome the havoc Trump has wrought with his disdain for democratic process, but it has been an increasingly prominent feature of Republican Party politics at least since Pat Robertson,[89] and, although the Russians may have intervened on Trump's side (when Trump declared his candidacy for 2016, the IRA opened an American department),[90] he is clearly not a Russian *creation*. Russia also stands accused of intervening on the side of socialist Bernie Sanders in the 2020 Democratic primary.[91]

The difference between the Cold War with the Soviet Union and the information war with Russia is that in the battle for domestic public opinion, technology and marketing were on the side of the United States in the former, and Russia in the latter. During the Cold War, the desirability of Coke, Levis, movies, rock 'n' roll, and other American products was underlined by the obviously more comfortable and attractive life in the United States and other democracies. In 2020, technology is being used, not least by Americans, to dissect American society, exposing the supposed rottenness at its core, and highlighting conflict, and many, not least the 45th president, seem happy to play along. The Internet also presents a broad attack surface, including social media, and algorithm-based information outlets. News Feed and Trending Topics on Facebook became manipulable agents, as all that was needed were the numbers to alter rankings, which could be provided by automation. Raw material might be generated by legitimate, if partisan, news outlets such as Fox News and Breitbart, but it could be amplified by an army of bots. Just before the 2016 election, Facebook had to close down 5.8 *million* fake accounts, while about 20 percent of the political conversation on Twitter was being produced by bots.[92] SNSs took the not unreasonable position that, in a culture like America's with very strong protection of free speech (especially political speech), it would be a minefield to try to decide between true and false. Twitter decided in 2019 to ban political advertising altogether,[93] and Facebook promised to follow suit after the polls closed in the 2020 election,[94] which put the campaigning industry into a flat spin.[95] One imagines that whatever rules they employ to define 'political' will ultimately be gamed by legitimate and illegitimate operators alike.[96]

Each tried to label content as misleading, especially in the chaotic aftermath of that election, when many of the president's own tweets claiming victory or fraud were labelled as misinformative. Ultimately, the president's Twitter account was permanently cancelled, when he was accused of provoking a lethal riot in the Capitol building in the final days of his administration, the event that led to a second attempt to impeach him. But by then he was already a diminished figure, his electoral defeat having been finally confirmed by Congress, and so cancelling him had become a politically easier route. Facebook did the same, with cover provided by its Oversight Board, which took the decision to review.

COUNTERING THE SPOILER

Lying is not illegal except in specially defined circumstances, nor should it be. Most liberal thinking defends freedom of expression, however cretinous. When it comes to outright lies, liberal thinking has usually fallen back on the idea of a marketplace of ideas, where—in an inverse of Gresham's Law—good thinking is supposed to drive out bad. Yet does this optimistic view stand up in the face of mechanized, weaponized social media? After all, many of the views expressed by troll farms such as the IRA are not lies at all, merely opinions that are actually held by substantial numbers of people—the idea that Hillary Clinton's commitment to civil rights was too weak was argued by many perfectly genuine activists.[97]

First, define your problem. The European Union's High Level Expert Group (HLEG) on Fake News and Online Disinformation, set up in 2018, reported on best practice to combat disinformation, basing it on five pillars: transparency about how online news is circulated; promoting media literacy; tools for empowering users and journalists; safeguarding the diversity and sustainability of the European media ecosystem; and continued research to evaluate and revise anti-disinformation strategies. This has an air of motherhood and apple pie, but its valuable contribution is its critique of the term 'fake news'. The term does not really capture the range of phenomena, which goes beyond news to include other kinds of misrepresentation, such as claiming fake followers, organized trolling, targeted advertising, automated accounts, and 'astroturfing' (making it appear that content is community-generated rather than orchestrated PR). Content may not be entirely fake, but simply misleading (e.g. presenting the work of a small minority of conspiracy theorists alongside genuine science to create the impression of a lack of consensus), or a mix of fact and falsehood.

Indeed, the cry of 'fake news' is often taken up by those who disagree with their coverage by the media, so that to many the term signals *more* tiresome partisan debate, rather than a threat to the body politic. The HLEG writes instead of 'disinformation', defined as 'false, inaccurate, or misleading information designed, presented and promoted to intentionally cause public harm or for profit. The risk of harm includes threats to democratic political processes and values, which can specifically target a variety of sectors, such as health, science, education, finance and more. It is driven by the production and promotion of disinformation for economic gains or for political or ideological goals, but can be exacerbated by how different audiences and communities receive, engage, and amplify disinformation.'[98]

It is worth drawing a distinction between those who are committed to misinformation, because they wish to pollute the information space, and those who are committed to hate speech, because they hate. These are two separate, though dangerous, phenomena. In Myanmar, for instance, Facebook (which has captured close to 100 percent of Burmese-language social media) is the medium of choice of Buddhist nationalist extremists, including politicians, soldiers, monks, and other religious figures, who deliberately stir up murderous hatred of minority groups, including the Muslim Rohingya.[99] This hatred no doubt includes dreadful lies, tapping into an Islamophobic tradition. But the nationalists primarily want to communicate hate, and to cause violence against minority groups. The adherents of the Moscow Spoiler, on the other hand, are more concerned with ushering in general chaos, which might include hatred, but also cynicism, lack of trust in authority, suspicion of neighbours, confusion about facts, uncertainty, and general suspicion of all information. No doubt these two tendencies blur together at the boundary, but today's SNSs are a tool of both them. Only the second of the two is a specific *product* of digital modernity.

Those worried by the spread of mendacious discourse are usually concerned with politics, although the COVID-19 pandemic has also focused attention on health advice and topics such as anti-vaccination propaganda. Fact-checking organizations and websites[100] can specialize either in correcting false statements made by individual public figures, or in understanding and countering the spread of viral rumours online.[101] Since the archetype of the fibbing politician has been with us since the year dot, the specific threat to the Internet comes from the viral sort, the pollution of our information space on an industrial scale. This distinction is not always clear-cut, as the utterances of the individual fibber can often go viral, and a focus on the ways in which misinformation travels through social groups might also help stem the flow of misinformation from social media. The efficacy of different techniques for fact checkers may vary, depending on the cultural and technological characteristics of the societies in which they are based.[102]

Google, with Delfi, a start-up in Vilnius, Lithuania, pioneered Demaskuok, a fact checker that tries to detect online misinformation in Lithuanian, Russian, and English, and trace it back to its origins. It has developed various heuristics to detect misinformation. Topics are important, with common themes being sexual assaults, health scares, and corruption. Emotive terms are used, often including children, sex, ethnicity, and national symbols. The speed with which a story goes viral is important, because misinformation is designed to go viral. And obviously if the story originated at or is forwarded from a site or identity already known to be dubious, then that is further evidence that it may be problematic. Together with the cooperation of journalists, the system is working to improve the detection of true but misleading stories (for example, a true story about an immigrant who has committed a crime may go viral, even though immigrants commit disproportionately few such crimes). The success rate for Demaskuok's flags is about 50 percent.[103]

Finland has received plaudits for its thorough education in media literacy, and its own home-grown fact-checking organization, Faktabaari, has adapted its disinformation-detection techniques for schools and universities. As with Lithuania, it benefits from a strong sense of a national resistance effort against the undermining of politics and the Internet from outside, taking as read the existence of a responsible political class and intellectual elite, as well as a cohort of concerned volunteers from civil society, willing to work together to support a small, beleaguered nation against a cyber-enabled aggressor.[104]

Sadly, not all political classes do pull together—how, for example, could a fact checker work in the hyper-partisan politics of the United States, for example? The University of Indiana's project Truthy, which maps partisan differences in social media and looks for the diffusion of false or misleading stories, has been strongly criticized as an attempt to close down free speech and debate.[105] We mention this not to judge Truthy's worth (although the authors of this book have long been aware of the project, and fully support what we believe to be excellent research), but more to highlight that when fact, truth, and science are not the foundation of a common political discourse, fact checking itself is absorbed into the debate (those who use fact checkers tend to be whiter, more politically engaged, more liberal, younger, and more educated than those who do not—in other words, across the fault lines of a number of existing political controversies).[106] Proposals for greater transparency in data use, even if globally feasible, would still require a coherent political response.[107] Another idea is to flag the provenance of content, to enable others to reason about it, but this also requires a concerned constituency of users.[108]

As noted earlier, misinformers don't mind getting caught. It helps establish the Spoiler's premise that objectivity is dead, that all 'fact' is really opinion, that no one has a reliable route to the truth. Every opinion is as valid as the next, and nothing can be trusted to be true, even if it comes from apparently reputable sources. The only difference between such sources and fake news farms is the good reputations of the former with elites and those in power. Hence, even if a fact checker highlights the disinformation circulating round a network, this doesn't obviously hinder the wider objective.

It especially doesn't when democrats, supposedly the enemies of fake news, play the same game. The United States had come to view corruption in Eastern Europe as an important tool of Russian influence. Hence, at least since the Ukrainian revolution of 2014, the rule of law had been not only a human rights issue but also part of the United States' security policy. President Trump's behaviour toward Ukraine, allegedly linking American aid to the investigation of a relative of his 2020 opponent, had the unfortunate effect of highlighting American post-truth decadence, backing up Russian claims of the subjectivity of truth (it also was the reason for the first attempt to impeach him). The damage to Western credibility is severe, enabling non-democrats to paint arguments about human rights and corruption as a hypocritical veneer of self-serving bluster.[109]

It also does not help when a well-known political party disguises a partisan Twitter account as a fact checker, as Britain's Conservative Party did during the 2019 General Election. The 'deceit' was not really a deceit, to the extent that the wheeze was signalled in advance, labelled @CCHQPress (the Conservative Party's press office's Twitter handle), and looked more like an attempt by the populist leadership of Boris Johnson and his advisor Dominic Cummings to annoy serious academic types who worry about truth. To that extent it was fashionably 'ironic'.[110] If fact checkers become part of the political landscape, this incident is probably a precursor of the general appearance of 'fake' fact checkers.

Neither does it help when companies persist in falsehoods in the face of regulatory suspicion, spinning out the process of investigation and normalizing the offence. Egregious examples include Facebook's consistent refusal to admit to tracking users with the 'like' button,[111] Verizon's deceptions about its tracking ID assigned to users that could not be turned off or opted out of,[112] and Google's 'deficiencies' and 'continued failure to provide a compliant declaration attesting to the veracity and completeness of its responses to the [Federal Communications] Commission's inquiries' when investigated by the FCC for its gathering of excessive WiFi data in its Google Street View cars. In the Google case, astonishingly, 'for many months, Google deliberately impeded and delayed the [FCC Enforcement] Bureau's investigation by failing to respond to requests for material information and to provide certifications and verifications of its responses. . . . Google apparently willfully and repeatedly violated Commission orders to produce certain information and documents that the Commission required for its investigation'.[113] None of these firms wants to upend the idea of truth per se, but they—as the Spoiler model would like to represent it—do seem to have the attitude that truth is for the 'little people'.

It remains problematic that tech giants have nurtured the idea that human oversight is a bottleneck, and that democratic measures of significance, such as Google's PageRank, have legitimacy at least as great. Whether companies who have invested in algorithms trained to count links and likes can retrain themselves to spot and eradicate egregious falsehoods, however well supported, remains an open question—especially when their business models depend on clicks. The tech giants have periodically promised to address disinformation and other problems such as hate speech in the face of ever-growing scandal; it is only fair to point out that Facebook in particular is an important source of funding for the fact-checking industry, and claims big successes in deterring users from clicking through to flagged content,[114] while in many countries such as Myanmar (discussed earlier), at least Facebook is trying to curb hate speech, unlike their governments, which are content to spectate mob violence. This debate will run, and we await developments with interest.[115]

CHAPTER 14

Policy Question

Is a Sovereign Internet Feasible?

Orwell argued, 'indifference to objective truth is encouraged by the sealing-off of one part of the world from another'.[1] The converse may also be the case. Russian suspicion of the Internet, and the information it brings and the access to Russia that it provides to its enemies, have long tempted the Putin government to attempt a genuine withdrawal, putting a complete barrier between the Russian Internet and the global one. The plan seems to have become concrete in 2014, during the Ukraine invasion. The Russian portion of the Internet (often called the RuNet) does appear to be well suited to this, as it is relatively centralized, with few 'joints' at which it could be carved. Despite its size, it has relatively few IXPs (about a dozen, while the US has nearer a hundred), and half the information traffic passes through one of them, in Moscow. Most passes through two cables which run to Scandinavia and Germany; there are a few lines in the East. In other words, there are enough bottlenecks to make a separation plausible.[2]

Why might the Russians worry about control of the Internet? Luminaries of the RuNet, such as Alexey Soldatov (head of the research centre that launched Russia's first ISP Relcom, and later a telecommunications minister)[3] and Igor Ashmanov (a founder of the IRA who believes that 'Google, Facebook and Twitter are ideological weapons aimed at Russia'),[4] are strong believers in 'Internet sovereignty',[5] alongside politicians such as Dmitry Medvedev,[6] while a Russian senator first proposed a domestic Internet in 2014.[7] It would be congruent with the development of the RuNet itself, which had always had a focus on local language, culture, and the nation.[8] The Snowden revelations demonstrated to the Russians the advantages for the United States of

Four Internets. Kieron O'Hara and Wendy Hall, Oxford University Press. © Oxford University Press 2021.
DOI: 10.1093/oso/9780197523681.003.0014

the presence of the servers of major service providers such as Google and Facebook on American soil. It soon passed a data law, demanding (as many nations now do, see Chapter 17) that Russian citizens' data be stored only in Russia. The ostensible (and no doubt genuine) reason was to protect citizens from foreign spying, but perhaps another reason was to bring data about its citizens into its jurisdiction.[9]

One possible scenario of Russian concern stems from the DNS and the role of ICANN. Most nations have a country code top-level domain (ccTLD: Russia's is .ru, Britain's is .uk, France's .fr, China's .cn, Mexico's .mx), run by a registry in that country. If the United States has preferential access to the root zone, then it could potentially delete the country code of an enemy. Then addresses ending in that code would cease to function because computers would be unable to get access via the root to that nation's registry. That would mean that those of its command and control defence systems that are attached to the Internet would lose connectivity, which is unthinkable in the digitally modern world.

This shouldn't work, however, for a number of reasons.[10] First, there are lots of other ways to get access to whatever IP address a domain is linked to (especially with respect to military computers, most of whose connections would be automatic via the IP address directly). Second, the United States' capacity to interfere in ICANN is undoubtedly less than it was, say, in 2010. Third, a nation which was prepared for the eventuality could copy the country code registry, and perhaps run it internally (thereby losing connectivity with the rest of the world, but preserving it at home), or back it up in another, hard-to-delete, top-level domain, such as .com. ISPs unwilling to take sides in a conflict might agree to cooperate and restore the country code domain in their own cached databases. Fourthly, perhaps most importantly, such an action by the United States would certainly result in a concerted effort by a large number of countries to re-establish the DNS in a new institution outside the US. The Russians had already mooted the possibility of a separate DNS, independent of the existing system, run by and for the BRICS—the group of large and increasingly influential developing nations consisting of Brazil, India, China, and South Africa, as well as Russia—though this proposal went nowhere.[11] Even if American interference with the ccTLD worked once, it couldn't work a second time.

Irrespective of that, in 2019 the sovereign RuNet moved closer to reality with the passage of a 'sovereign Internet' bill. The way was paved for this by the *Strategy of Information Society Development in Russia until 2030*, which includes such ambitions as the 'formation of a common information space, including for solving problems of ensuring national security', and to 'support the activities of state and non-state organizations to preserve cultural and moral values, the traditions of patriotism and humanism in society; propaganda of cultural and moral values of the Russian people', as well as many worthy goals about developing the knowledge economy and protecting the privacy of citizens.[12] The final trigger for the bill was not this strategy, however, but a reaction to the naming of Russia, along with China, Iran, and North Korea, as 'adversaries' conducting 'reckless cyber attacks' prompting 'a crisis short of war' in the Trump administration's National Cyber Strategy.[13]

The new law gives Roskomnadzor the power to route data across networks in Russia and, if deemed necessary, to prevent it entering or leaving the country, together with the responsibility to maintain critical digital infrastructure once RuNet is separated from the global Internet. Traffic exchanges on Russian territory will happen only at registered IXPs, and a national DNS will be created to be used if the RuNet is blocked from abroad. All Russian ISPs must therefore install hardware from Roskomnadzor to facilitate detection and blocking of unauthorized data sources.[14]

Experts are sceptical of the possibility of cutting the Internet off entirely, not least because Russia would cut itself off from important functionality that is only available on the Internet outside the RuNet, such as the SWIFT payments information network. If they replicated this functionality within Russia, then its international clients would need access to it. And the RuNet is bound to look different, as the information that makes up a webpage is often stored in a highly distributed manner (for example, a commenting function, a 'like' button, or an advertising space may rely on software and/or data held in a non-Russian cloud). The control measures envisaged by the sovereign Internet bill would enable Roskomnadzor to target specific people, organizations, or opinions, and close down their online presence, or to cut off particular parts of the country from the Internet (as already happened in the province of Ingushetia in 2018–2019), and this may be more germane to its purpose. The legislation might also conceivably be used as a lever to pressurize large foreign media companies such as Facebook or Twitter, if they resisted attempts to interfere with expression on their sites. But, as Andrew Sullivan of the Internet Society points out, if you craft your local Internet so that it can be separated from the global one, you of necessity create the possibility that it will separate by accident.[15] In late 2019, Russia announced that its first tests had been successful, and all traffic had been re-routed within Russia's borders for a period of time. It gave no technical details, and no one appears to have noticed until they were told; it may be that some scepticism is appropriate about the announcement.[16]

Iran has also mused for over a decade over the possibility of cutting itself off in the RuNet style, to create a so-called halal Internet (the National Information Network—NIN) upon which only approved content would circulate. A team from the University of Michigan took a valuable look at NIN's prospects in 2013, but it is difficult to generalize given that their testbed was just one device served by a single ISP. They discovered that control of that device was traceable to one centralized location, but that does not mean that other

ISPs do not have alternative loci of control, as they point out. Similarly, their experiment was time-limited, and the Iranian government is very proactive in adjusting its censorship strategies.[17] The call for a decisive break from the global Internet mainly comes from the religious wing, and the government's stated policy falls short of this drastic step. Certain services, such as Twitter, are associated with the malign influence of the United States, and are blocked. This has created a gap for the Telegram encrypted instant messaging service (launched by Pavel Durov and his brother), which has on occasion itself been blocked, but which is subject to far less interference. The widespread use of Telegram has been associated with the good performance of Reformist parties in the 2016 parliamentary elections.[18]

Iran has blacked out the Internet temporarily to control the flow of information, particularly during disputed elections in 2009, but also in response to certain public relations problems for the regime. It employs a number of techniques for censoring the Internet experience of its resident citizens: broadband speed limits, to hinder access to multimedia and video; DNS redirection, so certain addresses resolve into black holes; blocking access on the basis of keywords in the HTTP host header (originally blocking adult content, but in later years including more political keywords); and throttling connection speeds to certain services (such as Gmail) or protocols (such as HTTPS). But its efforts have so far only produced a vacuum, rather than a sovereign Internet.[19]

Shutting down the Internet without putting up a new one is very expensive, as Egypt discovered when it shut down its local DNS during the protests that led to the downfall of President Mubarak in 2011. All five of its ISPs went down within a few minutes of each other, and stayed down for some days, at an estimated impact to the Egyptian economy in excess of $100 million.[20] It is likely that the NIN would also incur great costs, if not as much as a total blackout, but, as a demonstration of technical acumen akin to Russia's RuNet, it could be a boost for the regime. It would also give the regime information as to who was accessing what information.

CHAPTER 15

Peaceful Coexistence

These visions of the Internet do not, and probably could not, exist in their pure forms, still less be so neatly ascribed to particular regimes. We caricature to make our main point: that the homogeneity of the Internet is not a given, and that scenarios about what is sometimes called its Balkanization or the Splinternet cannot be ruled out.[1] We caricature, but not inaccurately. Neither, we should say, are these the only Internets that could evolve—the four (plus spoiler) could become five, or six, or seven, or more. There could be a developing world Internet, or a feminist Internet, or an Islamic Internet, or a caring Internet, or a green Internet, or an Internet of cyborgs, if the appropriate ethical vision found a technological realization, and sufficiently powerful institutional backing. Different types of democracy might be enabled; media scholar Lincoln Dahlberg suggests liberal-individualist, deliberative, counter-publics, and autonomist Marxist democracies might be constructed digitally.[2] Mueller argues that we need to replace ideas of national sovereignty with net nationalism for non-territorial transnational popular sovereignty over cyberspace.[3] However, most visions of the Internet driven by concerns of democracy, justice, or equity lack either technical coherence or powerful political backing, or both.

As an example, media scholar Last Moyo blasts 'an undemocratic, colonial and exclusive model of the information society produced by a discriminatory Western modernity project', and proposes an alternative postcolonial Internet.[4] It is an absolutely fair point that the large amount of English (and other languages originating in the colonial powers) can crowd out other cultures online. But given that lots of people speak English and relatively few speak minority languages, what is the technical proposal to prevent this happening? More links will be generated and followed for English sites than ones in, say, Hausa or Tagalog, and it is hard to think of a technical intervention to

Four Internets. Kieron O'Hara and Wendy Hall, Oxford University Press. © Oxford University Press 2021.
DOI: 10.1093/oso/9780197523681.003.0015

ameliorate this that will simultaneously be practicable. Exclusion is surely an *outcome* of democracy, not its opposite.

That is not to say that the Internet is not accelerating the loss of languages, or that it is not a severe ethical issue. Moyo suggests 'democratizing [the Internet] beyond its neo-liberal character by confronting its various coloni-alities [and] re-conceptualizing it as a truly autonomous space for many lan-guages, cultures, identities, and knowledges. . . . European languages must stand side-by-side with languages from the border. This is already happening with languages like Mandarin in China and Korean/Hangul in Korea. This kind of information society is not top down, divisive, and colonially struc-tured, but truly democratic, decolonized, multicultural and lateral'.[5] But since there is little top-down control of content as it is, certain languages gain prominence precisely because the Internet is *already* multicultural and lateral. Mandarin and Korean are numerically important online because there are a lot of Mandarin and Korean speakers using the Internet. Whatever worked for Mandarin isn't going to work for an African language spoken by a smaller community with a modest Internet penetration unless it is accompanied by a concrete technical proposal about how to make it happen (such proposals can certainly be made, perhaps involving automatic translation—we certainly do not rule them out). The Internet is an engineered space; there is no point willing the ends without willing the (technical) means.[6]

The clamour of voices makes it clear that the battle between visions of the Internet is not the straight fight between China and the United States en-visaged by Eric Schmidt and Kai-Fu Lee. This underestimates the breadth of dispute between conflicting visions (not least within the US itself). It is also important to understand as well that these models do at the moment coexist in uneasy tension.

We single out Russia as the spoiler, free-riding on the efforts of others to produce a valuable information space,[7] but of course very many nations, includ-ing the United States, indulge in disinformation. The actions of the United States (under both Presidents Obama and Trump) in indicting cyberspies and cyberwarriors from China, Russia, Iran, and elsewhere have reportedly concerned members of its National Security Agency, who fear being pros-ecuted themselves outside the United States for similar crimes.[8] Meanwhile, although the Russians and others are happy to troll the Internet, they do re-quire a functioning Internet to troll, so they have no incentive to undermine it totally. Dishonesty requires a background of honesty.[9] The acceptability of dishonesty is likely to increase if the system as a whole is perceived as unfair, so spoilers still have incentives to highlight lapses in the standards of other nations with accusations of hypocrisy.[10]

Similarly, the Beijing Paternal vision appeals to the Chinese government, which is quick to close down conversation in its lively microblogging media, while valuing the openness that leads to the publication of dissent, which it uses as an early warning of problems. The Paternal Internet will appeal to any government, however democratic, that takes responsibility for social problems (such as obesity or climate change) and would rather impose a paternalistic solution than allow one to emerge from an autonomous citizenry. The kind of soft paternalism known as the 'nudge' philosophy is one means of leveraging data within an Internet environment to close choices down on grounds determined by liberal elites.[11]

In the United States, the breakdown of political consensus has made the distinction between the Silicon Valley Open Internet and the DC Commercial Internet far sharper than it traditionally has been (one of the last acts in office of President Trump's former attorney general Jeff Sessions was to sue the State of California for its decision to restore net neutrality regulation against the FCC's own reversal reported in Chapter 9),[12] but until fairly recently the two visions managed to rub along reasonably well, with businesses switching their evangelizing between openness and surveillance opportunistically as their situations demanded. Meanwhile, some of the tech giants are recruiting prominent European politicians to defend their positions in the European Union, such as Facebook's appointment of Sir Nick Clegg, as its head of Global Affairs.[13] Such cross-fertilization may also result in bringing the Eurocrats closer to the Americans; Margrethe Vestager's decision in 2017 to order Apple to pay back taxes to the Irish government (which didn't want the money) was criticized by one of her predecessors, Neelie Kroes, who had been appointed to Uber's Public Policy Advisory Board in 2016.[14]

Hence these models (and the spoilers that undermine them) are likely to coexist even within individual organizations and governments. Nevertheless, clear preferences exist for certain models, and these contribute to the tensions in global Internet governance. In Part III, we will look ahead to see how these tensions might develop, and how they might affect some of the burgeoning technologies upon which so much of our future depends.

PART III

Futures

Prediction is very difficult, especially about the future, as Niels Bohr may or may not have said. The narrative of the dialectic for and against openness in the context of networks, data, and digital modernity, which we developed in Part II, suggests two particular sets of questions. First, how will it play out? Will there be a winner? What will destabilize or cement equilibrium? Surely many of the important factors affecting these issues will depend on where the Internet grows, and the culture, experience, and resources that new users will bring. Will they accept, adapt, or reject digital modernity? Second, how will the narrative affect discernible technological trends currently under way? In this final part, we will look at a selection of issues both geopolitical and technological through the lens of our Four Internets, to consider how they might affect the growth and development of the Internet as a whole, and the ways in which it intersects with daily life.

To begin, we will consider the special case of India, as its Internet penetration grows remorselessly, the country becomes more networked, and increasing quantities of data are made available to that network by migration to online services. There is little doubt that it will be a key player, and it is already making its presence felt in global Internet and data policy. We will also consider data nationalism as a specific policy question posed by India's rise.

Following that, we will look at two technologies that are central to digital modernity—artificial intelligence and the Internet of Things. They may be hyped, but they both have great potential for transforming everyday life and the economy, for good or ill. Whether one is optimistic, pessimistic, or sceptical, these technological developments cannot be ignored by policymakers. The creation and use of data is once more a central part of the story. AI does not strictly depend on the Internet for its operation, but in its current manifestation it does depend on data, and both its chief source of data and its key deployment will be the networking of intelligent objects and systems (perhaps most ambitiously in smart cities).[1]

Chapter 20 is a little more speculative. We consider the conditions for the development of what have been called *social machines*, ad hoc groups of networked individuals working together at scale on a common practice, problem, or task, exploiting the affordances of the devices and websites they possess and understand. Yet again, the role of data turns out to be important, and we will also look at a new proposal to reinvigorate Silicon Valley Openness in the face of the forces described in Part II.

Our final chapter sums up. The major themes running through the book are the growth and maturity of the four visions of the Internet we have sketched, and how these affect and are affected by the massively increasing quantity of data we generate about ourselves and the world. To quote the late Johnny Nash, there are more questions than answers, but we hope that we can see (a little more) clearly now why questions of Internet governance and data regulation will be of central importance for the digital economy, and indeed geopolitical relations as a whole, as we prepare to navigate the second quarter of the twenty-first century.

CHAPTER 16

India, the 'Swing State'

Right at the beginning of this book, Table 1.1 covered Internet penetration across the globe. Notable was India's penetration of around 30% in 2016—plenty of room to grow. Its population is projected to reach 1.5 billion, having overtaken China's, by 2030, so if penetration increases to the level of China's in that time (a conservative assumption, given current growth rates), we are looking at 300 million–400 million new Internet users in that nation over the next decade—not an insignificant percentage of the whole, and possibly sufficient to provide a balance of power.

India is the world's largest democracy, while at the same time, under Prime Minister Narendra Modi, it is a fully paid-up member of the Axis of Incivility. It is also home to a world-class technology industry, with a number of bases, including Bengaluru, Mumbai, Pune, Hyderabad, and elsewhere. Its university research sector, particularly at the autonomous Indian Institutes of Technology, has an international reputation. In 2019 it boasted around 80,000 start-ups, which between them raised $10 billion in venture capital, and 18 unlisted companies valued at over $1 billion. Major IT firms that are household names include Infosys, Tata Consulting, Reliance/Jio Platforms, and Wipro, and the sector contributes a high percentage of India's GDP. Although much of that is export revenue, India is not reliant on external technologies for its growth, and there is also much inward investment, from US firms like Accel and Bessemer, Chinese firms such as Alibaba and Tencent, SoftBank of Japan, and the Singaporean sovereign wealth holding company Temasek.[1]

International relations scholar Christopher Coker, who created the notion of a civilizational state discussed in the opening chapter, writes that India is unlikely to become one. Since his definition includes the tendency to push against the international rules-based order, this means he judges it will not become undemocratic and disruptive like Russia and China, because of its

Four Internets. Kieron O'Hara and Wendy Hall, Oxford University Press. © Oxford University Press 2021.
DOI: 10.1093/oso/9780197523681.003.0016

highly diverse population, proud democratic history, and pluralist politics. It will surely become more assertive as it becomes the largest nation on Earth, and as its technological resources add greater value. Coker's claim is an optimistic one, and there is a subconscious double edge in his remark that 'India may even be the place where the future of human freedom is determined'.[2] Determined, yes—but in which direction?

Certainly, given the fine balance of the current Internet and its likely growth in India, it may be less of a stretch to suggest that the future of the *Internet* may be determined, and certainly strongly influenced, by developments in India, of which two seem especially relevant. The first is the dominance in general elections of 2014 and 2019 of Modi's Bharatiya Janata Party (BJP), a new direction following some years of indecisive and anti-incumbent election results. The second is the rapid increase in access to digital technology, driven by the public and private sectors in concert.

FROM HYDERABAD TO SILICON VALLEY? INDIAN OPENNESS

Prior to these developments, the Internet had long been championed as a means to empower the global poor, by providing access to crop prices, political and economic news, extreme weather events, educational opportunities, health information, and other worthy fare. Much aid has been premised on such virtuous and utilitarian use of technology. One early positive narrative of how the Open Internet could support development emerged from attempts to use Internet technology to improve governance, through transparency and deregulating.[3]

For instance, in the 1990s, populist policies, such as subsidized power, rice, or fertilizer for the poor or for farmers, often held sway in India, yet were at the same time expensive, ineffective (for instance, the benefits of power subsidies often went to richer people for whom it was a larger share of their expenditure), and easy to subvert corruptly, and so did little for development. One regional party, the Telugu Desam Party (TDP), had won a landslide in the large and relatively poor state of Andhra Pradesh in 1994 (population 76 million, with a 60% literacy rate at the time), and adhered to a fairly standard populist policy slate, until a palace coup in 1995 saw Chandrababu Naidu become TDP leader and Andhra Pradesh's chief minister. He liberalized the economy, but more to the point for our own inquiries, he deregulated to cut the number of interfaces between citizens and government, to remove inefficiencies, bottlenecks and opportunities for corruption. This was partly supported with a number of self-help schemes, but also with the use of technology. Every village was to be given a computer, to bypass layers of bureaucracy, and government services were regularly moved online, onto the APonline website. The state government developed the 'e-citizen lifecycle', covering the stages of the lives of its citizens, 'child', 'student', 'old age', and so on, pointing them to the appropriate set of services to which they might be entitled. A classic Bollywood blockbuster of 1987, *Mr India*, starring Sridevi and Anil Kapoor, featured an 'ordinary' Indian finding an invisibility device, and taking on the villains who thrived on the powerlessness and lack of voice of his fellow citizens. Invisibility was the means to make ordinary citizens visible; transparency through technology, on the Naidu vision, was intended to perform a similar trick.

In the cities, of which the largest was Hyderabad, e-Seva centres were created where clerks at computer terminals completed forms in the presence of claimants, and proved highly popular. Hyderabad grew a substantial technology industry, and the Hyderabad Information Technology and Engineering Consultancy City (HITEC City, otherwise known as Cyberabad) became its technology district, specializing in biotechnology and health informatics.[4] Corruption fell, quality and reach of service provision rose, and Naidu became the darling of the global elite, including Microsoft, and the United Kingdom's Department for International Development.[5] Conversely, he became a target of the anti-globalization brigade.

Could technology solve Andhra Pradesh's problems? To an extent, but not all the way. Government service improved, but many of the state's problems went beyond what could be remedied by technology imposed from the top down. A long-term insurgency of Naxalite (Maoist) guerrillas rumbled away, including two assassination attempts on Naidu. The agricultural region of Telangana, which saw its problems in terms of agrarian crisis rather than poor and corrupt service provision, nurtured a separatist movement. The opposition Congress Party developed a narrative (not unfamiliar in the richer world today) that the TDP had neglected rural, poor Indians, and their villages had been left behind in the scramble for technology.

Naidu was defeated in the election of 2004. Anti-globalists celebrated; British activist George Monbiot cheered that 'the voters of the Indian state of Andhra Pradesh may have destroyed the world's most dangerous economic experiment. . . . We can't yet vote [Tony] Blair out of office, but in Andhra Pradesh they have done the job on our behalf.'[6] Yet the new government broadly continued with the high-tech policies, and Greenpeace was able to take 'cyber action' against the successor government which had allowed shipbreaking units to threaten the livelihoods of fishermen and an ecologically sensitive nature reserve.

The ultimate outcome of the idealistic use of technology in Andhra Pradesh is hard to judge. It (especially Hyderabad) remains a centre of the industry. However, it is about average among Indian states, and below the median, in terms of the UNDP's Human Development Index in 2018, although it has improved its absolute score a lot (as have most other Indian states) since 1995.[7] In 1995, it was a little below the Indian average; now it is a little above. The territory of Telangana eventually did separate and became a new state in 2014. In the bewildering provincial politics of India, Naidu managed another term as chief minister of the rump state of Andhra Pradesh in 2014–2019, but was ejected once more in a landslide, amid corruption allegations. In his second period in office, he updated Andhra Pradesh's technology aims, launching real-time big data and IoT initiatives to gather and process data for governance. Since then, in opposition, his TDP has fractured, with its members of the upper house of India's Parliament joining their allies in Prime Minister Modi's BJP, while his coalition partners in the state legislature deserted him.

It is probably fair to say that Naidu's legacy is mixed, at best. Perhaps, like Mr India, he has helped citizens' voices be heard. At the same time, the negatives mean that the catchphrase of the super-villain of that film might also be relevant: 'Mogambo is pleased!'

FROM MUMBAI TO DC? INDIAN COMMERCIALISM

Given the rhetoric of openness for development, it may be surprising that the use of the Internet in emerging economies and poorer societies is not unlike that elsewhere, with the joys of social networking, gaming, dating, movies, and pornography looming rather larger than the reflective use of the medium for economic advantage and political deliberation. In India as elsewhere, the Internet reflects society in a dynamic where each subtly changes the other. The unintended consequences of the consumption of entertainment, especially enabled by the smartphone, have included greater privacy from family members and neighbours in small, crowded dwellings, and greater use of the Internet by women, although still with constraints and disadvantages.[8]

There have been noteworthy commercial developments that will affect the evolution of the Indian Internet. The telecommunications company Jio Platforms (part of Mukesh Ambani's Reliance Industries conglomerate) launched a strategy in 2015 for increasing India's digital profile, with itself as the main beneficiary. The telecoms market was crowded, with little money being made per user; most pricing models competed on call rates, which led to low prices and poor service. There was little to be gained by competing in that vein, but Jio marked out a completely new model—it abolished call rates, and charged only for data, differentiating itself immediately. It also provided services across the nation, unlike many of its regional competitors. Quality was aided by its not providing any services below 4G, unlike its competitors which were burdened by legacy services, and it partnered with Google to produce a cheap 4G smartphone, the JioPhone, that ran exclusively on its network. Reliance launched a number of Jio-branded apps, such as JioSaavn (music streaming), Jio TV, JioCinema, JioChat (messaging), JioMeet (videoconferencing), JioMart (e-commerce), JioCloud, and, last but not least, JioMoney for online payments. The MyJio service provides access to good deals, as well as all Jio apps.

Jio took off dramatically, with hundreds of millions of customers, and not only blasted its competitors, it—as intended—grew the market absolutely.[9] As of 2019, the average Indian smartphone user uses more data than those of many European nations. As in the richer world, growing the network is an expensive business, and Jio has yet to make a profit for the hundreds of billions of rupees it has spent—although it has put many of its rivals out of business. Indeed, even as the number of subscribers has increased, the aggregate revenues of the industry have shrunk. The government has helped, with regulations and judgments favouring Jio over both domestic and foreign competitors. The CEO of Vodafone has complained of 'unsupportive regulation [and] excessive taxes'.[10]

Unlike the early digital commerce pioneers, Jio's strategy was not to provide a specific service, but rather to follow the Tencent/Alibaba model of providing every service that users might wish, so that they never leave the 'Jio' ecosystem. The network effect operates by increasing the transaction costs of using another service; the Jio network is simple and cheap to join, and expensive to leave. These are the conditions for a network to grow quickly, and for its services within the walled garden to be monetized on the DC model.

And, as if by magic, up pops Mark Zuckerberg. In April 2020, Facebook bought a 9.9% stake in Jio for $5.7 billion, a useful sum of money for its parent Reliance, which had been struggling in the COVID-19 pandemic. India contains, surprisingly, the highest number of Facebook users, at 280 million. It also has 400 million WhatsApp users, and it is probably no coincidence that its owner bet on Jio while WhatsApp was negotiating India's tortuous bureaucracy to get approval for a payments-handling service (in the end, that became bogged down, and WhatsApp's first national payment service was launched in Brazil, not India, although *that* got blocked by the Brazilian government within a week). Now partners, both Jio and Facebook have designs on working with India's millions of *kirana*, or convenience stores, using their local knowledge together with WhatsApp and JioMart to set up a hybrid commerce system for quick home delivery or in-store collection.[11]

Is India heading for a Mumbai model, where Jio and Reliance are based, analogous to the DC model?

FROM NEW DELHI TO BEIJING? INDIAN PATERNALISM

As a factor in considering the future of the Internet in India, we mentioned earlier the recent dominance of Modi's BJP, whose governments' outlooks have been generally authoritarian, populist, and, unusually for India, openly sectarian. Modi himself came to international prominence in 2002 as chief minister of Gujarat state, following his inadequate response to a three-day anti-Muslim pogrom by Hindu mobs. Such is his sway that Prime Minister Modi and the BJP are likely to have a great deal of influence on the growth of the Internet in the short to medium term.

Coker's focus on illiberalism in his definition of civilizational states seems less valuable than the wider observation that such states should have, or perceive themselves to have, a civilization to project, and on that ground we would prefer to include India,[12] despite its palpable diversity and tradition of debate.[13] It has a rich tradition of narrative and storytelling to draw upon, and retelling of the epics of Indian literature has been common in mass media, and now online.[14] In the years following independence, its profile was somewhat low, known mostly for a series of Indian National Congress governments' experiments in autarkic socialism that kept the nation impoverished, for its robust and noisy democracy, and for a diplomatic cussedness that elevated it to seniority in the Non-Aligned Movement. The end of the Cold War and a monetary crisis prompted financial liberalization in the 1990s, reversing decades of policy and taking millions out of extreme poverty. It is hard for a ruling class to admit mistakes, and Congress was never the same force again (the assassination of Rajiv Gandhi in 1991 was also a factor—had he lived, he would have been 75 years old at the 2019 general election, a mere six years older than Modi, and younger than Joe Biden).

The BJP's ideology jettisons the secularism of Congress, along with the rich multicultural history upon which Coker lays stress, with the clear and distinct contributions made to art, culture, and law by Hellenic Greeks, Islam, the British Empire, Christianity, and socialism, among others. Instead, it champions *Hindutva*, a type of nationalism asserting that India is the one and only home of Hinduism and other Indic cultures, although it has a sometimes tense relationship with other indigenous cultures such as Sikhism. In this it has paradoxically been helped by the insistence of Muhammad Ali Jinnah's All-India Muslim League on creating the Muslim state of Pakistan at independence in 1947, against Mohandas Gandhi's policy of a religiously plural Greater India; if Pakistan (and now Bangladesh) are the Muslim states, what identity could India have but a majority Hindu/Indic one (despite being home to 172 million Muslims at the last census, the third largest Muslim population in the world)?

In terms of policy, this has taken the form of supporting Hindu groups in territorial disputes (e.g. over the Ayodhya dispute), promoting Hindu norms at the expense of others (e.g. attempting to ban the slaughter of cows), taking a sceptical view of the citizenship of Muslims (e.g. the 2019 Citizenship Amendment Act gave a route to Indian citizenship to illegal immigrants and refugees of several religious minorities, but not Muslims), revising history textbooks, arguing for the superiority of classical Indian science (e.g. that Ancient Hindus pioneered stem cell technology), and pushing both technology (e.g. via a multi-billion-dollar space programme), and modernity (e.g. the Clean India Mission promoting indoor plumbing). Diplomatically, the defence forces have received increased support, aggressive stances have been taken against Pakistan and China, the special status of the disputed state of Jammu and Kashmir has been removed, the Indian diaspora has been cultivated, economic protectionism has been dialled down, foreign investment attracted, environmental concerns downgraded, and President Trump courted. It should be fairly clear that this is a heady authoritarian/populist brew of the kind fashionable in the twenty-first century, that could create combustible politics when served up on the Internet.

Hence, given the interests of the government in promoting a particular set of ideas and social outcomes, we can also detect a precondition for an Indian version of the Paternal vision to express and implement those outcomes. India and China are of course very different places—one democratic, the other an autocracy; one relatively chaotic, the other relatively organized. They are regional rivals, and there is occasionally conflict near their disputed border. There are also similarities—in 2019, they were joint 80th in Transparency International's Corruption Perception Index. They are arguably both civilizational states, with a mission to project not only their geopolitical power but also their venerable cultures more widely.[15] It is therefore perhaps not surprising to find parallels between the Internet in India and the Beijing Paternal Internet.

That is not to say that the two countries see eye to eye, or that there is much cooperation between them with respect to Internet governance. The Internet is sometimes a victim of their rivalry. After a lethal confrontation in 2020 between their troops in the disputed territory of Ladakh near Kashmir, the Indian government retaliated by banning dozens of Chinese apps, including TikTok, at the time the most downloaded app in India, and WeChat, ostensibly to protect the data and privacy of Indian citizens from rapacious Chinese data-grabbing.[16]

The Indian business environment also has similarities to and differences from China. The Modi government, despite having a proud pro-business record that enabled its re-election in 2019, is not always business friendly, in a nation with a tradition of bureaucracy and red tape. All companies in India, big and small, have to deal with constantly changing rules, regulatory opacity, and complexity, all of which give scope for corruption. Listing on Indian exchanges requires meeting onerous rules; those to do with profitability are particularly obstructive, because few tech start-ups are profitable as they invest in growing their networks. Listing abroad is not an option for those who wish to keep their bases in India.[17]

To take one example, digital payments have had a roller-coaster ride. First, in 2016, the government invalidated all 500 and 1,000 rupee notes at very short notice, which caused massive disruption but boosted digital banking. In

2019, it banned companies from charging fees to merchants for payment services (the business model for Ant Financial, Tencent, Visa, and Mastercard), which was also disruptive but had the opposite effect. It also, despite there being a flourishing private sector with effective digital payment firms such as JioMart and Paytm, set up a competitor, the Unified Payment Interface (UPI). UPI is a real-time payment system run by a non-profit owned by a consortium of banks and backed by the Reserve Bank of India. Other payment systems, banks, and shops can use the infrastructure, while customers can switch between systems as easily as switching between apps, and even very small businesses such as street vendors are connected. Before the COVID-19 lockdown in India, it carried well over a billion transactions each month, about a fifth of all banking transactions; at the time of writing the shape of the post-pandemic economy is unknown, but while absolute numbers may be down, we might expect a higher percentage of transactions. Furthermore, the government has used UPI to make emergency payments to small businesses during the lockdown.[18]

This is an open system designed to support competition and to inhibit customer lock-in. It will also lower a number of barriers to entry—for example, enabling poor people to get loans by storing their transaction history, or helping small businesses join the formal economy. Is this a move towards an Indian version of Silicon Valley openness? Not quite, because the system rests on one of the most significant digital developments of our time, the *Aadhaar* system.

Aadhaar was an initiative in the early 2000s to develop a national identity register for Indians. The state supplies a number of benefits and subsidies for very poor people, and in the nature of the case it was not always easy to ensure the right people got the right benefits (more or less the same problems that Naidu was wrestling with in Andhra Pradesh in the 1990s). Large numbers of Indians found it hard to prove their identity, for instance to establish claims to property. It was also surprisingly easy to get multiple passports with different details. An ID register was deemed to be the solution to these problems— the UN's Sustainable Development Goals included the recommendation for nations to provide all their citizens with a unique identity by 2030—and so in 2010, Nandan Nilekani, founder of Infosys, was appointed to develop the system.[19]

This is not the place to go into details, but on any measure the enrolment in a decade of one and a quarter billion people, including millions of the world's poorest and least-educated, and making the system usable even by illiterate citizens, is an astonishing piece of logistics and administration. The system is biometric, capturing fingerprints, iris scans, and photographs in return for a 12-digit number which consolidates digital identities used in India. Hence the undocumented can be documented, corruption and money laundering are harder, and services such as welfare, subsidies, banking, and loans became easier. It is not a compulsory system, but the network effects suggest that opting out will be increasingly difficult. It is not linked to citizenship directly—it applies to residents. To access any of the services that use the infrastructure (such as UPI), you show your Aadhaar card (you can also identify yourself with an alternative method, but few do). Payments can then come from and go into your bank, and Aadhaar provides the glue to connect the two ends of the transaction.

We need not flag the complex politics of privacy, security, and trust which arise with large ID systems, even voluntary ones. Aadhaar has proved leaky, with a number of data breaches, if not always from the central database. These have allowed unauthorized individuals to get access cheaply to the data.[20] Meanwhile, despite not being compulsory, it has proved exclusionary; shockingly, several children starved to death after their family's ration cards were cancelled because they were not linked to Aadhaar.[21]

It is therefore important to understand both the affordances and the limitations of such a system in their social context. For example, an Aadhaar 'card' is only printed on paper, without a chip or hologram or other kind of security feature, and so is not suitable for use as an ID card proper. Aadhaar is in essence a database, not a token for a physical transaction. Indian law makes no mention of an Aadhaar card, so its use as photo ID occupies a legal grey area. As a verification confirms the number and connects it with the postcode and gender of the holder, it is quite possible to generate new fake cards with that information and a new photo. In other words, the advantage of Aadhaar is its ability to authenticate information; if that functionality is not used, then it is no better or worse than any other photo ID. Yet it *is* widely used as photo ID; this social reality negates much of the security engineering.[22]

Our point is less the imperfections of the system than its role in the ideological development of the Internet in India. The Modi government inherited the scheme in 2014, but ID systems are agreeable to governments with particular social philosophies. Aadhaar may be a vital building block in the development in India of a Beijing-style paternalism. Though participation in Aadhaar is voluntary, it is the most convenient delivery mechanism for a number of vital services. It has also been argued that media coverage has focused more on the business opportunities Aadhaar provides, rather than privacy, surveillance, and inclusion, and that in this and other respects it is not unlike the information the Chinese media provides about its social credit system.[23]

The Indian state is also interested in other methods of tracking and monitoring its population. In 2019, it began to explore the possibility of centralizing face recognition information from its network of surveillance cameras and linking it with other databases such as passports and fingerprints.[24] Its purpose would ostensibly be law enforcement (India has been the target of dozens of deadly terror attacks), although the use of a tethered surveillance balloon to monitor a COVID-19 curfew in the city of Vadodara shows the danger of function creep.[25] Conversely, face recognition has not been of much use in its intended humanitarian applications; after three years, despite hopes, it has made no contribution to the tracing of the thousands of missing children in Delhi.[26] Centralization creates vulnerabilities; details from a face recognition database in Tamil Nadu have leaked online, while there are suspicions about the opportunities for espionage created by the large number of Chinese cameras in India's CCTV network. Nevertheless, it is estimated that India's face-recognition industry will be worth billions of dollars by 2024, close to the size of China's.[27]

A proposed Data Protection Bill is intended to put a legal framework around India's growing personal data economy, to control collection, processing, and usage of data. Some aspects are modelled on GDPR—not least its ambition and high penalties. User consent is a pillar of the Bill, and unlike other data protection legislation, it explicitly proposes that data principals (i.e. what GDPR calls 'data subjects') are, at least in some cases, owners of their data. The Bill also eschews the strict nationalism of the Chinese approach and insists only that 'sensitive' and 'critical' data be held in India.

It also departs from GDPR in a couple of respects where citizens' privacy is no longer the imperative. In the first place, it applies in full to the private sector only, and the state can collect data without consent or demand it from others under a wide range of circumstances. Secondly, it attempts to reduce trolling by requiring digital companies to identify their users—a potential burden for SNSs who would have to determine which of their millions of accounts were fake.[28]

In business more generally, the government is also apt to co-opt and strong-arm businesses using techniques that are traditionally more familiar in Beijing than Delhi. Support for businesses is said by some to be not unconnected with their alignment with BJP policy, for example where they provide services such as loans, energy, or sanitation to poor villages at low rates.[29] This is hardly a bad thing in itself, but the flip side is that the government can play hardball too. The owner of a popular national coffee chain committed suicide after heavy pressure from the Income Tax Department, which some have associated with his connections with the opposition Congress Party.[30] In the tech sector, the Vodafone CEO mentioned earlier who complained about unreasonable taxes was forced to apologize and withdraw the complaint the next day.[31] Businesses' alignment with the business-friendly government, and not vice versa, would appear to be the order of the day.

India's Supreme Court has a long tradition of standing up to the government, and continues to do so. However, it has taken to delaying judgments so long that the situation on the ground becomes a fait accompli, impossible to reverse. As one example, it considered a privacy challenge to Aadhaar six years after it was filed, and found that Aadhaar was breaking privacy law. It decreed that the scheme should be scaled back, but in the interim it had enrolled a billion people. Privacy activist and legal scholar Gautam Bhatia has called this 'judicial evasion', a delay which allows the status quo to be maintained, in effect a decision for the government. He also emphasizes the creative deployment of equivocation or vagueness: 'although private parties were banned from accessing the Aadhaar database, the ambiguity in the court's holding meant that different parties interpreted the judgment differently—leading to an amendment to the Aadhaar Act that attempts to circumvent the judgment by letting in private parties through the backdoor. This is, once again, a reminder that—much like judicial evasion—ambiguity is not neutral: it primarily benefits the party that has the power to exploit it, and that party is invariably the government.'[32] Other examples of judicial cooperation include a series of delays in hearing challenges to Internet shutdowns, for example in Kashmir, thereby inevitably prolonging them.

FROM KASHMIR TO MOSCOW? INDIAN SPOILERS

India is democratic and speech is protected, but it has a problem with disinformation and misuse of the Internet. Whereas much misinformation across the Internet as a whole crosses borders, most of India's is home-grown, targeting politicians, minority groups, and journalists, and often fuelling sectarian tension. Several people have been lynched on the basis of social media rumours (for instance that they have been involved in slaughtering cows, or kidnapping children), using popular messaging services such as Facebook, WhatsApp, ShareChat, and Helo. Not all these attacks have a sectarian basis; for instance, in one Maharashtrian village, in a febrile atmosphere caused by constant rumours of bandits in the region, first a couple of doctors were attacked, and then two Hindu ascetics and their driver were murdered.[33] One public servant from the Tripura Information and Culture Affairs Department was actually campaigning against rumour-mongering when a rumour was spread about him that he was part of a child-kidnapping team, prompting his murder by a mob.[34]

Responsibility goes to the top. Chapter 13 has given examples of trolling associated with the BJP. The 2019 general election saw a number of messages circulated in BJP-supporting WhatsApp groups claiming falsely that, for instance, opposition Congress politicians gave the family of a Kashmiri suicide bomber financial support.[35]

In the field of culture, the Internet opens up the possibility of expression beyond the narrower confines and regulations of Indian society, so TV channels like Netflix and Amazon Prime are able to host programmes exploring themes of sexual violence and anti-Muslim prejudice. Open platforms also allow coordination of a backlash. For example, the Amazon Prime TV series

Rasbhari, a 2020 romance about a sexy teacher in a small town, was hit by a campaign claiming it was anti-Hindu. It was given preposterously low ratings, and within a week had several hundred one-sentence, one-star reviews. The show's award-winning star was an outspoken critic of the BJP, and had campaigned against the Citizenship Amendment Act the previous year.[36]

In February 2019, shocked, *shocked*, that such manipulation was going on, the government proposed to give itself powers to weaken encryption of data in apps such as WhatsApp, whose end-to-end encryption prevents even the app developers from having access to message content. Compulsory automatic filtering would prevent content of certain kinds reaching Indian citizens, while hate speech, invasions of privacy, and fake news would be the responsibility of platforms to remove—an onerous task that would massively increase the costs of hosting crowdsourced content, as well as privatizing judgments about censorship. Clegg, Facebook's global PR lead, met with a group of Indian ministers to argue the point, offering metadata of 'dubious or suspicious persons', but not retrospectively, and pressed the need for encryption to stay. Independently, WhatsApp had already put certain measures in place, such as restricting the number of messages someone could forward in India (thereby hoping to curb the use of bots), and in general making it harder to forward posts in haste. The trolls' workaround was simply to start more groups, so that they could forward from each one. The high-level talks were inconclusive.[37]

All things being equal, subversion of the Internet is likely to interfere with other government goals, and the BJP government has shown no interest in subverting the Internet outside its own borders (although at least one firm based in Delhi has been accused of providing hacking services for hire internationally).[38] Similarly, the terrible lynchings mentioned at the beginning of this section appear to be the outcome of hateful rumours and panics, rather than the serious attempts to undermine the information space characteristic of the Spoiler model.

There has been no Moscow-style suggestion about making a separate Hindu Internet, but the government is alive to the use of the Internet by opposition movements. It is fair to say that many political disputes in India have led to violence from both rebels and government, such as the conflicts in the North-West (a four-way contest between India, Pakistan, China, and local separatists, which led directly to the assassination of Indira Gandhi in 1984), the North-East (location of multiple separatist insurgencies for decades), and Naxalite rebellions across the East. Protests against the Citizenship Amendment Act also led to riots.

Following the removal of the limited autonomy of Jammu and Kashmir, and its split into two separate union territories, India launched the longest ever shutdown of the Internet in a democracy there, from August 2019 to its easing in January 2020 (but not removal—4G services were only restored in parts of Kashmir as a result of a Supreme Court ruling, in August 2020). This shutdown was accompanied by curfews, travel restrictions, and the detention of a number of prominent figures, and was clearly a tactic to prevent violence in the face of the removal of Kashmiri autonomy. It was certainly not the first shutdown in Kashmir (there had been a 133-day shutdown in 2016). Militant groups continued to mobilize online, for example by uploading short and low-quality video to get round the curbs on Internet speeds.[39] Respected political scientist and public intellectual Pratap Bhanu Mehta argued that, far from Indianizing Kashmir, this will bring on the Kashmirization of India—'a dry run for the political desecration that may follow in the rest of India'.[40]

Both national and individual state governments have resorted to lawful Internet shutdowns in affected regions many times (109 times over 4,000 hours, impacting over 8 million users in 2019 alone, including in Jammu and Kashmir and parts of Assam, West Bengal, and Uttar Pradesh, which cost the economy an estimated $1.3 billion);[41] this is the highest rate of shutdown in the world. As one commentator wrote, 'India is the country that has written the handbook on internet shutdowns'.[42] Thanks to a colonial-era law from 1885, the government has the ability to demand of ISPs that they block all data moving through mobile phone masts and fibre-optic cabling in the affected region. Judicial approval is not needed, and ISPs are obliged to allow government access to user data.[43] This may or may not be a reasonable response to security problems, but if shutdowns are going to remain a key part of Indian policy for the foreseeable future, it will add considerable risk to any attempt to promote the digital economy—for instance, electronic payments such as UPI.

The COVID-19 pandemic also provided opportunities for both government-level and privately organized interference in the Internet. The stringent Indian lockdown occasionally took the form of taking control of online resources. India developed the Aarogya Setu app for contact-tracing, connecting health services and advising users proactively about the risks, best practice, and current state of play. In the high-tech city of Noida near Delhi, download of the app onto smartphones was compulsory, and failure to do so was a violation of the lockdown rules, with a potential six-month sentence. Random checks were promised, and the police commissioner even said, 'If a person does not have a smartphone, they will be asked to get one or fetch it from their homes. Who does not have a smartphone these days?'[44] Er, well, quite a few people in India, as it happens (a mere 600 million). The central government also made it compulsory for air passengers. The app itself was controversial because of data centralization (and frequent shutdowns of the Internet hardly helped its operation!).[45]

More sinisterly, anti-Muslim feeling was exacerbated by a social media campaign against a so-called corona jihad, where Muslims were supposedly deliberately spreading the virus by spitting in food or licking plates. The starting point for this rumour appears to be a religious gathering in New Delhi in March, attended by a number of foreign Muslims, and which may have had the effect of spreading the virus around India. Tests focused only on the participants—it was never shown that they had a greater prevalence of the virus than the rest of the population. Video evidence of the deliberate spread of the virus was all faked, but the false rumour was widely believed, provoked violent incidents, and may well have resulted in Muslims failing to report symptoms of COVID-19 for fear of their own safety.[46]

There are grounds for both optimism and pessimism with respect to India. The quality of communication and quantity of misinformation are troubling, but the mud and scandal is largely internally directed. India does not seem to be adopting the Moscow Spoiler as its brand. The Internet has much space to grow in India, and although at the time of writing the BJP government seems solidly based, it is a democracy, and a change of government is always a possibility. The future influence of India on the global Internet is likely to be enormous, and the direction of that influence is still up for grabs.

Indeed, the very size and diversity of India,[47] combined with its robust private sector, means that it may be that no characteristic Internet emerges consistent with any of the visions we explored in Part II. It may be that two, three, or four of our Internet visions coexist, plagued and perhaps inspired by an enthusiastic body of hackers and spoilers, perhaps merely as a temporary politico-technical collision of styles and aspirations. Or it may be that India's growth and self-sufficiency might even create a stable new type of hybrid of some or all of those styles and visions. The assessment of that is work for the future to be sure—but not the distant future.[48]

Whether one considers its size, strategic importance, vibrant democratic scene, tech industry, or large economy, India ought to be a major player, and it is no surprise that a nationalistic government sees things that way. It is no longer content to be a passive observer of world affairs and recipient of aid, but aims to spread its influence. Considering this, we look at two areas where India is exerting international leadership: identity systems, to round off this chapter, and data nationalism, as the policy question explored in the next. Each of them inclines Indian influence towards support for the Paternal Internet over the other visions we have identified.

EXPORTING INDIAN IDENTITY

India's technological flagship is arguably Aadhaar, the national ID system discussed earlier. Identity is a vital tool of good government, often lacking in emerging economies. It is key to getting access to public services, such as health and education, protecting one's rights, such as property ownership, and getting financial services, such as loans. Governments too need to know who to tax, where to send welfare, who to draft into their armies, and may also want the means to identify wrongdoers. According to the World Bank, a billion of the poorest people lack official identities (one person in two in sub-Saharan Africa). And India has just enrolled a billion people in a decade.

The issue for some countries is a lack of formal registrations, even of births; for others, a transition from ad hoc paper systems to an integrated digital system is needed. Nigeria has three national identity schemes, and several others organized by states. It has a National Identity Management Commission (NIMC), but its programme of national unification and digitization has only reached about 20 percent of the population since 2007.

Aadhaar has already transformed the identity system industry. ID schemes were expensive, partly because providers would insist on locking in their customers with non-interoperable infrastructure, such as enrolment software, biometric scanners, databases, and ID cards, from the same proprietary source, thereby removing competition, raising costs, and minimizing incentives for innovation.[49] Aadhaar changed that, partly because India's size gave it unprecedented buying power, and partly because its scale increased production and reduced prices. It was also able to insist that those building the system used open source infrastructure, to enable competitive bidding across the range of services and hardware.

The industry responded with the development of an open standard, the Open Standards Identity API (OSIA), which is technology neutral with built-in privacy-by-design standards, allowing the modular and scalable construction of registries of citizens, voters, or welfare recipients compatible with each other and with legacy systems. The developers included most of the main companies in the area, such as Gemalto, De La Rue, and IDEMIA—a classic case of an industry being forced out of proprietary rent-seeking into standards-setting by organized buying power, in this case, India alongside others like Nigeria (the head of the NIMC leads OSIA's advisory board). Different companies could construct different parts of a system, while still others could supply services going forward. Note that standards are open, and software developed by one company could be modified by another, but the software would still be proprietary.[50]

As well as transforming the industry, India also has a player in the game. The Modular Open Source Identity Platform (MOSIP),[51] developed at the Institute of Information Technology Bangalore with philanthropic support, was a year or more ahead of OSIA. This is genuinely open source, unlike the OSIA initiative, with a set of modules designed for security and privacy sitting on a platform, with open standards based on ISO biometric standards. If a nation adopted the MOSIP platform, any company with the expertise could implement and integrate the components of the system (MOSIP is cultivating an 'ecosystem' of commercial partners). MOSIP researchers are also working to integrate state-of-the-art privacy-preserving analysis, encryption, public key infrastructure, zero knowledge authentication, access control, and auditing. MOSIP's academic background brings expertise in training, education, and consultancy; individual countries would use this guidance to design, implement, and launch a system based on the platform, depending not only on their requirements, but also on the technical resources they can bring to bear. MOSIP has initial deals with the governments of Morocco[52] and the Philippines.

Hence OSIA and MOSIP are both likely to lead to an acceleration of the number of people globally with a digital identity, opening doors to increased prosperity—and lowering the distance between those people and the Internet. If the two systems were interoperable, which may happen over time with their open philosophies, then so much the better. The effect will be transformative not only for poor populations in certain parts of the world, but also for the Internet as a whole.

Yet ID can be as much a curse as a cure—*apartheid* in South Africa would not have been possible without a robust ID system, and neither would the Rwandan genocide. In a world where ethnic strife is problematic, a set of easy labels is concerning, and biometrics are particularly sensitive, enabling linking across a wide range of databases. The problem is compounded by some nations restricting national citizenship for residents of particular ethnic groups. Kenya (using a proprietary system developed by IDEMIA) wants to register its whole population, for instance, but Nubians have to go through extra steps to prove their nationality. The Kenyan system, like Aadhaar, got ahead of data-protection law, which is easy to do in the system design phase. Not only the technical design, but also the development process, needs to be open to scrutiny and ideally to active participation by engineers, civil society representatives, and the public, in order to decrease the likelihood of the future misuse of the system.[53]

ID systems generally can help the poor and undocumented in important ways. The MOSIP open source approach should help empower governments as well, many of which are not in good bargaining positions, by enabling them to avoid lock-in via its open source methodology. However, although this helpful aspect restores a balance between governments and providers, it cannot by itself furnish parity between governments and their citizens. For this, as argued in a recent white paper, it is also required that the political procurement and design processes are open too, and that users of the system are accountable.[54] There also need to be multiple choices as to how to identify oneself as a citizen or resident, which need to be inclusive, so the choice doesn't affect the services one receives. Without these, ID systems will render the citizen legible to the state, without necessarily making the state equally legible to the citizen.[55]

It is currently unknown whether India will aspire to international leadership (as it did with the Non-Aligned Movement in the Cold War)[56] using Aadhaar/MOSIP strategically to create a sphere of influence in a similar way to China's BRI, or whether it will instead be content to support its technology sector's service export drive. We may speculate that, notwithstanding the diversity of approaches evident within India's borders, its externally facing dealings with Internet governance will be most influential upon the Internet as a whole. The export of ID systems is one aspect of this; another is its position on the free flow of data across borders and data nationalism, which will be the topic of the next chapter.

CHAPTER 17

Policy Question

When Should Personal Data Cross Borders?

It is a cliché to say that data is the new oil. It is certainly a combination of economic opportunity, fuel, lubricant, pollutant, and cause of grievance. Likewise, many nations are beginning to think of data not as a by-product of unregarded processes, but as a national asset to be curated, cosseted, and protected. Against that background, national data regulation is increasing globally, thanks to the cumulative effect of worries about privacy, the digital economy, and national security, and most regulatory changes have restricted rather than facilitated data crossing borders. The trend was already an American concern as early as 2001 in the USA PATRIOT Act, given a push elsewhere after the Snowden revelations of American and British mass surveillance, and accelerated further with the advent of cloud computing (particularly where governments wanted to use international cloud services).[1]

Some regional agreements, including the APEC CBPR (Chapter 7), have tried to liberalize, but as they differ widely in approach they can't constitute a de facto regime. Of the major players, the European Union typically prefers full compatibility with its own strict standards such as GDPR, while the United States is likelier to demand a more lenient data-protection framework alongside stronger prohibitions on data localization and nationalism. Hence the structure of an agreement will tend to vary depending on whether the European Union or the United States is prominent in the consortium. Furthermore, all such agreements include large exceptions for areas such as law enforcement.

In this chapter, we discuss data nationalism, or data sovereignty as it is also called, in more detail, because the flow of data (a) will affect how the

Four Internets. Kieron O'Hara and Wendy Hall, Oxford University Press. © Oxford University Press 2021.
DOI: 10.1093/oso/9780197523681.003.0017

digital economy develops, and (b) is the meat and drink of the Internet. Access controls at borders will inevitably affect its transnational governance.

E-COMMERCE AND CROSS-BORDER DATAFLOWS

The Indian view of data set out in its Data Protection Bill gives data principals a number of powers and rights which are generally subordinate to those abrogated to the state. Whereas in most jurisdictions, tech companies control the data as long as they stick to the law and manage consent, on the Data Protection Bill Indian citizens' data is a national resource, to be defended against foreign attacks and surveillance.[2] This was the pretext for banning TikTok and WeChat after a border skirmish with China in 2020.

Given such a premise, data and cross-border trade are a volatile mix. In a Four Internets world, can we expect agreement on cross-border dataflows, even given the immense economic benefits expected from them? The Europeans might want regulations against spam. Silicon Valley would prefer that digital resources whizzed through customs unmolested—but how would a protectionist American president in DC respond to that while globalization remains unfashionable, especially if the resources were whizzing into the United States and money whizzing out? Would the French (and the Cannes Film Festival in particular) be prepared to drop their counter-insurgency measures against Netflix?[3] Would China see a global data space as a means for allowing the US tech giants to circumvent national regulations and its own sovereignty? Would the European Union put the free flow of data before what it considers to be the human right of privacy, or the smooth running of its proposed Digital Single Market?[4] Would the Chinese or the Indians relax their insistence that data is a national security matter? And what kind of arrangements do hackers, spoilers, and cybercriminals prefer? For them, confusion works better than consensus.

At globalization's spiritual home, Davos, in 2019, trade ministers from seventy-five members of the WTO, between them responsible for 90% of global trade, issued a joint statement on the governance of electronic commerce, agreeing to begin negotiations, under WTO conditions and building on existing WTO commitments, on trade-related aspects of e-commerce. In the words of the Chinese Ministry of Commerce, WTO rules will serve 'the revitalization of the WTO negotiating function and the necessary reform of the WTO, and will help the WTO better respond to calls from the industry and boost the confidence of all in the multilateral trading system and economic globalization at large'.[5]

India, on the other hand, took a mercantilist position and led the holdouts. One commentator argued that the Davos statement 'turned the heat on India'. It would liberate stupendous flows of data, but 'if India is compelled by any future agreement at the WTO to allow unrestricted free flow of data across borders, then its ambition in the high-value digital segment would take a hit. In such a scenario, the country would be unable to monetize the raw material of the digital economy and would be reduced to becoming merely a consumer of digital products'.[6]

The potential for a global economic boost from free flows of data is enormous, but gridlock at the WTO, which requires consensus for agreement, has meant that some nations, not least India and South Africa, have been able to block progress towards lifting barriers to digital trade on this sort of ground.[7] The informal Davos meeting was intended to begin a process where a like-minded group could use WTO structures to dodge the refuseniks and go it alone with sufficient critical mass to make a difference.[8] The opponents of change, led by India, represent the majority of nations in the WTO, but a minority of world trade; they would prefer to stick to the letter of the WTO's 1998 program on e-commerce, which mandates continued exploratory work on trade issues to allow consensus to be achieved (i.e. kicking the issue into the long grass), using WTO amendment procedures to move at the pace of the most cautious, and not giving e-commerce a preferential position vis-à-vis other types of commercial transactions.[9]

Later that year, Japanese Prime Minister Shinzo Abe unveiled the 'Osaka Track' at the G20 group of wealthy nations, to support the 'free flow of data with trust'—the guarantor of trust being adequate protections for personal information and intellectual property, and strong cybersecurity.[10] The United States, China, and Russia were all signatories to the initial agreement, which suggests that pessimism about the likely level of mutual trust is in order; principles may come down to a lowest common denominator. India conspicuously refused to sign, together with other large emerging nations such as Egypt, South Africa, and Indonesia, again because it would undermine the WTO principle of consensus (despite support for the Osaka Track by the then-director general of the WTO).[11]

Data nationalism would be a hard road (India's government would in all likelihood be pressed to take part in these negotiations despite itself, by its IT sector and its multinationals), and the Osaka declaration included warm words about the 'unique challenges' faced by developing nations. It may prove impossible to hold the mercantilist line. As data flows across transnational networks, traditional hierarchies and autarkies historically struggle.

Unlike other cultures that have featured in this book so far, India laboured for some centuries under a colonial yoke, and *Hindutva* is to an extent a reaction against that. Indian politics remains significantly shaped by its colonial experience, and is unsurprisingly sensitive to the exploitative aspects of trade and technology, challenging the globalist view of trade as a straightforward win-win. From this perspective 'the empire building of the likes of Facebook, Google, and Amazon, through the aggressive scaling of their platforms worldwide, suggests neocolonial undertakings',[12] while others have worried that India's smart cities programme (see Chapter 19) is in the tradition of colonial urban planning.[13] This protective view also suits businesses with ambitions to be the one-stop shop for the Indian Internet; Jio has added its voice to complaints about the colonization of India by data-hungry foreigners.[14] Even those who don't subscribe to protectionist feeling, and see data as a significant source of growth, must agree that many developing countries do not have the capacity to participate in the digital economy with home-grown data-driven services, and so would benefit far less from the use of data about their citizens than outsiders.[15]

In the battles over data transfers, India is exercising a negative style of leadership, not unlike its experience as a founder member and driving force of the Non-Aligned Movement, resisting the hegemonic tendencies of the Cold War powers. Whether this will ensure diverse Internet governance or stymie worthwhile efforts at cooperation (or both) remains to be seen.

DATA NATIONALISM AND OUR FOUR INTERNETS

India may aspire to lead the reaction against cross-border dataflows, but it is not an outlier. Many nations are concerned with suppressing dataflow on a global scale. This development is an undoubted boost for those sharing the Beijing Paternal Internet vision.

The other three visions are not sympathetic to data nationalism. On the Silicon Valley Open Internet, data should be as free flowing as possible, shared copiously to create serendipitous opportunities for reuse, and economic and social value. From the DC point of view, economies of scale to be created by holding data in a cloud housed in large data centres hosted in areas with good telecoms, effective transport and power infrastructure, and sympathetic regulation should be exploited, wherever they are based. Indeed, they could also be hosted in such a way as to mitigate the immense impact of the cloud on carbon emissions.[16]

The European Union wants to encourage a single market in data, so the thrust of its policy (like the original data-protection legislation in the 1990s) is to balance economic development and human rights. This also pushes against data nationalism. In data nationalism, data about citizens is held in a particular nation and cannot leave its borders, giving the state a privileged role in its management. The government will almost certainly be able to get access to that data under some circumstances, depending on its data-protection laws and the condition of the rule of law. The Snowden revelations were also important in creating this mood, spreading a widespread sense of vulnerability of defence or commercial secrets to more technically advanced nations. Genuine concerns about privacy and legitimate demands of law enforcement are also drivers of data nationalism, but it still favours the Paternal Internet in ways that GDPR does not.

GDPR prevents personal data about EU citizens from leaving the European Union or the European Economic Area, except in specified circumstances. This is consistent with the Brussels Bourgeois Internet, protecting citizens first and foremost, but it is not a nationalist position. If another jurisdiction can prove equivalence—i.e. that their data protection is up to EU standards— then data can be transferred to them (assuming the transfer would be legal in the EU). The European Commission decides the equivalence of a non-EU country—i.e. whether it shows due respect for others.[17]

Hence the EU doctrine of equivalence is different from data nationalism/ sovereignty, the hallmark of the Paternal Internet. Data nationalism demands that data about citizens of a particular nation is held in that nation, as we have seen with the Indian Data Protection Bill. It differs, therefore, from GDPR, in two ways: first, GDPR isn't a national restriction, as the European Union and associated nations in the European Economic Area are already several jurisdictions (so, e.g. data about French citizens can legally be held in Romania and vice versa); and second, data can leave the European Union where protection is equivalent. Most European companies use US cloud providers, even though the US Cloud Act of 2018 allows local authorities to order US providers to turn over any company's data stored on servers regardless of where that company is based.

In short, on the Silicon Valley Open Internet, data should flow where it can be processed most efficiently and create the most value. On the DC Commercial Internet, pretty much the same holds, though with emphasis on economic value. The cloud, though, is increasingly sensitive to geographical boundaries. On the Brussels Bourgeois Internet, trust doesn't extend to all foreigners, and dataflow should be limited to like-minded trustworthy places. On the Beijing Paternal Internet, governmental access to the data and ultimate control of the data environment depend on keeping the data within the jurisdiction.

The US government presents a hybrid case, as it is similarly concerned with access to data, and is certainly not against putting Paternalist pressures on those holding data about US citizens, but it generally prefers to pursue surveillance through superior technical ability and/or commercial pressures. The legal stand-off in 2016 between Apple and the FBI when the former refused to disable security features on an iPhone belonging to a dead terrorist was an example of the complexities in this area. The long-running dispute between the US government and the tech industry, about limiting the spread of encryption strong enough to stymie law enforcement agencies, has been called the *crypto wars*. In the crypto wars, the US government is unusually at odds with both its Silicon Valley Openness advocates and the DC Commercial lobby, even though one of the arguments for open standards and strong encryption of data is that it makes the United States more secure.[18] The security would be provided not (directly) by the state's law enforcement arm, but rather by the skills and incentives of the cybersecurity industry, combined with American technological leadership, and so worries paternalists within the US national security sphere. Mueller goes so far as to say 'only a business-civil society alliance can prevent a dangerous alliance between state intelligence and law enforcement agencies and the major private sector Internet intermediaries who control so much data', and goes on to warn that by attacking business, 'anti-capitalist movements within civil society will . . . end up empowering territorial states and reinforcing alignment'.[19] As we have seen, similar arguments for openness have been made against the Trump administration's pursuit of Huawei.

However, data nationalism is unlikely to be applied rigidly or universally, because the economies of scale that cloud computing provides make it too valuable to reject. Many nations are prepared to take an economic hit for the principle of Internet sovereignty, but only within limits. China and India, and maybe Russia too, are large enough to sustain a local cloud, but smaller countries, if they cut themselves off from global providers, may end up without cloud services at all.

Technology may come to the rescue with federated storage and querying, but it is not clear how practical a solution that will be. It is also possible to imagine other groups of like-minded nations than the European Union coalescing around rules and standards to transfer data across their own borders, without letting the data go further. One or two schemes trade on this possibility, such as GAIA-X, a German initiative to produce a European cloud distributed across many countries (hence known as the 'Airbus Cloud'), to allow European data to be kept in Europe, away from the United States or elsewhere. GAIA-X is an example of paternal data regionalism, in addition to GDPR-style standards protection. Economically, it may struggle given its lack of scale compared to the major US providers, and consequent lack of ability to assure personalized service and tight security, and it is fair to say that there is scepticism about its prospects.[20]

CHAPTER 18

Artificial Intelligence

The data-driven AI revolution has been a theme running through this book; indeed, AI is perhaps the signature technology of digital modernity. There is a strong connection between the growth of the Internet, the production of data, and the development of AI, so that, as we argued at the beginning, today's AI is perhaps better thought of as a type of data science. AI has typically been characterized as the use of a machine to do something which, if performed by a human, would require intelligence. This isn't entirely satisfactory, partly because of the ambiguity of 'intelligence'—does it mean any kind of cognitive capacity, or some form of explicit reasoning, or could it include apparently instinctive things, such as pattern recognition? If the latter, then which instincts are 'intelligent' and which not? Is it necessarily creative and mysterious, or can it be algorithmic and rule-based? Must it include the ability to pose a problem and motivate its solution, or could it be merely problem-solving within an exogenously defined context? And does the machine have to solve the problem in the same way as the human? What if the machine does something that massively improves on human intelligence, that couldn't be achieved by humans in real time?

While these philosophical issues have rumbled on in the background, AI has become a buzzword, with lavish predictions of its ability to revolutionize industry. Here is where the data tsunami comes in; the AI we are concerned with today is different from the rule-based and knowledge-based systems of its pioneers. AI now exploits probabilistic machine learning (ML) algorithms, to (a) develop a model of relationships between what is expressed in the terms in a quantity of sample or training data, and then (b) improve the model in response to human correction or more data. The more data, the more interesting, accurate and surprising the models.

Four Internets. Kieron O'Hara and Wendy Hall, Oxford University Press. © Oxford University Press 2021.
DOI: 10.1093/oso/9780197523681.003.0018

ML and AI have moved closer to each other since the 1980s, when the probability focus of the former clashed with the logical base of the latter; *deep learning* (neural networks with several layers of nodes between the input and output nodes) has been a central advance,[1] and clever infrastructures such as Hadoop that support fast and efficient data storage, retrieval, and analysis have also been important.[2] Given sufficient data, ML algorithms can work out clusters (divide a domain into groups so that diversity is minimized within the groups and maximized between them), associations (people like you enjoyed this recommended book/film/news story), predictions (suggesting unknown values based on known values, such as who you vote for based on your spending patterns), and outliers (such as spotting unusual spending patterns on your credit card). This is their basic suite of functions, but given the massively increased computing power that Moore's Law and the cloud have given us, and the abundant data upon which to train the algorithms, ML is far more powerful than it was even a few years ago. It can now be the basis for intelligent problem-solving.

These models can be used for prediction or decision-making, and—particularly over very large datasets ('big data')—can discern relationships that would be impossible to detect manually. Why should this be? Humans make their inferences based on strong features that obviously correlate with outcomes, and often feature in causal models of the domain, but which are also psychologically salient. Someone explaining a car crash will look at the car's speed, the road conditions, the driver's alcohol levels, and so on. When we have sparse data and bounded (i.e. human) rationality, this is a very effective heuristic. Machines go further by taking into account unintuitive weak features, with no obvious correlations or psychological salience. Maybe, when we have zillions of examples in our dataset, unexpected or downright mysterious correlations can be identified; because of the large sample, they are unlikely to be mere artefacts of biased data. These correlations may not chime with common sense—they could correlate a car crash with occupation, diet, weather, time of day, or the recent performance of the driver's sports team. Knowing about these subtle correlations doesn't help explain why they should be so, or what the direction of causation is, if any. But it can provide inferential power in a number of areas, such as medical diagnosis and face recognition, that may often outdo that of a human, within the relevant timescale (i.e. in minutes rather than weeks). The key developments are the very large quantities of data that have become available, the improvement of computing hardware, and fast infrastructure for large-scale data storage, retrieval, and processing. Deep learning turns out to give particularly impressive results.[3]

AI is currently seen as a driver of the digital economy, and many companies are investing in the relevant technology and human resources; being a data scientist is currently a reliable route to a large monthly pay cheque. Nations also see AI as an important route to prestige and economic growth. President Putin has argued, with slight hyperbole, that 'whoever becomes the leader in this sphere will become the ruler of the world',[4] while President Xi told his Politburo that leadership in AI was essential for ensuring China's future.[5] AI is a key part of the Made in China 2025 initiative, via the IT and robotics industries. One of the authors of this book (Hall) jointly led a review of the AI industry in the United Kingdom in 2017,[6] and is at the time of writing the UK AI skills champion.

The promise of AI, then, is the promise of data and the techniques to unlock its secrets. Since the Internet is a prime supplier of data, as well as the main data transport infrastructure, the ideologies underlying our Four Internets are likely to have a powerful effect on how the AI industry develops in different contexts. Some assume that the United States and China have in-built advantages in AI, and that the future of the industry is therefore in the hands of these two nations.[7] Whether or not that assumption is accurate, the reason that the industry appears to be balanced in that way is largely because of the visions of the Internet espoused in those countries.

There are two important questions to be asked about the data involved in AI. First, what is the information it expresses about? To state the obvious, some topics are more interesting than others, depending on what problems you want to solve. Many industries have commercial opportunities for AI, and relevant data, for example about manufacturing processes or the performance of manufactured items, is consequently more valuable. Information about people is naturally relevant to a number of areas ranging from healthcare to policymaking, and often is highly adaptable to different contexts; it is also, of course, the most sensitive. Second, who can get at it? A lot of data is proprietary, so that it remains the property of the company which gathered it, or perhaps which inferred it from other datasets. It is quite possible that the answers to these two questions will reveal bias and special interests of which it is essential to be aware if we are to interpret the results.[8]

The more training data for an AI algorithm, the better, all things being equal. Hence it is important to pull as much data together in a single training dataset as possible. All things are not always equal, however. Sometimes, yoking together data from different sources leads to confusion. The datasets may not use the same representation formats and measurement standards, and aggregating data requires complex cleaning and integration. There are also techniques that allow several individual datasets to be queried without anyone getting an overview of the whole set; these are currently too specialized for routine use, but the field of federated ML improves all the time. Nevertheless, such algorithms still need to be granted access to the data in the first place.

Internet governance will crucially affect these issues, and particularly where they intersect, i.e. which types of data can be brought together easily and by whom? The Silicon Valley Open Internet espouses a disinterested, scientific ideal where data is maximally available, and as much data as possible is open, shared, or redistributed. Much can be done with open data, and opening up data to fresh eyes not only can add value to the data by allowing it to be reused in unanticipated contexts, but also can help the organization that created the datasets, for example by helping it understand the data resources it has, facilitating improvements in quality or improving insights. Like the environments in which we live, on this view the information environment should be a collective asset created and augmented by use of common resources, amalgamating our digitally extended selves or 'footprints'. Clearly there are issues and potential clashes between privacy and transparency, but these should be manageable, with proper precautions, and the risk has to be weighed against the potential benefits.[9]

The problem is that although there are incentives to open up and share data, there are also many blockers to doing it, not least a concern that collecting data entails costs to an organization which it may not get back if others use it for their own purposes. This worry about sharing was a major concern for Hall and Pesenti in their report on the AI industry.[10] Hence, although the Open Internet is a marvellous infrastructure for sending data around, without incentives data can't be guaranteed to be shared. We either need means or institutions to support sharing data, or alternatively to reduce the rights of data holders (for example, by increasing the rights of data subjects).[11] The unintended consequence, however, is that either of these measures might reduce the incentives to gather, store, and curate data in the first place, and so we would end up with less data than the current abundance. The open data field is also having to adapt to the world of disinformation ushered in by the Moscow Spoiler, so a laissez-faire attitude will be hard to commit to.[12] Attention therefore shifts to our other three Internets.

AI ON THE DC COMMERCIAL INTERNET

On the DC Commercial Internet, data is collected by companies to create economic value. Protections against abuse are triggered by tangible and quantifiable harms (i.e. physical, financial, or reputational harm), and it is the responsibility of the sufferer to sue. The so-called third-party doctrine in US law means that when someone shares their data or gives consent for data about them to be used, they cede their rights, so it can then be sold on to anyone who can put the data to better use by extracting even more value from it.[13] On this view, if data can be monetized, it should be.

It follows that companies have two potential routes to creating the critical mass to exploit data's predictive power. One is to pool data with others, creating the data-sharing problem described earlier. The other is to try to grow the network, to leverage network effects. This is the strategy of the big tech platforms, from Google to Facebook, and also of more domain-specific platforms, such as Netflix and Uber. Hence we see the growth of a strange type of economics where the associated network is seen as valuable, even in the absence of profits; the business model to exploit the network can follow the development of the network, and investors won't be impatient to see returns. The bet of the DC Commercial Internet is that more social value is created by such private networks than by networks which are not allowed to monopolize the data. Even if much of the value of the network goes to whoever builds it, many others benefit as a by-product of their activity, as when the development of private railways benefitted the entire community in Victorian Britain.

What this means in AI terms is that the major platforms, such as Google, Facebook, and Amazon, have built-in advantages in AI. Commercial rules prevent government, competitors, or civil society from diverting data from use by its owners, and so AI expertise will tend to agglomerate in certain large companies. They benefit disproportionately, but their quasi-monopolies will promote innovation (while over-regulation will hinder it), and they will be able to monetize their expertise and redistribute insight by selling AI services where there is demand. Where there is a public need, governments will be able to step in and buy services, as it does to provide other public goods, from roads to defence. AI for the public good could simply use commercial algorithms and other services on public data for a fee, or the service providers could receive access to the data under controlled conditions so that governments get expensive analyses for small financial outlay.[14]

If there are harms to individuals, they need to be litigated and compensated. This means that transparency is a key tool, so that companies can be held accountable for their actions. If benefits from AI turn out to be very unequal, so that large swathes of the population end up out of work for example, then it would be preferable for government to provide a safety net and help in reskilling, rather than for it to dampen innovation.[15] Another issue often raised about the tech industry is a problem with lack of diversity in its engineers; the response of the DC Commercial Internet is that diversity should increase profits, and therefore should eventually transpire without intervention. Rich data about diverse groups of people will help create products and services for a wider range of people; a more diverse cadre of engineers will promote the design of products for a wider range of customers. Problems such as these, on this view, should be self-correcting via the profit motive.[16]

The position is different with respect to the Beijing Paternal Internet. In his compelling account of Chinese AI, Lee argues that the age of massive AI break-throughs, led by American companies and scientists, is being superseded by an age of implementation, applying and adapting algorithms to the dull prob-lems of everyday life.[17] On this account, China has the advantage, in terms both of the national skillset, and of the numbers of scientists it can deploy on these incremental innovations.[18] AI is no longer, on this view, an elite busi-ness. Lee characterizes Chinese business as much more integrated, getting involved in all the details;[19] he also emphasizes how China's being a manufac-turing hub is important for the hardware.[20]

This has resulted in competitive advantage. Its Internet economy gener-ates far more data than any other.[21] Apps such as WeChat have become dom-inant for communication and mobile payments.[22] Many unglamorous aspects of life are being 'datafied'. Expatriate Chinese bring their online habits with them, which have started to spread throughout the West as a result. The data is stored in China and therefore accessible to the Chinese government. As a state with a large surveillance industry, it also has access to data from CCTV and other sources. All this data is immensely important to Chinese data sci-ence. It hopes to lead in AI, and has made advances in areas such as face rec-ognition and autonomous vehicles. Other aspects of the industry beyond the scope of this book, such as the development of special-purpose AI chips, are also being coordinated.[23] Its less-developed status helps as well in terms of social and industrial adaptability; whereas the United States is restricting the use of autonomous vehicles and worrying about pedestrian deaths, China is able to build and adapt cities to accommodate them.[24] It can create contact-tracing apps without worrying about data protection. Safety is far less of an issue—or put another way, China can afford to take a longer view than the United States, and hasten 'the implementation of technology that will save tens if not hundreds of thousands of lives in the not-too-distant future'.[25]

This is not to say that China's stance on AI is not informed by ethical prin-ciples. It released the Beijing AI Principles in 2019, which are similar to other sets of national guidelines, not least in being rather bland and focusing on promoting social good. Specifically Chinese twists included the exhortation that users of AI systems should be wise enough to use them properly, and in the mention of harmony as a goal, to be sought by the philosophy of 'opti-mizing symbiosis'.[26]

The reality of the application of AI in China challenges some of these Principles. Pervasive surveillance is hard to square with some of them, while their injunctions to be diverse and inclusive and to reduce bias doesn't sit too well with the state's treatment of minority populations and restive provinces such as Xinjiang and Tibet. It seems somewhat unlikely that the national AI strategy will be derailed by over-strict adherence to the Principles.[27]

Most commentators welcomed the Principles as evidencing a common view across the major AI powers about the ethical issues created by AI, and what can be done. This may be optimistic; the government of President Xi is fairly relaxed about obeying its own laws, and so it seems unlikely that it will feel any more bound by a set of ethical principles, although its companies may take it as an important steer. There is in any case not a great deal of evidence that the flurry of sets of unobjectionable AI ethics codes released in the last few years has actually affected anyone's behaviour very much in any jurisdiction.

The key point is that the state gets to define 'harmony'. AI is a particularly valuable technology because it supports the claim of technocratic efficiency (combined with the unique ability of the Communist Party to implement it) that underpins the government's account of its own legitimacy. AI is a signifier of digital modernity. It promises to boost the Chinese economy, and during Chinese-American trade tension becomes a critical industry for national security, because China will need to increase self-sufficiency. It is also a means for reconfiguring society, with the twin potential, (i) to improve provision of social services such as education and healthcare, and (ii) to suppress unrest and steer social development in 'harmonious' directions.[28]

Note that the Chinese government doesn't actually have to get at the data, or to force its companies to use it in particular ways. Like their American counterparts, Tencent, Alibaba, and Baidu have enough data to develop impressive AI independently. However, because of the alignment of Chinese business and government, activity in the former (as well as other business sectors such as capital investment) can usually be steered towards the policy goals of the latter, notably with respect to the BRI and the Made in China 2025 initiative. Chinese local government is also influential, as mayors turn their cities into AI hubs.[29] And if the worst comes to the worst, China's data nationalism means that the data is always within reach in its jurisdiction. All told, China is able to muster vital inputs—data, entrepreneurs, data scientists—within an AI-friendly policy environment.[30]

China's labour market affords other advantages, where willing human labour can perform low-level tasks essential for the smooth running of AI for a small wage. Content moderation is one such area; another is data labelling. A secret of AI is that a lot of preparation of data is needed before it is ready for automatic analysis, including checking quality. Data scientists devote much (no one quite knows how much, but it's a lot)[31] of their time to this prosaic work, understanding the data and getting it into shape. Data, recall, is merely 1s and 0s. It does not mean anything, but is crafted in order to be a vehicle for meaning, and without a grasp of what information the data expresses, scientists will find it harder to craft the algorithm to learn the statistical associations that will underpin their discoveries.

This is true of all data, but particularly obvious with image, pattern, or video recognition. To train an algorithm to recognize pictures of buildings requires a large set of images labelled as buildings or otherwise, some ontological relations between labels (such as, for instance, a *house* is a type of *building* and a *roof* is part of a *house*), and the ability to recognize ambiguities (for instance, do we class a *doll's house* or a *tipi* or *teepee* as a *building*?). This is simple for an individual image, but hard to generate the vast amount of labelled data needed for ML training data, because building-recognition is time-consuming and no one's hobby. And, of course, what goes for buildings also applies to any other concrete noun, from boats to cats to guns to rubbish to supernovae to thimbles.

Labelling data is a multi-billion-dollar business,[32] and a problem which different nations have to solve in different ways; we will see other solutions in Chapter 20 on social machines. China has used its vast labour resources to create a labelling industry, where for a small salary (but a tempting one in poor regions) hundreds of thousands of taggers label images to create enormous training sets for ML. This turns out to be important, as the general quality of Chinese data is lower than that of the United States, whose IT sectors use standardized business systems, which create AI-friendly datasets, far more routinely.[33]

China is *sui generis*, but other nations will wish to follow their Paternal vision. India, as we have argued, may well favour this model, and certainly has similarities to China, including a critical mass of users, a world-class AI industry, and an embedded data world in which increasingly many 'messy details of food delivery, car repairs, shared bikes and purchases at the corner store'[34] are being turned into data. Against this, India's government, though it carries weight, has far less leverage than China's to insist business goes in a particular direction, not least because in a democratic country there is always the possibility of it being replaced at the next election. A recent think tank strategy paper envisaged the government's role in developing the AI industry in relatively hands-off terms: setting up centres of excellence, training, and education, promoting data sharing, opening up government datasets, brokering partnerships, and drawing up the ethical code without which no national AI industry is complete.[35]

On the other hand, Indian citizens appear to have stronger privacy concerns than those of China, and we will have to wait for the full effects of implementation of the Data Protection Bill to emerge. Furthermore, the costs of failed innovation in India are somewhat higher than in wealthier countries, where moving fast and breaking things is unlikely to cause too much social harm. One commentator has even argued that the poor need less digital innovation, not more, at least with respect to education.[36]

As a democracy, the scope of Indian paternalism is limited. Authoritarian regimes have a greater ability to act, even if they are handicapped by small populations and relatively weak AI expertise. Saudi Arabia's Vision 2030 initiative is intended to transform the Saudi economy away from fossil fuels, to guarantee revenues to citizens well into the future, and not incidentally to secure the survival of the House of Saud. Oil revenue is parked in its sovereign wealth fund, the Public Investment Fund (PIF), which gives the government, driven by Crown Prince Mohammed bin Salman, extra leverage beyond the physical force which it is also prepared to use liberally. Augmenting overexcited symbolic gestures such as granting citizenship to a humanoid robot called Sophia, the PIF has committed $500 billion to build a new technology city the size of Belgium, called Neom, powered by renewable energy, where AI and robotics will be embedded into every aspect of life. It will sprawl into Jordanian and Egyptian territory, and will have an autonomous judicial system.[37] Neom at the time of writing sits largely on the drawing board, but its first phase is due for completion in 2025. It may end up as a white elephant, as so many artificial cities do (not least in China), but it is bound to influence the Saudi ambition to become a technology hub, and will no doubt lead to many discoveries about how such an environment may work.

AI ON THE BRUSSELS BOURGEOIS INTERNET

Lee (as do Hall and Pesenti in their UK AI report) lays emphasis on the local AI environment to deliver a world-class industry,[38] but can only see a 'bipolar world order' (by 'bipolar' he presumably doesn't mean 'manic-depressive', although relations between China and the Trump administration made that an all too plausible interpretation when he wrote his book). Rather, he is dismissive of the competition: 'Several other countries—the United Kingdom, France, and Canada, to name a few—have strong AI research labs staffed with great talent, but they lack the venture-capital ecosystem and large user bases to generate the data that will be key to the age of implementation.'[39]

This is somewhat defeatist, and the neat US/China distinction is, as we have argued, not nuanced enough anyway. In terms of expertise, good ideas, and va-va-voom, Europe is not in a bad position, especially if we continue to include London alongside Berlin, Paris, Amsterdam, and other tech hotspots. In terms of our overarching theme of data, however, the European Union may be behind the curve. In a world of giant private data monopolies, or where the government has power to influence how data is collected, stored, and used over a continent-sized swathe of territory, critical mass can be achieved and value extracted by first-rate data science. Relative to those contexts, the European Union suffers three major handicaps. First, it has a more fragmented AI industry, with fewer global players. Second, it is culturally fragmented, with different languages and jurisdictions across the continent (language doesn't matter in theory to data, but in practice mnemonic names for variables, classes, and other elements help in the interpretation and integration of data). Third, GDPR imposes a strong privacy-protective legal framework which hinders opportunistic exploitation of personal data, likely to be the most valuable in many important domains.

There are five main reasons to think GDPR will hinder big data analysis of personal data. First, its fines are swingeing, and the costs of compliance are high, so it's expensive if you're legal and eye-watering if you aren't. This presents a particular challenge for small and medium-sized enterprises, and as Europe has a lot of those and few deep-pocketed giants, it's self-harming.

Second, the GDPR principle that personal data has to be collected for a specific purpose goes against the big data idea of serendipitous reuse. It is intended to limit misuse of data, on the civil law strategy of anticipating harms and neutralizing them, rather than the common law principle of remedying and regulating harms as they happen (common law would allow more experimentation from data processors). The result again handicaps small start-ups, which often take information in one market and apply it elsewhere, and favours larger monopolies with horizontal integration and access to data subjects.[40]

Third, the data minimization principle, that data held should be limited to what is necessary for the specified purpose, in terms of scope, categories of data, and duration of holding, means that it should be deleted a short period of time after processing. Again, this intuitively pushes against the promise of big data as improvements in data science create more opportunities for analysis, as well as (currently) unspecifiable longitudinal research.[41]

Fourth, GDPR puts emphasis on protecting some specific categories of personal data, about topics such as ethnic origin, political views, healthcare, genetic data, and biometric data. The problem with big data is that it cuts across these categories, so that one might infer health-related information from itemized supermarket credit card bills, location, and orientation data from a smartphone (from which the owner's speed and mode of travel can be estimated), or address data (combined with non-personal data on pollution or population density), so the GDPR sensitive categories are either too expansionary, or alternatively won't do the protective job that they are intuitively meant to. Discrimination in ML is usually unanticipated, because it abstracts away from hard, psychologically salient concepts with obvious causal connections. ML, when it is discriminatory, is rarely intentional, but rather is an unanticipated and unpredictable result of weak correlations in the data that happen to produce discriminatory outcomes if we act upon them. The question then is whether the layered regime of different categories of data adds anything other than complexity and expense.[42]

Fifth and finally, the GDPR demands that automated decision-making must be explained to data subjects, who should be able to remove themselves from its scope. The uncertainties this brings may inhibit the use of ML and automatic processing of data for efficiency or scalability in problem-solving.[43]

This inhibition is merely the flip side of the less transactional Brussels Bourgeois Internet. Its vision is concerned with human rights and avoiding harms, prepared to forgo potential benefits, whether in terms of profits, engineering efficiency, social stability, or security, when individual rights are put at risk. Hence it is unsurprising that it is at a disadvantage with respect to those regimes which aim at one of these particular benefits, when they amalgamate data freely and process personal data opportunistically.

Nevertheless, there are stronger Bourgeois responses than merely noting the trade-off. One, focusing on the 'Brussels effect', is that GDPR has set a global standard in rights-respecting data analysis, and that the combination of the size of the European Union's markets and the extent of its data protection expertise means that companies from outside the EU will ultimately have to adapt to its ethical concerns.[44] A second view is that the standard itself will allow data subjects to 'have their cake and eat it'; trustworthy and rights-respecting data analytics are likely to produce a very high level of provision anyway, while mitigating breaches in rights.[45]

A third, Burkean, view is that when we discuss the potential benefits of 'runaway' AI, we rarely focus on the key word: 'potential'. The industry has not yet achieved the levels of productivity promised, and may never do. Accuracy is likely to remain a problem (consider a recent case when a smart camera with 'in-built, AI, ball-tracking technology' live-streaming a Scottish football match repeatedly confused the linesman's bald head with the ball).[46] To sacrifice existing, concrete rights and levels of respect for the abstract, projected benefits of untrammelled surveillance or overweening monopoly is premature if not irrational.

A fourth response is that the AI industry thrives on trust, which has been hit by data misuse scandals such as Cambridge Analytica (which acquired data on millions of Facebook users without their consent in 2016 for use in political advertising),[47] and it would be undermined in large parts of the world if such misconduct went unchecked. GDPR (or some variant) is essential in the long run to define and support the trustworthy data stewardship that is required for the AI industry to flourish.

All told, if the technology is effective, its prospects are currently unfulfilled, and may remain so. GDPR symbolizes what would be sacrificed if we genuflect to the hype. What is certain is that decisions about the implementation of GDPR will have to be made before the trajectory of the industry is known. As case law is made, the CJEU will interpret it broadly or narrowly, and will be more or less tolerant of data-protection breaches, exceptions, and loopholes, and then we will have more of a sense of how restrictive it will be. By then, though, the course will be set, and too late to change.

We should finally note that strong data protection can be accommodated by functional anonymization,[48] privacy-preserving ML, or secure multiparty computation,[49] where cryptographic techniques and access controls to data combine to allow querying of datasets without revealing the individual pieces of data. A number of systems aim to provide privacy-preserving ML as a service for customers who have data but lack the expertise, concealing the training data from the service operator, and the training algorithm and the model structure from the user. The model is presented to the outside world as a black box. Training performance and accuracy of the resulting models are practical for common uses of ML-as-a-service.[50]

One example drew attention as an analysis of COVID-19-related health data. OpenSAFELY is an initiative of Ben Goldacre and Liam Smeeth of the United Kingdom's National Health Service (NHS), who brought together academic researchers and private-sector data analysts to query pseudonymized NHS data in situ, rather than centralizing it; the level of pseudonymization (a weaker type of anonymization) is sensitive to the needs of the research. An added advantage in the fast-moving environment of COVID-19 of leaving the data in its secure NHS data centres is that it is then always up to date, as well as being protected. Code and procedures are open for inspection, auditing, and reuse. The project produced valuable scientific insights within a few weeks of being set up in 2020. This solution will not be available everywhere (impossible in the fragmented US healthcare industry), but the NHS, with its near-universal coverage of a large population, is an unusual resource, particularly in Europe, which has enabled this approach to bear fruit.[51]

We can view these creative and innovative techniques in two ways. One view is that they demonstrate the possibility of innovation in realizing the value of personal data while preserving the dignity of and respect for data subjects. The problems set by GDPR are hardly insurmountable. The alternative, and not contradictory, position is that these are difficult and expensive techniques, understandable only by a tiny cadre of experts, to overcome the self-inflicted obstacle posed by an over-prescriptive view of a disputed human right.

Either way, it seems clear that the AI industry can certainly function within the parameters set by GDPR. But the contrast between the rarefied cutting-edge expertise demanded by the self-constraint of the Brussels Bourgeois Internet and the pugnacious opportunism that flourishes within the Beijing and DC Internets couldn't be more telling.

CHAPTER 19

Smart Cities and the Internet of Things

The data that powers AI has arrived in waves. The first wave consisted of online interactions, and then as e-commerce, business-to-business, and e-government took off, we saw a second wave of business data. Instrumenting the physical world is producing a third wave, and as AI develops autonomous systems, we are beginning to see a fourth wave of extremely detailed and rich data generated by automated production.[1] In the third of these waves, data is released from the bottleneck of the keyboard or device interface; no longer do people have to type stuff in, because sensors will be able to gather more. In the fourth wave, machine-to-machine (M2M) interactions can create quantities of data equivalent to many thousands of complex human transactions on very short timescales. As a couple of examples of this, AlphaGo, which beat the world (human) Go champion, amassed data by playing against itself millions of times,[2] while the Chinese news company Toutiao came to understand fake news by competing against an algorithm to write false stories.[3]

THE INTERNET OF THINGS

The instrumented world is usually referred to as the Internet of Things (IoT), the result of the use of Internet protocols to allow wireless M2M communication, when the machines have IP addresses and are embedded in objects in the environment.[4] These could be household gadgets, items worn by people, things carried by people, transport vehicles, components of larger machines, the built environment (doors, floors, lights, etc.), the natural environment,[5] or anything. Technologies such as RFID, Bluetooth, and ubiquitous wireless, the cloud, GPS, and improved APIs to support M2M communication have all played their part. Thanks to Moore's Law,

Four Internets. Kieron O'Hara and Wendy Hall, Oxford University Press. © Oxford University Press 2021.
DOI: 10.1093/oso/9780197523681.003.0019

these communicators can be highly miniaturized, and therefore practically invisible or ambient. As the first important paper about the IoT (or 'ubiquitous computing') argued, 'the most profound technologies are those that disappear. They weave themselves into the fabric of everyday life until they are indistinguishable from it.'[6]

The 'things' of the IoT can be physical or virtual, existing only in software realizations. They are usually quite simple and so not intelligent on their own. But when a group of them are networked, the system as a whole can exhibit intelligent behaviour. This is a type of AI distributed over a network of objects, usually indicated by the adjective *smart*: we talk of smart homes, smart workplaces, and as we shall see, smart cities.

The communicating chips typically send messages to or receive them from other machines. The most important items are *sensors*, which detect parameter values about the objects in which they are embedded and communicate those values wirelessly, and *actuators*, which receive instructions and cause their objects to do something. So, for instance, part of an aero-engine can tell its owner when it is getting worn or overheated; a door can count the number of people entering a room and close when it has reached capacity; a wrist-worn device can gather data about its wearer's heart-rate or the number of steps they have taken; autonomous vehicles can send data about speed and congestion to a central planning system, as well as receiving instructions updating maps or routes to the destination; a hospital application can monitor patients' vital signs, increase or lower oxygen supplies, and alert medical staff to emergencies; smart shelves in supermarkets can tell when supplies are running low and send instructions to retrieve more from the store or order more from the warehouse. The IoT has impacted most directly on individuals via smart speakers hosting voice-controlled virtual assistants such as Amazon Echo/Alexa, Tmall Genie/AliGenie, or Google Nest Hub, and smart meters to monitor utility use in the home. It is routine to predict that the IoT will be of enormous economic value and size in terms of devices enabled. Current figures suggest spending on the IoT is in the hundreds of billions of dollars annually and is on course to pass $1 trillion in the early 2020s, which is about the point at which there will be more devices connected to the Internet than people on the planet (there are already more devices than people connected to the Internet).[7]

There are, of course, ethical and political problems raised by increasing the intelligence of our environment, homes, and workplaces. One recent survey set out five broad problem headings.[8] First, there is *informed consent*. Since IoT devices are ambient, they literally recede into the background, and may be passing information on, unknown to the data subject.[9] One particular surprise was an Internet-enabled sex toy that passed email addresses of registrants, together with times of use and vibration settings, to the manufacturer (no doubt to improve future generations of products rather than to spy voyeuristically, but still . . .).[10] Had that been clear in the original granting of consent, it wouldn't have been a shock for the owner. The second issue is *privacy*, which is intuitively threatened by an instrumented environment, and the sex toy again illustrates this.[11] Third, there is a *security* issue, in that these devices are generally exposed in the open, with wireless connections that can easily be intercepted, and miniaturization which requires a trade-off between battery life and processing power, and therefore limited scope for encryption of data.[12] In one widely reported incident, a hacking attack on a casino was launched through the Internet-enabled thermometer of a smart fishtank.[13] Security and privacy go together: imagine a hack into an augmented reality system so an unknown intruder could see exactly what your smart glasses could see as you looked through them. Fourth, there is *physical safety*, the importance of ensuring that the IoT device doesn't lead to real-world harm or financial loss—consider medical equipment or autonomous vehicles. Finally, there is *trust*, the need for people to be comfortable in an environment seeded with Internet-enabled devices as described. How transparent will such devices be? Would one even know one was in such an environment (for example, in a room rented through Airbnb)?[14]

The legal question of liability could also get very complex (for example, if two autonomous vehicles crash, which is responsible? Given an answer to that question, does the buck stop with the designer, the software creator, the producer, the owner, the occupant, or the administrators of servers or data infrastructure?). Some commentators have despaired at the possibility of regulating the IoT effectively with binding law, and prefer an industry-based self-regulatory regime set by international convention.[15]

Legal and social systems, democratic practice, and individual choice are being transformed, often without debate, by *data-driven agency*[16] or *economies of action*.[17] The inclusion of our familiar city, town, home, transport, and workplace environments into the Internet transforms them into spaces where our preferences, desires. and needs are probabilistically calculated and anticipated, very possibly before we realize there was a choice to be made, and our behaviour at that point is fed back into the system as even more data. The IoT backed by AI techniques turbocharges this kind of agency, allowing interventions which shape choices and possibly even modify behaviour by exploiting psychological insight, challenging a range of assumptions about how plural societies negotiate conflict, underpinned by democratic choice and the rule of law. Furthermore, opting out of surveillance and oversight may mean that one becomes invisible to the state or service providers;[18] if service provision becomes tied to the flow of data from the environment, then trying to exit or avoid the system will mean one effectively waives one's rights (remember the cases of starvation in India where ration cards were not connected to Aadhaar). This will always be a risk of a 'digital by default' strategy.

SMART CITIES

One important application of the IoT and AI combined is the so-called *smart city*. Smart cities are research programmes integrating a heterogeneous set of technologies to use the power of data to manage technology to regulate a location, which is usually an estate or neighbourhood rather than an entire town or city. Efficiency in this sense tends to mean achieving public goals by either 'nudging' the behaviour of individuals, or closing down choices.[19] Typical aims include eliminating some of the collective action problems of urban society, such as reducing traffic congestion, pollution, carbon emissions, energy usage, or water usage. Smart cities technology can be used to upgrade existing cities, or on occasion is integrated in a new built environment at the design stage. The ideal of smart cities goes beyond merely using IT systems, but includes data feedback from pervasive surveillance and monitoring, and an active environment that both adapts to and shapes the behaviour of those within it. There are a number of more precise theories of smart cities, but surveys tend to reveal heterogeneous, ad hoc approaches, rather than convergence.[20]

Smart cities may well be an important global battleground for projecting visions of the Internet.[21] As we will see in the following, the Paternal Internet looks to develop security, measured against national plans using technology commissioned by central governments across the globe. China includes the technology in the BRI, but other paternal states with advanced smart city programmes, such as Singapore and India, are less ambitious exporters of their own model. The Brussels Bourgeois Internet aims for sustainable cities in which privacy is preserved, with local-level planning, allowing a balance between top-down and bottom-up approaches. European tech companies, smaller than their international competitors, tend to provide complete solutions in alliances and consortia. The DC Commercial Internet is far more opportunistic; most US firms implement solutions in America itself. The British government sees smart city technology largely as a business opportunity; it focuses on smart infrastructure and digital twins of real-world environments, developing standards for resilient data sharing for operating and maintaining built assets.[22] As trade and security concerns grow, and especially if 5G standards bifurcate, these differing visions of the city and methods of delivery will become increasingly salient.

THE IOT ON THE SILICON VALLEY OPEN INTERNET

The idealism of the Silicon Valley Open Internet tends to underpin programmes for the democratic, bottom-up improvement of life, ignoring collective action problems, and describing a world of 'digital omniscience'[23] where the technology empowers individuals, increases transparency, broadens information access, and closes digital divides.[24] For that, citizens have to engage with technology companies and local government to demand accountability and privacy in data processing and governance. Calls for smart cities to be citizen-centric, co-created by residents, and respectful of social justice and individual and collective liberty abound.[25]

But are they practical? The alternative top-down approach by civic leaders and technology companies imposing technology solutions assumes that the interests and preferences of those who live in the environment are known or easily knowable, and that resistance to modernization will be overcome by glorious results. No amount of contrary evidence seems to shift this stubborn perspective. However, the advantage of top-down is that it inherits all the benefits of a hierarchical control layer over a network, making it easier to achieve coherence. An open IoT would have to solve a number of problems, both technical (who ensures, and how, interoperability of the devices?) and social (who ensures, and to what extent, the privacy of those being monitored in the instrumented environment? Who is responsible for failure?). Some issues combine the social and technical, such as ensuring data quality or cybersecurity. It would be a brave local government which left these matters to the techies, as it would have to carry the can in the event of failure.

These problems are non-trivial—consider that a smart fridge may come supplied with sensors and actuators to communicate with other household gadgets or a central server for a utility company. The typical lifespan of expensive white goods currently exceeds a decade, and it is desirable for that figure to increase, if only for environmental reasons. Yet twenty years in the life of a digital component, and certainly in the life of the software standards it requires, is a very long time to design for. Just as phones' OSs have to be updated every so often, the same will be true of each device in the home. How many times should a user have to replace components, or passwords, or biometrics, to ensure the data is good and safe? And who would be responsible for the updates? The consumer, or a service provider, or the manufacturer?

A bottom-up IoT may struggle to achieve hoped-for synergies because the collaboration is not under anyone's control. Control over a particular environment (such as an owner's over a smart home) produces efficiencies in its management, but that may only be a serious option for those with the technical facility, education, and financial resources to buy and coordinate the requisite gadgets. It would be unlikely to catch on with the time-poor precariat. The same is true of cooperatives (an example often given is of a group of utility consumers in a neighbourhood pooling their data to give themselves greater bargaining power with their suppliers). This may result in increased digital divides rather than otherwise. Ideas such as the United Kingdom's Midata scheme,[26] to give consumers more power over and access to the data they generate, have not lived up to early hopes.

All too rarely is data presented to civil society groups in palatable form, although there are successes in the use of open data for service provision or advocacy. For instance, Data:In Place is an open source tool supporting citizens in accessing, interpreting, and making sense of open data in the context of their urban environment with visual map-based querying. They can access official statistics about their community, interrogate the data, and map their own data sources to create data visualizations.[27] Spokespeople is a system to enable cyclists to collect information about their everyday journeys, to allow cycling advocates and local authority transport planners to mine their experiences to suggest possible routes for cycling activism.[28] The problem with these is that they require investment of expert time and support, meaning they tend to be well-meaning but resource-heavy proofs of concept which lack a business model and are unlikely to scale.

THE IOT ON THE DC COMMERCIAL INTERNET

Zuboff reminds us that the key elements of IoT or smart cities, the platform and the infrastructure, rarely feature in 'blue sky' discussion.[29] For example, if we think of a smart building, we tend to list as stakeholders the local government which wants high-quality service provision while keeping tax and borrowing down, civil society groups which want a sustainable, fair, and liveable environment, individual citizens and residents, who want to promote their own well-being, and utility companies who want to administer their own services while meeting regulators' demands. A medical device may seem to concern a patient, a medical team, a hospital, and an insurance company. The stakeholder missed in each case is the platform used by the technology to manipulate data. But the platform certainly has an interest. For instance, smart dolls (which can talk to children and answer some of their questions) need to be connected to a data network, to transmit and decode the children's chat and formulate replies, or to connect with some of their apps. All of that will be stored. A parent might not realize that this perpetual connection means that the doll remains to an extent under the control of the company, so its vocabulary, range of topics, and even its functionality might change with software upgrades.[30]

With regard to both the DC Commercial Internet and the Beijing Paternal Internet, clearly the platform's ownership will make a difference. For the Commercial Internet, the incidental data captured within the IoT ecosystem will be rich and revealing of the lifestyles of its clients, and companies like Facebook and Google are moving into the 'extraction architecture'[31] of the IoT. Eric Schmidt has looked forward to the day when 'the Internet will disappear. . . . It will be part of your presence all the time. Imagine you walk into a room and the room is dynamic.'[32] For example, commercial voice assistants such as Alexa, Nest, Apple's Siri, and Microsoft's Cortana can do basic tasks in response to a human voice, such as dealing with messages in several media, answering queries, managing diaries and appointments, giving reminders, playing media, controlling other IoT devices such as thermostats and alarms, and interfacing with other apps and bank accounts so they can order a coffee or a taxi.[33] These give a very detailed picture of the user's daily life and routine, and clearly raise serious security and privacy issues.[34] One tactic to help assuage consumer anxiety is to leverage gendered stereotypes of women as nurses, mothers, and wives by giving the assistants female names and voices, deflecting attention from their surveillance and revenue-generating functions, framing them instead as carers and providers.[35]

Smart cities also put an extra spring in the steps of the commercial tech giants. The combination of the aspirations of digital modernity and the methods of the DC Commercial Internet produces ubiquitous architectures, observation without awareness, a narrative of inevitability, and the transformation of space into cyberspace. Alphabet contains an urban innovation company called Sidewalk Labs, which focuses on building platforms for gathering data, allowing city administrators to run experiments on traffic flow or environmental issues. CEO Dan Doctoroff has mused about innovations such as 'performance-based zoning', where building codes and standards can be superseded by algorithms that are able to judge whether standards (e.g. noise levels) are exceeded—replacing democratic decision-making with black box algorithms.[36] Sidewalk spent 2017–2020 attempting to develop five hectares of the Quayside area of Toronto, in a project blessed by dignitaries but dogged by controversy. Plans were said by an advisory panel to be too 'abstract', and innovations 'irrelevant and unnecessary', and full government approval never arrived. Inevitably, privacy and data were at the epicentre of concerns, with the Canadian Civil Liberties Association unimpressed by the proposal to set up a 'data trust', warning of 'ubiquitous and intensive sensor-laden infrastructure', and insisting that 'Waterfront Toronto never had the jurisdiction to sign off on a data surveillance test bed with a Google sibling'. The project was cancelled in 2020, citing the COVID-19 pandemic, but less ambitious projects on a smaller scale abound. The incremental approach would seem to be much less likely to alienate civil society than a Toronto-style big bang.[37]

THE IOT ON THE BRUSSELS BOURGEOIS INTERNET

As far as the Brussels Bourgeois Internet goes, the issues are parallel to those for AI—is it possible to reap the benefits, or most of them anyway, from the technology while minimizing risk, and if so how? If not, should the European Union, and nations with a similarly low risk appetite, accept an economic hit, or project power aggressively through the GDPR? Some commentators have bullishly asserted that, given the potential for a 'data-sharing storm' without controls and safeguards, GDPR is the only framework around that could possibly legitimize the IoT in the eyes of citizens and users.[38]

As already noted, the IoT poses an obvious issue for privacy, and the application of standard risk management techniques such as consent and anonymization will be hard. Cybersecurity will also be a serious problem. It is quite likely that many IoT devices will collect data from which individuals are identifiable—these may be the owners of the devices, or people who live or work in or near an IoT-enabled environment. If they do collect personal data, then the purpose of processing must be declared, processing of personal data must be limited to whatever necessary to achieve that purpose, there must be a ground for processing (including but not limited to consent), and it must be fair and transparent. Data subjects need to be informed about this too, and also have the right under GDPR to download their data and use it elsewhere.

The relevance of GDPR does not have to be stressed, but it may struggle to accommodate the technology (or vice versa). The rights it affords are individual, but IoT data may well concern groups or communities. Indeed, if a device gathers personal data from a range of people, the exercise of one person's data-protection rights may jeopardize the rights of the others. Furthermore, in a complex, distributed, and highly automated application, it may be hard to identify the data controller responsible. Managing such matters, and giving people the opportunity to assert their rights and apply for remedies for harms, will get harder as the devices recede into the background, and environments are equipped with data-driven agency. These problems are universal—no one is given an absolute right to abuse data—but the European Union has the most far-reaching solution. The FTC has a set of recommendations that are weaker than GDPR but still challenging.[39]

It may need technical expertise to come to the rescue. There is a range of measures one could imagine, including aggregating data and deleting the raw data as soon as possible. Devices could be designed to allow consent to be given, withdrawn, or modified, or to make data demands apparent to those being sensed, for example deploying icons, light displays, smart interfaces, or even SMS messages.[40] Standardization may allow users to exercise their GDPR data-portability rights.[41] Blockchains have been proposed as a means to generate a secure audit trail, or to create smart contracts that restrict what devices may do. Processing is likely to migrate to the 'edge', i.e. to the nodes in an IoT network of devices, as opposed to a hub-and-spoke architecture with all the data being sent to a central server. Edge computing has the advantage of making data minimization and devolving control easier. In short, computing is taken to the data, not the data to the computing.[42]

However, the ultimate strategy for implementing the IoT must surely be premised on transparency and trustworthiness, which the Bourgeois vision highlights.[43] European smart cities are often local government initiatives, rather than national programmes, and they may be easier to develop in nations where trust in government is relatively high, and where technology might therefore be imposed in a relatively structured way, while being clear about what was being done, and providing opportunities for citizens to make their voices heard and discontent obvious. Clearly in an IoT-enabled world, privacy preservation will be extremely difficult to manage; being honest about the risks is likely to pay dividends. Also being prepared for disputes, with lines of communication open to stakeholders, not only makes sense, but will also make for a more openly understood environment. This is more likely to be of use than expecting citizens to engage enthusiastically with arcane planning and design processes.

THE IOT ON THE BEIJING AND OTHER PATERNAL INTERNETS

Unsurprisingly, smart cities, with their potential for direction and control, loom large in the Paternal Internet. Singapore is a smart city/state, and has been known to call itself a smart nation.[44] China is experimenting with 500 of them, and also includes smart city development services in its BRI. Its ideas, as with AI, are inherently more pragmatic, less concerned with cutting-edge research than with applying known technologies in familiar situations to maximum effect. The national government makes a top-level five-year plan, including standards and funding, jealously guarding its agenda-setting role for 'exemplary smart cities, focusing on developing smart infrastructure, convenient public services, and refined social governance'.[45] Private companies develop the tools, systems, and components, and local government implements the cities themselves—a major contrast to the bottom up citizen-centric empowerment approach advocated by most academic commentators. Many of the smart cities are impressive, but its coastal showcases may be exceptional, as a recent study of Wuhan (described as an 'ordinary' smart city, but perhaps, post-pandemic, ordinary never again) reveals. Publicized smart activities are often unknown to the residents, and in many cases actually remain on the drawing board, with the city concept viewed 'as a passing fad mobilized instrumentally to attract funding'. However, the fact that the smart aspects of the city are embedded in the background, invisibly monitoring and predicting behaviour, enhances their capacity for surveillance. Populations are not conceptualized in this approach as creative, civic actors, but rather as recipients of government services.[46]

Chinese smart cities were originally branded as 'safe cities', betraying their emphasis on security over usability, and still are often called 'smart-safe cities'. Huawei, a leader in the field, continues to market 'safety solutions'. Security can include avoiding vulnerabilities such as flood or fire, but law enforcement and social control are prominent in this style of urban planning. Shame is a powerful tool; an increasingly common police tactic is to place large screens at road junctions, and use face recognition cameras to display faces, names, and

ID numbers of jaywalkers and other minor transgressors. China's Skynet network combines CCTV and face recognition, as well as other sensors, in order to create a centralized surveillance system for smart environments. At the time of writing, Skynet is under development, and it may suit both its proponents and detractors to exaggerate its capabilities. As with other ideas, such as the social credit system, much depends on integrating myriad subsystems in a nation where individual local governments, hungry for recognition from above, often fail to cooperate with others. Nevertheless, Chinese business technologies such as ubiquitous wireless connectivity, sensors, e-payments, and cloud services place it in the smart city vanguard.[47]

China's BRI safe city programme is equipped to export its model of 'an intelligent and data-driven society'[48] to places such as Central Asia, the Middle East, and sub-Saharan Africa, with a specific focus on public security, terrorism, and crime (and there are many parts of the world where these are genuinely serious issues). Digital and smart city technology is designed to integrate with other BRI infrastructure, such as ports and transport networks.[49] Huawei is an important player, providing integrated and interoperable services around the kinds of connectivity that it is selling (for instance, its surveillance solutions are interoperable with its broadband services). After providing the technologies to coordinate the Hajj for some years, it has received the contract to build the Saudi 5G network, and has a strong presence in other Gulf States.[50] It is also 'deeply embedded' in Europe.[51]

With respect to the wider IoT, the Chinese government has been prominent in pushing for traceability and social control, for example in its attempts to adopt DOA, described in Chapter 11. It is also interested in its own effectiveness, and so has developed a number of important standards and mechanisms for exploiting IoT for administration. For example, it has suffered a number of food-quality scandals in recent years, and in response set up a platform to trace food during production, using unique DOA identifiers to follow an item through the production process, and identify moments of malpractice. This is surveillance and control, but with a positive aspect.[52]

India also has a smart city programme driven by AI, intended to improve urban life and the efficiency of administration in a nation transformed by rapid, chaotic, and unplanned urbanization. Its Smart Cities Mission is aimed at improving 99 cities with investments in AI and IoT of 2 trillion rupees ($25–30 billion), addressing problems of poor planning and land use, while improving utility provision, service delivery, and design and surveillance to combat crime. The role of AI is to transform the data into 'predictive intelligence'.[53] One survey of the literature found a number of barriers to development, of which existing problems of governance (lack of coordination of agencies, unclear management vision, political instability, lack of trust in government, poor interaction between public and private sectors, and a lack of common system models) were the most prominent.[54] Since one of the aims of smart cities is to improve governance, this may be a chicken-and-egg problem, unless some better-run cities can develop best practice and bootstrap their way to improvement. A positive result from the survey was that legal and ethical issues were relatively insignificant. Geographer Ayona Datta argued that support for smart cities across India was a matter of 'technocratic nationalism' among the urban young, a manifestation of digital modernity that bodes well for future support for such schemes.[55]

SMART CITIES AND THE FUTURE OF THE INTERNET

The IoT in general and smart cities in particular are signifiers of digital modernity, and their affordances will be influenced dramatically by the governance of the Internet in the jurisdictions in which they, or the servers that process the data, sit. Sociologist Philip Howard has argued that digital networks weaken ideologies, and that as a consequence governance through the IoT and the 'clash of civilizations' will in all likelihood be replaced by competition between device networks.[56] This seems unlikely. Depoliticization may be detectable within jurisdictions, as data-driven agency closes off undesirable behaviours, to give us what law professor Roger Brownsword has called a switch from law to technological management or administration,[57] but if our survey of the Internet is correct, the networks that connect the devices may themselves have ideological value designed into them. Hence any competition between them may be 'managed' by governments keen to establish the conditions under which their citizens' data is processed. The nature of the IoT, for example, is the root of the wrangle between the United States and China over Huawei's 5G networks, and ideology may result in two completely separate standards for 5G, perhaps one using DOA so that objects have persistent identifiers, resulting in the 'Splinternet of Things'. That would not in itself cleave the Internet in two, but it would hardly help keep it optimally connected.

Some of the areas to which China is exporting, like sub-Saharan Africa, may not look like promising business opportunities, because of their poor infrastructure, iffy governance, and digital divides, but they provide a platform for a growing industry. It will also be hard to break into such markets once they are open, because interoperability will be a key factor in smart city development. Bifurcation of standards would only make it harder for Western business down the line. Chinese technological development will be slowed in the short term if it is unable to rely on American inputs and components, but in the medium term it will diversify supply chains and become more self-sufficient, financially supported by the deep pockets of its central government. This looming fork in the road, as we have argued, cannot be in America's interests, but it will also be to the detriment of all.

CHAPTER 20

Social Machines

D ata, data everywhere. We have focused so far on the weight of technology and data pressing down on individuals, but it would be wrong not to consider how individuals benefit from them as well. Obviously there are directly consumed services, such as social networking, file storage, search, and so on, but in this section we will consider new social structures that may become even more salient in the post-COVID-19 world. First we will look at a particular type of social organizing principle, and then we will describe a new initiative for individuals and groups to manage the data that they generate through their Internet-enabled activity.

WHAT IS A SOCIAL MACHINE?

The Internet is now a familiar part of life, via SNSs, smartphones, smart speakers, and Internet-enabled devices ranging from wearables to TV sets. It is, therefore, unsurprising that its affordances are woven into everyday social life. People connect to cooperate, negotiate, exchange information, document and augment lived reality, solve problems, work, keep up with the latest news or gossip, or just to play, and this can now be done socially, at scale, in real time. Existing social groups and practices can be scaled up and new ones enabled. These new groups exhibit network effects; each new participant adds greater power, because although no one knows everything relevant to a problem, everyone knows something. These new informal and ad hoc groups have been called *social machines*.[1]

They are increasingly common, Wikipedia and Pokémon Go being prominent examples.[2] Some have enabled communities to provide a social response to modern problems of transport, such as Waze, a navigation app which uses

Four Internets. Kieron O'Hara and Wendy Hall, Oxford University Press. © Oxford University Press 2021.
DOI: 10.1093/oso/9780197523681.003.0020

community-derived real-time data about traffic congestion and accidents.[3] Healthcare is another area, where patient groups may discuss their experiences and treatments (sufferers from chronic illnesses are often far more expert about their own conditions than specialists), or well-being groups may form around specific devices such as activity trackers like Fitbit.[4] For instance, CrowdMed crowdsources diagnoses of user-submitted medical conditions from 'medical detectives', who generally don't practice medicine, although many have or are seeking medical qualifications.[5] Managing crime is also sometimes amenable to the social machine approach; BlueServo crowdsources immigration policing on the Texas-Mexico border,[6] and *Onde Tem Tiroteio* (Where the Shootouts Are) connects a million people on Facebook, Twitter, Instagram, WhatsApp, and Telegram to a special-purpose app to provide real-time information about shootings and gang-related crime in Brazil.[7] Social machines can be transitory, existing only while there is a problem. For instance, coordinated rescue and disaster responses have supplied bottom-up support for state efforts, such as the Cajun Navy, for which leisure boat owners in Louisiana located victims of floods in 2016 via a Facebook group, and organized rescues using GPS app Glympse and walkie-talkie app Zello.[8] Not all social machines are problem-related; Pokémon Go has already been mentioned, and the level of coordination that fans of K-pop in South Korea achieve, in attempting to make sure their heroes reach the charts, shows a set of highly successful social machines in action.[9] Social machines will only have grown in salience as families, associations, and workforces have tried to adapt during the COVID-19 pandemic using resources such as Zoom, FaceTime, WhatsApp, Trello, and YouTube. Facebook alone facilitated 300 coronavirus support groups in the United Kingdom with a million members between them.[10] Social games platforms such as Twitch and Steam have had record traffic, and games companies are among the few to have increased their share prices during the pandemic.

Some social machines have been devised to get particular jobs of work done. In Chapter 18, we discussed the resource-heavy problem of labelling data, and the Chinese solution of using human labour. Elsewhere, where labour is more expensive, researchers have devised clever ways of getting people to do it for free, as a by-product of something they actually want to do. Luis von Ahn, who pioneered research into 'games with a purpose', devised the ESP game where two players, randomly paired and unable to communicate directly, try to agree on an original label for a picture. This entertains the players, but more to the point results in free and effective labelling of images, which can then be used as data for ML down the line.[11]

As another type of social machine, citizen science involves interested publics in scientific endeavour by crowdsourcing and organizing contributions to experiments and classifications. An early example was Galaxy Zoo, where a DPhil student in astronomy, faced with the tedious and time-consuming task of classifying 900,000 images of galaxies, set up a platform for volunteers to be trained and help in the work. This attracted well over 100,000 participants, and led to genuine scientific discoveries and dozens of peer-reviewed publications (many of which included Zoo volunteers as co-authors). On the back of this extraordinary success, a portal called the Zooniverse was set up at Oxford University to coordinate citizen science projects (on all kinds of subjects ranging from astronomy, nature and the climate, biology, and history) and discover best practice for nurturing citizen science social machines, fostering genuine communities via discussion and Talk pages, and including lay participants in the scientific publication and reward system. Well over a million people have participated in at least one project, and many spend a lot of time on the site contributing to a range of projects.[12]

Those who call for citizen involvement in the co-creation of smart cities have argued that this will turn them into social machines, where the citizens become participants in the city, driving development and innovating sustainable systems of systems.[13] Bottom-up participation in innovation, regulation, automation, and administration is likelier to identify quick solutions to small problems, based on the deep knowledge participants have of their own neighbourhoods and neighbours,[14] facilitated by community support apps such as Nextdoor.[15] Cities have been characterized as 'urban machinery',[16] and social machines may be a way of resisting the unwelcome metaphor of residents as mere cogs. A smart city is likely to be not a single social machine, but a whole ecosystem of smaller social machines working not only at local community level, but also globally as well, connecting participants in the smart city with residents elsewhere in intra-city interest groups. Crowdsourcing data about transport, for instance, might include annotating cycle routes with points of interest and real-time safety information, collecting data about accidents, near-accidents, pollution, potholes or danger spots, designing new routes or experiences, organizing cycling groups, and advocating cyclists' interests. These can all be social activities using the resources that many have to hand, particularly smartphones.[17]

Common platforms play the important role of hosting social machines; indeed, their history is inseparable from that of social machines. Many of the familiar platforms upon which most social machines sit have evolved from more focused social machines themselves, only to become general purpose as their affordances became repurposed (Facebook began life as a searchable directory of Harvard students).

It is unsurprising that the role of the platform that carries data and communication between the participants will affect both the practicalities and the politics of a social machine, in different ways depending on which vision of the Internet is operative. The Zooniverse citizen science platform is an academic design informed by evaluations of Zooniverse projects, gathering data about the interactions of the participants, including their often informative debates on the Talk pages. The data is used to improve the system, and to discover new scientific concepts; for example, a new type of starburst galaxy (one undergoing a rapid rate of new star formation) was identified following analysis of a Talk thread in Galaxy Zoo in which lay participants discussed images that reminded them of green peas.[18] Other analyses are used to discover useful facts about the workflow, such as which tasks participants find tedious or boring, and how participation varies when a project is featured in the media or on television. This transparent arrangement between system administrators and participants creates new opportunities to invest back into the system, assumes a platform that is neutral, or whose interests coincide with the participants', and is characteristic of the Silicon Valley Open Internet. Its consent-based approach also makes it compatible with the Brussels Bourgeois Internet.

However, Zooniverse is a top-down system developed and run by academic scientists. In general, this would not be the case for bottom-up social machines. The data gathered by platforms will include both the matter of the social machine, likely to be valuable in areas such as transport and health, and the social connections within the network that populate it. In the case of the Beijing Paternal Internet, this would give the platform, and indirectly the government, a lot of data about what social activities were going on independently of state control. Obviously online activism is risky in China,[19] but other social tasks have been less controversial, such as sharing advice about food quality concerns, translating and subtitling foreign computer games, augmenting children's education, socially distributed manufacturing, and distributing food to the poor.[20] The social machine is inevitably exposed to the view of the authorities via its use of social media.

To expand on the last example, Free Lunch for Children (FL4C) organizes around the Sina Weibo microblogging platform, and so is visible to outsiders (which would not have been the case had it organized around, say, WeChat). As noted earlier, the Chinese government does monitor social media to inform itself of upcoming problems, and there was government interest in this social machine. FL4C became an important conduit for raising awareness of the problem of child poverty and malnutrition, but the government didn't appreciate being embarrassed, so the framing of the issue was important—did FL4C pave the way for government action, or was it a partner all along? The affordances of Weibo were used by FL4C in order to curry legitimacy with the government (and with the public, often sceptical of charities, too). The public microblogging platform both enforced and enabled transparency, providing a route for publication of evidence of the scale of the problem. It enhanced accountability, as the statements of the group's founders were open to scrutiny, and it also helped build public trust by supporting feedback and interaction.[21]

Chinese tech companies are also interested in gathering data for the other obvious purpose: making money.[22] In that, they also have interests which are shared on the DC Commercial Internet. Data tracking the activities of a social machine are likely to be very informative of the interests of its participants, and it is no surprise to see, for example, Alphabet/Google purchasing devices around which users have tended to socialize, such as Fitbit. At the time of writing, that deal has yet to find favour with either regulators worried about antitrust issues, or privacy campaigners concerned with the sensitive information this would provide.[23] Entire social machines have been purchased, such as Waze, bought by Google,[24] and CureTogether, a crowdsourced treatment-rating website with data on hundreds of medical conditions, bought out by genomics company 23andMe.[25]

Zuboff has argued that the collection of data and the provision of services are not only intrusive, they also modify behaviour covertly, and so reduce autonomy.[26] In that case, the platform's interference with the collective in a social machine may be even greater. Informatics professors Hamid Ekbia and Bonnie Nardi point out that in a social machine, many people contribute their labour for free, and the extraction of value from such networks by platforms is inequitable, yielding profits for the platform with no return for those doing the labour.[27] This is the inevitable background of bottom-up organizing using familiar platforms, but may be less visible or evident to social machine organizers and participants than is the hand of the state in the Paternal Internet.

Is this necessarily a bad thing? Defenders of the commercial Internet would reply that the social machine is enabled by the technological affordances of the platforms on offer, and it is no coincidence that the most useful platforms are commercial systems based in the United States, because the commercial emphasis facilitates customer-centric innovation. The reason there is no alternative is that no one else has the business model to innovate so radically, in a customer-centred way.

RE-DECENTRALIZING THE WEB

One consistent lesson that has emerged throughout this and the previous two chapters is that platforms control dataflow, and can exploit it, whether for social control or profit. Any new social structure or practice on the Internet is going to have to acknowledge that the data it generates via the online portion of its activity will be sucked up and used by the facilitators, and possibly not at all by the practitioners. The Brussels Bourgeois Internet will look for a solution in regulation, but this option does not appeal to the original pioneers of openness. Is there an answer that will enable the Silicon Valley Open Internet to reassert its values without undermining accessible means for users to get onto the Internet in the first place?

Tim Berners-Lee, the original developer of the Web, has been arguing for some time about the problems of data being out of the control of the people it describes. Along similar lines to Zittrain, he locates the problem in the walled gardens that the major tech firms construct in order to grow large networks. Such networks need to be hard to leave, to promote growth, so they use languages and identifiers that are not interoperable with other systems (so the information within the walled garden becomes essentially meaningless when transplanted outside).[28]

Berners-Lee locates the problem in the way that walled gardens undo the decentralization of the Web. The tech giants' business model is to centralize data in silos. They work to maximize the amount of data they have exclusive access to, rather than working either to open non-sensitive data to as many people as possible, or to secure the data privacy of individuals. In this way, the DC Commercial vision cuts across both the Silicon Valley and Brussels visions, creating centripetal forces driving the Web towards a hub/spoke information-flow model. This provokes power asymmetries between users (at the spokes) and the corporations (hubs), creates inefficiencies in dataflow and storage, and suppresses innovation by making it harder for developers to build on top of existing popular platforms.

His radical proposal is to *re-decentralize* the Web, meaning: to get data back out of the walled gardens, or at least make them interoperable with everything else.[29] Decentralization, especially P2P architectures, have long been seen as a potential solution to deficits of trust, where the nodes of the network take charge and reject any overall authority.[30] For instance, blockchain has emerged since 2008 as the go-to solution for any problem where a ledger is needed, but no one trusts anyone to keep it.[31]

Berners-Lee's solution is called *Solid* (Social Linked Data), a decentralized platform for social applications on the Web, in which users' data is managed separately from the applications that create it and those that consume it. This means that the app doesn't funnel data, or the inferences from it, to the centralized data consumers (the tech companies). Rather than being ceded to the app's special-purpose back-end storage, the data is stored in a *pod* (Personal Online Datastore). Users can have a range of Web-accessible pods from which data is portable, and which may be provided by a market of independent pod providers, enabling simple switching between pods or providers. In this way, the app works for the user, rather than performing a service for the user while simultaneously creating data about the user's activity, which goes to the app company to be aggregated with the rest of its data and monetized. Solid protocols are based on W3C recommendations, which are open, interoperable standards, allowing developers to create applications which can read or write to pods, or control access securely. Such apps can range over all the data under the user's control wherever it is stored on the Web.[32]

The Solid vision therefore counters the centripetal forces of the walled gardens with centrifugal ones, reusing current Web protocols to engineer a P2P network. Solid is not intended to replace the existing Web or Internet, as, for example, are the ambitions of rival re-decentralization schemes, such as the blockchain-based Elastos,[33] and Dfinity, which wants to replace IP with an-other protocol that allows software to run anywhere on the Internet rather than the corporate cloud.[34] Instead, Solid sits on top of existing infrastruc-ture, alongside existing social media and large data consumers, competing against their walled gardens with its ecosystem of services.

On the Solid view, the centripetal forces threaten not only privacy, but also the Web's USP, its universality. Walled gardens threaten axioms of the Web, such as uniform identifiers and permissionless development. The Solid coun-termove is to give individuals complete control of their data, so that they can engage in contacts with their networks without necessarily contributing to anyone's store of surveillance metadata about who is in contact with whom and when, in order to create targeted advertisements, political messages, or other types of manipulation of the surveillance economy. It uses a linked data model (RDF, based on uniform identifiers), so data can still be shared and linked to other relevant data easily, but only using processes authorized by the user. A Solid server is therefore basically an ordinary Web server plus those two requirements of access control and support for linked data. Individuals can run multiple identities as chosen by them on a range of servers, and even achieve near-anonymity by minting an ID and using it a single time. The par-ticipants in social machines could cooperate privately by devoting a pod to the machine, and giving permission for apps to access not only the social machine's pod but also participants' pods, where safe and necessary.[35]

Solid is administered jointly via an academic project at the Massachusetts Institute of Technology[36] and Inrupt, a company to provide the commercial context for some of the development work.[37] Solid currently fosters a commu-nity from which one can receive a pod situated in the cloud, and the aim is that other providers will emerge, thus providing choice as to where data is stored and how it is managed (and how much, if anything, is paid for the storage ser-vice). Hardier souls may wish to develop or administer their own pods. The in-dependence of the pod completes the separation of data from application, or, put another way, the front end from the back end. App developers would only need to design the front, because in effect the pod system creates a common back end (i.e. the back end of all Solid apps is the Web as a whole), and the data produced by the app would be distributed across the user's pods. This means that different apps could be run over the same data, or that a single app could provide a seamless experience combining data from an individual's pod(s) with data from others' pods for which access permission has been obtained. So far, the main development effort up to now has been on the Solid servers, rather than apps. Hence the ecosystem is currently sparse.[38] Security, authen-tication, and access control remain important technical problems to solve.[39]

App developers in the Solid ecosystem only get to design the interface with the user. Hence, they lose control of the data, which may impact their business model. They could refuse to adopt the Solid architecture, or to supply services to users who wished to keep control over their data. There may be interesting compromises—for instance, an app developer may define a back end to integrate with a particular pod design. Use of the app might require the user's consent to put all the resulting data into a pod controlled by the user, but hosted by the developer. This may help the developer, for instance ensuring the pod's API makes data transfer easier, or alternatively preventing competing developers from accessing the data.

Business models could doubtless emerge. An app developer might join the Solid ecosystem as a pod provider, using the pods as loss leaders to drive demand towards its apps. If the use of its pods was voluntary, would there be any objection? Or conversely, could such a developer refuse to register someone for an app if they didn't also subscribe to one of its pods? A developer could decide that Solid would be a useful architecture for GDPR-compliant data management. Whether any of this would be sufficient to tempt app developers to enter the Solid ecosystem may depend more on the network effects of doing so, i.e. whether enough data subjects are concerned enough about privacy issues to take more responsibility in the management of their data, and to create a large network. As Lalana Kagal, Solid's project manager, admits, progress is slow.[40]

Even in the context of a thriving ecosystem and consequent network effects for providers and users alike, this must entail a degree of uncertainty for developers. Data will quite possibly have to be taken from multiple servers, each of which may have unexpected properties and incompatibilities. It will be hard to create application-specific queries or requests for data, in the absence of widely followed standards.

The uncertainty follows from Solid's focus on the preferences of the individual, which need be neither consistent nor persistent, and so are fundamentally unpredictable. By ceding control of the back end, app developers could advance such noble aims as GDPR-compliance, but the development environment will be more complex as data representation inevitably becomes less application-specific. One response has been to link Solid with the Data Transfer Project (DTP), an open-source initiative from Google, also involving Apple, Facebook, Microsoft, and Twitter, to provide a platform for individuals to move their data across different platforms, in line with their GDPR rights. DTP could be a useful way of creating network effects around Solid.[41]

Ultimately, Solid is an insurgent of the Silicon Valley Open Internet fighting back against the forces of Part II. The question we must ask is: can it function as a global standard and still remain compatible with the other Internets we describe? They are not going to go away.

CHAPTER 21

The Unity of Freedom

This is not a book about saving the world. Whether capitalism, human rights, authoritarianism, or free speech are a boon or a curse, these are not within the range of questions amenable to computer science. Our necessarily limited aim is to map the Internet in a world which, for good or ill, does contain capitalism and other diverse voices. We may not like the ways in which, for instance, China, or the United States, or the European Union, or Russia, or India do their business, but we cannot wish them away. It is not our job to judge which of our Four Internets is 'superior', and neither do we have any better ideas. We only emphasize that, in the absence of political change, they have to coexist. It is not our job to work out how to eradicate the Spoiler, only to argue that the Internet needs to be resilient against it.

The Internet was designed by its foresighted pioneers to be resilient, and so far it has passed that test with flying colours. Patterns of Internet use changed overnight at massive scale when the COVID-19 pandemic hit in early 2020, and the system hardly flinched. We should not forget what an extraordinary engineering achievement that is. In this book, we have described some of the sources of that resilience, and in this final chapter we will try to draw the threads together, and think more widely about how risks might be managed, opportunities created, and benefits preserved.

Different views on governance have emerged, and some have gained technical and geopolitical currency. So many actors and interests are involved that our picture has necessarily been broad-brush. To caricature:

- In DC and Silicon Valley, something is permitted if it's not forbidden.
- In Brussels, it's forbidden if it's not permitted.
- In Beijing, it's discouraged, even if it's permitted.
- In Moscow, it's encouraged, especially if it's forbidden.

Four Internets. Kieron O'Hara and Wendy Hall, Oxford University Press. © Oxford University Press 2021.
DOI: 10.1093/oso/9780197523681.003.0021

As we have noted, none of the visions of the Internet we have reviewed could stand on its own. It is, however, worth making the point at the outset that, had the Silicon Valley Open Internet not been the first historically, then *we would not have an Internet*. Openness has been key to building and sustaining the network that brings the value. Restrictions and bottlenecks, whether to support human rights, as in the Brussels Bourgeois Internet, or private-sector profits, as in the DC Commercial Internet, or social values, as in the Beijing Paternal Internet, would have strangled it at birth. Through its history, the technical standards of the Internet and Web—brilliantly conceived by Cerf, Kahn, Berners-Lee, and their collaborators—have held. The network has remained connected, has grown, scaled, and still delivered positive network effects. Having grown, the Internet now has survival characteristics, and so its openness—which has undeniably led to problems—can be dialled down, but surely not abandoned.

It would be a colossal error for adherents to any of these models to attempt a power-grab. It would have been a huge mistake to allow a private equity company to buy the .org domain for a debt-fuelled $1 billion, *even if the .org domain had continued to be well and equitably run*. It would be a massive blunder to transfer responsibility for some aspects of Internet governance to the ITU, *even if it worked to ensure that dictatorships didn't take over and to keep civil society representatives in the loop*. It would be an awful misjudgement to expand the projection of the European Union's values upon the rest of the world, *even if it did not push its rights-based thinking into governance and turn the Internet into an ideological battlefield*. And it would be a gigantic omission not to address the fake news and conspiracy theory phenomenon, *even if Russia and other nations stood down their troll farms and even if SNSs took their responsibilities as publishers seriously*. We need to establish an imperfect space where all parties are able to compromise on terms they can recognize as their own.

At the moment, the United States is *primus inter pares*, which naturally does not sit well with rival nations, nor with many commentators and academics. Neither of the present authors is American or has any loyalty to the United States, but it is surely germane to observe that the US predominates *because it built and fostered the Internet*, through a potent combination of technological expertise, economic heft, thriving telecommunications businesses, and military efficiency, and it is hard to imagine that any other nation, or combination of nations, could have managed that feat. As Berners-Lee explained when he moved from CERN in Europe to the Massachusetts Institute of Technology to set up the W3C in 1994, the United States was the 'centre of gravity' of the Internet.[1]

Even if its information dominance is waning,[2] the United States still plays an outsize role because of its positive contribution—its soft power is enhanced by restraint on its hard power.[3] This argument is not helped, though, by America's abuse of its analogous dominance in other areas, such as finance.[4]

The United States is dominant there because the dollar is the world's reserve currency, the most convertible and well supported, and because various crucial bits of financial machinery, such as the SWIFT system, Visa, and Mastercard, are based there. It does flex its financial muscles, justifiably in the case of the Bush administration's pursuit of al Qaeda via money-laundering regulations, defensibly in the case of the Obama administration's sanctions on Russia following the annexation of Crimea, and irresponsibly in the case of the Trump administration's wide-ranging sanctions on Iran, China, and various European banks in pursuit of narrow American interests. When Americans throw their weight around like this, international cooperation on their terms looks less palatable. This is particularly worrying given their offensive against Huawei, which only makes sense on the premise that Internet infrastructure can be a vehicle for national interests. If they believe that is possible for the Chinese, then critics will ask, what is to stop them misusing it for American purposes?

The future form of the Internet is absolutely up for grabs—and, although this is not our prediction, there is certainly a risk that it will cease to be a *global information space* as we currently understand it. Though at some level it is likely to remain connected as a unified network, as we have seen, it is possible to constrain or monitor the data that crosses national borders, which is likely to have a chilling effect at best, or at worst to strangle certain sections. Russia's efforts have even included trying to separate its Internet from the global Internet, although the efficacy of that experiment is currently unknown. If enough large nations foolishly tried to do this, then the Splinternet would become more likely than not.

As the preceding chapters in Part III have all confirmed, the attitude towards data will be central. It is the key by-product of the Internet, and one of its main sources of value. Data, when interpreted as information, brings power: to *communicate* at speed, to *influence* friends and enemies, to improve *decision-making*, and to create *wealth*. The Internet is intended to move data around, and by doing so creates even more. Recent developments in Artificial Intelligence have supersized its importance; at least part of the rationale for data nationalism is to grow indigenous AI industries. The IoT also stands out among current technologies, as it has brought the physical world online: places, spaces, and things you can drop on your foot now have avatars which are first-class objects in cyberspace, which will generate even more data about real-world interactions, which will then go to feed the AI beast, and so the cycle continues. The Internet has blended the physical and the digital in a riffle shuffle that presents the world to us as a single pack.

This means that we need to think about virtuous data stewardship. Data expresses information, and information is about things, especially people, and these things and people are ends in themselves, not means to the perfection of some algorithm. Data science is a complex discipline, not a magic wand to resolve policy difficulties, nor a magic machine for coining profits. Processing data means that one is interacting, if only indirectly, with the things and the people that it purports to describe. They must be treated with respect, whatever openness allows one to do.

Should we always keep the data we generate? The temptation of big data is to save as much as possible, for it is impossible to know what will be valuable in the future; anything may correlate with the parameters a scientist, doctor, or policymaker is legitimately interested in. But the process of datafication is already a covert intrusion into the autonomy of the individuals whose behaviour is being transcribed. Should there be limits? At a minimum we should get to know data better, and understand how it is produced, so as to appreciate its inadequacies. It will make us better citizens, better equipped to be the humans in the AI loop. Not for us the Bismarckian maxim: if you like data and sausages, you should never watch either being made. *Au contraire*, you should get familiar with the slaughterhouse.

Ideology is another important vector. The moderator of an OECD governance forum in 2011 drew attention to the bewildering variety of meanings that speakers gave to the terms 'freedom' and 'openness' (and the OECD is a relatively homogeneous club).[5] Given these different wavelengths, crossed lines, and wrong ends of the stick, it will be impossible to reach global agreement on technical matters without compromise between stakeholders. Attempts to ground the Internet on human rights or free trade or national sovereignty (or whatever) are likelier to fail than succeed. That does not mean that we shouldn't be ambitious, and as Arora argues, openness is still a powerful ideal for which there is much nostalgia in the Global South.[6] But the *very existence* of the Internet is *already* a vital contributor to the world's prosperity and freedom. Other improvements to global rights, while undeniably welcome, are risky if they threaten present benefits.[7]

Lee Bygrave, a scholar of computing law, draws attention to 'the sheer clutter of the ideological landscape in which conventions must now be brokered',[8] and it is an enormous task. Our survey helps convey the geopolitical and ethical parts of the mess, and there are many other related aspects, such as human rights, national sovereignty, national security, law enforcement, and the global digital economy. No single overarching organization can realistically solve all these. The ITU has proved sympathetic to nations which are less than comfortable with free flows of information, and its attention is very much focused on governments, which are more often problems than solutions. The World Trade Organization is struggling for relevance as multilateral treaty-making has fallen out of fashion. The OECD, as a club of rich countries, is unlikely to represent the interests of the emerging nations which will provide the Internet's future growth. For instance, the OECD's Global Partnership on AI is an initiative pushed by France and Canada to try to make sure AI is used to do nice things and not nasty ones, with buy-in from a number of democracies (including India), but excluding China. Granted, China is unlikely to endorse the initiative's respect for 'democratic values and the primacy of human beings', but equally, without China's involvement it is unlikely to be the last word on AI.[9]

There are vulnerabilities and risks as we move forward. The Internet is becoming the battleground for various proxy wars. The United States is in pursuit of Huawei, on supposed national security grounds, in order to prevent its technology dominating 5G (Chapter 12). The European Union's GDPR and competition laws project European standards well beyond its borders.[10] China meanwhile exerts power to suppress debate; for instance, in 2020 it leant on videoconferencing company Zoom (a Californian company whose servers are nonetheless in China) to close the accounts of activists in the United States and Hong Kong who were organizing meetings to commemorate the massacre of protestors in Tiananmen Square in 1989,[11] and has applied similar pressure variously to LinkedIn, Yahoo! TikTok, Google, and Facebook.

Another vulnerability is the prominence of influential individuals. Sometimes, the individuals are disruptive—President Trump was known to drop a bombshell or two over the course of an evening's tweeting. For instance, in 2020 the president, enjoying himself in a war of words with Twitter which had suggested that some of his tweets might be run through a fact-checker, suddenly announced an executive order to repeal section 230 of the Communications Decency Act, which covers platforms from liability for the content they host. This freedom from liability is what makes large-scale fast-paced social content-sharing feasible, and its removal (amendment would have its supporters)[12] would completely change the nature of Internet use.[13] As another example, President Putin has no succession plan in place, so no one, least of all his closest cronies, has any idea of who or what will follow him.[14]

Other individuals are influential in more positive, or at least less stochastic, ways. The active presence of Internet and Web pioneers defending their achievements has conserved both their creation and the Silicon Valley Open Internet ideals behind it. The ascendency of ISOC/IETF and the W3C, for example, are intertwined with the personal authority of their creators, Vinton Cerf and Tim Berners-Lee, respectively. Where Internet pioneers have not been able to protect their legacy, institutions formed to continue their work have not avoided controversy; ICANN was an attempt to institutionalize Jon Postel's work on consistent naming, for instance, but has become a lightning rod for governance disputes.

Treaty and regulation seem to be slow and blunt instruments for Internet governance, but they help to reduce uncertainty, constrain undesirable behaviour, and cement principles in place without relying on individual evangelists. On a smaller scale, contracts may serve, with more flexibility making it easier to adjust to technological and social change.[15] But law is not everything; cooperative communities are often able to build practical functional systems that can create a new reality to be tested and scaled up. However the Internet is governed, the different roles of ideology, law, technology, and economics will be fluid over time. Space must be left for new systems to be built and used, and the multiple benefits of a connected information space (tempered with firewalls, censors, content moderators, and bottlenecks) should not be sacrificed on the altar of morality, national security, privacy, or other ideals. As President Kennedy said in his final State of the Union Address, 'the unity of freedom has never relied on uniformity of opinion'.

Rather than making the perfect the enemy of the good, Internet governance processes should be premised on *expressing common interests between all participants*, and *respecting cultural diversity* as non-negotiable desiderata. We believe that the multistakeholder model is the best way of doing this. Deliberately setting out to reduce the role of the United States will result in increasing the role of other governments (what we might call the ITU route), because the only effective counterweight to a government is other governments. The ITU route would be to the detriment of civil society and commercial interests, many of which are not popular in government circles, and would be secondary citizens in a purely diplomatic environment.

Scientific and engineering concerns are important—the Internet has to *work* before it can be useful—but cannot rule the show either, because engineers often have tin ears to political issues. The rough and ready combination of voices that multistakeholderism produces is necessary to find the mean between too much politics on the one hand and too much technocracy on the other. Naïve demands for even more (usually ill-defined) democracy risk the functioning structure that we now have. A United Nations report in 2019 in the context of the Internet helping the Sustainable Development Goals promoted the idea of *digital interdependence*, a multilateral view of governance shared between governments and businesses, academics, and NGOs in permanent platforms of cooperation.[16]

Broadly, our prescription is to focus on the power of decentralization, the network over the hierarchy, the square over the tower. This will make it harder to focus the Internet on a particular set of problems, or to make it perform some specific function, but this is partly the point. We must always remember that it is a *global* Internet, a *World Wide* Web. Californian common sense can seem bizarre in Paris or New Delhi (and vice versa). No one view should prevail. We roundly endorse Thomas Jefferson's principle that 'it is not by the consolidation, or concentration of powers, but by their distribution, that good government is effected'.[17] A well-governed Internet will be governed by many, if not everybody.

But this cannot be the whole story. Openness, as we have seen, is a vector of risk, disruption, and unfamiliarity, which are meat and drink to the innovator, but less attractive to users and consumers, who take usability and legibility into account. Within a commercial framework at least, openness and what Zittrain calls 'tethered' apps can coexist.[18] Google manages Android with relatively little oversight, while Apple's iTunes was successful for many years under similar circumstances, until its business model was superseded by subscription streaming services (Apple began the process of breaking it up in 2019).[19] We need an understanding of openness that enables this coexistence, promotes useful attributes like interoperability, and supports governance mechanisms for responsible development, while denying control of the Internet to any small group of actors.

As Cave puts it, 'it is appropriate—even essential—to have separate internets, with different characteristics and sometimes-clear boundaries'.[20] He is thinking in particular of the many economic and other pressures favouring walled gardens, and so suggests that there should be an 'affirmative duty' on those involved in Internet governance to protect openness and mobility where possible. A licence has the effect of closing off a portion of the Internet, but there may be economic reasons why the owner of an Internet resource wished to use one, and there may be social value to be gained (e.g. if the owner can institute some useful service with the licence, and had no incentive to do it otherwise). In that case, the aim should be to make the licence available to anyone who wanted it and was prepared and able to meet its conditions, so the fee, the decision to grant the licence, and its allocation shouldn't be discriminatory.

A key factor in a functioning Internet is its support for innovation. This aspect is most emphasized in the two American visions. In Silicon Valley, it is an axiom that openness will produce innovation, because nothing stands in the way of the innovator. On the DC vision, innovation is the single source of legitimacy for large and powerful closed networks. An Internet that stands still, and does not periodically provide new services and renew existing markets, has no business being there, on this view, and should be shaken up. The Spoiler also prizes innovation; at its most benign form in the hacking ethic of Anonymous, it celebrates the hackers' abilities to second guess and counter the security measures of corporate suits, and to become equal protagonists in a cybersecurity arms race. The Brussels and Beijing visions are more ambivalent about innovation, but many places in the world have to innovate, as their most tradeable and renewable resource is human capital. The European Union springs to mind, while others include Israel, Singapore, Japan, and the United Kingdom.

We need to understand that innovation has a context, which it needs to respect. There needs to be enough social and political control to dampen temptations towards 'solutionism', where innovation is seen as the answer to every problem. Old-fashioned institutions are not simply there to be 'disrupted'; we must not fall for the axiom of digital modernity that *to exist is to be backward*. Digital modernity prizes disruption, but we cannot ignore the transaction costs of constant reorganization. An education system that is clearly failing (for example, on the measure of PISA scores) may well seem like a waste of money, but may still provide value—socializing children, helping mix social classes and genders, providing baseline knowledge and skills, instilling trust and love of village, neighbourhood, town, and nation, or providing a framework of discipline such as attendance at a particular time every day. One might supplement this with clever educational apps on free smartphones, but if the app is intended to replace the school, then 'the private sector gets to be innovative while the public sector takes the risk'.[21]

Nevertheless, more disruptive technologies will arrive, some anticipated, some not, but they will have to be incorporated, and resilience somehow preserved. For example, consider quantum computing, which, if it is realized, will replace bits with qubits, using phenomena such as superposition and entanglement (which Einstein labelled 'spooky action at a distance') to do the computation instead of voltages, amplifiers, and switches.[22] Though a quantum computer is technically equivalent to a digital one, it can perform certain tasks speedily that digital computers never could in a feasible amount of time, such as factorizing integers into prime numbers. Unfortunately, many cybersecurity methods, and the security of the Internet itself, depend precisely on the intractability of such tasks. If quantum computing became practicable and robust, then security infrastructure would be immediately upended. Could the rest of the Internet live alongside a Quantum Internet?

The common tendency of these preceding thoughts is that the Internet is surely critical infrastructure and needs to be handled with care, its strengths and weaknesses understood, and its value preserved. The COVID-19 pandemic, still playing out at the time of writing, has highlighted its role in so many ways.

- It has become a vital way for individuals, families, communities, and work colleagues to communicate safely.[23]
- New forms of digital congestion occurred and needed to be solved, for example as residential accounts were used for work.[24]
- New forms of engagement were developed to replace spatially focused collective activities, for instance by museums and orchestras, but also in political demonstrations.[25]
- It became a tool for governments and health services in contact tracing.[26]
- It was source of data, and means of data-sharing, for scientists, pharmacologists, and epidemiologists.[27]
- It was an attack vector for misinformation.[28]

Maybe research in the immediate aftermath of the pandemic will suggest a fifth Internet has appeared, the COVID-19 Internet: where scientific and medical data flows freely; where misinformation is rigorously policed; where inclusion is a key value and digital divides closed; where consumer and citizen services, such as e-commerce, e-government, e-payments, and telemedicine are supported and protected; where virtual reality and other technologies (e.g. haptic technology)[29] are closely integrated to provide a more immersive experience; but where data protection and privacy (for instance of location data for contact tracing, or medical data) are moderated and subordinated to greater public goods; where opting out, anonymity, and obscurity are strongly discouraged; and to the resources of which governments have greater access. Civil liberties might seem less important than social and national security. It would be a powerful technology for fighting a future pandemic, *and one that might emerge through our common cooperation to fight this one*—but a technology that would also be open to massive abuse and potential dystopian futures. How could we stop or police that globally?

Or perhaps it might be argued that a new post-pandemic vision for the Internet *should* have emerged, but didn't. How could we tell? That's not easy to say. It seems evident from our work that the number of disciplines involved in understanding how the Internet works has no real limit. Computer engineers can no longer seriously claim to have no responsibility to consider the effects and outcomes of their technologies. We have vacated our comfort zones numerous times in the course of writing this book. Computers, politics, networks, social groups, law, philosophy, business, history, mathematics, organized crime, culture, economics: virtually any type of study of any type of interaction could be relevant to this kind of inquiry. We label our research *Web Science*, deliberately multidisciplinary, but we have our biases, like everyone else. Our narrative will surely not convince everyone, and we welcome alternative views and debate.[30]

There are two major, perhaps contradictory, lessons from our survey of Four Internets. First, the scalability of the Internet means that it will always be able to reap the benefits of *network effects*. It is an infrastructure for moving data around, and the bigger the network, the greater the potential for productive use of the data. These benefits are too large to sacrifice.

Second, interpretation turns data into information. Information has meaning, and therefore also can bring costs, whether as malware, spam, misinformation, privacy breaches, deepfakes, obscene or hateful content, revelation of state secrets or intellectual property. *Moving information efficiently is not always a good thing*, when the information itself is harmful. But different people and cultures have very different views of what is harmful, and so restrictions cannot be determined technically.

The contradiction can be described in terms of the OSI layered model of the Internet from Chapter 3. The first lesson is that the lower, transport layers need to be robust against interference, so that the network is connected and the network effects realized. The second lesson is that when dysfunction emerges at the upper, policy layers because the interpretations of the data reveal its harmfulness, policymakers need to have licence to interfere. If they don't, they—as the Russians or the Iranians would prefer—will simply pull the plug.

Somehow, between those two lessons, we need to craft an information infrastructure that will respect them both, allow for scaling, and permit the technical specification of even more Internets than the four we describe in this book. The growth of the Internet at the global scale simply *is* the creation of more Internets. As Part II shows, worries about openness translated into new ways of exploiting the Internet to preserve human rights, to enable market solutions, and to establish particular social values. This process cannot stop as ever-more diverse groups are connected.

That will mean, however, that the interactions between the stakeholders are managed and conflicts resolved, and the basic technical standards have to hold, and must remain open, because sometimes they will be all that keeps the network connected.

GLOSSARY OF ABBREVIATIONS

AEPD	Agencia Española de Protección de Datos (Spanish data protection authority)
AI	Artificial Intelligence
AOL	America Online
APEC	Asia-Pacific Economic Cooperation
API	Application Programming Interface
App	Application, application software
ARPA	Advanced Research Projects Agency
ASCII	American Standard Code for Information Interchange
BGP	Border Gateway Protocol
BJP	Bharatiya Janata Party
BRI	Belt and Road Initiative
CAA	Certification Authority Authorization
CBM	Confidence-Building Measure
CBPR	Cross-Border Privacy Rules
ccTLD	Country Code Top-Level Domain
CCTV	Closed-circuit television
CDU	Christlich Demokratische Union Deutschlands (German Christian Democratic Union)
CEO	Chief executive officer
CJEU	Court of Justice of the European Union
CNIL	Commission Nationale de l'Informatique et des Libertés (French data protection authority)
CSIRT	Computer Security Incident Response Team
DARPA	Defense Advanced Research Projects Agency
DDoS	Distributed Denial of Service
DNC	Democratic National Committee
DNS	Domain Name System
DOA	Digital Object Architecture
DOC	(US) Department of Commerce
DOI	Digital Object Identifier

DPD	(EU 1995) Data Protection Directive
DPI	Deep Packet Inspection
DRM	Digital Rights Management
DSTA	(Singapore) Defence Science and Technology Agency
DTP	Data Transfer Project
ECHR	European Court of Human Rights
EEA	European Economic Area
EU	European Union
FCC	Federal Communications Commission
FDI	Foreign direct investment
FIRST	Forum of Incident Response and Security Teams
FL4C	Free Lunch for Children
FoI	Freedom of Information
FTC	Federal Trade Commission
GAC	(ICANN) Government Advisory Committee
GDPR	General Data Protection Regulation
GNU	GNU's Not UNIX
GPS	Global Positioning System
HCSEC	Huawei Cyber Security Evaluation Centre
HLEG	High Level Expert Group on Fake News and Online Disinformation
HTML	Hypertext Markup Language
HTTP	Hypertext Transfer Protocol
HTTPS	Hypertext Transfer Protocol Secure
IAB	Internet Architecture Board
IANA	Internet Assigned Numbers Authority
ICANN	Internet Corporation for Assigned Names and Numbers
IEEE	Institute of Electrical and Electronics Engineers
IETF	Internet Engineering Task Force
IFTF	Institute for the Future
IMDb	Internet Movie Database
iOS	originally iPhone Operating System, the mobile OS developed by Apple
IoT	Internet of Things
IP	Internet Protocol
IPv4	Internet Protocol Version 4
IPv6	Internet Protocol Version 6
IRA	Internet Research Agency
ISO	International Organization for Standardization
ISOC	Internet Society
ISP	Internet Service Provider
ITU	International Telecommunication Union

IXP	Internet Exchange Point
JIT	Joint Investigation Team
M2M	Machine-to-Machine
ML	Machine Learning
MOSIP	Modular Open Source Identity Platform
NAFTA	North American Free Trade Agreement
NCSC	(UK) National Cyber Security Centre
NHS	(UK) National Health Service
NIC	Network Information Center
NIMC	(Nigerian) National Identity Management Commission
NIN	(Iranian) National Information Network
OECD	Organisation for Economic Co-operation and Development
ONA	Open Network Architecture
OS	Operating System
OSI	Open Systems Interconnection model
OSIA	Open Standards Identity API
P2P	Peer-to-Peer
P3P	Platform for Privacy Preferences
PIF	(Saudi) Public Investment Fund
PII	Personally identifying information
PIR	Public Interest Registry
PLA	(Chinese) People's Liberation Army
Pod	Personal online datastore
PRC	People's Republic of China
RDF	Resource Description Framework
RFC	Request for comments
RFID	Radio Frequency Identification
RIR	Regional Internet Registry
RT	Russia Today
RuNet	Russian Internet
SNS	Social networking site
Solid	Social Linked Data
SOPA	(US) Stop Online Piracy Act 2012
STS	Science and Technology Studies
TCP	Transmission Control Protocol
TCP/IP	Internet Protocol Suite
TDP	Telugu Desam Party
TLD	Top-level domain
UNDP	United Nations Development Programme
UPI	Unified Payment Interface
URI	Uniform Resource Identifier
URL	Uniform Resource Locator

USMCA	United States-Mexico-Canada Agreement
USP	Unique Selling Proposition
VOIP	Voice Over Internet Protocol
VPN	Virtual Private Network
W3C	World Wide Web Consortium
WHO	World Health Organization
WTO	World Trade Organization

NOTES

PREFACE
1. Blum 2012, DeNardis 2014a.
2. Berners-Lee et al. 2006; O'Hara et al. 2013; and O'Hara & Hall 2013 for the interdisciplinary study of web-like technology-mediated networks from an engineering perspective, which has been called *Web Science*. Similar important and valuable research from a sociological perspective has gone under the umbrella title of *Internet Studies*: Dutton 2013; Graham & Dutton 2014.

CHAPTER 1
1. Cave 2013, 163. 'Our' in this case refers to the European tradition.
2. The latest penetration figures can be found at https://www.internetworldstats.com/stats.htm or https://www.statista.com/statistics/269329/penetration-rate-of-the-internet-by-region/. For an early prediction that 'the boom years of Internet explosion are over', Modis 2005.
3. Arora 2019.
4. There is a debate over whether 'data', as a borrowing from Latin, is the plural of 'datum', or whether it is a singular mass noun. We prefer the latter usage, because we see 'data' as a complementary concept to 'information', and so we might expect them to have parallel grammar. Hence we treat 'data' as singular in this book, and 'a piece of data' refers to a single item, rather as we would talk about 'a piece of information'. For a complete argument that 'data' is a singular term in English, Kieron O'Hara, '"Data are" or "data is"? A pedant writes', *Web Science Trust*, 24 October 2020, https://www.webscience.org/2020/10/24/data-are-or-data-is-a-pedant-writes/.
5. Caldarelli & Catanzaro 2012; Estrada & Knight 2015.
6. Technically, the theoretical number of connections is of the order of N^2, where N is the number of nodes, but for a large real-world network where it is unlikely that every pair of nodes is directly connected, it is closer to $N(\log_2 N)$—a figure that will still grow faster than any linear relationship between N and the number of connections. Thanks to Vint Cerf for pointing this out.
7. Ferguson 2017; Raymond 2001.
8. Hayek 1935; Nye 2011, 114–118.
9. Guilluy 2019.
10. Cross & Woozley 1964, 98–101.
11. O'Hara et al. 2013.
12. Brook 2008.
13. Boutang 2011, 107–112, quote from 110.

14. O'Hara 2009.
15. On smart vs. 'sledgehammer' regulation, see Brown & Marsden 2013, 20.
16. O'Hara et al. 2013.
17. For national Internets, Mueller 2017, 48–54. For North Korea, Ko et al. 2009; Gerschewski & Dukalskis 2018.
18. The upgrade from IPv4 to IPv6, despite the support of governments and tech giants alike, is taking forever, precisely because of the positive network effects of IPv4. Yet the creation of IPv6 is just such an incompatible invention of a new protocol. Thanks to Carolyn Nguyen for this perspicuous point. We explain and discuss the upgrade in Chapter 3.
19. Laura Kolodny, 'Former Google CEO predicts the internet will split in two—and one part will be led by China', *CNBC*, 20 September 2018, https://www.cnbc.com/2018/09/20/eric-schmidt-ex-google-ceo-predicts-internet-split-china.html. Griffiths 2019, 317–318 also takes the binary view.
20. Mueller 2017, 3.
21. For language, Kralisch & Mandl 2006.
22. Mueller 2017, 43, his emphases.
23. Carolyn Nguyen points out that this definition emphasizes technical incompatibilities, but that we also need to think about regulatory and governance incompatibilities too. Indeed—although it is likely that the latter will lead to technical difficulties anyway.
24. It may be thought that American incivility is a passing phase associated with the period in office of President Trump. Though it is true that he brought incivility to a fine art, he didn't invent it, and it won't disappear under President Biden. It is too early to tell how the Biden regime will evolve at the time of writing, and President Biden may not make such a point of 'putting America first', although the finely balanced Senate may also have its say. But the point is not that America acts in its own interests to the exclusion of everyone else, but rather that its policymakers tend to assume that its interests *are* everyone else's. US foreign policy has always been unilateral internationalism, driven by an exceptionalist identity of America as the exemplar, with a mission to lead and use its military and economy power wisely, requiring less of a responsibility to respect the bounds that restrain other nations. See Restad 2012 for an elaboration.
25. Coker 2019.
26. Macfarlane 2018.
27. Coker 2019, 167.
28. Kaplan 2018. And in this context, Huntington 1996 once more appears relevant.
29. Nye 2011, 119.
30. For alternative characterizations of 'data' in different disciplines, Kitchin 2014, 2–4.
31. For a historical note about TTL and its competitors in the early days of computing, https://www.computerhistory.org/siliconengine/standard-logic-ic-families-introduced/.
32. Roberts 2019, 34.
33. Cf. Freiman & Miller 2020 for a survey of some of the complexities of 'hybrid testimony'.
34. Vosoughi et al. 2012.
35. John Herrman, 'Twitter is a truth machine', *Buzzfeed*, 30 October 2012, https://www.buzzfeednews.com/article/jwherrman/twitter-is-a-truth-machine.
36. Arendt 1963.

37. Illari & Floridi 2014.

38. O'Hara 2013; Kitchin 2014, 12–21 (although he does not make the same data/information distinction as us).

39. Kitchin 2014. Boutang 2011, 144, argues on the contrary that 'knowledge goods' are non-excludable.

40. World Economic Forum, *Personal Data: The Emergence of a New Asset Class*, 17 February 2011, https://www.weforum.org/reports/personal-data-emergence-new-asset-class,

41. Rosenbach & Mansted 2019; Diane Coyle, Stephanie Diepeveen, Julia Wdowin, Jeni Tennison & Lawrence Kay, *The Value of Data*, February 2020, https://www.bennettinstitute.cam.ac.uk/research/research-projects/valuing-data/.

42. Kelleher & Tierney 2018.

43. Alpaydin 2016.

44. Hetherington & West 2020.

45. Kitchin 2014, 67–127.

46. Foucault 1981.

47. Proudhon 1923, 293–294.

48. Scott 1998.

49. Zuboff 2019.

50. O'Hara 2020a.

51. Wagner 2012.

52. Wagner 2012.

53. Giddens 1990.

54. O'Hara 2020a, 2020c, 2021.

55. As argued implicitly in O'Hara & Stevens 2006a.

56. O'Hara 2020a.

57. Thomas & Thomas 1928, 571–572.

58. Francis Fukuyama, 'After neoconservatism', *New York Times*, 19 February 2006, http://www.nytimes.com/2006/02/19/magazine/after-neoconservatism.html.

59. For positive narratives of digital modernity, Kurzweil 2005; Schmidt & Cohen 2013; Brynjolfsson & McAfee 2014; Schwab 2016. Negative examples include Barrat 2015; Zuboff 2019.

60. Koenis 2014. Erikson 1976 is a classic account of how collective trauma undermined a community.

61. Harvey 1990.

62. Sumter et al. 2017.

63. Christensen 1997.

64. Curley & Salmelin 2018, 15–25; Yang et al. 2016.

65. Schumpeter 1950.

66. Colombo et al. 2015.

67. Guttentag 2015; Tristan Greene, 'Winding Tree is the new kid on the blockchain set on disrupting Airbnb and Expedia', *The Next Web*, 8 September 2017, https://thenextweb.com/money/2017/09/08/1075124/.

68. Cramer & Krueger 2016; Yang et al. 2016; Christopher Langner, 'Uber, disrupted', *Bloomberg*, 15 April 2016, https://www.bloomberg.com/opinion/articles/2016-04-15/uber-disrupted.

PART I

1. Thanks to Vint Cerf for emphasizing this point, and for the wording we have used in the last two sentences.
2. Clark's slogan was from a meeting of the Internet Engineering Task Force. For the IETF's current position on rough consensus and running code, P. Resnick, *On Consensus and Humming in the IETF*, IETF Request for Comments 7282, June 2014, https://tools.ietf.org/html/rfc7282.
3. Braman 2020.

CHAPTER 2

1. In this chapter, we are indebted to narratives from Abbate 2000; Castells 2001; Carpenter 2013; Ziewitz & Brown 2013; DeNardis 2014a; Naughton 2016; Evans 2018; Cerf 2019b; and comments from Vint Cerf.
2. Waldrop 2001.
3. Evans 2018, 111–122.
4. We give a standard, relatively US-centric, narrative here. For an antidote to the Americanism, see Carpenter 2013.
5. Cerf 2009, 2019b.
6. As an example of the collaboration between Cerf and Kirstein, their (1978) is a fascinating early discussion of the technical, legal, and political problems of the internetworking scheme.
7. Van Schewick 2010.
8. Cerf 2019c.
9. Naughton 2016.
10. Mueller 2013.
11. Greenstein 2015.
12. Castells 2001.
13. Philip Elmer-Dewitt, 'First nation in cyberspace', *Time*, 6 December 1993, http://content.time.com/time/magazine/article/0,9171,979768,00.html.
14. Ziewitz & Brown 2013.
15. https://www.ietf.org/rfc/rfc1958.
16. Wardrip-Fruin 2004. Evans 2018, 153–174, discusses the contribution of Wendy Hall to the development of hypertext.
17. Cerf 2019b argues that the URI needs to be replaced by something more persistent, because 'they have embedded in them domain names and the domain names go away if you forget to pay the rent or if your company goes out of business so all the URLs that reference content in the Internet may no longer resolve'. The Digital Object Architecture (DOA), developed by Robert Kahn, is one response to this, to try to create identifiers that will last through time. We discuss this in a surprising context in Chapter 11.
18. Priestley et al. 2020.
19. Berners-Lee & O'Hara 2013.
20. https://www.imdb.com/.
21. Battelle 2005; Stross 2008.
22. Shadbolt et al. 2006; Berners-Lee & O'Hara 2013.
23. Berners-Lee et al. 1994.
24. Kirkpatrick 2010.
25. Frier 2020.
26. Hogan & Wellman 2014.

27. Ellison & boyd 2013.
28. DeNardis 2014b.

CHAPTER 3

1. Bygrave 2013, 171–181.
2. Powell 2013.
3. Greenleaf 2013, 247–248.
4. https://www.itu.int/net/wsis/wgig/index.html.
5. Budnitsky 2020.
6. UN Secretary-General's High-level Panel on Digital Cooperation 2019. Thanks to Carolyn Nguyen for emphasizing this historical context to us.
7. Negro 2020; Mueller & Badiei 2020, 65–71.
8. Weber 2013; Lyall 2016.
9. See e.g. Alex Fitzgerald, 'United States to UN: keep your hands off the Internet', *Mashable*, 3 August 2012, https://mashable.com/2012/08/03/us-un-internet/?europe=true. For a robust opposing view, Bill Thompson, 'Damn the Constitution: Europe must take back the Web', *The Register*, 9 August 2002, https://www.theregister.com/2002/08/09/damn_the_constitution_europe_must/.
10. For the latest elected membership of the UN Human Rights Council, which usually contains some eye-popping members, https://www.ohchr.org/EN/HRBodies/HRC/Pages/CurrentMembers.aspx.
11. Bygrave 2013, 174.
12. DeNardis 2014a, 226–230; Weber 2020, 111–117; Hofmann 2020.
13. Padovani & Pavan 2007, 100.
14. Brown & Marsden 2013, 173.
15. See Brown & Marsden 2013, 15–17; DeNardis 2014a.
16. See Daniel Karrenberg, *The Internet Domain Name System Explained for Non-Experts*, Internet Society Briefing #16, 1 March 2004, https://www.internetsociety.org/resources/doc/2004/the-internet-domain-name-system-explained-for-non-experts-by-daniel-karrenberg/.
17. For a pungent criticism of Esther Dyson's stewardship of ICANN, Milton Mueller, 'New ORG stewards? Or vultures circling?' *Internet Governance Project*, 8 January 2020, https://www.internetgovernance.org/2020/01/08/new-org-stewards-or-vultures-circling/.
18. For the power struggles around the creation of ICANN, Griffiths 2019, 217–225; Mueller & Badiei 2020, 63–65.
19. For a critique of ICANN's apparent failures of accountability, Kieren McCarthy, 'As internet pioneers fight to preserve.org's non-profit status, those in charge are hiding behind dollar signs', *The Register*, 9 January 2020, https://www.theregister.co.uk/2020/01/09/org_preservation/. Bill Thompson, 'Damn the Constitution: Europe must take back the Web', *The Register*, 9 August 2002, https://www.theregister.com/2002/08/09/damn_the_constitution_europe_must/, is an early swipe at US control of the Internet that includes ICANN in its scope.
20. Becker 2019.
21. Jeremy Rabkin, *Careful What You Wish For: Why ICANN 'Independence' Is a Bad Idea*, 22 June 2009, http://www.circleid.com/posts/20090622_careful_what_you_wish_icann_independence_bad_idea/126.

22. Soldatov & Borogan 2017, 228–237; Griffiths 2019, 227–233; Vinton G. Cerf, 'Keep the Internet open', *New York Times*, 24 May 2012, https://www.nytimes.com/2012/05/25/opinion/keep-the-internet-open.html.
23. Froomkin 2013.
24. Froomkin 2013; Bygrave 2013, 179–180.
25. Parks & Starosielski 2015.
26. http://www.itu.int/rec/dologin_pub.asp?lang=e&id=T-REC-X.200-199407-I!!PDF-E&type=items.
27. Cerf 2018.
28. On value neutrality, Shilton 2018.
29. Mueller 2013.
30. Cerf 2019a.
31. Mueller 2013.
32. Internet Society, *State of IPv6 Deployment 2018*, 6 June 2018, https://www.internetsociety.org/resources/2018/state-of-ipv6-deployment-2018/.
33. Carpenter 2013, 102.
34. Cf. Mueller & Badiei 2020, 60–63.
35. Mogridge 1997 for this counterintuitive discovery about the traffic network.
36. Zittrain 2006, 1981–1982.

CHAPTER 4

1. Mueller & Badiei 2020, 60–63. For a strong rebuttal of the exceptionalist view, Bill Thompson, 'Damn the Constitution: Europe must take back the Web', *The Register*, 9 August 2002, https://www.theregister.com/2002/08/09/damn_the_constitution_europe_must/.
2. David Isenberg & David Weinberger, *The Paradox of the Best Network*, https://net-paradox.com/.
3. Reglitz 2020. Also Tim Berners-Lee, 'Covid-19 makes it clearer than ever: Access to the internet should be a universal right', *The Guardian*, 4 June 2020.
4. https://www.eff.org/cyberspace-independence.
5. Benkler 2006.
6. Coates 2011.
7. Brown & Marsden 2013, 36.
8. Dolmans & Piana 2010; Brown & Marsden 2013, 38–43; Kahin & Abbate 1995.
9. Boutang 2011, 81–87, 108–109.
10. Kernighan & Pike 1983.
11. Surowiecki 2004; Tapscott & Williams 2006, 2010; Leadbeater 2008.
12. Stross 2008, 21–45; Hal Varian, *Open Source and Open Data*, 12 September 2019, https://www.blog.google/technology/research/open-source-and-open-data/.
13. Mark Zuckerberg, 'Standing for voice and free expression', *Facebook*, 17 October 2019, https://www.facebook.com/notes/mark-zuckerberg/standing-for-voice-and-free-expression/10157267502546634/.
14. Lessig 2001; Boutang 2011, 104–117.
15. Diderot 1995, 19.
16. For the contrast between open data and shared data, Jeni Tennison, 'Open data is a public good. It should not be confused with data sharing', *The Guardian*, 12 May 2014, https://www.theguardian.com/commentisfree/2014/may/12/response-confuse-open-data-sharing-government.
17. Kitchin 2014, 48–66.
18. Pitt-Payne 2007.

19. For the distribution of skills to work with structured data, Koesten et al. 2017.
20. Bowles et al. 2014; Shadbolt & O'Hara 2013; O'Hara 2014a.
21. For a broad history of openness, Johns 2009.
22. For the advantages of sharing data, Jarvis 2011. For the value of open data during the Covid-19 pandemic, Jeni Tennison, 'Why isn't the government publishing more data about coronavirus deaths?' *The Guardian*, 2 April 2020, https://www.theguardian.com/commentisfree/2020/apr/02/government-publish-data-coronavirus-deaths.
23. Eggers 2013.
24. https://wikileaks.org/.
25. https://www.starlink.com/.
26. Brown & Marsden 2013, 36; Cannon 2003.
27. Marsden 2013.
28. Brown & Marsden 2013, 141–144, 152–155.

CHAPTER 5

1. https://en.wikipedia.org/wiki/Main_Page, for the English version.
2. https://stats.wikimedia.org/EN/TablesPageViewsMonthlyCombined.htm.
3. Quoted in Fallis 2011, 297.
4. https://en.wikipedia.org/wiki/Trevor_Philips, https://en.wikipedia.org/wiki/Elisabeth_Lutyens.
5. 'North Korea blows up the South's de facto embassy', *The Economist*, 20 June 2020, https://www.economist.com/asia/2020/06/18/north-korea-blows-up-the-souths-de-facto-embassy.
6. Richard Cooke, 'Wikipedia is the last best place on the Internet', *Wired*, 17 February 2020, https://www.wired.com/story/wikipedia-online-encyclopedia-best-place-internet/.
7. For the principles, https://en.wikipedia.org/wiki/Wikipedia:No_original_research, https://en.wikipedia.org/wiki/Wikipedia:Verifiability, https://en.wikipedia.org/wiki /Wikipedia:Neutral_point_of_view and https://en.wikipedia.org/wiki/Ignore_all_rules.
8. https://en.wikipedia.org/wiki/Jimmy_Wales.
9. Fallis 2011.
10. Giles 2005.
11. Clauson et al. 2008; Brown 2011.
12. https://wiki.dbpedia.org/.
13. Ferrucci et al. 2010.
14. Niederer & van Dijck 2010; Tsvetkova et al. 2017.
15. Witnessed (but not perpetrated) by Kieron O'Hara. For the general online reaction, Barney Ronay, 'Hands-on Thierry Henry becomes public enemy numéro un', *The Guardian*, 19 November 2009, https://www.theguardian.com/football/2009/nov/19/thierry-henry-france-football-worldcup.
16. Leitch 2014, 37, 74.
17. https://en.wikipedia.org/wiki/Wikipedia:List_of_hoaxes_on_Wikipedia, which of course may or may not be reliable.
18. Kumar et al. 2016; Ruprechter et al. 2019.
19. Leitch 2014, 35.
20. Sanger 2006, 319.
21. Leitch 2014, 37–38; O'Neil 2010.

22. Oliver Balch, 'Making the edit: Why we need more women in Wikipedia', *The Guardian*, 28 November 2019, https://www.theguardian.com/careers/2019/nov/28/making-the-edit-why-we-need-more-women-in-wikipedia; Lir 2019; Hinnosaar 2019; Frost-Arnold 2019; Menking et al. 2019.

23. https://en.wikipedia.org/wiki/Wikipedia:Arbitration/Requests/Case/GamerGate/Statement.

24. Gauthier & Sawchuk 2017.

25. Evgeny Morozov, 'Can the US government stem the tide of "fake news" in a postmodern world?' *The Guardian*, 31 October 2019, https://www.theguardian.com/global/commentisfree/2019/oct/31/can-the-us-government-stem-the-tide-of-fake-news-in-a-postmodern-world.

26. Noam Cohen, 'How Wikipedia prevents the spread of coronavirus misinformation', *Wired*, 15 March 2020, https://www.wired.com/story/how-wikipedia-prevents-spread-coronavirus-misinformation/.

27. Julia Carrie Wong, 'Tech giants struggle to stem "infodemic" of false coronavirus claims', *The Guardian*, 10 April 2020, https://www.theguardian.com/world/2020/apr/10/tech-giants-struggle-stem-infodemic-false-coronavirus-claims.

28. Menking et al. 2019.

PART II

1. For instance, Amol Rajan, 'No such thing as the internet', *BBC News*, 19 October 2020, https://www.bbc.com/news/entertainment-arts-54514574, misinterprets our thesis in this way. He cites the Indian and Indonesian governments' paternal interventions in the Internet as showing that other nations than China and the United States can intervene. This is obvious, of course they can—but their interventions are both paternal. The adjective is important, not the geographical label. This is the key point.

2. Froomkin 2013, 30.

3. Brown & Marsden 2013, 4–5.

CHAPTER 6

1. For China's early problems with the Internet, O'Hara 2009; and for the failure of the Open Internet to intimidate dictators, Morozov 2011.

2. Benkler 2006.

3. 'Why startups are leaving Silicon Valley', *The Economist*, 1 September 2018, https://www.economist.com/leaders/2018/08/30/why-startups-are-leaving-silicon-valley.

4. 'Silicon Valley is changing, and its lead over other tech hubs narrowing', *The Economist*, 1 September 2018, https://www.economist.com/briefing/2018/09/01/silicon-valley-is-changing-and-its-lead-over-other-tech-hubs-narrowing.

5. For the squeeze on minor artists, Lanier 2011.

6. For the exploitation of user-generated content, Ekbia & Nardi 2017.

7. For the five cases, Brown & Marsden 2013 *passim*, and for the straw man point, xvi.

8. Cave 2013, 162–163.

9. Mark Scott, Laurens Cerulus, & Janosch Delcker, 'Coronavirus is forcing people to work from home. Will it break the internet?' *Politico*, 17 March 2020, https://www.politico.eu/article/coronavirus-covid19-internet-data-work-home-mobile-internet/; Laura Kayali, 'Brussels in talks with Netflix about reducing internet congestion', *Politico*, 18 March 2020,

https://www.politico.eu/article/brussels-in-talks-with-netflix-about-reducing-internet-congestion/; Mark Sweney, 'Netflix to slow Europe transmissions to avoid broadband overload', *The Guardian*, 19 March 2020, https://www.theguardian.com/media/2020/mar/19/netflix-to-slow-europe-transmissions-to-avoid-broadband-overload. Thanks to Bill Thompson for pointing out that the measures may not have been necessary.

10. For the Brazilian pursuit of online rights, before its recession and corruption scandals, Bygrave 2013, 190.

11. Morozov 2011.

12. DeNardis 2014a, 84.

13. DeNardis 2014a, 199–221.

14. DeNardis 2014a, 95.

15. Hunter 2008.

16. For alignment and fragmentation, Mueller 2017, 49, and for national Internets more generally 48–54. For the structural difficulty of alignment, Boutang 2011, 111.

17. Aryan et al. 2013.

18. Louise Matsakis, 'What happens if Russia cuts itself off from the Internet?' *Wired*, 2 December 2019, https://www.wired.com/story/russia-internet-disconnect-what-happens/.

19. 'Weird but wired', *The Economist*, 1 February 2007, https://www.economist.com/asia/2007/02/01/weird-but-wired; 'Black hats for hire', *The Economist*, 9 August 2011, https://www.economist.com/banyan/2011/08/09/black-hats-for-hire; 'What North Koreans learn from their smartphones', *The Economist*, 10 August 2017, https://www.economist.com/asia/2017/08/10/what-north-koreans-learn-from-their-smartphones.

20. Zittrain 2006, 1977.

21. Brown & Marsden 2013, 139–162.

22. O'Hara & Hall 2010.

23. Elle Hunt, 'Tay, Microsoft's AI chatbot, gets a crash course in racism from Twitter', *The Guardian*, 24 March 2016, https://www.theguardian.com/technology/2016/mar/24/tay-microsofts-ai-chatbot-gets-a-crash-course-in-racism-from-twitter.

24. For positive accounts of the value of big data, Mayer-Schönberger & Cukier 2013; Pentland 2014. For a sustained attack on Pentland, Zuboff 2019, 416–444.

25. Elkhodr et al. 2016; Maple 2017.

26. Brown & Marsden 2013, 145; Anderson 2008, 633–678; Day 2017, Matthias Jung, 'Cloud security and the end-to-end principle', *Elastic Security*, 14 June 2011, https://elasticsecurity.wordpress.com/2011/06/14/cloud-security-and-the-end-to-end-principle/.

27. Rössler 2005; Conti 2009; Greenwald 2014; Christl & Spiekermann 2016; Lyon 2018; Zuboff 2019; Hildebrandt & O'Hara 2020.

28. Suler 2004; Bishop 2014; Griffiths 2014; Lallas 2014; Buckels et al. 2019.

29. Davenport 2002.

30. Coles-Kemp et al. 2019; Zanzotto 2019.

31. Noam Cohen, 'Google's algorithm isn't biased, it's just not human', *Wired*, 14 December 2018, https://www.wired.com/story/google-algorithm-conservatives-biased-its-just-not-human/; 'Did AI teach itself to "not like" women?' *Mind Matters*, 11 October 2018, https://mindmatters.ai/2018/10/did-ai-teach-itself-to-not-like-women/.

32. Kirkpatrick 2010; Marichal 2012.

33. 'The unexpected brightness of new satellites could ruin the night sky', *The Economist*, 30 May 2019, https://www.economist.com/science-and-technology/2019/05/30/the-unexpected-brightness-of-new-satellites-could-ruin-the-night-sky.

34. 'Virtual reality continues to make people sick', *The Economist*, 23 November 2019, https://www.economist.com/science-and-technology/2019/11/23/virtual-reality-continues-to-make-people-sick.

35. Sidney Fussell, 'Why can't this soap dispenser identify dark skin?' *Gizmodo*, 17 August 2017, https://gizmodo.com/why-cant-this-soap-dispenser-identify-dark-skin-1797931773.

36. Nye 2011, 122–132.

CHAPTER 7

1. Fawcett 2018.
2. Berlin 2002.
3. Berlin 2002, 171, quoting Tawney 1938, 208.
4. Habermas 1996; Sunstein 2007; Mossberger et al. 2008; Dutton 2009; Coleman & Blumler 2009; Hindman 2009; Loader & Mercea 2011; Stevens & O'Hara 2015.
5. Habermas 1989, 27.
6. For duffing up the bourgeoisie, the *locus classicus* is Marx & Engels 2002, 219–233, berating it for, among other things, emancipating the serfs, ending feudal and hierarchical relations, increasing trade, commerce, science, and navigation, revolutionizing industrial production, showing 'what man's activity can bring about', accomplishing 'wonders far surpassing Egyptian pyramids, Roman aqueducts and Gothic cathedrals', creating a cosmopolitan society, satisfying material wants, expanding people's horizons, lowering prices, urbanizing, creating 'more massive and more colossal productive forces than have all preceding generations together', and other heinous crimes.
7. McCloskey 2006, 85.
8. McCloskey 2006, 85.
9. Burke 1968, 90.
10. Hall & Soskice 2001, 8.
11. Whitman 2004.
12. EDPS Ethics Advisory Group 2018.
13. Bradford 2012, 15.
14. 'The backlash against Airbnb', *The Economist*, 21 July 2018, https://www.economist.com/news/europe/21746287-protests-will-meet-holidaymakers-charlemagne-backlash-against-airbnb.
15. For Vestager, 'Is Margrethe Vestager championing consumers or her political career?' *The Economist*, 14 September 2017, https://www.economist.com/business/2017/09/14/is-margrethe-vestager-championing-consumers-or-her-political-career; 'Europe has so many issues with Big Tech it hardly knows where to begin', *The Economist*, 5 October 2019, https://www.economist.com/business/2019/10/03/europe-has-so-many-issues-with-big-tech-it-hardly-knows-where-to-begin.
16. Thomas Macaulay, 'Automated facial recognition breaches GDPR, says EU digital chief', *The Next Web*, 17 February 2020, https://thenextweb.com/neural/2020/02/17/automated-facial-recognition-breaches-gdpr-says-eu-digital-chief/.
17. For Macron's ambitions, 'Emmanuel Macron on Europe's fragile place in a hostile world', *The Economist*, 7 November 2019, https://www.economist.com/briefing/2019/11/07/emmanuel-macron-on-europes-fragile-place-in-a-hostile-world;

Angelique Chrisafis, 'France's digital minister says tax on big tech is just the start', *The Guardian*, 12 January 2020, https://www.theguardian.com/world/2020/jan/12/frances-digital-minister-tax-on-tech-giants-just-the-start-cedric-o-gafa.

18. Konstantinos Komaitis, 'Europe's pursuit of digital sovereignty could affect the future of the Internet', *tech.eu*, 7 September 2020, https://tech.eu/features/32780/europe-digital-sovereignty/.

19. 'The Redmond doctrine', *The Economist*, 14 September 2019, https://www.economist.com/business/2019/09/12/the-redmond-doctrine.

20. Brown & Marsden 2013, 64; Bradford 2020; Layton & Mclendon 2018.

21. Brown & Marsden 2013, 191.

22. For the de-indexing case, Case C-131/12, *Google Spain SL, Google Inc. v Agencia Española de Protección de Datos, Mario Costeja González*; O'Hara 2015b; O'Hara & Shadbolt 2015; O'Hara et al. 2016; Politou et al. 2018.

23. Petkova 2019.

24. For the institutional political economy of privacy, Brown & Marsden 2013, 59–63.

25. 'A controversial new copyright law moves a step closer to approval', *The Economist*, 15 September 2018, https://www.economist.com/business/2018/09/13/a-controversial-new-copyright-law-moves-a-step-closer-to-approval.

26. Marcus et al. 2008, quoted at DeNardis 2014a, 130.

27. Tocqueville 2011, 68.

28. Thanks to Carolyn Nguyen for this formulation.

29. Rössler 2005.

30. Grimm & Rossnagel 2000; Reay et al. 2007, 2009; Leon et al. 2010,

31. Fairfield 2012, 2013; Ferden 2015; Ed Bott, 'Why Do Not Track is worse than a miserable failure', *ZDNet*, 21 September 2012, https://www.zdnet.com/article/why-do-not-track-is-worse-than-a-miserable-failure/.

32. Bamberger & Mulligan 2015.

33. Prosser 1960.

34. Narayanan & Shmatikov 2010.

35. Greenleaf 2013, 230.

36. Heisenberg & Fandel 2004, 109, although as late as 2013, even as shrewd a judge as Lilian Edwards called the international expansion of EU privacy laws a 'non-starter' (Edwards 2013, 336).

37. Bradford 2020; Brown & Marsden 2013, 59–63.

38. Quoted in Christou 2018, 185.

39. Greenwald 2014.

40. Soma & Rynerson 2008, 259–280.

41. Greenwald 2014.

42. Bender 2016, 117.

43. For a critique of the CJEU on these and other cases, Pfisterer 2019.

44. Bradford 2020, 151–152.

45. Stuart D. Levi, Eve-Christie Vermynck, & Daniel Millard, '*Schrems II*: EU-US Privacy Shield struck down, but European Commission standard contractual clauses survive', *skadden.com*, 17 July 2020, https://www.skadden.com/insights/publications/2020/07/schrems-ii-eu-us-privacy-shield-struck-down.

46. For a critique of the label 'right to be forgotten', Markou 2015. For the 2010 aspiration, Greenleaf 2013, 242.

47. O'Hara 2015b tells the story of the Google Spain decision without the benefit of hindsight.

48. *Opinion of Advocate General Jääskinen*, 25 June 2013, http://curia.europa.eu/juris/document/document.jsf?docid=138782&doclang=EN.

49. For the Canadian firm (AggregateIQ), Jonathan Chadwick, 'AggregateIQ hit with first GDRP [sic] enforcement notice', *Computer Business Review*, 21 September 2018, https://www.cbronline.com/news/gdpr-enforcement.

50. 'Mark Zuckerberg says he wants more regulation for Facebook', *The Economist*, 6 April 2019, https://www.economist.com/business/2019/04/06/mark-zuckerberg-says-he-wants-more-regulation-for-facebook.

51. https://ec.europa.eu/digital-single-market/en/proposal-eprivacy-regulation, Joanna de Fonseka, Benjamin Slinn, John McGovern, Andre Walter, & Magdalena Kogut-Czarkowska, 'Cookies under e-Privacy regulation: A developing story as Europe is drifting apart', *Lexology*, 25 March 2020, https://www.lexology.com/library/detail.aspx?g=e2064f70-4979-4b98-8ef7-1698779e8458.

52. Goldsmith & Wu 2006.

53. Bradford 2012, 2020.

54. Bradford 2020.

55. Greenleaf 2019.

56. http://cbprs.org/. For comparison with GDPR, Greenleaf 2013, 231–232; Andrei Gribakov, 'Cross-border privacy rules in Asia: An overview', *Lawfare*, 3 January 2019, https://www.lawfareblog.com/cross-border-privacy-rules-asia-overview.

57. Schwartz 2019.

58. Soma & Rynerson 2008, 183–184.

59. https://iapp.org/resources/article/privacy-by-design-the-7-foundational-principles/.

60. Dan McCrum, 'Wirecard: The timeline', *Financial Times*, 25 June 2020, https://www.ft.com/content/284fb1ad-ddc0-45df-a075-0709b36868db.

61. 'Who will be the main loser from Europe's new data-privacy law?' *The Economist*, 26 May 2018, https://www.economist.com/business/2018/05/26/who-will-be-the-main-loser-from-europes-new-data-privacy-law; 'The power of privacy', *The Economist*, 23 March 2019, https://www.economist.com/briefing/2019/03/23/big-tech-faces-competition-and-privacy-concerns-in-brussels.

62. 'Europe's GDPR offers privacy groups new ways to challenge adtech', *The Economist*, 23 March 2019, https://www.economist.com/briefing/2019/03/23/europes-gdpr-offers-privacy-groups-new-ways-to-challenge-adtech; Chris Shuptrine, 'GDPR and ad tech: The definitive guide of 2019', *adzerk*, 15 February 2019, https://adzerk.com/blog/gdpr-ad-tech/.

63. EDPS Ethics Advisory Group 2018, 6.

CHAPTER 8

1. Petkova 2019.

2. Mueller & Badiei 2020, 71–74, place security and privacy at the centre of Internet governance issues at the present time.

3. Parkinson et al. 2018.

4. Polanyi 1944, Zuboff 2019, 100.

5. O'Hara 2020a, 2021.

6. Kendall-Taylor et al. 2020, 104; see also Xu 2020.

7. Blaydes 2018, 31–60.

8. Guriev & Treisman 2015.

9. Razaghpanah et al. 2018. Other examples in Zuboff 2019, 136–137; Vallina-Rodriguez 2016.
10. McDonald & Cranor 2008.
11. For apparency, schraefel et al. 2020.
12. Zuboff 2019, 139–140.
13. Berle 2020.
14. Thomas Macaulay, 'Automated facial recognition breaches GDPR, says EU digital chief', *The Next Web*, 17 February 2020, https://thenextweb.com/neural/2020/02/17/automated-facial-recognition-breaches-gdpr-says-eu-digital-chief/; Parth Misra, 'Here's how face recognition tech can be GDPR compliant', *The Next Web*, 29 October 2018, https://thenextweb.com/contributors/2018/10/29/heres-how-face-recognition-tech-can-be-gdpr-compliant/; David Meyer, 'Facebook really wants to bring back its face-scanning tech in Europe. Problem is, it might be illegal', *Fortune*, 19 April 2018, https://fortune.com/2018/04/19/facebook-facial-recognition-gdpr-eu/.
15. 'Facebook settles facial recognition dispute', *BBC News*, 30 January 2020, https://www.bbc.com/news/technology-51309186.
16. Hong 2017.
17. Macnish 2018, 30–47.
18. Giddens 1991; Scott 1998.
19. Giddens 1990.
20. O'Hara 2021.
21. Lyon 2001, 151–154; Macnish 2018, 118–129.
22. Etzioni 1999, 43–137; Macnish 2018, 77–117.
23. Cf. Clarke et al. 2014.
24. Coles-Kemp et al. 2019.
25. For ten tests of intrusion, RUSI 2015 (a report, for which one of the current authors, Hall, sat on the review panel).
26. Brohé 2016.
27. Li & Shapiro 2020, 70–75.
28. 'Coronavirus forces Christian Democrats to postpone crucial conference', *DW*, 26 October 2020, https://www.dw.com/en/coronavirus-forces-christian-democrats-to-postpone-crucial-conference/a-55400660; 'Germany: Angela Merkel's party to decide her successor in January', *DW*, 31 October 2020, https://www.dw.com/en/germany-angela-merkels-party-to-decide-her-successor-in-january/a-55461472. Thanks to Gefion Thuermer for discussions and advice about the German Basic Law.
29. O'Hara & Stevens 2006b.
30. Oliver et al. 2020.
31. 'Countries are using apps and data networks to keep tabs on the pandemic', *The Economist*, 28 March 2020, https://www.economist.com/briefing/2020/03/26/countries-are-using-apps-and-data-networks-to-keep-tabs-on-the-pandemic.
32. Ahmed et al. 2020.
33. Judah Ari Gross, 'Shin Bet says it found 500 coronavirus carriers with its mass surveillance', *Times of Israel*, 26 March 2020, https://www.timesofisrael.com/shin-bet-says-it-found-500-coronavirus-carriers-with-its-mass-surveillance/.
34. https://www.healthhub.sg/apps/38/tracetogether-app, https://www.tech.gov.sg/media/technews/tracetogether-behind-the-scenes-look-at-its-development-process.

35. Hariz Baharudin, 'Coronavirus: S'pore contact tracing app now open-sourced, 1 in 5 here have downloaded', *Straits Times*, 10 April 2020, https://www.straitstimes.com/singapore/coronavirus-spore-contact-tracing-app-now-open-sourced-1-in-5-here-have-downloaded.

36. 'Binyamin Netanyahu boasted too soon of defeating the coronavirus', *The Economist*, 23 July 2020, https://www.economist.com/middle-east-and-africa/2020/07/23/binyamin-netanyahu-boasted-too-soon-of-defeating-the-coronavirus.

37. Oliver et al. 2020.

38. Hart et al. 2020.

39. https://www.top10vpn.com/news/surveillance/covid-19-digital-rights-tracker/.

40. 'Some countries want central databases for contact-tracing apps', *The Economist*, 2 May 2020, https://www.economist.com/europe/2020/04/30/some-countries-want-central-databases-for-contact-tracing-apps; John Naughton, 'Contact apps won't end lockdown. But they might kill off democracy', *The Guardian*, 25 April 2020, https://www.theguardian.com/commentisfree/2020/apr/25/contact-apps-wont-end-lockdown-but-they-might-kill-off-democracy; Paul Lewis, David Conn, & David Pegg, 'UK government using confidential patient data in coronavirus response', *The Guardian*, 12 April 2020, https://www.theguardian.com/world/2020/apr/12/uk-government-using-confidential-patient-data-in-coronavirus-response. For the use of SNS data, https://dataforgood.fb.com/tools/social-connectedness-index/. *COVID-19 Rapid Evidence Review: Exit through the App Store?* Ada Lovelace Institute, 20 April 2020, https://www.adalovelaceinstitute.org/our-work/covid-19/covid-19-exit-through-the-app-store/; Kenan Malik, 'Yes, expect more surveillance during a crisis, but beware it once the danger has passed', *The Guardian*, 12 April 2020, https://www.theguardian.com/commentisfree/2020/apr/12/yes-expect-more-surveillance-during-a-crisis-but-beware-it-once-the-danger-has-passed.

41. *Contact Tracing for COVID-19: Current Evidence, Options for Scale-up and an Assessment of Resources Needed*, European Centre for Disease Prevention and Control, April 2020, https://www.ecdc.europa.eu/sites/default/files/documents/COVID-19-Contract-tracing-scale-up.pdf.

42. Keeling et al. 2020.

43. Dan Sabbagh & Alex Hern, 'UK abandons contact-tracing app for Apple and Google model', *The Guardian*, 18 June 2020, https://www.theguardian.com/world/2020/jun/18/uk-poised-to-abandon-coronavirus-app-in-favour-of-apple-and-google-models.

44. James Tapper, 'NHS Covid app developers "tried to block rival symptom trackers"', *The Guardian*, 20 June 2020, https://www.theguardian.com/technology/2020/jun/20/nhs-covid-app-developers-tried-to-block-rival-symptom-trackers.

45. 'Norway suspends virus-tracing app due to privacy concerns', *The Guardian*, 15 June 2020, https://www.theguardian.com/world/2020/jun/15/norway-suspends-virus-tracing-app-due-to-privacy-concerns.

46. 'Dutch coronavirus app rolls out nationally Oct. 10 after months of talks', *NL Times*, 6 October 2020, https://nltimes.nl/2020/10/06/dutch-coronavirus-app-rolls-nationally-oct-10-months-talks.

47. Ieva Ilves, 'Why are Google and Apple dictating how European democracies fight coronavirus?' *The Guardian*, 16 June 2020, https://www.theguardian.com/commentisfree/2020/jun/16/google-apple-dictating-european-democracies-coronavirus.

48. Hildebrandt & Gurwirth 2008; Bayamlioğlu et al. 2018.

CHAPTER 9

1. Priestley et al. 2020.
2. Hayek 1935, 1960.
3. Coase 1937.
4. Baumol 2002.
5. Ferguson 2017.
6. Sorescu 2017; Boutang 2011, 20–37.
7. Hall & Soskice 2001, 8.
8. Layton & Mclendon 2018, 235.
9. Voss & Houser 2019, 308.
10. Bamberger & Mulligan 2015.
11. 'American tech giants are making life tough for startups', *The Economist*, 2 June 2018, https://www.economist.com/business/2018/06/02/american-tech-giants-are-making-life-tough-for-startups; 'Silicon Valley is changing, and its lead over other tech hubs narrowing', *The Economist*, 1 September 2018, https://www.economist.com/briefing/2018/09/01/silicon-valley-is-changing-and-its-lead-over-other-tech-hubs-narrowing.
12. Zuboff 2019, 124.
13. For Obama and Barroso, Brown & Marsden 2013, xi.
14. Brown & Marsden 2013, 22.
15. Brown & Marsden 2013, 37–38.
16. Zuboff 2019, 86–87; Zittrain 2008.
17. Jones 2020.
18. https://amturing.acm.org/vp/berners-lee_8087960.cfm.
19. Zittrain 2008; Brown & Marsden 2013, 190–192.
20. Brown & Marsden 2013, 124–125; DeNardis 2014b.
21. Berners-Lee 2010, quoted in DeNardis 2014a, 241.
22. https://www.w3.org/blog/2014/12/opensocial-foundation-moves-standards-work-to-w3c-social-web-activity/.
23. In Wu 2003.
24. 'A vote on "net neutrality" has intensified a battle over the internet's future', *The Economist*, 23 December 2017, https://www.economist.com/news/business/21732823-americas-fcc-repeals-obama-era-rules-ensure-all-web-traffic-treated-equally-vote; 'Another debate about net neutrality in America', *The Economist*, 22 April 2017, http://www.economist.com/news/business/21721245-new-head-fcc-will-roll-back-obama-era-rules-another-debate-about-net-neutrality.
25. Samuelson 2001.
26. Brown & Marsden 2013, 140–141.
27. Greenstein et al. 2016; Vogelsang 2018, Jamison 2018.
28. Glass & Tardiff 2019.
29. Hooton 2020.
30. Nunziato 2009; Zuboff 2019, 109.
31. DeNardis 2014a, 108ff.
32. Brown & Marsden 2013, 84–85.
33. Ashlee Vance, 'Facebook: The making of 1 billion users', *Bloomberg*, 5 October 2012, https://www.bloomberg.com/news/articles/2012-10-04/facebook-the-making-of-1-billion-users; 'Facebook's (FB) CEO Mark Zuckerberg on Q4 2014 results–earnings call transcript', *Seeking Alpha*, 28 January 2015, https://seekingalpha.com/article/2860966-facebooks-fb-ceo-mark-zuckerberg-on-q4-2014-results-earnings-call-transcript.

34. Nick Statt, 'Facebook is shifting its Libra cryptocurrency plans after intense regulatory pressure', *The Verge*, 3 March 2020, https://www.theverge.com/2020/3/3/21163658/facebook-libra-cryptocurrency-token-ditching-plans-calibra-wallet-delay.

35. Mark Zuckerberg, 'Is connectivity a human right?' *Facebook*, n.d. [2013], https://www.facebook.com/isconnectivityahumanright.

36. Taylor 2016.

37. https://info.internet.org/en/. The list of countries in which Free Basics has been launched is at https://info.internet.org/en/story/where-weve-launched/, and the platform, together with some discussion of how to join it, is described at https://info.internet.org/en/story/platform/.

38. Biddle et al. 2017, 2–3.

39. Taylor 2016. See also Arora 2019.

40. Roberts 2019, 27.

41. Kieren McCarthy, 'Internet world despairs as non-profit.org sold for $$$$ to private equity firm, price caps axed', *The Register*, 20 November 2019, https://www.theregister.co.uk/2019/11/20/org_registry_sale_shambles/; Kieren McCarthy, 'Protestors in Los Angeles force ICANN board out of hiding over.org sale—for a brief moment, at least', *The Register*, 25 January 2020, https://www.theregister.co.uk/2020/01/25/icann_board_org/.

42. 'Controversial sale of.org web domain blocked', *BBC News*, 1 May 2020, https://www.bbc.com/news/technology-52501456.

43. Zuboff 2019, 53–54.

44. Evgeny Morozov, 'The tech "solutions" for coronavirus take the surveillance state to the next level', *The Guardian*, 15 April 2020, https://www.theguardian.com/commentisfree/2020/apr/15/tech-coronavirus-surveillance-state-digital-disrupt.

45. Morozov 2019a, 2019b; Arora 2019.

46. Battelle 2005; Stross 2008; Zuboff 2019, 67–68.

47. Oddly, Sandberg, an immensely important figure in the history of the Internet, does not feature in Evans 2018.

48. Kirkpatrick 2010, 256–273; Zuboff 2019, 457.

49. Ekbia & Nardi 2017.

50. Zuboff 2019, 102.

51. Jamie Harris, 'Zuckerberg wants West to lead the way on internet laws before China does', *Yahoo! Finance*, 18 May 2020, https://uk.finance.yahoo.com/news/zuckerberg-wants-west-lead-way-214343057.html.

52. Brailovskaia et al. 2018; Turkle 2011, 293–294.

53. O'Hara 2012, 68–82.

CHAPTER 10

1. Zuboff 2019, 134.

2. Ebenstein 2015; Schumpeter 1950.

3. Lee 2018, 170–172.

4. Bajgar et al. 2019.

5. Farhi & Gourio 2019.

6. Autor et al. 2020.

7. Rochet & Tirole 2003.

8. Quotes from Layton & Mclendon 2018, 242–243. For a DC critique of 'hipster' antitrust, Wright et al. 2019.

9. Page & Lopatka 2007.

10. https://www.statista.com/statistics/276623/number-of-apps-available-in-leading-app-stores/.

11. 'Why Apple's developers are cross', *The Economist*, 27 June 2020, https://www.economist.com/business/2020/06/27/why-apples-developers-are-cross.

12. https://www.statista.com/statistics/672747/amazons-consolidated-net-revenue-by-segment/.

13. 'How to dismantle a monopoly', *The Economist*, 26 October 2019, https://www.economist.com/business/2019/10/24/dismembering-big-tech.

14. Naughton 2016.

15. 'The economic crisis will expose a decade's worth of corporate fraud', *The Economist*, 18 April 2020, https://www.economist.com/business/2020/04/18/the-economic-crisis-will-expose-a-decades-worth-of-corporate-fraud.

16. Negroponte 1995.

17. Christensen 1997.

18. For Facebook's supposed anti-conservative bias, Jon Kyl, 'Covington Interim Report', August 2019, https://fbnewsroomus.files.wordpress.com/2019/08/covington-interim-report-1.pdf.

19. For foreign policy, Sitaraman 2020.

20. The Stop BEZOS Act was aimed at Amazon's alleged low pay; Jeff Bezos is the billionaire head of Amazon.

21. Sunny Kim, 'Elizabeth Warren proposes criminal penalties for spreading voting disinformation online', *CNBC*, 29 January 2020, https://www.cnbc.com/2020/01/29/warren-proposes-criminal-penalties-for-spreading-disinformation-online.html; Matthew Sheffield, 'Poll: Most Americans not interested in new regulations for big tech companies', *The Hill*, n.d. [March 2019], https://thehill.com/hilltv/what-americas-thinking/433482-poll-americans-not-interested-in-extra-regulations-for-big-tech; Casey Newton, 'Read the full transcript of Mark Zuckerberg's leaked internal Facebook meetings', *The Verge*, 1 October 2019, https://www.theverge.com/2019/10/1/20892354/mark-zuckerberg-full-transcript-leaked-facebook-meetings.

22. Mark Zuckerberg, 'The Internet needs new rules. Let's start in these four areas', *Washington Post*, 30 March 2019, https://www.washingtonpost.com/opinions/mark-zuckerberg-the-internet-needs-new-rules-lets-start-in-these-four-areas/2019/03/29/9e6f0504-521a-11e9-a3f7-78b7525a8d5f_story.html.

23. Nick Clegg, 'I'm joining Facebook to build bridges between politics and tech', *The Guardian*, 19 October 2018, https://www.theguardian.com/commentisfree/2018/oct/19/nick-clegg-facebook-politics-tech; Nancy Scola, 'How Nick Clegg is trying to fix Facebook's global image', *Politico*, 15 May 2020, https://www.politico.eu/article/how-nick-clegg-is-trying-to-fix-facebooks-global-image-2/.

24. Ben Brody & Naomi Nix, 'Google hires Republican Senate aide to head lobby office', *Bloomberg*, 27 September 2019, https://www.bloomberg.com/news/articles/2019-09-27/google-hires-former-republican-senate-aide-to-head-lobby-shop; Zuboff 2019, 126.

25. For a summary with links to this bewildering activity, Makena Kelly, 'Google under antitrust investigation by 50 attorneys general', *The Verge*, 9 September 2019, https://www.theverge.com/2019/9/9/20857440/google-antitrust-investigation-attorneys-general-advertising-search.

26. Adi Robertson & Russell Brandom, 'Congress releases blockbuster tech antitrust report', *The Verge*, 6 October 2020, https://www.theverge.com/2020/10/6/

21504814/congress-antitrust-report-house-judiciary-committee-apple-google-amazon-facebook.

27. Natasha Lomas, 'Trump just noticed Europe's $5BN antitrust fine for Google', *TechCrunch*, 19 July 2018, https://techcrunch.com/2018/07/19/trump-just-noticed-europes-5bn-antitrust-fine-for-google/.

28. Jonathan Shieber & Ingrid Lunden, 'The Justice Department has filed its antitrust lawsuit against Google', *TechCrunch*, 20 October 2020, https://techcrunch.com/2020/10/20/justice-department-will-reportedly-file-its-antitrust-lawsuit-against-google-today/.

29. Quoted in Lauren Feiner, 'House Democrats say Facebook, Amazon, Alphabet, Apple enjoy "monopoly power" and recommend big changes', *CNBC*, 6 October 2020, https://www.cnbc.com/2020/10/06/house-democrats-say-facebook-amazon-alphabet-apple-enjoy-monopoly-power.html#close.

30. Only a matter of weeks after the US action was brought, the EU brought antitrust charges against Amazon, India launched an investigation into Google's app store Play, and Chinese regulators drafted a set of antitrust rules.

CHAPTER 11

1. Mueller 2013.
2. Aycan 2006, 445.
3. Dworkin 1972. 'Paternalism' and 'maternalism' are gendered terms, based on traditional parental roles. A paternalist is usually taken to mean someone who decides where another's interests lie without taking their opinion into account. A maternal person is someone who cares unconditionally for the other. Clearly one could be a paternal female, or a maternal man. Clearly, one could also be both paternal and maternal at the same time, although there will be points of tension when the other decides not to follow the paternal injunction.
4. Hayek 1935.
5. Mark Zuckerberg, 'Standing for voice and free expression', *Facebook*, 17 October 2019, https://www.facebook.com/notes/mark-zuckerberg/standing-for-voice-and-free-expression/10157267502546634/.
6. Coker 2019, 96–111; Macfarlane 2018, 23–59.
7. Hansen 1991, 70; Vallor 2016, 69–72.
8. Ronan & Needham 1978, 282.
9. Lee 2018, 57–58; Wu 2020.
10. For Xi Jinping, Xue & Li 2019.
11. Griffiths 2019, 131–158, 195–201; 'China has turned Xinjiang into a police state like no other', *The Economist*, 2 June 2018, https://www.economist.com/briefing/2018/05/31/china-has-turned-xinjiang-into-a-police-state-like-no-other; 'How Xinjiang's gulag tears families apart', *The Economist*, 17 October 2020, https://www.economist.com/china/2020/10/17/how-xinjiangs-gulag-tears-families-apart.
12. Griffiths 2019, 26–29, 95–113.
13. Griffiths 2019, 185–192.
14. Chase & Mulvenon 2004.
15. For Google's marginalization, Griffiths 2019, 61–67, 115–127, 165–174.
16. Naaman Zhou, 'China to relax its internet restrictions for 100,000 students hit by Australia's coronavirus travel ban', *The Guardian*, 13 February 2020, https://www.theguardian.com/world/2020/feb/13/china-to-open-up-its-internet-for-100000-students-hit-by-australias-coronavirus-travel-ban.

17. Wübbeke et al. 2016.
18. Li 2018.
19. Zaagman 2018.
20. 'The smartphone will see you now', *The Economist*, 7 March 2020, https://www.economist.com/business/2020/03/05/millions-of-chinese-cooped-up-and-anxious-turn-to-online-doctors.
21. Griffiths 2019, 227–238.
22. Anna Gross & Madhumita Murgia, 'China shows its dominance in surveillance technology', *Financial Times*, 27 December 2019, https://www.ft.com/content/b34d8ff8-21b4-11ea-92da-f0c92e957a96.
23. Creemers 2017a; Negro 2020.
24. Chip Sharp, *Overview of the Digital Object Architecture (DOA)*, Internet Society, 25 October 2016, https://www.internetsociety.org/resources/doc/2016/overview-of-the-digital-object-architecture-doa/,
25. Eli Dourado, 'How Russia and the UN are actually planning to take over the Internet', *The Hill*, 12 September 2016, https://thehill.com/blogs/congress-blog/technology/295320-how-russia-and-the-un-are-actually-planning-to-take-over-the. For the relaxed view, Karim Farhat, *Digital Object Architecture and the Internet of Things: Getting a 'Handle' on Techno-Political Competition*, Georgia Tech Internet Governance Project, n.d., https://www.internetgovernance.org/wp-content/uploads/Karim_Farhat_IoT_IGP.pdf; *ITU WTSA 2016 Outcomes: An Internet Society Perspective*, Internet Society, 22 November 2016, https://www.internet-society.org/resources/doc/2016/itu-wtsa-2016-outcomes-an-internet-society-perspective/.
26. Daniel Hurst, Lily Kuo, & Charlotte Graham-McLay, 'Zhenhua Data leak: Personal details of millions around world gathered by China tech company', *The Guardian*, 14 September 2020, https://www.theguardian.com/world/2020/sep/14/zhenhua-data-full-list-leak-database-personal-details-millions-china-tech-company.
27. Creemers 2017b; Guy 2018.
28. 'The economic crisis will expose a decade's worth of corporate fraud', *The Economist*, 18 April 2020, https://www.economist.com/business/2020/04/18/the-economic-crisis-will-expose-a-decades-worth-of-corporate-fraud.
29. Griffiths 2019, 190.
30. Lee 2018, 51–53.
31. 'Networking the "Belt and Road": The future is digital', *Mercator Institute*, 28 August 2019, https://www.merics.org/en/bri-tracker/networking-the-belt-and-road.
32. Samm Sacks, *New China Data Privacy Standard Looks More Far-Reaching than GDPR*, Center for Strategic and International Studies, 29 January 2018, https://www.csis.org/analysis/new-china-data-privacy-standard-looks-more-far-reaching-gdpr; Michael Gentle, 'China's data-privacy law vs. GDPR', *medium.com*, 11 October 2018, https://medium.com/the-balance-of-privacy/chinas-data-privacy-law-vs-gdpr-566fde8c213c.
33. Liu 2020.
34. 'China's new $15bn tech fund emulates SoftBank's Vision Fund', *The Economist*, 5 July 2018, https://www.economist.com/business/2018/07/05/chinas-new-15bn-tech-fund-emulates-softbanks-vision-fund.
35. 'Alibaba and Tencent have become China's most formidable investors', *The Economist*, 4 August 2018, https://www.economist.com/business/2018/08/02/alibaba-and-tencent-have-become-chinas-most-formidable-investors.

36. Lee 2018, 64.

37. 'America and the EU are both toughening up on foreign capital', *The Economist*, 28 July 2018, https://www.economist.com/finance-and-economics/2018/07/26/america-and-the-eu-are-both-toughening-up-on-foreign-capital; 'Silicon Valley gets queasy about Chinese money', *The Economist*, 11 August 2018, https://www.economist.com/business/2018/08/09/silicon-valley-gets-queasy-about-chinese-money.

38. Kevin Webb, 'China is cracking down on new video games entering the country and it's costing publishing giants billions in profit', *Business Insider*, 25 October 2018, https://www.businessinsider.nl/china-video-games-crackdown-costing-billions-2018-10/.

39. Barclay Bram, 'Jack Ma was China's most vocal billionaire. Then he vanished', *Wired*, 13 January 2021, https://www.wired.co.uk/article/jack-ma-disappear-ant-group-ipo, is one of the fullest accounts of this episode, although written while Ma's whereabouts were still unknown following his very public humiliation.

40. 'Xiaomi's forthcoming IPO shows how the rules of business are changing', *The Economist*, 9 June 2018, https://www.economist.com/business/2018/06/07/xiaomis-forthcoming-ipo-shows-how-the-rules-of-business-are-changing; Lee 2018, 25–28, 137.

41. O'Hara 2009.

42. Creemers 2017a; Arora 2019, 35–37; Roberts et al. 2021.

43. Negro 2020.

44. 'A diarist in Wuhan faces fury for sharing her story with the West', *The Economist*, 18 April 2020, https://www.economist.com/china/2020/04/16/a-diarist-in-wuhan-faces-fury-for-sharing-her-story-with-the-west.

45. Xue & Li 2019, 25–26. The English of this quote is not of the best, but the meaning is clear and we have left it as published in Singapore.

46. *Provisions on the Governance of the Online Information Content Ecosystem*, China Law Translate, 21 December 2019, https://www.chinalawtranslate.com/en/provisions-on-the-governance-of-the-online-information-content-ecosystem/.

47. 'Some people in China help the party police the internet', *The Economist*, 18 January 2020, https://www.economist.com/china/2020/01/18/some-people-in-china-help-the-party-police-the-internet.

48. McDougall 2002; Feuchtwang 2002.

49. Roberts et al. 2021.

50. 'The first face-off', *The Economist*, 9 November 2019, https://www.economist.com/china/2019/11/09/a-lawsuit-against-face-scans-in-china-could-have-big-consequences; Cao Yin & Aybek Ashkar, 'Facial recognition sparks debate', *China Daily*, 19 November 2019, http://www.chinadaily.com.cn/global/2019-11/19/content_37523904.htm.

51. 'How covid-19 is interrupting children's education', *The Economist*, 21 March 2020, https://www.economist.com/international/2020/03/19/how-covid-19-is-interrupting-childrens-education.

52. 'Sealed off', *The Economist*, 1 February 2020, https://www.economist.com/china/2020/01/30/tough-quarantine-measures-have-spread-across-china.

53. Bolsover 2018.

54. Griffiths 2019, 9–10, 74–77.

55. Lu et al. 2018.

56. Jiang & Fu 2018.

57. 'Sealed off', *The Economist*, 1 February 2020, https://www.economist.com/china/2020/01/30/tough-quarantine-measures-have-spread-across-china; 'Casualties of war', *The Economist*, 22 February 2020, https://www.economist.com/china/2020/02/22/in-china-newly-confirmed-cases-of-coronavirus-infection-are-falling.

58. 'To curb covid-19, China is using its high-tech surveillance tools', *The Economist*, 29 February 2020, https://www.economist.com/china/2020/02/29/to-curb-covid-19-china-is-using-its-high-tech-surveillance-tools.

59. Griffiths 2019, 275–283; Lee 2018, 16–17, 56–61.

60. Lim 2019, 137–144; Zaagman 2018; Li et al. 2018.

61. Lee 2018, 119–121.

62. Helen Davidson, 'China starts major trial of state-run digital currency', *The Guardian*, 28 April 2020, https://www.theguardian.com/world/2020/apr/28/china-starts-major-trial-of-state-run-digital-currency.

63. Liang et al. 2018; Creemers 2017b; Lewis 2020.

64. Engelmann et al. 2019.

65. Wong & Dobson 2019; Shahin & Zheng 2020; Dai 2020.

66. James Cartledge, 'Councils explain use of microchips on household bins', *letsrecycle.com*, 1 September 2006, https://www.letsrecycle.com/news/latest-news/councils-explain-use-of-microchips-on-household-bins/.

67. Griffiths 2019, 10–11.

68. Catalin Cimpanu, 'Kazakhstan government is now intercepting all HTTPS traffic', *ZDNet*, 18 July 2019, https://www.zdnet.com/article/kazakhstan-government-is-now-intercepting-all-https-traffic/.

69. Tham Yuen-C, 'Singapore's fake news law to come into effect Oct 2', *Straits Times*, 1 October 2019, https://www.straitstimes.com/politics/fake-news-law-to-come-into-effect-oct-2; 'The ministries of truth', *The Economist*, 8 February 2020, https://www.economist.com/asia/2020/02/06/singaporean-ministers-can-decide-what-is-fake-news.

70. Brown & Marsden 2013, 93ff.

71. Natasha Lomas, 'UK health minister leans on social media platforms to delete anti-vax content', *TechCrunch*, 25 April 2019, https://techcrunch.com/2019/04/25/u-k-health-minister-leans-on-social-media-platforms-to-delete-anti-vax-content/.

72. Department for Digital, Culture, Media and Sport/Home Office, *Online Harms White Paper*, 8 April 2019, https://www.gov.uk/government/consultations/online-harms-white-paper.

73. Brown & Marsden 2013, 94ff.

74. For issues around intermediary liability, Brown & Marsden 2013, 76–79.

75. Josh Taylor, 'Not just nipples: How Facebook's AI struggles to detect misinformation', *The Guardian*, 16 June 2020, https://www.theguardian.com/technology/2020/jun/17/not-just-nipples-how-facebooks-ai-struggles-to-detect-misinformation.

76. Roberts 2019; Accenture, *Content Moderation: The Future Is Bionic*, 2017, https://www.accenture.com/ie-en/_acnmedia/PDF-47/Accenture-Webscale-New-Content-Moderation-POV.pdf.

77. James Vincent, 'YouTube says China-linked comment deletions weren't caused by outside parties', *The Verge*, 28 May 2020, https://www.theverge.com/2020/5/28/21272983/youtube-deleting-comments-chinese-communist-censorship-explanation.

78. 'China talks of building a "digital Silk Road"', *The Economist*, 2 June 2018, https://www.economist.com/china/2018/05/31/china-talks-of-building-a-digital-silk-road.

79. 'Networking the "Belt and Road": The future is digital', *Mercator Institute*, 28 August 2019, https://www.merics.org/en/bri-tracker/networking-the-belt-and-road.

80. Adrian Shahbaz, *Freedom on the Net 2018: The Rise of Digital Authoritarianism*, Freedom House, https://freedomhouse.org/report/freedom-net/2018/rise-digital-authoritarianism.

81. Adrian Shahbaz & Allie Funk, *Freedom on the Net 2019: The Crisis of Social Media*, Freedom House, 13, https://freedomhouse.org/report/freedom-net/2019/crisis-social-media.

82. For bKash, 'Rules are made to be broken', *The Economist*, 7 March 2020, https://www.economist.com/asia/2020/03/05/a-new-mobile-money-firm-in-bangladesh-is-benefiting-from-special-treatment.

83. 'Why some countries are turning off the internet on exam days', *The Economist*, 7 July 2018, https://www.economist.com/middle-east-and-africa/2018/07/05/why-some-countries-are-turning-off-the-internet-on-exam-days.

84. Dominic Ziegler, 'Return to centre', *The Economist*, 8 February 2020, https://www.economist.com/special-report/2020/02/06/china-wants-to-put-itself-back-at-the-centre-of-the-world.

85. Lee 2018, 34–35.

86. 'Chinese and US tech giants go at it in emerging markets', *The Economist*, 7 July 2018, https://www.economist.com/business/2018/07/07/chinese-and-us-tech-giants-go-at-it-in-emerging-markets.

87. David Gilbert, 'Zimbabwe is trying to build a China style surveillance state', *Vice*, 2 December 2019, https://www.vice.com/en_uk/article/59n753/zimbabwe-is-trying-to-build-a-china-style-surveillance-state.

88. 'Viva Laos Vegas', *The Economist*, 1 February 2020, https://www.economist.com/asia/2020/01/30/south-east-asia-is-sprouting-chinese-enclaves.

CHAPTER 12

1. Tao et al. 2017; Wang 2020, 229–290.

2. Triollo 2020.

3. Milton Mueller, 'Part 2: Let's have an honest conversation about Huawei', *Internet Governance Project*, 25 October 2019, https://www.internetgovernance.org/2019/10/25/part-2-lets-have-an-honest-conversation-about-huawei/.

4. *Huawei Cyber Security Evaluation Centre Oversight Board: Annual Report 2019*, UK Cabinet Office, 28 March 2019, https://www.gov.uk/government/publications/huawei-cyber-security-evaluation-centre-oversight-board-annual-report-2019; Amit Katwala, 'Here's how GCHQ scours Huawei hardware for malicious code', *Wired*, 22 February 2019, https://www.wired.co.uk/article/huawei-gchq-security-evaluation-uk.

5. Rachel Kraus, 'Welp, the U.S. is already ending its ZTE sanctions. Here's how it happened', *Mashable*, 7 June 2018, https://mashable.com/2018/06/07/us-ends-zte-sanctions-trump/.

6. 'Old export regulations get a new use', *The Economist*, 18 January 2020, https://www.economist.com/united-states/2020/01/16/old-export-regulations-get-a-new-use.

7. *Huawei Annual Report 2019*, https://www.huawei.com/en/press-events/annual-report/2019; 'America's latest salvo against Huawei is aimed at chipmaking in China', *The Economist*, 23 May 2020, https://www.economist.com/business/2020/05/23/americas-latest-salvo-against-huawei-is-aimed-at-chipmaking-in-china.

8. 'America closes the last loophole in its hounding of Huawei', *The Economist*, 18 August 2020, https://www.economist.com/business/2020/08/18/america-closes-the-last-loophole-in-its-hounding-of-huawei.

9. 'America's war on Huawei nears its endgame', *The Economist*, 16 July 2020, https://www.economist.com/briefing/2020/07/16/americas-war-on-huawei-nears-its-endgame.

10. Dan Sabbagh & Lily Kuo, 'Huawei to be stripped of role in UK's 5G network by 2027, Dowden confirms', *The Guardian*, 14 July 2020, https://www.theguardian.com/technology/2020/jul/14/huawei-to-be-stripped-of-role-in-uk-5g-network-by-2027-dowden-confirms.

11. Patrick Wintour, '"Westlessness": is the west really in a state of peril?' *The Guardian*, 16 February 2020, https://www.theguardian.com/world/2020/feb/16/westlessness-is-the-west-really-in-a-state-of-peril; Triollo 2020, 26–27.

12. Dominic Ziegler, 'The future stage', *The Economist*, 8 February 2020, https://www.economist.com/special-report/2020/02/06/the-digital-side-of-the-belt-and-road-initiative-is-growing; Griffiths 2019, 304; 'Young Africans want more democracy', *The Economist*, 7 March 2020, https://www.economist.com/middle-east-and-africa/2020/03/05/young-africans-want-more-democracy; Jonathan E. Hillman & Maesea McCalpin, *Watching Huawei's 'Safe Cities'*, Center for Strategic and International Studies brief, 4 November 2019, https://www.csis.org/analysis/watching-huaweis-safe-cities.

13. Shi Jiangtao, 'Chinese ambassador accused of threatening German car industry if Huawei is frozen out', *South China Morning Post*, 15 December 2019, https://www.scmp.com/news/china/diplomacy/article/3042190/chinese-ambassador-accused-threatening-german-car-industry-if, Philip Heijmans, 'The U.S.-China tech war is being fought in Central Europe', *The Atlantic*, 6 March 2019, https://www.theatlantic.com/international/archive/2019/03/czech-zeman-babis-huawei-xi-trump/584158/; Filip Jirouš & Jichang Lulu, 'Huawei in CEE: From "strategic partner" to potential threat', *Sinopsis*, 17 May 2019, https://sinopsis.cz/en/huawei-in-cee-from-strategic-partner-to-potential-threat/; Tom McEnchroe & Janek Kroupa, 'Former Huawei employees say client information was discussed at Chinese embassy', *Radio Prague International*, 22 July 2019, https://www.radio.cz/en/section/curraffrs/former-huawei-employees-say-client-information-was-discussed-at-chinese-embassy.

14. Ryan Broderick, 'Forget the trade war. TikTok is China's most important export right now', *BuzzFeed News*, 16 May 2019, https://www.buzzfeednews.com/article/ryanhatesthis/forget-the-trade-war-tiktok-is-chinas-most-important-export; 'TikTok time bomb', *The Economist*, 9 November 2019, https://www.economist.com/business/2019/11/07/tiktoks-silly-clips-raise-some-serious-questions.

15. 'Who are the TikTok saga's biggest winners?', *The Economist*, 16 September 2020, https://www.economist.com/business/2020/09/16/who-are-the-tiktok-sagas-biggest-winners.

16. 'Will Beijing derail the TikTok deal?' *The Economist*, 3 September 2020, https://www.economist.com/business/2020/09/03/will-beijing-derail-the-tiktok-deal.

17. Joseph McCormick, 'Egyptian police use Grindr to lure gay men to hotel rooms', *Pink News*, 29 October 2017, https://www.pinknews.co.uk/2017/10/29/egyptian-police-use-grindr-to-lure-gay-men-to-hotel-rooms/; Elisabeth Braw, 'China's Grindr strategy', *Foreign Policy*, 13 December 2019, https://foreignpolicy.com/2019/12/13/grindr-tech-company-china-acquire-strategy-buying-cutting-edge-western-firms/; Zack Whittaker, 'Grindr sold by Chinese owner after US raised

national security concerns', *TechCrunch*, 6 March 2020, https://techcrunch.com/2020/03/06/grindr-sold-china-national-security/; Pan Yue, 'Baidu Vice President James Lu steps down', *China Money Network*, 26 May 2017, https://www.china-moneynetwork.com/2017/05/26/baidu-vice-president-james-lu-steps-down.

18. The lobbying industry is tracked at https://www.opensecrets.org/.
19. Patrick Foulis, 'Dynamism has declined across Western economies', *The Economist*, 17 November 2018, https://www.economist.com/special-report/2018/11/15/dynamism-has-declined-across-western-economies.
20. *Attorney General William P. Barr Delivers the Keynote Address at the Department of Justice's China Initiative Conference*, US Dept of Justice, 6 February 2020, https://www.justice.gov/opa/speech/attorney-general-william-p-barr-delivers-keynote-address-department-justices-china; Chris Strohm & Alyza Sebenius, 'Barr rips China's dominance of 5G technology as major threat', *Bloomberg Quint*, 6 February 2020, https://www.bloombergquint.com/politics/barr-rips-china-s-dominance-of-5g-technology-as-major-threat.
21. Jan Wolfe & Stephen Nellis, 'FTC antitrust victory on Qualcomm questioned by appeals court', *Reuters*, 13 February 2020, https://www.reuters.com/article/us-qualcomm-ftc-argument/ftc-antitrust-victory-on-qualcomm-questioned-by-appeals-court-idUSKBN2071Q6; 'The Qualcommunist manifesto', *The Economist*, 15 February 2020, https://www.economist.com/business/2020/02/13/american-state-capitalism-will-not-beat-china-at-5g.
22. Michael R. Pompeo, *Announcing the Expansion of the Clean Network to Safeguard America's Assets*, press statement, Department of State, 5 August 2020, https://www.state.gov/announcing-the-expansion-of-the-clean-network-to-safeguard-americas-assets/; James Clayton, 'Is the US about to split the internet?' *BBC News*, 6 August 2020, https://www.bbc.com/news/technology-53686390.
23. Alan Burkitt-Gray, 'Rakuten and NEC deliver first cloud 5G unit ahead of June launch', *Capacity Media*, 24 March 2020, https://www.capacitymedia.com/articles/3825160/rakuten-and-nec-deliver-first-cloud-5g-unit-ahead-of-june-launch.

CHAPTER 13

1. Himanen 2001; Tirri 2014; Boutang 2011, 87–91.
2. Mosco 2004, 48.
3. United States Pirate Party (n.d.).
4. Coleman 2013.
5. Arora 2019, 50–68, long quote from 51.
6. Halpin 2012.
7. David Gilbert, 'Anonymous declared war on Trump, and then disappeared', *Vice News*, 28 November 2016, https://www.vice.com/en_us/article/ywna4w/anonymous-declared-war-on-trump-and-then-disappeared.
8. Jarvis 2014.
9. Wong & Brown 2013.
10. Powell 2013, 210–213.
11. Halpin 2012, 27.
12. Feyerabend 1975; Barnes & Bloor 1982; Sismondo 2010. For a robust response to the strong programme, Hollis 1982, and other papers in that volume.
13. Freeden 2018, 2. Also Margetts et al. 2016.
14. Snyder 2018; Coker 2019, 111–126; Budnitsky 2020. For imperial geography, Kaplan 2018.

15. Cherniavsky 1958.
16. Ilyin quoted in Snyder 2018, 10.
17. Pomerantsev 2015, 234.
18. Snyder 2018; Pomerantsev 2015; Soldatov & Borogan 2017, 335–337; Belton 2020.
19. Pomerantsev 2015, 76–90; Snyder 2018, 159–160; 'An ideologue's exit', *The Economist*, 11 May 2013, https://www.economist.com/europe/2013/05/11/an-ideologues-exit; Katri Pynnöniemi, 'Surkov and the three pillars of Putinism', Aleksanteri Institute, 24 April 2019, https://www.helsinki.fi/en/news/society-economy/surkov-and-the-three-pillars-of-putinism.
20. For the Night Wolves, Snyder 2018, 140; and for their philosophy, Pomerantsev 2015, 216–221.
21. 'Russian disinformation distorts American and European democracy', *The Economist*, 24 February 2018, https://www.economist.com/briefing/2018/02/22/russian-disinformation-distorts-american-and-european-democracy.
22. For the history of the Russian Internet, Soldatov & Borogan 2017, *passim*, and for Ukraine, 279–285.
23. Soldatov & Borogan 2017, 151–152.
24. Pomerantsev 2019, 82–90; Kertu Ruus, 'Cyber War I: Estonia attacked from Russia', *European Affairs*, Spring 2008, http://www.europeaninstitute.org/index.php/component/content/article?id=67:cyber-war-i-estonia-attacked-from-russia.
25. Graham et al. 2013.
26. Soldatov & Borogan 2017, 320–321.
27. Rosenbach & Mansted 2019.
28. Cormac & Aldrich 2018; Snyder 2018, 163–164.
29. Pogrund & Maguire 2020, 75–87.
30. Snyder 2018, 138–139, 162ff, 225–227. For the quote, 162.
31. Pomerantsev 2019, 33–40.
32. Kadri Liik, *Winning the Normative War with Russia: An EU-Russia Power Audit*, European Council on Foreign Relations, 21 May 2018, https://www.ecfr.eu/publications/summary/winning_the_normative_war_with_russia_an_eu_russia_power_audit.
33. Chris Marshall, 'Russians "tried to discredit 2014 Scots independence vote"', *The Scotsman*, 13 December 2017, https://www.scotsman.com/news/politics/russians-tried-to-discredit-2014-scots-independence-vote-1-4638210.
34. Snyder 2018, 106.
35. Asmolov 2018.
36. Broniatowski et al. 2018.
37. Freeden 2018.
38. Rebecca Heilweil & Shirin Ghaffary, 'Facebook and Twitter are struggling to get coronavirus disinformation details from the government', *Vox*, 6 March 2020, https://www.vox.com/recode/2020/3/6/21166982/coronavirus-conspiracy-theories-state-department-social-media-russia; Jennifer Rankin, 'Russian media "spreading Covid-19 disinformation"', *The Guardian*, 18 March 2020, https://www.theguardian.com/world/2020/mar/18/russian-media-spreading-covid-19-disinformation.
39. Alex Hern & Luke Harding, 'Facebook uncovers Russian-led troll network based in west Africa', *The Guardian*, 13 March 2020, https://www.theguardian.com/technology/2020/mar/13/facebook-uncovers-russian-led-troll-network-based-in-west-africa.

40. Elena Sánchez Nicolás, 'EU: China, Russia responsible for Covid-19 disinformation', *EU Observer*, 11 June 2020, https://euobserver.com/eu-china/148618,

41. 'The Trump campaign', *The Economist*, 14 March 2020, https://www.economist.com/united-states/2020/03/14/the-trump-campaign.

42. O'Hara 2015a.

43. Aro 2016, Reporters Without Borders (RSF), *RSF Unveils 20/2020 List of Press Freedom's Digital Predators*, https://rsf.org/en/news/rsf-unveils-202020-list-press-freedoms-digital-predators.

44. Pomerantsev 2019, 89.

45. Soldatov & Borogan 2017, 30–43.

46. Soldatov & Borogan 2017, 101ff.

47. Soldatov & Borogan 2017, 311.

48. Soldatov & Borogan 2017, 166–173.

49. Soldatov & Borogan 2017, 198.

50. Soldatov & Borogan 2017, 200, and for the example of Twitter blocking a Ukrainian political site at the behest of Moscow despite having no Russian presence, 216–217.

51. http://www.ligainternet.ru/en/; Soldatov & Borogan 2017, 201. For examples of voluntary nationalist censorship elsewhere (of theatre companies), 'Pursued by a bear', *The Economist*, 1 February 2020, https://www.economist.com/books-and-arts/2020/01/30/the-many-ways-to-censor-cutting-edge-art-in-russia.

52. Soldatov & Borogan 2017, 215–216.

53. For Skolkovo, Pomerantsev 2015, 88–90; and Mike Butcher, 'Chill out—Russia's Skolkovo project attempts a re-boot with a new venture fund', *TechCrunch*, 9 June 2017, https://techcrunch.com/2017/06/09/chill-out-russias-skolkovo-project-attempts-a-re-boot-with-a-new-venture-fund/.

54. For Russian failure to suppress a crowdsourced map of electoral fraud in 2011, Soldatov & Borogan 2017, 137–139.

55. Soldatov & Borogan 2017, 307–309.

56. Soldatov & Borogan 2017, 110–115.

57. For the Western threat, particularly around the Arab Spring, Soldatov & Borogan 2017, 124–125, 163, 223; Mark Pfeifle, 'A Nobel Peace Prize for Twitter?' *Christian Science Monitor*, 6 July 2009, https://www.csmonitor.com/Commentary/Opinion/2009/0706/p09s02-coop.html; Morozov 2011, 1–31; Griffiths 2019, 110–112, 264.

58. Soldatov & Borogan 2017, 238.

59. Snyder 2018, 223–227. For a brief history of DDoS attacks by hacker patriots, Soldatov & Borogan 2017, 149ff.

60. Soldatov & Borogan 2017, 277–279.

61. Soldatov & Borogan 2017, 279–285.

62. Pomerantsev 2015, 276–277; Snyder 2018, 212–215.

63. For Russia Today, Pomerantsev 2015, 54–58; and 'Top 15 Youtube news channels to follow', *Feedspot*, 6 February 2020, https://blog.feedspot.com/news_youtube_channels/.

64. Soldatov & Borogan 2017, 291–294; Ingrid Lunden, 'Durov, out for good from VK.com, plans a mobile social network outside Russia', *TechCrunch*, 22 April 2014, https://techcrunch.com/2014/04/22/durov-out-for-good-from-vk-com-plans-a-mobile-social-network-outside-russia/.

65. Soldatov & Borogan 2017, 295–297; 'UPDATE 1-Russia's Yandex to close offices in Ukraine's Odessa and Kiev', *Reuters*, 1 June 2017, https://www.reuters.

com/article/russia-yandex-ukraine/update-1-russias-yandex-to-close-offices-in-ukraines-odessa-and-kiev-idUSL8N1IY5W8; 'Russia's Yandex resists pressure to share encryption keys with state', *Reuters*, 4 June 2019, https://www.reuters.com/article/us-yandex-privacy/russias-yandex-resists-pressure-to-share-encryption-keys-with-state-idUSKCN1T51JY.

66. Soldatov & Borogan 2017, 341–342.
67. Pomerantsev 2015, 57.
68. Kollars & Petersen 2019.
69. Soldatov & Borogan 2017, 312–317.
70. Howard 2020.
71. Rid 2020, Orwell quoted in Dwan 2018, 140.
72. Woolley & Howard 2017.
73. Craig Timburg, 'Facebook, Twitter remove hundreds of disinformation pages created by Russia, Iran', *Sydney Morning Herald*, 22 August 2018, https://www.smh.com.au/world/north-america/facebook-removes-652-disinformation-pages-created-by-russia-iran-20180822-p4zyyi.html.
74. Nyst & Monaco 2018.
75. Ong & Cabañes 2018.
76. Nyst & Monaco 2018, 17–21, Arora 2019, 85.
77. Griffiths 2019, 212–215.
78. See also Reporters Without Borders (RSF), *RSF Unveils 20/2020 List of Press Freedom's Digital Predators*, 12 March 2020, https://rsf.org/en/news/rsf-unveils-202020-list-press-freedoms-digital-predators.
79. Salge & Karahanna 2018.
80. 'Turkish politicians quit over sex tapes', *al-Jazeera*, 22 May 2011, https://www.aljazeera.com/news/europe/2011/05/2011521132012679960.html.
81. 'The humiliation of Katie Hill offers a warning', *The Atlantic*, 31 October 2019, https://www.theatlantic.com/ideas/archive/2019/10/katie-hill-and-many-victims-revenge-porn/601198/.
82. Reporters Without Borders (RSF), *RSF Unveils 20/2020 List of Press Freedom's Digital Predators*, 12 March 2020, https://rsf.org/en/news/rsf-unveils-202020-list-press-freedoms-digital-predators. See also Arora 2019, 46–47.
83. Quote from Emma Batha, 'Women standing in Iraq election battling abuse including sex tapes', *Reuters*, 11 May 2018, https://www.reuters.com/article/us-iraq-women-abuse/women-standing-in-iraq-election-battling-abuse-including-sex-tapes-idUSKBN1IC18V.
84. Nicolas Kristen, 'Rana Ayyub on online harassment in India: "I get daily rape & death threats"', *medium.com*, 27 June 2019, https://medium.com/global-editors-network/rana-ayyub-on-online-harassment-in-india-i-get-daily-rape-death-threats-c970f542e554.
85. Thomas Erdbrink, 'She won a seat in Iran's Parliament, but hard-liners had other plans', *New York Times*, 11 May 2016, https://www.nytimes.com/2016/05/12/world/middleeast/iran-parliament-minoo-khaleghi.html.
86. Zarni Mann, 'Minister's wife shares fake Facebook photo of Suu Kyi in Islamic headscarf', *The Irrawaddy*, 6 June 2014, https://www.irrawaddy.com/news/burma/ministers-wife-shares-fake-facebook-photo-suu-kyi-islamic-headscarf.html.
87. Soldatov & Borogan 2017, 329–331; Robert Farley, 'Misrepresenting Stone's prescience', FactCheck.org, 28 March 2017, updated 28 January 2019, https://www.factcheck.org/2017/03/misrepresenting-stones-prescience/.

88. Snyder 2018, 219.
89. Snyder 2018, 255–257.
90. Snyder 2018, 226;
91. Brian Barrett, 'Russia doesn't want Bernie Sanders. It wants chaos', *Wired*, 21 February 2020, https://www.wired.com/story/bernie-sanders-russia-chaos-2020-election/.
92. For the figures, Snyder 2018, 227–229.
93. Makena Kelly, 'Twitter will ban all political advertising starting in November', *The Verge*, 30 October 2019, https://www.theverge.com/2019/10/30/20940587/twitter-political-ad-ban-election-2020-jack-dorsey-facebook.
94. Adi Robertson, 'Facebook will ban US political ads indefinitely after election', *The Verge*, 7 October 2020, https://www.theverge.com/2020/10/7/21506798/facebook-ban-political-ads-after-us-presidential-election-trump-biden-results-notification.
95. Elena Schneider, 'The "rug has been pulled out": Campaigns flop amid Facebook, Google ad bans', *Politico*, 27 January 2021, https://www.politico.com/news/2021/01/27/facebook-google-political-ad-ban-462948.
96. Emily Stewart, 'Twitter is walking into a minefield with its political ads ban', *Vox*, 15 November 2019, https://www.vox.com/recode/2019/11/15/20966908/twitter-political-ad-ban-policies-issue-ads-jack-dorsey; 'Glitches allow banned Facebook election ads to recirculate', *Yahoo! Finance*, 2 November 2020, https://uk.finance.yahoo.com/news/glitches-allow-banned-facebook-election-145644246.html; Tate Ryan-Mosley, 'Five ways political groups are getting around ad bans', *M.I.T. Technology Review*, 3 November 2020, https://www.technologyreview.com/2020/11/03/1011618/five-ways-political-groups-are-getting-around-ad-bans/.
97. Pomerantsev 2019, 40. One of the authors of this book has defended the marketplace of ideas, in Stevens & O'Hara 2015.
98. Final report of the High Level Expert Group on Fake News and Online Disinformation, 12 March 2018, https://ec.europa.eu/digital-single-market/en/news/final-report-high-level-expert-group-fake-news-and-online-disinformation, 10. For audience reactions to the term 'fake news', Nielsen & Graves 2017. Also Freeden 2018, 3.
99. 'In Myanmar, Facebook struggles with a deluge of disinformation', *The Economist*, 24 October 2020, https://www.economist.com/asia/2020/10/22/in-myanmar-facebook-struggles-with-a-deluge-of-disinformation.
100. For a potted justification and history of fact checking that traces its pre-Internet origins holding the mass media to account, Seaton et al. 2020.
101. Graves & Mantzarlis 2020.
102. Cunliffe-Jones 2020; Dias & Sippitt 2020.
103. 'Lie detector', *The Economist*, 26 October 2019, https://www.economist.com/science-and-technology/2019/10/24/lithuanians-are-using-software-to-fight-back-against-fake-news.
104. *Fact-Checking for Educators and Future Voters*, https://www.faktabaari.fi/assets/FactBar_EDU_Fact-checking_for_educators_and_future_voters_13112018.pdf.
105. Truthy is at http://truthy.indiana.edu/. Ratkiewicz et al. 2011; Lazer et al. 2018; Mario Trujillo, 'Five things to know about "Truthy"', *The Hill*, 22 October 2014, https://thehill.com/policy/technology/221565-five-things-to-know-about-truthy.
106. Dias & Sippitt 2020.
107. For a recent plea for transparency, Howard 2020.

108. Jatin Aythora, 'Project Origin', *About the BBC Blog*, 8 September 2020, https://www.bbc.co.uk/blogs/aboutthebbc/entries/46f5eb33-b7b8-4a9b-a24e-2c38e0cf8c2a.

109. 'The dirty mop', *The Economist*, 23 November 2019, https://www.economist.com/europe/2019/11/23/americas-losing-battle-against-corruption-in-eastern-europe.

110. 'The Tories' dodgy "factcheckUK" tweets are a taste of what's to come', *The Economist*, 23 November 2019, https://www.economist.com/britain/2019/11/21/the-tories-dodgy-factcheckuk-tweets-are-a-taste-of-whats-to-come.

111. Roosendaal 2012; Julia Angwin, 'It's complicated: Facebook's history of tracking you', *ProPublica*, 17 June 2014, https://www.propublica.org/article/its-complicated-facebooks-history-of-tracking-you.

112. Jonathan Mayer, 'The Turn-Verizon zombie cookie', *Web Policy Blog*, 14 January 2015, http://webpolicy.org/2015/01/14/turn-verizon-zombie-cookie/.

113. *Notice of Apparent Liability for Forfeiture in the Matter of Google Inc.*, Federal Communications Commission, 13 April 2012, https://docs.fcc.gov/public/attachments/DA-12-592A1.pdf, quotes at 15, 2.

114. Graves & Mantzarlis 2020; Guy Rosen, 'An update on our work to keep people informed and limit misinformation about COVID-19', *Facebook*, 16 April 2020, https://about.fb.com/news/2020/04/covid-19-misinfo-update/.

115. Evgeny Morozov, 'Can the US government stem the tide of "fake news" in a post-modern world?' *The Guardian*, 31 October 2019, https://www.theguardian.com/global/commentisfree/2019/oct/31/can-the-us-government-stem-the-tide-of-fake-news-in-a-postmodern-world; Alex Heath, 'Mark Zuckerberg: Facebook will "proceed carefully" with fighting fake news and won't block "opinions"', *Business Insider*, 16 December 2016, https://www.businessinsider.nl/mark-zuckerberg-on-how-facebook-will-fight-fake-news-2016-12/; 'Zuckerberg outlines steps for fighting fake news on platform', *CNBC*, 1 May 2018, https://www.cnbc.com/video/2018/05/01/zuckerberg-outlines-steps-for-fighting-fake-news-on-platform.html; Asha Barbaschow, 'Facebook announces election changes, hate speech fight as advertisers pull out', *ZDNet*, 29 June 2020, https://www.zdnet.com/article/facebook-announces-election-changes-hate-speech-fight-as-advertisers-pull-out/; John Naughton, 'Facebook can't control its users. And it has no incentive to do so', *The Guardian*, 26 August 2018, https://www.theguardian.com/commentisfree/2018/aug/26/facebook-cant-control-its-users-real-trouble-is-it-doesnt-want-to; John Naughton, 'Nick Clegg is on the wrong side of history at Facebook', *The Guardian*, 20 June 2020, https://www.theguardian.com/commentisfree/2020/jun/20/nick-clegg-is-on-the-wrong-side-of-history-at-facebook; Howard 2020.

CHAPTER 14

1. Quoted in Dwan, 146.
2. Soldatov & Borogan 2017, 304–305.
3. Alexey Soldatov is the estranged father of journalist Andrei Soldatov, whose book with Irina Borogan we have extensively quoted.
4. Pomerantsev 2019, 109–110.
5. For national information spaces, Mueller 2017.
6. Soldatov & Borogan 2017, 121.
7. Soldatov & Borogan 2017, 302.
8. Asmolov & Kolozaridi 2017.
9. Soldatov & Borogan 2017, 195–222, 237–238.

10. Froomkin 2013.
11. 'Russia to launch "independent internet" for BRICS nations: Report', *RT*, 28 November 2017, https://www.rt.com/russia/411156-russia-to-launch-independent-internet/.
12. *Strategy of Information Society Development in Russia until 2030*, 12 August 2018, http://interkomitet.com/foreign-policy/basic-documents/strategy-of-information-society-development-in-russia-until-2030/.
13. *National Cyber Strategy of the United States of America*, September 2018, https://www.whitehouse.gov/wp-content/uploads/2018/09/National-Cyber-Strategy.pdf, 11–12.
14. Diana Rossokhovatsky & Olga Khvostunova, 'Why Russia needs a "Sovereign Runet"', *Institute of Modern Russia*, 25 July 2019, https://imrussia.org/en/analysis/3029-why-russia-needs-a-"sovereign-runet".
15. Louise Matsakis, 'What happens if Russia cuts itself off from the Internet?' *Wired*, 2 December 2019, https://www.wired.com/story/russia-internet-disconnect-what-happens/.
16. Catalin Cimpanu, 'Russia successfully disconnected from the internet', *ZDNet*, 23 December 2019, https://www.zdnet.com/article/russia-successfully-disconnected-from-the-internet/.
17. Aryan et al. 2013.
18. For the opposition's use of the Internet, Mohammadi 2019, 215–239; and for its use of Telegram, Alimardani & Milan 2018. DFRLab, '#TrollTracker: Outward influence operation from Iran', *medium.com*, 31 January 2019, https://medium.com/dfrlab/trolltracker-outward-influence-operation-from-iran-cc4539684c8d.
19. Brown & Marsden 2013, 98–99; Aryan et al. 2013; Sara Reardon, 'Inside Iran's "halal" internet', *New Scientist*, 216(2886), 13 October 2012, https://doi.org/10.1016/S0262-4079(12)62625-6; Daniel Van Boom, 'Iran's internet freedom is on life support', *CNet*, 8 December 2019, https://www.cnet.com/news/irans-president-plans-to-cut-countrys-internet-off-from-the-rest-of-the-world/; Hamid Enayat, 'Iran's insoluble paradox of cutting off the Internet', *GlobePost*, 13 January 2020, https://theglobepost.com/2020/01/13/iran-internet-paradox/.
20. Karagiannopoulos 2012; Taylor Reynolds & Arthur Mickoleit, 'The economic impact of shutting down Internet and mobile phone services in Egypt', OECD, 4 February 2011, http://www.oecd.org/countries/egypt/theeconomicimpactofshuttingdowninternetandmobilephoneservicesinegypt.htm.

CHAPTER 15

1. *One Internet*, Global Commission on Internet Governance, 2016, https://www.cigionline.org/publications/one-internet.
2. Dahlberg 2011.
3. Mueller 2017, 131–151.
4. Moyo 2018, 143.
5. Moyo 2018, 143; and see Arora 2019, 109.
6. O'Hara 2018 expands on the argument in this paragraph.
7. Rid 2020.
8. 'America's government is putting foreign cyber-spies in the dock', *The Economist*, 15 September 2018, https://www.economist.com/united-states/2018/09/13/americas-government-is-putting-foreign-cyber-spies-in-the-dock.
9. Nyberg 1997; Iñiguez et al. 2014.
10. Zhang 2008.

11. Thaler & Sunstein 2008; Brown & Marsden 2013, 39.

12. 'US justice department sues California over new net neutrality law', *The Guardian*, 1 October 2018, https://www.theguardian.com/technology/2018/oct/01/us-justice-department-sues-california-to-over-new-net-neutrality-law.

13. Nick Clegg, 'I'm joining Facebook to build bridges between politics and tech', *The Guardian*, 19 October 2018, https://www.theguardian.com/commentisfree/2018/oct/19/nick-clegg-facebook-politics-tech.

14. 'Is Margrethe Vestager championing consumers or her political career?' *The Economist*, 14 September 2017, https://www.economist.com/business/2017/09/14/is-margrethe-vestager-championing-consumers-or-her-political-career.

PART III

1. The connection is made explicitly in *Paths to Our Digital Future*, Internet Society Global Internet Report 2017, https://future.internetsociety.org/2017/wp-content/uploads/sites/3/2017/09/2017-Internet-Society-Global-Internet-Report-Paths-to-Our-Digital-Future.pdf, 31–36.

CHAPTER 16

1. Sharma 2015; 'India's booming startup scene is showing signs of trouble', *The Economist*, 12 March 2020, https://www.economist.com/business/2020/03/12/indias-booming-startup-scene-is-showing-signs-of-trouble.

2. Coker 2019, 126–140, quote from 140.

3. These developments are discussed in greater detail in O'Hara & Stevens 2006a, 152–166, with further references in that volume.

4. Das 2015.

5. Naidu & Ninan 2000.

6. George Monbiot, 'This is what we paid for', *The Guardian*, 18 May 2004, https://www.theguardian.com/politics/2004/may/18/foreignpolicy.india.

7. https://globaldatalab.org/shdi/shdi/IND/?levels=1%2B4&interpolation=0&extrapolation=0&nearest_real=0.

8. Arora 2019.

9. 'Mukesh Ambani wants to be India's first internet tycoon', *The Economist*, 26 January 2019, https://www.economist.com/business/2019/01/26/mukesh-ambani-wants-to-be-indias-first-internet-tycoon.

10. 'Vodafone's future in doubt after Supreme Court ruling', *The Hindu*, 12 November 2019, https://www.thehindu.com/business/Industry/vodafones-future-in-doubt-after-supreme-court-ruling/article29953866.ece.

11. 'Facebook bets on a different sort of e-commerce in India', *The Economist*, 25 April 2020, https://www.economist.com/business/2020/04/25/facebook-bets-on-a-different-sort-of-e-commerce-in-india; 'Facebook aims to extend products, tech built with Jio to other markets', *The Hindu*, 30 April 2020, https://www.thehindu.com/business/Industry/facebook-aims-to-extend-products-tech-built-with-jio-to-other-markets/article31471900.ece.

12. Khilnani 2012.

13. For India's diversity and argumentative tradition, Sen 2005.

14. Thanks to Srinath Srinivasa for this point. He also argues that Amazon Prime and Netflix have not taken off in India, partly because of their cost, but also because they neglect this tradition.

15. P. B. Mehta argues, in the context of the 2019 crackdown in Kashmir (see later discussion), that India is actively aping China's centralizing ambitions. 'The

international climate is propitious. We can do what China is doing: Remake whole cultures, societies. We can take advantage of the fact that human rights is not even a hypocrisy left in the international system.' Pratap Bhanu Mehta, 'The story of Indian democracy written in blood and betrayal', *The Indian Express*, 6 August 2019, https://indianexpress.com/article/opinion/columns/jammu-kashmir-article-370-scrapped-special-status-amit-shah-narendra-modi-bjp-5880797/.

16. Yuthika Bhargava, 'Government bans 59 apps including China-based TikTok, WeChat', *The Hindu*, 29 June 2020, https://www.thehindu.com/news/national/govt-bans-59-apps-including-tiktok-wechat/article31947445.ece.

17. 'India's booming startup scene is showing signs of trouble', *The Economist*, 12 March 2020, https://www.economist.com/business/2020/03/12/indias-booming-startup-scene-is-showing-signs-of-trouble.

18. Gochhwal 2017, 'In bleak times for banks, India's digital-payments system wins praise', *The Economist*, 9 May 2020, https://www.economist.com/finance-and-economics/2020/05/09/in-bleak-times-for-banks-indias-digital-payments-system-wins-praise.

19. Nilekani & Shah 2015.

20. Gautam S. Mengle, 'Major Aadhaar data leak plugged: French security researcher', *The Hindu*, 20 March 2019, https://www.thehindu.com/sci-tech/technology/major-aadhaar-data-leak-plugged-french-security-researcher/article26584981.ece; Srinath Vudali, 'Aadhaar details of 7.82 crore from Telangana and Andhra found in possession of IT Grids (India) Pvt Ltd', *Times of India*, 13 April 2019, https://timesofindia.indiatimes.com/city/hyderabad/aadhaar-details-of-7-82-crore-from-telangana-and-andhra-found-in-possession-of-it-grids-india-pvt-ltd/articleshow/68865938.cms; Zack Whittaker, 'Indian state government leaks thousands of Aadhaar numbers', *TechCrunch*, 1 February 2019, https://tech-crunch.com/2019/01/31/aadhaar-data-leak/; Jon Russell, 'India's national ID database is reportedly accessible for less than $10', *TechCrunch*, 5 January 2018, https://techcrunch.com/2018/01/04/indias-national-id-database-is-reportedly-accessible-for-less-than-10/.

21. 'Aadhaar linked to half the reported starvation deaths since 2015, say researchers', *HuffPost*, 26 September 2018, https://www.huffingtonpost.in/2018/09/25/aadhaar-linked-to-half-the-reported-starvation-deaths-since-2015-say-researchers_a_23539768.

22. Mir et al. 2020; Aria Thaker, 'Aadhaar's most common use is also one of its most dangerous problems', *Quartz India*, 25 September 2018, https://qz.com/india/1399518/whatever-indias-supreme-court-says-aadhaar-was-never-a-photo-id/; Mayank Jain, 'The dangers of Aadhaar-based payments that no one is talking about', *BloombergQuint*, 17 January 2017, https://www.bloombergquint.com/business/the-dangers-of-aadhaar-based-payments-that-no-one-is-talking-about; Parth Shastri, 'Jobless engineer made over 100 fake Aadhaar cards', *Times of India*, 28 April 2017, https://timesofindia.indiatimes.com/city/ahmedabad/jobless-engineer-made-over-100-fake-aadhaar-cards/articleshow/58406979.cms.

23. Shahin & Zheng 2020.

24. Archana Chaudhary, 'India is planning a huge China-style facial recognition program', *Bloomberg*, 19 September 2019, https://www.bloomberg.com/news/articles/2019-09-19/india-seeks-to-adopt-china-style-facial-recognition-in-policing.

25. Simon Sharwood, 'Indian city floats camera-packing surveillance balloon to zoom in on quarantine-quitters', *The Register*, 15 April 2020, https://www.theregister.com/2020/04/15/vadodara_balloon_surveillance/

26. 'Unacceptable that facial recognition software was not helpful in missing kids cases: HC to police', *Outlook*, 30 January 2019, https://www.outlookindia.com/newsscroll/unacceptable-that-facial-recognition-software-was-not-helpful-in-missing-kids-cases-hc-to-police/1468658.

27. Archana Chaudhary, 'India is planning a huge China-style facial recognition program', *Bloomberg*, 19 September 2019, https://www.bloomberg.com/news/articles/2019-09-19/india-seeks-to-adopt-china-style-facial-recognition-in-policing.

28. Govindarajan et al. 2019.

29. 'India Inc is growing disenchanted with Narendra Modi', *The Economist*, 17 August 2019, https://www.economist.com/business/2019/08/17/india-inc-is-growing-disenchanted-with-narendra-modi.

30. Mihir Sharma, 'Suicide of Indian coffee king VG Siddhartha should be a lesson', *Economic Times*, 1 August 2019, https://economictimes.indiatimes.com/news/company/corporate-trends/view-suicide-of-indian-coffee-king-vg-siddhartha-should-be-a-lesson/articleshow/70482923.cms.

31. Yuthika Bhargava, 'Now, Vodafone CEO says it is committed to Indian market', *The Hindu*, 13 November 2019, https://www.thehindu.com/business/now-vodafone-ceo-says-committed-to-indian-market/article29965535.ece.

32. Gautam Bhatia, 'Judicial evasion and the status quo: On SC judgments', *The Hindu*, 10 January 2019, https://www.thehindu.com/opinion/lead/judicial-evasion-and-the-status-quo/article25953052.ece.

33. Debasish Panigrahi, 'Everything you need to know about the Palghar attack where Sadhus were lynched by a mob', *Mumbai Mirror*, 30 October 2020, https://mumbaimirror.indiatimes.com/mumbai/crime/everything-you-need-to-know-about-the-palghar-attack-where-sadhus-were-lynched-by-a-mob/articleshow/75248136.cms.

34. Biswendu Bhattacharjee, 'Man hired by Tripura to dispel child-lifting rumours lynched', *Times of India*, 30 June 2018, https://timesofindia.indiatimes.com/india/man-hired-by-tripura-to-dispel-child-lifting-rumours-lynched/articleshow/64800628.cms. For a tally of the lynchings, https://www.thequint.com/quintlab/lynching-in-india/.

35. Snigdha Poonam & Samarth Bansal, 'Misinformation is endangering India's election', *The Atlantic*, 1 April 2019, https://www.theatlantic.com/international/archive/2019/04/india-misinformation-election-fake-news/586123/.

36. https://www.imdb.com/title/tt9096108/reviews?ref_=tt_ov_rt; Devarsi Ghosh, 'Is the controversy about the web series "Rasbhari" the best thing about it?' *Scroll.in*, 4 July 2020, https://scroll.in/reel/966171/is-the-controversy-about-the-web-series-rasbhari-the-best-thing-about-it; 'Swara Bhasker starrer web series gets record low ratings, leftist elites claim it is because she opposes BJP, not because it is bad', *Opindia*, 2 July 2020, https://www.opindia.com/2020/07/swara-bhasker-web-series-rasbhari-low-ratings-imdb-amazon-prime-leftists/; Manish Gaekwad, 'There's no silencing Swara', *The Hindu*, 21 December 2018, https://www.the-hindu.com/entertainment/theres-no-silencing-swara/article25798056.ece.

37. Shelley Singh & Anandita Singh Mankotia, 'Facebook still at odds with government over WhatsApp monitoring', *Economic Times*, 14 September 2019, https://economictimes.indiatimes.com/tech/internet/facebook-still-at-odds-with-govt-over-whatsapp-monitoring/articleshow/71120821.cms.

38. John Scott-Railton, Adam Hulcoop, Bahr Abdul Razzak, Bill Marczak, Siena Anstis, & Ron Deibert, *Dark Basin: Uncovering a Massive Hack-for-Hire Operation*, CitizenLab, 9 June 2020, https://citizenlab.ca/2020/06/

dark-basin-uncovering-a-massive-hack-for-hire-operation/. It has also been claimed that BJP trolling is creating conflict, intentionally or otherwise, in India's large diaspora: Mostafa Rachwani, 'Fears of escalating violence as online "hate factories" sow division within Australia's Indian community', *The Guardian*, 19 March 2021, https://www.theguardian.com/australia-news/2021/mar/19/fears-of-escalating-violence-as-online-hate-factories-sow-division-within-australias-indian-community.

39. Khalid Shah, 'How the world's longest internet shutdown has failed to counter extremism in Kashmir', *Observer Research Foundation*, 22 August 2020, https://www.orfonline.org/expert-speak/how-the-worlds-longest-internet-shutdown-has-failed-to-counter-extremism-in-kashmir/; Kabir Taneja & Kriti M. Shah, The *Conflict in Jammu and Kashmir and the Convergence of Technology and Terrorism*, Royal United Services Institute/Observer Research Foundation Global Research Network on Terrorism and Technology Paper No. 11, 2019, https://www.rusi.org/sites/default/files/20190807_grntt_paper_11.pdf.

40. Pratap Bhanu Mehta, 'The story of Indian democracy written in blood and betrayal', *The Indian Express*, 6 August 2019, https://indianexpress.com/article/opinion/columns/jammu-kashmir-article-370-scrapped-special-status-amit-shah-narendra-modi-bjp-5880797/.

41. Sindhu Hariharan, 'India lost $1.3 billion due to 4,196 hours of no internet', *Times of India*, 10 January 2020, https://timesofindia.indiatimes.com/business/india-business/india-lost-1-3bn-due-to-4196-hours-of-no-internet/articleshow/73179287.cms. This is consistent with the trends from 2012–2017, in Rajat Kathuria, Mansi Kedia, Gangesh Varma, Kaushambi Bagchi, & Richa Sekani, *The Anatomy of an Internet Blackout: Measuring the Economic Impact of Internet Shutdowns in India*, Indian Council for Research on International Economic Relations, April 2018, https://think-asia.org/handle/11540/8248.

42. Selva 2019, 19.

43. 'What is internet ban in India?' *Times of India*, 27 March 2020, https://timesofindia.indiatimes.com/india/what-is-internet-ban-in-india/articleshow/74849820.cms; Jeremy Hsu, 'How India, the world's largest democracy, shuts down the Internet', *IEEE Spectrum*, 27 January 2020, https://spectrum.ieee.org/tech-talk/telecom/internet/how-the-worlds-largest-democracy-shuts-down-the-internet.

44. Ashna Butani, 'Not having Aarogya Setu app is a punishable offence, say Noida police', *The Indian Express*, 6 May 2020, https://indianexpress.com/article/cities/delhi/coronavirus-noida-aarogya-setu-app-police-6395945/.

45. Binayak Dasgupta, 'Protection or threat? Experts say Aarogya Setu poses national security risk', *Hindustan Times*, 23 May 2020, https://www.hindustantimes.com/india-news/aarogya-setu-protection-or-threat/story-QmpSP3H60ohkLV3l5ywhBI.html.

46. Payal Mohta, 'Fuelled by social media, in India Muslims are "a convenient scapegoat" for the coronavirus', *Equal Times*, 6 May 2020, https://www.equaltimes.org/fuelled-by-social-media-in-india#.XtJjl25FzD4.

47. Sen 2005.

48. Thanks to Srinath Srinivasa and Bill Thompson, who independently and cogently urged this option upon us.

49. 'African countries are struggling to build robust identity systems', *The Economist*, 5 December 2019, https://www.economist.com/middle-east-and-africa/2019/12/05/african-countries-are-struggling-to-build-robust-identity-systems.

50. Secure Identity Alliance, *Secure Identity Alliance Announces Global Availability of OSIA: The Open Standards Identity API*, 16 June 2019, https://secureidentityalliance.org/news-events/news/entry/secure-identity-alliance-announces-global-availability-of-osia-the-open-standards-identity-api; Chris Burt, 'Two ideas to break down vendor lock-in in foundational biometric ID systems launch at ID4Africa 2019', *Biometric Update*, 20 June 2019, https://www.biometricupdate.com/201906/two-ideas-to-break-down-vendor-lock-in-in-foundational-biometric-id-systems-launch-at-id4africa-2019.

51. https://www.mosip.io/.

52. Aditi Gyanesh, 'IIITB to develop Aadhaar-like database for Morocco', *Times of India*, 30 August 2018, https://timesofindia.indiatimes.com/city/bengaluru/iiitb-to-develop-aadhaar-like-database-for-morocco/articleshow/65599637.cms.

53. Lucas Laursen, 'Countries debate openness of future national IDs', *IEEE Spectrum*, 30 January 2020, https://spectrum.ieee.org/tech-talk/computing/it/countries-debate-openness-of-future-national-ids.

54. Kak et al. 2020.

55. Scott 1998.

56. Abraham 2008.

CHAPTER 17

1. Irion 2012; Mueller 2017, 79–80; Casalini & López González 2019; OECD, *Trade in the Digital Era*, March 2019, https://www.oecd.org/going-digital/trade-in-the-digital-era.pdf.

2. Govindarajan et al. 2019.

3. Charlie Lyne, 'French resistance: Can Netflix win over its harshest critics?' *The Guardian*, 9 November 2016, https://www.theguardian.com/film/2016/nov/19/divines-netflix-france; Alissa Wilkinson, 'Netflix vs. Cannes: Why they're fighting, what it means for cinema, and who really loses', *Vox*, 13 April 2018, https://www.vox.com/culture/2018/4/13/17229476/netflix-versus-cannes-ted-sarandos-thierry-fremaux-okja-meyerowitz-orson-welles-streaming-theater.

4. https://ec.europa.eu/commission/priorities/digital-single-market_en.

5. http://english.mofcom.gov.cn/article/newsrelease/counselorsoffice/bilateralexchanges/201901/20190102830342.shtml.

6. Abhijit Das, 'E-comm talks: India must stand firm', *The Hindu*, 25 January 2019, https://www.thehindubusinessline.com/opinion/e-comm-talks-india-must-stand-firm/article26092215.ece.

7. For the opponents of change (the Third World Network), http://www.twn.my/title2/wto.info/2019/ti190110.htm.

8. For Chinese support for change, Jing Shuiyu & Ouyang Shijia, 'China, WTO will start talks on e-commerce rules', *China Daily*, 26 January 2019, http://www.chinadaily.com.cn/a/201901/26/WS5c4b9792a3106c65c34e69da.html.

9. https://www.wto.org/english/tratop_e/ecom_e/wkprog_e.htm.

10. Satoshi Sugiyama, 'Abe heralds launch of "Osaka Track" framework for free cross-border data flow at G20', *Japan Times*, 28 June 2019, https://www.japantimes.co.jp/news/2019/06/28/national/abe-heralds-launch-osaka-track-framework-free-cross-border-data-flow-g20/#.XmeYukB2vIU; Walter Sim, 'Osaka Track on digital rules launched at G-20 summit', *Straits Times*, 28 June 2019, https://www.straitstimes.com/asia/east-asia/osaka-track-on-digital-rules-launched.

11. D. Ravi Kanth, 'India boycotts "Osaka Track" at G20 summit', *LiveMint*, 30 June 2019, https://www.livemint.com/news/world/india-boycotts-osaka-track-at-g20-summit-1561897592466.html.
12. Arora 2019, 201–202; Couldry & Mejias 2019.
13. Datta 2015.
14. 'Mukesh Ambani wants to be India's first internet tycoon', *The Economist*, 26 January 2019, https://www.economist.com/business/2019/01/26/mukesh-ambani-wants-to-be-indias-first-internet-tycoon.
15. Aaronson 2018.
16. On cloud computing and the environment, Khosravi & Buyya 2018.
17. For the equivalence rules, https://gdpr-info.eu/issues/third-countries/. 'At the time that the General Data Protection Regulation became applicable, the third countries which ensure an adequate level of protection were: Andorra, Argentina, Canada (only commercial organizations), Faroe Islands, Guernsey, Isle of Man, Israel, Japan, Jersey, New Zealand, Switzerland, Uruguay, and USA (if the recipient belonged to the Privacy Shield).'
18. McLaughlin 2016; Kaminski 2018; Etzioni 2018.
19. Mueller 2017, 147.
20. Catherine Stupp, 'European cloud project draws backlash from U.S. tech giants', *Wall Street Journal*, 1 November 2019, https://www.wsj.com/articles/european-cloud-project-draws-backlash-from-u-s-tech-giants-11572600600; Will Bedingfield, 'Europe has a plan to break Google and Amazon's cloud dominance', *Wired*, 27 January 2020, https://www.wired.co.uk/article/europe-gaia-x-cloud-amazon-google; Ludwig Siegele, 'Virtual nationalism', *The Economist*, 22 February 2020, https://www.economist.com/special-report/2020/02/20/governments-are-erecting-borders-for-data; Lucas Wojcik, 'Europe's Gaia-X cloud service faces a difficult future', *HelpNet Security*, 9 March 2020, https://www.helpnetsecurity.com/2020/03/09/gaia-x-cloud-service/.

CHAPTER 18

1. Kelleher 2019.
2. White 2015.
3. Mayer-Schönberger & Cukier 2013; Kelleher & Tierney 2018.
4. James Vincent, 'Putin says the nation that leads in AI "will be the ruler of the world"', *The Verge*, 4 September 2017, https://www.theverge.com/2017/9/4/16251226/russia-ai-putin-rule-the-world.
5. Zhou Xin & Choi Chi-Yuk, 'Develop and control: Xi Jinping urges China to use artificial intelligence in race for tech future', *South China Morning Post*, 31 October 2018, https://www.scmp.com/economy/china-economy/article/2171102/develop-and-control-xi-jinping-urges-china-use-artificial.
6. Hall & Pesenti 2017.
7. Lee 2018.
8. Langlois et al. 2015.
9. Jarvis 2011; Shadbolt & O'Hara 2013; Pentland 2014; O'Hara 2014a, 2014b; Parkinson et al. 2018; Smith & Browne 2019, 269–286; Hawken et al. 2020.
10. Hall & Pesenti 2017.
11. O'Hara 2019 and Hardjono et al. 2016 consider possible solutions.
12. Colborne & Smit 2020.
13. Kerr 2009.

14. *Preparing for the Future of Artificial Intelligence*, Executive Office of the President National Science and Technology Council Committee on Technology, October 2016, https://obamawhitehouse.archives.gov/sites/default/files/whitehouse_files/microsites/ostp/NSTC/preparing_for_the_future_of_ai.pdf. This seems to have been removed from government websites by the succeeding administration. For the implications for China of this expertise, see Lee 2018, 91–92.
15. On training and reskilling, Smith & Browne 2019, 231–247.
16. On diversity, David Rock & Heidi Grant, 'Why diverse teams are smarter', *Harvard Business Review*, 4 November 2016, https://hbr.org/2016/11/why-diverse-teams-are-smarter.
17. Lee 2018, 12, 53–56.
18. Lee 2018, 83–84.
19. Lee 2018, 71–73.
20. Lee 2018, 125–126.
21. Lee 2018, 55–56.
22. Lee 2018, 16–17.
23. Lee 2018, 96–97.
24. Lee 2018, 101–103, 132–134; 'A pedestrian has been killed by a self-driving car', *The Economist*, 24 March 2018, https://www.economist.com/science-and-technology/2018/03/22/a-pedestrian-has-been-killed-by-a-self-driving-car; Shunsuke Tabeta, 'China intends for self-driving cars to propel smart megacity', *Nikkei Asian Review*, 20 May 2018, https://asia.nikkei.com/Economy/China-intends-for-self-driving-cars-to-propel-smart-megacity; Sarah Dai, 'Baidu to build self-driving test facility in Chongqing as the Chinese city pushes ahead with smart city infrastructure', *South China Morning Post*, 20 March 2020, https://www.scmp.com/tech/big-tech/article/3076088/baidu-build-self-driving-test-facility-chongqing-western-city-pushes.
25. Lee 2018, 102.
26. Beijing Academy of Artificial Intelligence 2019.
27. Gal 2020; Roberts et al. 2021.
28. Creemers 2020.
29. Lee 2018, 98–100.
30. Lee 2018, 4, 14–15.
31. Leigh Dodds, 'Do data scientists spend 80% of their time cleaning data? Turns out, no?' *Lost Boy blog*, 31 January 2020, https://blog.ldodds.com/2020/01/31/do-data-scientists-spend-80-of-their-time-cleaning-data-turns-out-no/.
32. Jeremy Kahn, 'If data is the new oil, these companies are the new Baker Hughes', *Fortune*, 4 February 2020, https://fortune.com/2020/02/04/artificial-intelligence-data-labeling-labelbox/.
33. Lee 2018, 112.
34. Lee 2018, 55.
35. The think tank piece is NITI Aayog, *National Strategy for Artificial Intelligence #AIforAll*, June 2018, https://niti.gov.in/writereaddata/files/document_publica-tion/NationalStrategy-for-AI-Discussion-Paper.pdf; Aditi Chandrasekar, 'State of Artificial Intelligence in India', *Analytics Insight*, 20 March 2020, https://www.analyticsinsight.net/state-of-artificial-intelligence-in-india/.
36. Arora 2019, 147.
37. Hassan 2020.
38. Lee 2018, 168–170; Hall & Pesenti 2017.
39. Lee 2018, 20.

40. Zarsky 2017, 1005–1009.
41. Zarsky 2017, 1009–1011.
42. Zarsky 2017, 1012–1015.
43. Zarsky 2017, 1015–1018; Narayanan & Shmatikov 2010; O'Hara 2020b.
44. Bradford 2020.
45. Hildebrandt 2015, 211.
46. James Vincent, 'AI camera operator repeatedly confuses bald head for soccer ball during live stream', *The Verge*, 3 November 2020, https://www.theverge.com/tldr/2020/11/3/21547392/ai-camera-operator-football-bald-head-soccer-mistakes. Thanks to Tom Scutt for bringing this to our attention.
47. Venturini & Rogers 2019.
48. Elliot et al. 2016; Elliot et al. 2018; Elliot et al. 2020.
49. Evans et al. 2018.
50. Hunt et al. 2018; Kairouz et al. 2019.
51. https://opensafely.org/; Williamson et al. 2020.

CHAPTER 19

1. Lee 2018, 104–139.
2. Chen 2016.
3. Lee 2018, 108–109.
4. Greengard 2015.
5. Hart & Martinez 2006.
6. Weiser 1991.
7. Steve Ranger, 'What is the IoT? Everything you need to know about the Internet of Things right now', *ZDNet*, 3 February 2020, https://www.zdnet.com/article/what-is-the-internet-of-things-everything-you-need-to-know-about-the-iot-right-now/.
8. Allhoff & Henschke 2018.
9. Gomer et al. 2014.
10. Ashley Carman, 'Sex toy company admits to recording users' remote sex sessions, calls it a "minor bug"', *The Verge*, 10 November 2017, https://www.theverge.com/2017/11/10/16634442/lovense-sex-toy-spy-surveillance; Flore & Pienaar 2020.
11. Weber 2010; Weber 2015; Wachter 2018a.
12. O'Hara 2014c; Maple 2017.
13. Oscar Williams-Grut, 'Hackers stole a casino's high-roller database through a thermometer in the lobby fish tank', *Business Insider*, 15 April 2018, https://www.businessinsider.in/Hackers-stole-a-casinos-high-roller-database-through-a-thermometer-in-the-lobby-fish-tank/articleshow/63769685.cms.
14. Wachter 2018b; Airbnb example suggested by Bill Thompson.
15. Weber & Weber 2010, 127.
16. Hildebrandt 2015; Hildebrandt & O'Hara 2020.
17. Zuboff 2019, 202.
18. Scott 1998.
19. Thaler & Sunstein 2008.
20. Shapiro 2006; Schaffers et al. 2011; Batty et al. 2012; Townsend 2013; Zanella et al. 2014; Albino et al. 2015; Ching & Ferreira 2015; Allam & Dhunny 2019.
21. Ekman 2019.
22. Hetherington & West 2020.
23. Joseph A. Paradiso, 'Our extended sensoria: How humans will connect with the Internet of Things', *MIT Technology Review*, 1 August 2017, https://www.

technologyreview.com/2017/08/01/68061/our-extended-sensoria-how-humans-will-connect-with-the-internet-of-things/.

24. The dialectic between techno-optimists and techno-pessimists about digital divides was mapped in Norris 2001, 3–92.

25. Hawken et al. 2020. Calls for co-creation include Howard 2015; Cardullo et al. 2019; Ho 2017; Le Dantec 2016.

26. Shadbolt 2013.

27. Puussaar et al. 2018.

28. Maskell et al. 2018.

29. Zuboff 2019, 247.

30. Keymolen & Van der Hof 2019.

31. Zuboff 2019, 129.

32. Chris Matyszczyk, 'The Internet will vanish, says Google's Eric Schmidt', *CNET*, 22 January 2015, https://www.cnet.com/news/the-internet-will-vanish-says-googles-schmidt/.

33. Hoy 2018.

34. Maras & Wandt 2019.

35. Woods 2018,

36. Zuboff 2019, 227–232.

37. Adam Carter & John Rieti, 'Sidewalk Labs cancels plan to build high-tech neighbourhood in Toronto amid COVID-19', *CBC News*, 7 May 2020, https://www.cbc.ca/news/canada/toronto/sidewalk-labs-cancels-project-1.5559370.

38. Ni Loideain 2019.

39. Hildebrandt 2015; Maple 2017; Wachter 2018a; Crabtree et al. 2018; Lindqvist 2018.

40. Barati et al. 2019; schraefel et al. 2020.

41. Urquhart et al. 2018.

42. Crabtree et al. 2018; Pacheco Huamani & Ziegler 2019.

43. Wachter 2018b; as well as the splendidly named Bourgeois et al. 2018.

44. Cavada et al. 2019.

45. Cowley et al. 2019, 56.

46. Han 2020.

47. Ekman 2019.

48. Ma Si, 'Nation leads race for data-driven societies', *China Daily*, 2 January 2019, https://www.chinadaily.com.cn/a/201901/02/WS5c2c0da7a310d91214051fa6.html

49. Ekman 2019.

50. John Calabrese, 'The Huawei Wars and the 5G revolution in the Gulf', *Middle East Institute*, 30 July 2019, https://www.mei.edu/publications/huawei-wars-and-5g-revolution-gulf.

51. Mathieu Duchâtel & François Godement, 'Europe and 5G: The Huawei Case Part 2', *Institut Montaigne*, June 2019, https://www.institutmontaigne.org/en/publications/europe-and-5g-huawei-case-part-2.

52. Kshetri 2017.

53. NITI Aayog, *National Strategy for Artificial Intelligence #AIforAll*, June 2018, https://niti.gov.in/writereaddata/files/document_publication/NationalStrategy-for-AI-Discussion-Paper.pdf.

54. Rana et al. 2019.

55. Datta 2015.

56. Howard 2015.

57. Brownsword 2019.

CHAPTER 20

1. Shadbolt et al. 2019; Berners-Lee & Fischetti 1999, 172; Hendler & Berners-Lee 2010; O'Hara et al. 2013.
2. Shadbolt et al. 2019, 2–3, 27–28, 31–33.
3. https://www.waze.com/.
4. Shadbolt et al. 2019, 186–200.
5. https://www.crowdmed.com/.
6. http://www.blueservo.net/.
7. https://www.ondetemtiroteio.com.br/.
8. https://www.facebook.com/groups/TheCajunNavy/, https://www.glympse.com/, https://zello.com/.
9. 'What's bigger than K-pop?' *The Economist*, 5 November 2020, https://www.economist.com/asia/2020/11/05/whats-bigger-than-k-pop.
10. John Harris, 'Facebook is still far too powerful. It's also how millions are coping with this crisis', *The Guardian*, 22 March 2020, https://www.theguardian.com/commentisfree/2020/mar/22/facebook-powerful-crisis-coronavirus-communities-online; Kirkpatrick 2010, 27–41.
11. Von Ahn & Dabbish 2004, 2008; von Ahn 2006.
12. Shadbolt et al. 2019, 121–135.
13. Ahlers et al. 2016.
14. Batty et al. 2012.
15. https://nextdoor.nl/.
16. Hård & Misa 2008.
17. Maskell et al. 2018.
18. Shadbolt et al. 2019, 50–51; https://en.wikipedia.org/wiki/Pea_galaxy.
19. Griffiths 2019, 195–201; Clothey et al. 2016.
20. For these social machines, Schumilas & Scott 2016; Wang & Zhang 2017; Huang & Lin 2019; Jiang & Leng 2017; Zheng & Yu 2016.
21. Zheng & Yu 2016.
22. Jiang & Fu 2018.
23. Dieter Bohn, 'Google is buying Fitbit: Now what?' *The Verge*, 1 November 2019, https://www.theverge.com/2019/11/1/20943993/google-fitbit-acquisition-smartwatch-wearable-fitness-nest-htc-hardware-software; Jonathan Heller, 'Will a Fitbit-Alphabet merger actually happen?' *Real Money*, 18 May 2020, https://realmoney.thestreet.com/investing/will-a-fitbit-alphabet-merger-actually-happen--15325311.
24. Zuboff 2019, 152.
25. Rip Empson, '23andMe makes first acquisition, nabs CureTogether to double down on crowdsourced genetic research', *TechCrunch*, 11 July 2012, https://techcrunch.com/2012/07/11/23andme-first-acquisition/.
26. Zuboff 2019, 128–175.
27. Ekbia & Nardi 2017.
28. Alex Hern, 'Sir Tim Berners-Lee speaks out on data ownership', *The Guardian*, 8 October 2014, https://www.theguardian.com/technology/2014/oct/08/sir-tim-berners-lee-speaks-out-on-data-ownership; Zittrain 2008.
29. See also https://redecentralize.org/, for a wider perspective on re-decentralization. Our aim here is to discuss an approach that might be congenial for individuals and groups in social machines.
30. Waldman et al. 2001.

31. Welfare 2019.

32. Mansour et al. 2016.

33. https://www.elastos.org/.

34. https://dfinity.org/, Will Douglas Heaven, 'A plan to redesign the internet could make apps that no one controls', *M.I.T. Technology Review*, 1 July 2020, https://www.technologyreview.com/2020/07/01/1004725/redesign-internet-apps-no-one-controls-data-privacy-innovation-cloud/.

35. See Berners-Lee's talk at MozFest, https://www.youtube.com/watch?v= elfSz-MATcB4. For Solid and social machines, Shadbolt et al. 2019, 211–214.

36. https://solid.mit.edu/.

37. https://inrupt.com/.

38. K. G. Orphanides, 'How Tim Berners-Lee's Inrupt project plans to fix the web', *Wired*, 15 February 2019, https://www.wired.co.uk/article/inrupt-tim-berners-lee.

39. Liam Tung, 'Berners-Lee's Solid project: Schneier joins team to give you back control over data', *ZDNet*, 24 February 2020, https://www.zdnet.com/article/berners-lees-solid-project-schneier-joins-team-to-give-you-back-control-over-data/.

40. Will Douglas Heaven, 'A plan to redesign the internet could make apps that no one controls', *M.I.T. Technology Review*, 1 July 2020, https://www.technologyreview.com/2020/07/01/1004725/redesign-internet-apps-no-one-controls-data-privacy-innovation-cloud/.

41. Liam Tung, 'Berners-Lee's Solid project: Schneier joins team to give you back control over data', *ZDNet*, 24 February 2020, https://www.zdnet.com/article/berners-lees-solid-project-schneier-joins-team-to-give-you-back-control-over-data/.

CHAPTER 21

1. Berners-Lee & Fischetti 1999, 96.

2. Rosenbach & Mansted 2019.

3. Nye 2011.

4. Matthieu Favas, 'Geopolitics and technology threaten America's financial dominance', *The Economist*, 9 May 2020, https://www.economist.com/special-report/2020/05/07/geopolitics-and-technology-threaten-americas-financial-dominance.

5. Cited in Brown & Marsden 2013, 194.

6. Arora 2019, 168.

7. This is contrary to the arguments of many, such as Brown & Marsden 2013, 192–203. However, we certainly agree with their plea for holistic interdisciplinary study of the operation of the Internet.

8. Bygrave 2013, 190.

9. Audrey Plonk, 'The Global Partnership on AI takes off—at the OECD', *OECD.AI Policy Observatory*, 9 July 2020, https://oecd.ai/wonk/oecd-and-g7-artificial-intelligence-initiatives-side-by-side-for-responsible-ai.

10. Bradford 2020.

11. Helen Davidson & Lily Kuo, 'Zoom admits cutting off activists' accounts in obedience to China', *The Guardian*, 12 June 2020, https://www.theguardian.com/world/2020/jun/12/zoom-admits-cutting-off-activists-accounts-in-obedience-to-china; Naomi Xu Elegant, 'Zoom's censorship stumble is a familiar narrative for tech stuck between U.S. and Beijing', *Fortune*, 12 June 2020, https://fortune.com/2020/06/12/zooms-censorship-stumble-is-a-familiar-narrative-for-tech-stuck-between-u-s-and-beijing/.

12. Spiccia 2013.
13. Gian Volpicelli, 'Trump's feud with Twitter might change the internet as we know it', *Wired*, 30 May 2020, https://www.wired.co.uk/article/donald-trump-twitter; Kosseff 2010; Roberts 2019, 212–213; Fishback 2020.
14. Snyder 2018, 37–66.
15. Bygrave 2013.
16. UN Secretary-General's High-Level Panel on Digital Cooperation 2019.
17. Jefferson 1993, 78.
18. Zittrain 2006, 2008; Brown & Marsden 2013, 22.
19. For the iTunes break-up, Michael Kan, 'Apple to kill iTunes, split into 3 different apps', *PCMag*, 3 June 2019, https://www.pcmag.com/news/368750/apple-to-kill-itunes-split-into-3-different-apps. For criticism of iTunes, Scott Gilbertson, 'The top ten reasons iTunes sucks', *Wired*, 11 May 2008, https://www.wired.com/2008/11/the-top-ten-reasons-itunes-sucks/.
20. Cave 2013, 159.
21. Arora 2019, 101–151, quote from 149.
22. Bernhardt 2019.
23. Jacob Kastrenakes, 'Zoom saw a huge increase in subscribers—and revenue—thanks to the pandemic', *The Verge*, 2 June 2020, https://www.theverge.com/2020/6/2/21277006/zoom-q1-2021-earnings-coronavirus-pandemic-work-from-home.
24. Laura Kayali, 'Brussels in talks with Netflix about reducing internet congestion', *Politico*, 18 March 2020, https://www.politico.eu/article/brussels-in-talks-with-netflix-about-reducing-internet-congestion/.
25. Rosamond Hutt, 'World-famous cultural institutions closed due to coronavirus are welcoming virtual visitors', *World Economic Forum*, 17 March 2020, https://www.weforum.org/agenda/2020/03/world-famous-cultural-institutions-closed-due-to-coronavirus-are-welcoming-virtual-visitors/.
26. Kirsten Grind, Robert McMillan, & Anna Wilde Mathews, 'To track virus, governments weigh surveillance tools that push privacy limits', *Wall Street Journal*, 17 March 2020, https://www.wsj.com/articles/to-track-virus-governments-weigh-surveillance-tools-that-push-privacy-limits-11584479841.
27. Dan Brickley, R. V. Guha, & Tom Marsh, 'Schema for coronavirus special announcements, covid-19 testing facilities and more', *Schema Blog*, 16 March 2020, http://blog.schema.org/2020/03/schema-for-coronavirus-special.html.
28. Jennifer Rankin, 'Russian media "spreading Covid-19 disinformation"', *The Guardian*, 18 March 2020, https://www.theguardian.com/world/2020/mar/18/russian-media-spreading-covid-19-disinformation.
29. Jones 2018.
30. O'Hara & Hall 2013. For a discussion of the complexities of the study of Internet governance, DeNardis 2020.

REFERENCES TO BOOKS AND ACADEMIC PAPERS

Susan Ariel Aaronson (2018). *Data Is Different: Why the World Needs a New Approach to Governing Cross-Border Data Flows*, Centre for International Governance Innovation paper no. 197, https://www.cigionline.org/publications/data-different-why-world-needs-new-approach-governing-cross-border-data-flows.

Janet Abbate (2000). *Inventing the Internet*, Cambridge, MA: MIT Press.

Itty Abraham (2008). 'From Bandung to NAM: Non-alignment and Indian foreign policy, 1947–65', *Commonwealth and Comparative Politics*, 46(2), 195–219, https://doi.org/10.1080/14662040801990280.

Dirk Ahlers, Patrick Driscoll, Erica Löfström, John Krogstie, & Annemie Wyckmans (2016). 'Understanding smart cities as social machines', in *WWW '16 Companion: Proceedings of the 25th International Conference Companion on World Wide Web*, New York: ACM, 759–764, https://doi.org/10.1145/2872518.2890594.

Nadeem Ahmed, Regio A. Michelin, Wanli Xue, Sushmita Ruj, Robert Malaney, Salil S. Kanhere, Aruna Seneviratne, Wen Hu, Helge Janicke, & Sanjay K. Nha (2020). 'A survey of COVID-19 contact tracing apps', *IEEE Access*, 8, 134577–134601, https://doi.org/10.1109/ACCESS.2020.3010226.

Vito Albino, Umberto Berardi, & Rosa Maria Dangelico (2015). 'Smart cities: Definitions, dimensions, performance, and initiatives', *Journal of Urban Technology*, 22(1), 3–21, https://doi.org/10.1080/10630732.2014.942092.

Mahsa Alimardani & Stefania Milan (2018). 'The Internet as a global/local site of contestation: The case of Iran', in Esther Peeren, Robin Celikates, Jeroen de Kloet & Thomas Poell (eds.), *Global Cultures of Contestation: Mobility, Sustainability, Aesthetics & Connectivity*, Cham: Palgrave Macmillan, 171–192, https://doi.org/10.1007/978-3-319-63982-6_9.

Zaheer Allam & Zaynah A. Dhunny (2019). 'On big data, artificial intelligence and smart cities', *Cities*, 89, 80–91, https://doi.org/10–1016/j.cities.2019.01.032.

Fritz Allhoff & Adam Henschke (2018). 'The Internet of Things: Foundational ethical issues', *Internet of Things*, (1–2), 55–66, https://doi.org/10–1016/j.iot.2018.08.005.

Ethem Alpaydin (2016). *Machine Learning*, Cambridge, MA: MIT Press.

Ross Anderson (2008). *Security Engineering: A Guide to Building Dependable Distributed Systems*, 2nd edition, Indianapolis: Wiley.

Hannah Arendt (1963). *Eichmann in Jerusalem: A Report on the Banality of Evil*, New York: Viking Press.

Jessikka Aro (2016). 'The cyberspace war: Propaganda and trolling as warfare tools', *European View*, 15(1), 121–132, https://doi.org/10.1007/s12290-016-0395-5.

Payal Arora (2019). *The Next Billion Users: Digital Life beyond the West*, Cambridge, MA: Harvard University Press.

Simurgh Aryan, Homa Aryan, & J. Alex Halderman (2013). 'Internet censorship in Iran: A first look', in *Proceedings of the 3rd USENIX Workshop on Free and Open Communications on the Internet (FOCI '13)*, https://www.usenix.org/conference/foci13/workshop-program/presentation/aryan.

Gregory Asmolov (2018). 'The disconnective power of disinformation campaigns', *Journal of International Affairs*, 71(1.5), 69–76.

Gregory Asmolov & Polina Kolozaridi (2017). 'The imaginaries of RuNet: The change of the elites and the construction of online space', *Russian Politics*, 2(1), 54–79, https://doi.org/10.1163/2451-8921-00201004.

David Autor, David Dorn, Lawrence F. Katz, Christina Patterson, & John Van Reenen (2020). 'The fall of the labor share and the rise of superstar firms', *Quarterly Journal of Economics*, 135(2), 645–709, https://doi.org/10.1093/qje/qjaa004.

Zeynep Aycan (2006). 'Paternalism: Towards conceptual refinement and operationalization', in Uichol Kim, Kuo-Shu Yang, & Kwang-Kuo Hwang (eds.), *Indigenous and Cultural Psychology: Understanding People in Context*, Boston: Springer, 445–466, https://doi.org/10.1007/0-387-28662-4_20.

Matej Bajgar, Giuseppe Berlingieri, Sara Calligaris, Chiara Criscuolo, & Jonathan Timmis (2019). 'Industry concentration in Europe and North America', *OECD Productivity Working Papers*, No. 18, https://doi.org/10.1787/2ff98246-en.

Kenneth A. Bamberger & Deirdre K. Mulligan (2015). *Privacy on the Ground: Driving Corporate Behavior in the United States and Europe*, Cambridge, MA: MIT Press.

Masoud Barati, Ioan Petri, & Omer F. Rana (2019). 'Developing GDPR compliant user data policies for Internet of Things', in *UCC '19: Proceedings of the 12th IEEE/ACM International Conference on Utility and Cloud Computing*, New York: ACM, 133–141, https://doi.org/10.1145/3344341.3368812.

Barry Barnes & David Bloor (1982). 'Relativism, rationalism and the sociology of knowledge', in Martin Hollis & Steven Lukes (eds.), *Rationality and Relativism*, Oxford: Basil Blackwell, 21–47.

James Barrat (2015). *Our Final Invention: Artificial Intelligence and the End of the Human Era*, New York: Thomas Dunne Books.

John Battelle (2005). *The Search: How Google and Its Rivals Rewrote the Rules of Business and Transformed Our Culture*, London: Nicholas Brealey.

M. Batty, K. W. Axhausen, F. Giannotti, A. Pozdnoukhov, A. Bazzani, M. Wachowicz, G. Ouzounis, & Y. Portugali (2012). 'Smart cities of the future', *European Physical Journal Special Topics*, 214(1), 481–518, https://doi.org/10.1140/epjst/e2012-01703-3.

William J. Baumol (2002). *The Free-Market Innovation Machine: Analyzing the Growth Miracle of Capitalism*, Princeton, NJ: Princeton University Press.

Emre Bayamlioğlu, Irina Baraliuc, Liisa Janssens, & Mireille Hildebrandt (eds.) (2018). *Being Profiled: Cogitas Ergo Sum*, Amsterdam: Amsterdam University Press.

Manuel Becker (2019). 'When public principals give up control over private agents: The new independence of ICANN in internet governance', *Regulation and Governance*, 13(4), 561–576, https://doi.org/10.1111/rego.12250.

Beijing Academy of Artificial Intelligence (2019). 'Beijing AI Principles', in Marc Rotenberg (ed.), *The AI Policy Sourcebook 2020*, Washington DC: Electronic Privacy Information Center, 8–10.

Catherine Belton (2020). *Putin's People: How the KGB Took Back Russia and Then Turned on the West*, London: William Collins.

David Bender (2016). 'Having mishandled Safe Harbor, will the CJEU do better with Privacy Shield? A US perspective', *International Data Privacy Law*, 6(2), 117–138, https://doi.org/10.1093/idpl/ipw005.

Yochai Benkler (2006). *The Wealth of Networks: How Social Production Transforms Markets and Freedom*, New Haven, CT: Yale University Press.

Jake A. Berkowsky & Thaier Hayajneh (2017). 'Security issues with certificate authorities', in *IEEE 8th Annual Ubiquitous Computing, Electronics and Mobile Communication Conference (UEMCON)*, IEEE, https://doi.org/10.1109/UEMCON.2017.8249081.

Ian Berle (2020). *Face Recognition Technology: Compulsory Visibility and Its Impact on Privacy and the Confidentiality of Personal Identifiable Images*, Cham: Springer.

Isaiah Berlin (2002). 'Two concepts of liberty', in Henry Hardy (ed.), *Liberty*, Oxford: Oxford University Press, 166–217.

Tim Berners-Lee (2010). 'Long live the Web: A call for continued open standards and neutrality', *Scientific American*, 303(6), 80–85, https://www.scientificamerican.com/article/long-live-the-web/.

Tim Berners-Lee, Robert Cailliau, Ari Luotonen, Henrik Frystyk Nielsen, & Arthur Secret (1994). 'The World-Wide Web', *Communications of the ACM*, 37(8), 76–82, https://doi.org/10.1145/179606.179671.

Tim Berners-Lee & Tim Fischetti (1999). *Weaving the Web: The Original Design and Ultimate Destiny of the World Wide Web*, New York: HarperCollins.

Tim Berners-Lee, Wendy Hall, James A. Hendler, Kieron O'Hara, Nigel Shadbolt, & Daniel J. Weitzner (2006). 'A framework for Web Science', *Foundations and Trends in Web Science*, 1(1), 1–134.

Tim Berners-Lee & Kieron O'Hara (2013). 'The read–write Linked Data Web', *Philosophical Transactions of the Royal Society A: Mathematical, Physical and Engineering Sciences*, 371(1987), https://doi.org/10–1098/rsta.2012.0513.

Chris Bernhardt (2019). *Quantum Computing for Everyone*, Cambridge, MA: MIT Press.

Ellery Roberts Biddle, Lauren Lee Finch, & Sarah Myers West (eds.) (2017). *Free Basics in Real Life: Six Case Studies on Facebook's Internet 'On Ramp' Initiative from Africa, Asia and Latin America*, Amsterdam: Global Voices, https://advox.globalvoices.org/wp-content/uploads/2017/08/FreeBasicsinRealLife_FINALJuly27.pdf.

Jonathan Bishop (2014). 'Representations of "trolls" in mass media communication: A review of media-texts and moral panics relating to "internet trolling"', *International Journal of Web Based Communities*, 10(1), 7–24, https://doi.org/10.1504/IJWBC.2014.058384.

Lisa Blaydes (2018). *State of Repression: Iraq under Saddam Hussein*, Princeton, NJ: Princeton University Press.

Andrew Blum (2012). *Tubes: Behind the Scenes at the Internet*. London: Viking.

Gillian Bolsover (2018). 'Slacktivist USA and authoritarian China? Comparing two political public spheres with a random sample of social media users', *Policy and Internet*, 10(4), 454–482, https://doi.org/10.1002/poi3.186.

Jacky Bourgeois, Gerd Kortuem, & Fahim Kawsar (2018). 'Trusted and GDPR-compliant research with the internet of things' in *IOT '18: Proceedings of the 8th International Conference on the Internet of Things*, New York: ACM, Article 13, https://doi.org/10.1145/3277593.3277604.

Yann Moulier Boutang (2011). *Cognitive Capitalism*, Cambridge: Polity Press.

Nigel Bowles, James T. Hamilton, & David A. L. Levy (eds.) (2014). *Transparency in Politics and the Media: Accountability and Open Government*, London: I. B. Tauris.

Anu Bradford (2012). 'The Brussels Effect', *Northwestern University Law Review*, 107(1), 1–67, http://scholarlycommons.law.northwestern.edu/cgi/viewcontent.cgi?article=1081&context=nulr.

Anu Bradford (2020). *The Brussels Effect: How the European Union Rules the World*, New York: Oxford University Press.

Julia Brailovskaia, Elke Rohmann, Hans-Werner Bierhoff, & Jürgen Margraf (2018). 'The brave blue world: Facebook flow and Facebook Addiction Disorder (FAD)', *PLoS One*, 13(7), e0201484, https://dx.doi.org/10.1371/journal.pone.0201484.

Sandra Braman (2020). 'The irony of Internet governance research: Metagovernance as context', in Laura DeNardis, Derrick L. Cogburn, Nanette S. Levinson, & Francesca Musiani (eds.), *Researching Internet Governance: Methods, Frameworks, Futures*, Cambridge, MA: MIT Press, 21–57.

Arnaud Brohé (2016). *The Handbook of Carbon Accounting*, Abingdon: Greenleaf.

David A. Broniatowski, Amelia M. Jamison, SiHua Qi, Lulwah AlKulaib, Tao Chen, Adrian Benton, Sandra C. Quinn, & Mark Dredze (2018). 'Weaponized health communication: Twitter bots and Russian trolls amplify the vaccine debate', *American Journal of Public Health*, 108(10), 1378–1384, https://ajph.aphapublications.org/doi/10.2105/AJPH.2018.304567.

Timothy Brook (2008). *Vermeer's Hat: The Seventeenth Century and the Dawn of the Global World*, London: Profile.

Adam R. Brown (2011). 'Wikipedia as a data source for political scientists: Accuracy and completeness of coverage', *PS: Political Science and Politics*, 44(2), 339–343, https://doi.org/10.1017/S1049096511000199.

Ian Brown & Christopher T. Marsden (2013). *Regulating Code: Good Governance and Better Regulation in the Information Age*, Cambridge, MA: MIT Press.

Roger Brownsword (2019). *Law, Technology and Society: Re-Imagining the Regulatory Environment*, Abingdon: Routledge.

Erik Brynjolfsson & Andrew McAfee (2014). *The Second Machine Age: Work, Progress and Prosperity in a Time of Brilliant Technologies*, New York: W. W. Norton.

Erin E. Buckels, Paul D. Trapnell, Tamara Andjelovic, & Delroy L. Paulhus (2019). 'Internet trolling and everyday sadism: Parallel effects on pain perception and moral judgment', *Journal of Personality*, 87(2), 328–340, https://doi.org/10.1111/jopy.12393.

Stanislav Budnitsky (2020). 'Russia's great power imaginary and pursuit of digital multipolarity', *Internet Policy Review*, 9(3), https://doi.org/10–14763/2020.3.1492.

Edmund Burke (1968). *Reflections on the Revolution in France*, Harmondsworth: Penguin.

Lee Bygrave (2013). 'Contract vs. statute in internet governance', in Ian Brown (ed.), *Research Handbook on Governance of the Internet*, Cheltenham: Edward Elgar, 168–197.

Guido Caldarelli & Michele Catanzaro (2012). *Networks: A Very Short Introduction*, Oxford: Oxford University Press.

Robert Cannon (2003). 'The legacy of the Federal Communications Commission's computer inquiries', *Federal Communications Law Journal*, 55(2), 167–205, https://www.repository.law.indiana.edu/fclj/vol55/iss2/2/.

Paolo Cardullo, Cesare Di Feliciantonio, & Rob Kitchin (eds.) (2019). *The Right to the Smart City*, Bingley: Emerald.

Brian E. Carpenter (2013). *Network Geeks: How They Built the Internet*, London: Springer.

Francesca Casalini & Javier López González (2019). 'Trade and cross-border data flows', *OECD Trade Policy Papers 220*, Paris: OECD, http://dx.doi.org/10.1787/b2023a47-en.

Manuel Castells (2001). *The Internet Galaxy: Reflections on the Internet, Business and Society*, Oxford: Oxford University Press.

Marianna Cavada, Miles R. Tight, & Christopher D. F. Rogers (2019). 'A smart city case study of Singapore: Is Singapore truly smart?' in Leonidas Anthopolous (ed.), *Smart City Emergence: Cases from around the World*, Amsterdam: Elsevier, 295–314, https://doi.org/10.1016/B978-0-12-816169-2.00014-6.

Jonathan Cave (2013). 'Policy and regulatory requirements for a future internet', in Ian Brown (ed.), *Research Handbook on Governance of the Internet*, Cheltenham: Edward Elgar, 143–167.

Vinton G. Cerf (2009). 'The day the Internet age began', *Nature*, 461, 1202–1203, https://doi.org/10.1038/4611202a.

Vinton G. Cerf (2018). 'The upper layers of the Internet', *Communications of the ACM*, 61(11), 5, https://doi.org/10.1145/3281164.

Vinton G. Cerf (2019a). 'Ownership vs. stewardship', *Communications of the ACM*, 62(3), 6, https://doi.org/10.1145/3310251.

Vinton G. Cerf (2019b). 'The last 40, the next 40: The Internet's arc', *Human Behavior and Emerging Technologies*, 1(1), 9–14, https://doi.org/10.1002/hbe2.114.

Vinton G. Cerf (2019c). 'In debt to the NSF', *Communications of the ACM*, 62(4), 5, https://doi.org/10.1145/3313989.

V. G. Cerf & P. T. Kirstein (1978). 'Issues in packet-network interconnection', *Proceedings of the IEEE*, 66(11), 1386–1408, https://doi.org/10.1109/PROC.1978.11147.

Michael Chase & James Mulvenon (2004). *You've Got Dissent! Chinese Dissident Use of the Internet and Beijing's Counter-Strategies*, Santa Monica, CA: RAND.

Jim X. Chen (2016). 'The evolution of computing: AlphaGo', *Computing in Science and Engineering*, 18(4), 4–7, https://doi.org/10.1109/MCSE.2016.74.

Michael Cherniavsky (1958). ' "Holy Russia": A study in the history of an idea', *American Historical Review*, 63(3), 617–637.

Tuan-Yee Ching & Joseph Ferreira Jr (2015). 'Smart cities: Concepts, perceptions and lessons for planners', in Stan Geertman, Joseph Ferreira Jr, Robert Goodspeed, & John Stillwell (eds.), *Planning Support Systems and Smart Cities*, Cham: Springer, 145–168, https://doi.org/10.1007/978-3-319-18368-8_8.

Clayton M. Christensen (1997). *The Innovator's Dilemma: When New Technologies Cause Great Firms to Fail*, Boston: Harvard Business Review Press.

Wolfie Christl & Sarah Spiekermann (2016). *Networks of Control: A Report on Corporate Surveillance, Digital Tracking, Big Data and Privacy*, Vienna: Facultas.

George Christou (2018). 'European Union privacy and data protection policy', in Nikolaos Zahariadis & Laurie Buonanno (eds.), *The Routledge Handbook of European Public Policy*, Abingdon: Routledge, 179–190.

Richard A. Clarke, Michael J. Morell, Geoffrey R. Stone, Cass R. Sunstein, & Peter Swire (2014). *The NSA Report: Liberty and Security in a Changing World*, Princeton, NJ: Princeton University Press.

Kevin A. Clauson, Hyla H. Polen, & Maged N. Kamel Boulos (2008). 'Scope, completeness, and accuracy of drug information in Wikipedia', *Annals of Pharmacotherapy*, 42(12), 1814–1821, https://doi.org/10.1345/aph.1L474.

Rebecca A. Clothey, Emmanuel F. Koku, Erfan Erkin, & Husenjan Emat (2016). 'A voice for the voiceless: Online social activism in Uyghur language blogs and state control of the Internet in China', *Information, Communication and Society*, 19(6), 858–874, https://doi.org/10.1080/1369118X.2015.1061577.

Ronald Coase (1937). 'The nature of the firm', *Economica*, 4(16), 386–405, https://doi.org/10.1111/j.1468-0335.1937.tb00002.x.

Kevin Coates (2011). *Competition Law and Regulation of Technology Markets*, New York: Oxford University Press.

Christopher Coker (2019). *The Rise of the Civilizational State*, Cambridge: Polity Press.

Adrienne Colborne & Michael Smit (2020). 'Characterizing disinformation risk to open data in the post-truth era', article 13, *Journal of Data and Information Quality*, 12(3), https://doi.org/10–1145/3328747.

Gabriella Coleman (2013). 'Anonymous and the politics of leaking', in Benedetta Brevini, Arne Hintz, & Patrick McCurdy (eds.), *Beyond WikiLeaks: Implications for the Future of Communications, Journalism and Society*, London: Palgrave Macmillan, 209–228, https://doi.org/10–1057/9781137275745_13.

Stephen Coleman & Jay G. Blumler (2009). *The Internet and Democratic Citizenship: Theory, Practice and Policy*, New York: Cambridge University Press.

Lizzie Coles-Kemp, Debi Ashenden, & Kieron O'Hara (2019). 'Why should I? Cybersecurity, the security of the state and the insecurity of the citizen', *Politics and Governance*, 6(2), https://www.cogitatiopress.com/politicsandgovernance/article/view/1333.

Massimo Colombo, Chiara Franzoni, & Reinhilde Veugelers (2015). 'Going radical: Producing and transferring disruptive innovation', *Journal of Technology Transfer*, 40(4), 663–669.

Greg Conti (2009). *Googling Security: How Much Does Google Know about You?* Boston: Pearson Education.

Rory Cormac & Richard J. Aldrich (2018). 'Grey is the new black: Covert action and implausible deniability', *International Affairs*, 94(3), 477–494, https://doi.org/10.1093/ia/iiy067.

Nick Couldry & Ulises A. Mejias (2019). 'Data colonialism: Rethinking big data's relation to the contemporary subject', *Television & New Media*, 20(4), 336–349, https://doi.org/10.1177/1527476418796632.

Robert Cowley, Federico Caprotti, Michele Ferretti, & Chen Zhong (2019). 'Ordinary Chinese smart cities: The case of Wuhan', in Andrew Karvonen, Federico Cugurullo, & Federico Caprotti (eds.), *Inside Smart Cities: Place, Politics and Urban Innovation*, Abingdon: Routledge, 45–64.

Andy Crabtree, Tom Lodge, James Colley, Chris Greenhalgh, Kevin Glover, Hamed Haddadi, Yousef Amar, Richard Mortier, Qi Li, John Moore, Liang Wang, Poonam Yadav, Jianxin Zhao, Anthony Brown, Lachlan Urquhart, & Derek McAuley (2018). 'Building accountability into the Internet of Things: The IoT Databox model', *Journal of Reliable Intelligent Environments*, 4, 39–55, https://doi.org/10.1007/s40860-018-0054-5.

Judd Cramer & Alan B. Krueger (2016). 'Disruptive change in the taxi business: The case of Uber', *American Economic Review*, 106(5), 177–182.

Rogier Creemers (2017a). 'Cyber China: Upgrading propaganda, public opinion work and social management for the twenty-first century', *Journal of Contemporary China*, 26(103), 85–100, https://doi.org/10.1080/10670564.2016.1206281.

Rogier Creemers (2017b). 'Disrupting the Chinese state: New actors and new factors', *Asiascape: Digital Asia*, 5(3), 169–197, https://doi.org/10.1163/22142312-12340094.

Rogier Creemers (2020). 'The ideology behind China's AI strategy', in *The AI Powered State: China's Approach to Public Sector Innovation*, London: Nesta, 63–69, https://media.nesta.org.uk/documents/Nesta_TheAIPoweredState_2020.pdf.

R. C. Cross & A. D. Woozley (1964). *Plato's Republic: A Philosophical Commentary*, Basingstoke: Macmillan.

Peter Cunliffe-Jones (2020). 'From church and mosque to WhatsApp—Africa Check's holistic approach to countering "fake news"', *Political Quarterly*, 91(3), 596–599, https://doi.org/10.1111/1467-923X.12899.

Martin Curley & Bror Salmelin (2018). *Open Innovation 2.0: The New Mode of Digital Innovation for Prosperity and Sustainability*, Cham: Springer.

Lincoln Dahlberg (2011). 'Re-constructing digital democracy: An outline of four "positions"', *New Media & Society*, 13(6), 855–872, https://doi.org/10.1177/1461444810389569.

Xin Dai (2020). 'Enforcing law and norms for good citizens: One view of China's social credit system project', *Development*, 63, 38–43, https://doi.org/10.1057/s41301-020-00244-2.

Diganta Das (2015). 'Hyderabad: Visioning, restructuring and making of a high-tech city', *Cities*, 43, 48–58, https://doi.org/10.1016/j.cities.2014.11.008.

Ayona Datta (2015). 'A 100 smart cities, a 100 utopias', *Dialogues in Human Geography*, 5(1), 49–53, https://doi.org/10.1177/2043820614565750.

David Davenport (2002). 'Anonymity on the Internet: Why the price may be too high', *Communications of the ACM*, 45(4), 33–35, https://doi.org/10.1145/505248.505267.

Graham Day (2017). *Security in the Digital World: For the Home User, Parent, Consumer and Home Office*, Ely: IT Governance.

Laura DeNardis (2014a). *The Global War for Internet Governance*, New Haven, CT: Yale University Press.

Laura DeNardis (2014b). 'The social media challenge to Internet governance', in Mark Graham & William H. Dutton (eds.), *Society and the Internet: How Networks of Information and Communication Are Changing Our Lives*, Oxford: Oxford University Press, 348–359.

Laura DeNardis (2020). 'Introduction: Internet governance as an object of research inquiry', in Laura DeNardis, Derrick L. Cogburn, Nanette S. Levinson, & Francesca Musiani (eds.), *Researching Internet Governance: Methods, Frameworks, Futures*, Cambridge, MA: MIT Press, 1–20.

Nicholas Dias & Amy Sippitt (2020). 'Researching fact checking: Present limitations and future opportunities', *Political Quarterly*, 91(3), 605–613, https://doi.org/10.1111/1467-923X.12892.

Denis Diderot (1995). 'Encyclopédie', in Isaac Kramnick (ed.), *The Portable Enlightenment Reader*, New York: Penguin, 17–21.

Maurits Dolmans & Carlo Piana (2010). 'A tale of two tragedies: A plea for open standards', *International Free and Open Source Software Law Review*, 2(2), 115–138, https://www.ifosslr.org/index.php/ifosslr/article/view/46.

Zakir Durumeric, James Kasten, Michael Bailey, & J. Alex Halderman (2013). 'Analysis of the HTTPS certificate ecosystem', in *IMC '13: Proceedings of the 2013 Conference on Internet Measurement*, New York: ACM, 291–304, https://doi.org/10.1145/2504730.2504755.

William H. Dutton (2009). 'The fifth estate emerging through the network of networks', *Prometheus*, 27(1), 1–15, https://doi.org/10.1080/08109020802657453.

William H. Dutton (ed.) (2013). *The Oxford Handbook of Internet Studies*, Oxford: Oxford University Press.

David Dwan (2018). *Liberty, Equality and Humbug: Orwell's Political Ideals*, Oxford: Oxford University Press.

Gerald Dworkin (1972). 'Paternalism', *The Monist*, 56(1), 64–84.

Lanny Ebenstein (2015). *Chicagonomics: The Evolution of Chicago Free Market Economics*, New York: St Martin's Press.

EDPS Ethics Advisory Group (2018). *Towards a Digital Ethics*, European Data Protection Supervisor, https://edps.europa.eu/sites/edp/files/publication/18-01-25_eag_report_en.pdf.

Lilian Edwards (2013). 'Privacy, law, code, and social networking sites', in Ian Brown (ed.), *Research Handbook on Governance of the Internet*, Cheltenham: Edward Elgar, 309–352.

Dave Eggers (2013). *The Circle*, London: Hamish Hamilton.

Hamid R. Ekbia & Bonnie A. Nardi (2017). *Heteromation: And Other Stories of Computing and Capitalism*, Cambridge, MA: MIT Press.

Alice Ekman (2019). *China's Smart Cities: The New Geopolitical Battleground*, Études de l'Ifri, Paris: Institut Français des Relations Internationales, https://www.ifri.org/sites/default/files/atoms/files/ekman_smart_cites_battleground_2019.pdf.

Mahmoud Elkhodr, Seyed Shahrestani, & Hon Cheung (2016). 'The Internet of Things: New interoperability, management and security challenges', *International Journal of Network Security & Its Applications*, 8(2), 85–102, https://doi.org/10.5121/ijnsa.2016.8206.

Mark Elliot, Elaine Mackey, & Kieron O'Hara (2020). *The Anonymisation Decision-Making Framework 2nd Edition: European Practitioners' Guide*, Manchester: UKAN.

Mark Elliot, Elaine Mackey, Kieron O'Hara, & Caroline Tudor (2016). *The Anonymisation Decision-Making Framework*, Manchester: UKAN.

Mark Elliot, Kieron O'Hara, Charles Raab, Christine M. O'Keeffe, Elaine Mackey, Chris Dibben, Heather Gowans, Kingsley Purdam, & Karen McCullagh (2018). 'Functional anonymisation: Personal data and the data environment', *Computer Law and Security Review*, 34(2), 204–221, https://doi.org/10.1016/j.clsr.2018.02.001.

Nicole B. Ellison & danah m. boyd (2013). 'Sociality through social network sites', in William H. Dutton (ed.), *The Oxford Handbook of Internet Studies*, Oxford: Oxford University Press, 151–172.

Severin Engelmann, Mo Chen, Felix Fischer, Ching-yu Kao, & Jens Grossklags (2019). 'Clear sanctions, vague rewards: How China's social credit system currently defines "good" and "bad" behavior', in *FAT* '19: Proceedings of the Conference on Fairness, Accountability, and Transparency*, New York: ACM, 69–78, https://doi.org/10.1145/3287560.3287585.

Kai T. Erikson (1976). *Everything in Its Path: Destruction of Community in the Buffalo Creek Flood*, New York: Simon & Schuster.

Ernesto Estrada & Philip A. Knight (2015). *A First Course in Network Theory*, Oxford: Oxford University Press.

Amitai Etzioni (1999). *The Limits of Privacy*, New York: Basic Books.

Amitai Etzioni (2018). 'Encryption wars: Who should yield?' in Derek S. Reveron, Nikolas K. Gvosdev, & John A. Cloud (eds.), *The Oxford Handbook of U.S. National Security*, New York: Oxford University Press, 417–434.

Claire L. Evans (2018). *Broad Band: The Untold Story of the Women Who Made the Internet*, New York: Portfolio/Penguin.

David Evans, Vladimir Kolesnikov, & Mike Rosulek (2018). 'A pragmatic introduction to secure multi-party computation', *Foundations and Trends in Privacy and Security*, 2(2–3), 70–246, http://dx.doi.org/10.1561/3300000019.

Joshua A. T. Fairfield (2012). '"Do-not-track" as contract', *Vanderbilt Journal of Entertainment and Technology Law*, 14(3), 545–602.

Joshua A. T. Fairfield (2013). '"Do-not-track" as default', *Northwestern Journal of Technology and Intellectual Property*, 11(7), article 2, http://scholarlycommons.law.northwestern.edu/njtip/vol11/iss7/2.

Don Fallis (2011). 'Wikipistemology', in Alvin I. Goldman & Dennis Whitcomb (eds.), *Social Epistemology: Essential Readings*, New York: Oxford University Press, 297–313.

Emmanuel Farhi & François Gourio (2019). 'What is driving the return spread between "safe" and "risky" assets?' *Chicago Fed Letter Essays on Issues 2019*, 416, https://doi.org–10.21033/cfl-2019-416.

Edmund Fawcett (2018). *Liberalism: The Life of an Idea*, 2nd edition, Princeton, NJ: Princeton University Press.

Kyle Ferden (2015). 'The Swanson Paradox: Do-Not-Track and the intersection of data autonomy and the free market', *Journal of Corporation Law*, 41(2), 493–508.

Niall Ferguson (2017). *The Square and the Tower: Networks, Hierarchies and the Struggle for Global Power*, London: Allen Lane.

David Ferrucci, Eric Brown, Jennifer Chu-Carroll, James Fan, David Gondek, Aditya A. Kalyanpur, Adam Lally, J. William Murdock, Eric Nyberg, John Prager, Nico Schlaefer, & Chris Welty (2010). 'Building Watson: An overview of the DeepQA project', *AI Magazine*, 31(3), 59–79, https://doi.org/10.1609/aimag.v31i3.2303.

Stephan Feuchtwang (2002). 'Reflections on privacy in China', in Bonnie S. McDougall & Anders Hansson (eds.), *Chinese Concepts of Privacy*, Leiden: Brill, 211–230.

Paul Feyerabend (1975). *Against Method*, London: Verso.

George Fishback (2020). 'How the Wolf of Wall Street shaped the Internet: A review of Section 230 of the Communications Decency Act', *Texas Intellectual Property Law Journal*, 28(2), 275–296.

Jacinthe Flore & Kiran Pienaar (2020). 'Data-driven intimacy: Emerging technologies in the (re)making of sexual subjects and 'healthy' sexuality', *Health Sociology Review*, 29(3), 279–293, https://doi.org/10.1080/14461242.2020.1803101.

Michel Foucault (1981). *Power/Knowledge: Selected Interviews and Other Writings 1972–1977*, London: Harvester.

Michael Freeden (2018). 'Loose talk costs . . . nothing', *Journal of Political Ideologies*, 23(1), 1–9, https://doi.org/10.1080/13569317.2018.1413825.

Ori Freiman & Boaz Miller (2020). 'Can artificial entities assert?' in Sanford G. Goldberg (ed.), *The Oxford Handbook of Assertion*, New York: Oxford University Press, 415–434.

Sarah Frier (2020). *No Filter: The Inside Story of How Instagram Transformed Business, Celebrity and Our Culture*, London: Random House Business.

A. Michael Froomkin (2013). 'ICANN and the domain name system after the "Affirmation of Commitments"', in Ian Brown (ed.), *Research Handbook on Governance of the Internet*, Cheltenham: Edward Elgar, 27–51.

Karen Frost-Arnold (2019). 'How an epistemology of ignorance maintains Wikipedia's gender gap', *AoIR Selected Papers of Internet Research*, https://journals.uic.edu/ojs/index.php/spir/article/view/10052.

Danit Gal (2020). 'China's approach to AI ethics', in *The AI Powered State: China's Approach to Public Sector Innovation*, London: Nesta, 53–61, https://media.nesta.org.uk/documents/Nesta_TheAIPoweredState_2020.pdf.

Maude Gauthier & Kim Sawchuk (2017). 'Not notable enough: Feminism and expertise in Wikipedia', *Communication and Critical/Cultural Studies*, 14(4), 385–402, https://doi.org/10–1080/14791420.2017.1386321.

Johannes Gerschewski & Alexander Dukalskis (2018). 'How the Internet can reinforce authoritarian regimes: The case of North Korea', *Georgetown Journal of International Affairs*, 19(1), 12–19, https://doi.org/10.1353/gia.2018.0002.

Rebecca Giblin (2014). 'When ISPs become copyright police', *IEEE Internet Computing*, 18(2), 84–87, https://doi.org/10.1109/MIC.2014.37.

Anthony Giddens (1990). *The Consequences of Modernity*, Cambridge: Polity Press.

Anthony Giddens (1991). *Modernity and Self-Identity: Self and Society in the Late Modern Age*, Cambridge: Polity Press.

Jim Giles (2005). 'Internet encyclopaedias go head to head', *Nature*, 438, 900–901, https://www.nature.com/articles/438900a.

Victor Glass & Timothy Tardiff (2019). 'A new direction for the net neutrality debate', *Telecommunications Policy*, 43(3), 199–212, https://doi.org/10.1016/j.telpol.2018.05.002.

Rahul Gochhwal (2017). 'Unified Payment Interface: An advancement in payment systems', *American Journal of Industrial and Business Management*, 7(10), 1174–1191, https://doi.org/10–4236/ajibm.2017.710084.

Jack Goldsmith & Tim Wu (2006). *Who Controls the Internet? Illusions of a Borderless World*, Oxford: Oxford University Press.

Richard Gomer, m. c. schraefel & Enrico Gerding (2014). 'Consenting agents: Semi-autonomous interactions for ubiquitous consent', in *Proceedings of the 2014 ACM International Joint Conference on Pervasive and Ubiquitous Computing: Adjunct Publication (UbiComp '14)*, New York: ACM, 653–658, https://doi.org/10.1145/2638728.2641682.

Vijay Govindarajan, Anup Srivastava, & Luminita Enache (2019). 'How India Plans to Protect Consumer Data', *Harvard Business Review*, 18 December 2019, https://hbr.org/2019/12/how-india-plans-to-protect-consumer-data.

Mark Graham & William H. Dutton (eds.) (2014). *Society and the Internet: How Networks of Information and Communication Are Changing Our Lives*, Oxford: Oxford University Press.

Mark Graham, Matthew Zook, & Andrew Boulton (2013). 'Augmented reality in urban places: Contested content and the duplicity of code', *Transactions of the Institute of British Geographers*, 38(3), 464–479, https://doi.org/10.1111/j.1475-5661.2012.00539.x.

Lucas Graves & Alexios Mantzarlis (2020). 'Amid political spin and online misinformation, fact checking adapts', *Political Quarterly*, 91(3), 585–591, https://doi.org/10.1111/1467-923X.12896.

Samuel Greengard (2015). *The Internet of Things*, Cambridge, MA: MIT Press.

Graham Greenleaf (2013). 'Data protection in a globalised network', in Ian Brown (ed.), *Research Handbook on Governance of the Internet*, Cheltenham: Edward Elgar, 221–259.

Graham Greenleaf (2019). *Global Data Privacy Laws 2019: 132 National Laws & Many Bills*, https://papers.ssrn.com/sol3/papers.cfm?abstract_id=3381593.

Shane Greenstein (2015). *How the Internet Became Commercial: Innovation, Privatization, and the Birth of a New Network*, Princeton, NJ: Princeton University Press.

Shane Greenstein, Martin Peitz, & Tommaso Valleti (2016). 'Net neutrality: A fast lane to understanding the trade-offs', *Journal of Economic Perspectives*, 30(2), 127–150, https://doi.org/10.1257/jep.30.2.127.

Glenn Greenwald (2014). *No Place to Hide: Edward Snowden, the NSA and the Surveillance State*, London: Hamish Hamilton.

James Griffiths (2019). *The Great Firewall of China: How to Build and Control an Alternative Version of the Internet*, London: Zed Books.

M. D. Griffiths (2014). 'Adolescent trolling in online environments: A brief overview', *Education and Health*, 32(3), 85–87.

Rüdiger Grimm & Alexander Rossnagel (2000). 'Can P3P help to protect privacy worldwide?', in *MULTIMEDIA '00: Proceedings of the 2000 ACM Workshops on Multimedia*, New York: ACM, 157–160, https://doi.org/10.1145/357744.357917.

Christophe Guilluy (2019). *Twilight of the Elites: Prosperity, the Periphery, and the Future of France*, New Haven, CT: Yale University Press.

Sergei Guriev & Daniel Treisman (2015). *How Modern Dictators Survive: An Informational Theory of the New Authoritarianism*, National Bureau of Economic Research working paper no. 21136, https://www.nber.org/papers/w21136.

Daniel Guttentag (2015). 'Airbnb: Disruptive innovation and the rise of an informal tourism accommodation sector', *Current Issues in Tourism*, 18(12), 1192–1217.

Peter Guy (2018). 'Consumers, corporations and government: Computing in China', *Communications of the ACM*, 61(11), 46–47, https://doi.org/10.1145/3239538.

Jürgen Habermas (1989). *The Structural Transformation of the Public Sphere: An Inquiry into a Category of Bourgeois Society*, Cambridge: Polity Press.

Jürgen Habermas (1996). *Between Facts and Norms*, Cambridge: Polity Press.

Peter A. Hall & David Soskice (2001). 'An introduction to Varieties of Capitalism', in Peter A. Hall & David Soskice (eds.), *Varieties of Capitalism: The Institutional Foundations of Comparative Advantage*, Oxford: Oxford University Press, 1–68.

Wendy Hall & Jérôme Pesenti (2017). *Growing the Artificial Intelligence Industry in the UK*, London: Department for Digital, Culture, Media & Sport and Department for Business, Energy & Industrial Strategy, https://www.gov.uk/government/publications/growing-the-artificial-intelligence-industry-in-the-uk.

Harry Halpin (2012). 'The philosophy of Anonymous: Ontological politics without identity', *Radical Philosophy*, 176, 19–28.

Eugeniu Han (2020). 'From traffic management to smart courts: China's approach to smart cities', in *The AI Powered State: China's Approach to Public Sector Innovation*, London: Nesta, 35–41, https://media.nesta.org.uk/documents/Nesta_TheAIPoweredState_2020.pdf.

Chad Hansen (1991). 'Classical Chinese ethics', in Peter Singer (ed.), *A Companion to Ethics*, Malden MA: Blackwell, 69–81.

Mikael Hård & Thomas J. Misa (eds.) (2008). *Urban Machinery: Inside Modern European Cities*, Cambridge, MA: MIT Press.

Thomas Hardjono, David Shrier, & Alex Pentland (eds.) (2016). *Trust::Data: A New Framework for Identity and Data Sharing*, Visionary Future.

Jane K. Hart & Kirk Martinez (2006). 'Environmental Sensor Networks: A revolution in the earth system science?' *Earth Science Reviews*, 78(3–4), 177–191, https://doi.org/10.1016/j.earscirev.2006.05.001.

Vi Hart, Divya Siddarth, Bethan Cantrell, Lila Tretikov, Peter Eckersley, John Langford, Scott Leibrand, Sham Kakade, Steve Latta, Dana Lewis, Stefano Tessaro, & Glen Weyl (2020). *Outpacing the Virus: Digital Response to Containing the Spread of COVID-19 While Mitigating Privacy Risks*, Edmond J. Safra Center for Ethics

COVID-19 Rapid Response Impact Initiative White Paper 5, https://ethics.harvard.edu/files/center-for-ethics/files/white_paper_5_outpacing_the_virus_final.pdf

David Harvey (1990). *The Condition of Postmodernity: An Enquiry Into the Origins of Social Change*, Oxford: Blackwell.

Oz Hassan (2020). 'Artificial Intelligence, Neom and Saudi Arabia's economic diversification from oil and gas', *Political Quarterly*, 91(1), 222–227, https://doi.org/10.1111/1467-923X.12794.

Scott Hawken, Hoon Han, & Chris Pettit (eds.) (2020). *Open Cities, Open Data: Collaborative Cities in the Information Era*, Singapore: Springer Nature.

F. A. Hayek (1935). 'The use of knowledge in society', *American Economic Review*, 35(4), 519–530.

F. A. Hayek (1960). *The Constitution of Liberty*, London: Routledge & Kegan Paul.

Dorothee Heisenberg & Marie-Hélène Fandel (2004). 'Projecting EU regimes abroad: The EU Data Protection Directive as global standard', in Sandra Braman (ed.), *The Emergent Global Information Policy Regime*, Basingstoke: Palgrave Macmillan, 109–129.

James Hendler & Tim Berners-Lee (2010). 'From the semantic web to social machines: A research challenge for AI on the World Wide Web', *Artificial Intelligence*, 174(2), 156–161, https://doi.org/10.1016/j.artint.2009.11.010.

James Hetherington & Matthew West (2020). *The Pathway Towards an Information Management Framework: A 'Commons' for Digital Built Britain*, National Digital Twin Programme, Cambridge: Centre for Digital Built Britain, https://www.cdbb.cam.ac.uk/files/the_pathway_towards_an_imf.pdf.

Mireille Hildebrandt (2015). *Smart Technologies and the End(s) of Law*, Cheltenham: Edward Elgar.

Mireille Hildebrandt & Serge Gutwirth (eds.) (2008). *Profiling the European Citizen: Cross-Disciplinary Perspectives*, Dordrecht: Springer.

Mireille Hildebrandt & Kieron O'Hara (eds.) (2020). *Life and the Law in the Era of Data-Driven Agency*, Cheltenham: Edward Elgar.

Pekka Himanen (2001). *The Hacker Ethic and the Spirit of the Information Age*, London: Vintage.

Matthew Hindman (2009). *The Myth of Digital Democracy*, Princeton, NJ: Princeton University Press.

Marit Hinnosaar (2019). 'Gender inequality in new media: Evidence from Wikipedia', *Journal of Economic Behavior & Organization*, 163, 262–276, https://doi.org/10.1016/j.jebo.2019.04.020.

Ezra Ho (2017). 'Smart subjects for a Smart Nation? Governing (smart)mentalities in Singapore', *Urban Studies*, 54(13), 3101–3118, https://doi.org/10.1177/0042098016664305.

Jeanette Hofmann (2020). 'The multistakeholder concept as narrative: A discourse analytical approach', in Laura DeNardis, Derrick L. Cogburn, Nanette S. Levinson, & Francesca Musiani (eds.), *Researching Internet Governance: Methods, Frameworks, Futures*, Cambridge, MA: MIT Press, 253–268.

Bernie Hogan & Barry Wellman (2014). 'The relational self-portrait: Selfies meet social networks', in Mark Graham & William H. Dutton (eds.), *Society and the Internet: How Networks of Information and Communication Are Changing Our Lives*, Oxford: Oxford University Press, 53–66.

Martin Hollis (1982). 'The social destruction of reality', in Martin Hollis & Steven Lukes (eds.), *Rationality and Relativism*, Oxford: Basil Blackwell, 67–86.

Sun-ha Hong (2017). 'Criticising surveillance and surveillance critique: Why privacy and humanism are necessary but insufficient', *Surveillance and Society*, 15(2), 187–203, https://doi.org/10.24908/ss.v15i2.5441.

Christopher Alex Hooton (2020). 'Testing the economics of the net neutrality debate', *Telecommunications Policy*, 44(5), https://doi.org/10.1016/j.telpol.2019.101869.

Philip N. Howard (2015). *Pax Technica: How the Internet of Things May Set Us Free or Lock Us Up*, New Haven, CT: Yale University Press.

Philip N. Howard (2020). *Lie Machines: How to Save Democracy from Troll Armies, Deceitful Robots, Junk News Operations, and Political Operatives*, New Haven, CT: Yale University Press.

Matthew B. Hoy (2018). 'Alexa, Siri, Cortana, and more: An introduction to voice assistants', *Medical Reference Services Quarterly*, 37(1), 81–88, https://doi.org/10.1080/02763869.2018.1404391.

Hua Huang & Xun Lin (2019). 'Chinese parental involvement and class-based inequality in education: The role of social networking sites', *Learning, Media and Technology*, 44(4), 489–501, https://doi.org/10.1080/17439884.2019.1620767.

Tyler Hunt, Congzheng Song, Reza Shokri, Vitaly Shmatikov, & Emmett Witchel (2018). 'Chiron: Privacy-preserving machine learning as a service', *arXiv*, https://arxiv.org/abs/1803.05961v1.

Philip Hunter (2008). 'Pakistan YouTube block exposes fundamental Internet security weakness: Concern that Pakistani action affected YouTube access elsewhere in world', *Computer Fraud and Security*, 4, 10–11, https://doi.org/10.1016/S1361-3723(08)70065-4.

Samuel Huntington (1996). *The Clash of Civilizations: And the Remaking of the World Order*, New York: Simon & Schuster.

Phyllis Illari & Luciano Floridi (2014). 'Information Quality, Data and Philosophy', in Luciano Floridi & Phyllis Illari (eds.), *The Philosophy of Information Quality*, Cham: Springer, 5–23, https://doi.org/10.1007/978-3-319-07121-3_2.

Gerardo Iñiguez, Tzipe Govezensky, Robin Dunbar, Kimmo Kaski, & Rafael A. Barrio (2014). 'Effects of deception in social networks', *Proceedings of the Royal Society B: Biological Sciences*, 281(1790), https://doi.org/10.1098/rspb.2014.1195.

Kristina Irion (2012). 'Government cloud computing and national data sovereignty', *Policy and Internet*, 4(3–4), 40–71, https://doi.org/10.1002/poi3.10.

Mark A. Jamison (2018). 'Net neutrality policies and regulation in the United States', *Review of Network Economics*, 17(3), 151–174, https://doi.org/10.1515/rne-2018-0041.

Jason L. Jarvis (2014). 'Digital image politics: The networked rhetoric of Anonymous', *Global Discourse*, 4(2–3), 326–349, https://doi.org/10.1080/23269995.2014.923633.

Jeff Jarvis (2011). *Public Parts: How Sharing in the Digital Age Improves the Way We Work and Live*, New York: Simon & Schuster.

Thomas Jefferson (1993). 'Autobiography', in *The Life and Selected Writings of Thomas Jefferson*, New York: Random House, 3–104.

Min Jiang & King-Wa Fu (2018). 'Chinese social media and big data: Big data, big brother, big profit?' *Policy and Internet*, 10(4), 372–392, https://doi.org/10.1002/poi3.187.

Pingyu Jiang & Jiewu Leng (2017). 'The configuration of social manufacturing: A social intelligence way toward service-oriented manufacturing', *International Journal of Manufacturing Research*, 12(1), 4–19, https://doi.org/10.1504/IJMR.2017.083647.

Adrian Johns (2009). *Piracy: The Intellectual Property Wars from Gutenberg to Gates*, Chicago: University of Chicago Press.

Lynette A. Jones (2018). *Haptics*, Cambridge, MA: MIT Press.

Meg Leta Jones (2020). 'Cookies: A legacy of controversy', *Internet History*, 4(1), 87–104, https://doi.org/10.1080/24701475.2020.1725852.

Philippe Jougleux & Tatiana-Eleni Synodinou (2016). 'Prevention of cyber attacks', in Ioannis Iglezakis (ed.), *The Legal Regulation of Cyber Attacks*, Alphen aan den Rijn: Kluwer.

Brian Kahin & Janet Abbate (eds.) (1995). *Standards Policy for Information Infrastructure*, Cambridge, MA: MIT Press.

Peter Kairouz, H. Brendan McMahan, Brendan Avent, Aurélien Bellet, Mehdi Bennis, Arjun Nitin Bhagoji, Keith Bonawitz, Zachary Charles, Graham Cormode, Rachel Cummings, Rafael G. L. D'Oliveira, Salim El Rouayheb, David Evans, Josh Gardner, Zachary Garrett, Adrià Gascón, Badih Ghazi, Phillip B. Gibbons, Marco Gruteser, Zaid Harchaoui, Chaoyang He, Lie He, Zhouyuan Huo, Ben Hutchinson, Justin Hsu, Martin Jaggi, Tara Javidi, Gauri Joshi, Mikhail Khodak, Jakub Konečný, Aleksandra Korolova, Farinaz Koushanfar, Sanmi Koyejo, Tancrède Lepoint, Yang Liu, Prateek Mittal, Mehryar Mohri, Richard Nock, Ayfer Özgür, Rasmus Pagh, Mariana Raykova, Hang Qi, Daniel Ramage, Ramesh Raskar, Dawn Song, Weikang Song, Sebastian U. Stich, Ziteng Sun, Ananda Theertha Suresh, Florian Tramèr, Praneeth Vepakomma, Jianyu Wang, Li Xiong, Zheng Xu, Qiang Yang, Felix X. Yu, Han Yu, & Sen Zhao (2019). 'Advances and open problems in federated learning', *arXiv*, https://arxiv.org/abs/1912.04977v1.

Amba Kak, Jochai Ben-Avie, Alice Munyua, & Adbhav Tiwari (2020). *Bringing Openness to Identity: Technical and Policy Choices for Open National ID Systems*, Mozilla White Paper, https://blog.mozilla.org/netpolicy/files/2020/01/Mozilla-Digital-ID-White-Paper.pdf.

Liz Kaminski (2018). 'Calling a truce to the crypto wars: Why Congress and tech companies must work together to introduce new solutions and legislation to regulate encryption', *Seton Hall Law Review*, 48(2), 507–533.

Robert D. Kaplan (2018). *The Return of Marco Polo's World: War, Strategy, and American Interests in the Twenty-First Century*, New York: Random House.

Vasileios Karagiannopoulos (2012). 'The role of the Internet in political struggles: Some conclusions from Iran and Egypt', *New Political Science*, 34(2), 151–171, https://doi.org/10.1080/07393148.2012.676394.

James Kasten, Eric Wustrow, & J. Alex Halderman (2013). 'CAge: Taming certificate authorities by inferring restricted scopes', in Ahmad-Reza Sadeghi (ed.), *Financial Cryptography and Data Security*, Berlin: Springer, 329–337, https://doi.org/10.1007/978-3-642-39884-1_28.

Matt J. Keeling, T. Deirdre Hollingsworth, & Jonathan M. Read (2020). 'Efficacy of contact tracing for the containment of the 2019 novel coronavirus (COVID-19)', *Journal of Epidemiology & Community Health*, 74(10), 861–866, http://dx.doi.org/10.1136/jech-2020-214051.

John D. Kelleher (2019). *Deep Learning*, Cambridge, MA: MIT Press.

John D. Kelleher & Brendan Tierney (2018). *Data Science*, Cambridge, MA: MIT Press.

Andrea Kendall-Taylor, Erica Frantz, & Joseph Wright (2020). 'The digital dictators: How technology strengthens autocracy', *Foreign Affairs*, 99(2), 103–115.

Brian W. Kernighan & Rob Pike (1983). *The UNIX Programming Environment*, Englewood Cliffs, NJ: Prentice-Hall.

Orin S. Kerr (2009). 'The case for the third-party doctrine', *Michigan Law Review*, 107(4), 561–602.

Esther Keymolen & Simone Van der Hof (2019). 'Can I still trust you, my dear doll? A philosophical and legal exploration of smart toys and trust', *Journal of Cyber Policy*, 4(2), 143–159, https://doi.org/10.1080/23738871.2019.1586970.

Sunil Khilnani (2012). *The Idea of India*, 4th edition, London: Penguin.

Atefeh Khosravi & Rajkumar Buyya (eds.) (2018). *Energy and Carbon Footprint-Aware Management of Geo-Distributed Cloud Data Centers: A Taxonomy, State of the Art, and Future Directions*, IGI Global, https://www.igi-global.com/chapter/energy-and-carbon-footprint-aware-management-of-geo-distributed-cloud-data-centers/189954.

David Kirkpatrick (2010). *The Facebook Effect: The Inside Story of the Company That Is Connecting the World*, New York: Simon & Schuster.

Rob Kitchin (2014). *The Data Revolution: Big Data, Open Data, Data Infrastructures and Their Consequences*, London: Sage.

Kyungmin Ko, Heejin Lee, & Seungkwon Jang (2009). 'The Internet dilemma and control policy: Political and economic implications of the Internet in North Korea', *Korean Journal of Defense Analysis*, 21(3), 279–295, https://doi.org/10.1080/10163270903087204.

Sjaak Koenis (2014). *Voices of the People: Pluralism in Dutch Politics (1994–2014)*, Amsterdam: VU University Press.

Laura M. Koesten, Emilia Kacprzak, Jenifer F. A. Tennison, & Elena Simperl (2017). 'The trials and tribulations of working with structured data: A study on information seeking behaviour', in *CHI '17: Proceedings of the 2017 CHI Conference on Human Factors in Computing Systems*, 1277–1289, https://doi.org/10.1145/3025453.3025838.

Nina A. Kollars & Michael B. Petersen (2019). 'Feed the bears, starve the trolls: Demystifying Russia's cybered information confrontation strategy', *The Cyber Defense Review*, 2019 special edition, 145–160.

Steve Kornacki (2018). *The Red and the Blue: The 1990s and the Birth of Political Tribalism*, New York: Ecco.

Jeff Kosseff (2010). 'Defending Section 230: The value of intermediary immunity', *Journal of Technology Law and Policy*, 15(2), 123–158.

A. Kralisch & T. Mandl (2006). 'Barriers to information access across languages on the Internet: Network and language effects', in *Proceedings of the 39th Annual Hawaii International Conference on System Sciences (HICSS '06)*, IEEE, https://doi.org/10.1109/HICSS.2006.71.

Nir Kshetri (2017). 'The economics of the Internet of Things in the Global South', *Third World Quarterly*, 38(2), 311–339, https://doi.org/10.1080/01436597.2016.1191942.

Srijan Kumar, Robert West, & Jure Leskovec (2016). 'Disinformation on the Web: Impact, characteristics, and detection of Wikipedia hoaxes', in *WWW '16: Proceedings of the 25th International Conference on World Wide Web*, New York: ACM, 591–602, https://doi.org/10.1145/2872427.2883085.

Ray Kurzweil (2005). *The Singularity Is Near*, New York: Viking Penguin.

Demetrios Jason Lallas (2014). 'On the condition of anonymity: Disembodied exhibitionism and oblique trolling strategies', in Gustav Verhulsdonck & Marohang Limbu (eds.), *Digital Rhetoric and Global Literacies: Communication Modes and Digital Practices in the Networked World*, IGI Global, 296–311, https://10.4018/978-1-4666-4916-3.ch015.

Ganaele Langlois, Joanna Redden, & Greg Elmer (eds.) (2015). *Compromised Data: From Social Media to Big Data*, New York: Bloomsbury Academic.

Jaron Lanier (2011). *You Are Not a Gadget*, updated edition, London: Penguin.

Roslyn Layton & Julian Mclendon (2018). 'The GDPR: What it really does and how the U.S. can chart a better course', *Federalist Society Review*, 19, 234–248.

David M. J. Lazer, Matthew A. Baum, Yochai Benkler, Adam J. Berinsky, Kelly M. Greenhill, Filippo Menczer, Miriam J. Metzger, Brendan Nyhan, Gordon Pennycook, David Rothschild, Michael Schudson, Steven A. Sloman, Cass R. Sunstein, Emily A. Thorson, Duncan J. Watts, & Jonathan L. Zittrain (2018). 'The science of fake news', *Science*, 359(6380), 1094–1096, https://doi.org/10.1126/science.aao2998.

Christopher A. Le Dantec (2016). *Designing Publics*, Cambridge, MA: MIT Press.

Charles Leadbeater (2008). *We-Think: Mass Innovation, Not Mass Production*, London: Profile.

Kai-Fu Lee (2018). *AI Superpowers: China, Silicon Valley and the New World Order*, New York: Houghton Mifflin Harcourt.

Thomas Leitch (2014). *Wikipedia U: Knowledge, Authority, and Liberal Education in the Digital Age*, Baltimore, MD: Johns Hopkins University Press.

Pedro Giovanni Leon, Lorrie Faith Cranor, Aleecia M. McDonald, & Robert McGuire (2010). 'Token attempt: The misrepresentation of website privacy policies through the misuse of P3P compact policy tokens', in *WPES '10: Proceedings of the 9th Annual ACM Workshop on Privacy in the Electronic Society*, New York: ACM, 93–104, https://doi.org/10.1145/1866919.1866932.

Laurence Lessig (2001). *The Future of Ideas: The Fate of the Commons in a Connected World*, New York: Random House.

Dev Lewis (2020). 'Separating myth from reality: How China's social credit system uses public data for social governance', in *The AI Powered State: China's Approach to Public Sector Innovation*, London: Nesta, 43–50, https://media.nesta.org.uk/documents/Nesta_TheAIPoweredState_2020.pdf.

Ling Li (2018). 'China's manufacturing locus in 2025: With a comparison of "Made-in-China 2025" and "Industry 4.0"', *Technological Forecasting and Social Change*, 135, 66–74, https://doi.org/10–1016/j.techfore.2017.05.028.

Xiang-Yang Li, Jianwei Qian, & Xiaoyang Wang (2018). 'Can China lead the development of data trading and sharing markets?' *Communications of the ACM*, 61(11), 50–51, https://doi.org/10.1145/3239542.

Yifei Li & Judith Shapiro (2020). *China Goes Green: Coercive Environmentalism for a Troubled Planet*, Cambridge: Polity Press.

Fan Liang, Vishnupriya Das, Nadiya Kostyuk, & Muzammil M. Hussain (2018). 'Constructing a data-driven society: China's social credit system as a state surveillance infrastructure', *Policy and Internet*, 10(4), 415–453, https://doi.org/10.1002/poi3.183.

Tai Wei Lim (2019). *Industrial Revolution 4.0, Tech Giants, and Digitized Societies*, Singapore: Palgrave Macmillan.

Jenna Lindqvist (2018). 'New challenges to personal data processing agreements: Is the GDPR fit to deal with contract, accountability and liability in a world of the Internet of Things?' *International Journal of Law and Information Technology*, 26(1), 45–63, https://doi.org/10.1093/ijlit/eax024.

Shlomit Aharoni Lir (2019). 'Strangers in a seemingly open-to-all website: The gender bias in Wikipedia', *Equality, Diversity and Inclusion*, https://doi.org/10.1108/EDI-10-2018-0198.

Jinhe Liu (2020). 'China's data localization', *Chinese Journal of Communication*, 13(1), 84–103, https://doi.org/10.1080/17544750.2019.1649289.

Brian Loader & Dan Mercea (2011). 'Networking democracy? Social media innovations and participatory politics', *Information, Communication & Society*, 14(6), 757–769, https://doi.org/10.1080/1369118X.2011.592648.

Shuning Lu, Wenhong Chen, Xiaoqian Li, & Pei Zheng (2018). 'The Chinese smog crisis as media event: Examining Twitter discussion of the documentary *Under the Dome*', *Policy and Internet*, 10(4), 483–508, https://doi.org/10.1002/poi3.191.

Francis Lyall (2016). *International Communications: The International Telecommunication Union and the Universal Postal Union*, Abingdon: Routledge.

David Lyon (2001). *Surveillance Society: Monitoring Everyday Life*, Buckingham: Open University Press.

David Lyon (2018). *The Culture of Surveillance*, Cambridge: Polity Press.

Alan Macfarlane (2018). *China, Japan, Europe and the Anglo-Sphere: A Comparative Analysis*, Cambridge: Cam Rivers.

Kevin Macnish (2018). *The Ethics of Surveillance: An Introduction*, Abingdon: Routledge.

Essam Mansour, Andrei Vlad Sambra, Sandro Hawke, Maged Zereba, Sarven Capadisli, Abdurrahman Ghanem, Ashraf Aboulnaga, & Tim Berners-Lee (2016). 'A demonstration of the Solid platform for Social Web applications', in *Proceedings of the 25th International Conference Companion on World Wide Web*, New York: ACM, 223–226, https://doi.org/10.1145/2872518.2890529.

Carsten Maple (2017). 'Security and privacy in the internet of things', *Journal of Cyber Policy*, 2(2), 155–184, https://doi.org/10.1080/23738871.2017.1366536.

Marie-Helen Maras & Adam Scott Wandt (2019). 'Enabling mass surveillance: Data aggregation in the age of big data and the Internet of Things', *Journal of Cyber Policy*, 4(2), 160–177, https://doi.org/10.1080/23738871.2019.1590437.

J. Scott Marcus, Dieter Elixmann, & Kenneth R. Carter (2008). *The Future of IP Interconnection: Technical, Economic and Public Policy Aspects*, Bad Honnef: WIK-Consult, http://publications.europa.eu/resource/genpub/PUB_KK0114635ENN.1.1.

Helen Margetts, Peter John, Scott Hale, & Taha Yasseri (2016). *Political Turbulence: How Social Media Shape Collective Action*, Princeton, NJ: Princeton University Press.

José Marichal (2012). *Facebook Democracy: The Architecture of Disclosure and the Threat to Public Life*, Farnham: Ashgate.

Christiana Markou (2015). 'The *"Right to Be Forgotten"*: Ten reasons why it should be forgotten', in Serge Gutwirth, Ronald Leenes, & Paul de Hert (eds.), *Reforming European Data Protection Law*, Dordrecht: Springer, 203–226, https://doi.org/10.1007/978-94-017-9385-8_8.

Christopher T. Marsden (2013). 'Network neutrality: A research guide', in Ian Brown (ed.), *Research Handbook on Governance of the Internet*, Cheltenham: Edward Elgar, 419–444.

Karl Marx & Friedrich Engels (2002). *The Communist Manifesto*, London: Penguin.

Thomas Maskell, Clara Crivellaro, Robert Anderson, Tom Nappey, Vera Araújo-Soares, & Kyle Montague (2018). 'Spokespeople: Exploring routes to action through citizen-generated data', in *CHI '18: Proceedings of the 2018 CHI Conference on Human Factors in Computing Systems*, Paper No. 405, https://doi.org/10.1145/3173574.3173979.

Viktor Mayer-Schönberger & Kenneth Cukier (2013). *Big Data: A Revolution That Will Transform How We Live, Work and Think*, London: John Murray.

Deirdre N. McCloskey (2006). *The Bourgeois Virtues: Ethics for an Age of Commerce*, Chicago: University of Chicago Press.

Aleecia M. McDonald & Lorrie Faith Cranor (2008). 'The cost of reading privacy policies', *I/S: A Journal of Law and Policy for the Information Society*, 4(3), 543–568.

Bonnie S. McDougall (2002). 'Particulars and universals: Studies on Chinese privacy', in Bonnie S. McDougall & Anders Hansson (eds.), *Chinese Concepts of Privacy*, Leiden: Brill, 3–24.

Paul McLaughlin (2016). 'Crypto wars 2.0: Why listening to Apple on encryption will make America more secure', *Temple International and Comparative Law Journal*, 30(2), 353–384.

Amanda Menking, Ingrid Erickson, & Wanda Pratt (2019). 'People who can take it: How women Wikipedians negotiate and navigate safety', in *CHI '19: Proceedings of the 2019 CHI Conference on Human Factors in Computing Systems*, New York: ACM, Paper no. 472, https://doi.org/10.1145/3290605.3300702.

Umar Bashir Mir, Arpan K. Kar, Yogesh K. Dwivedi, M. P. Gupta, & R. S. Sharma (2020). 'Realizing digital identity in government: Prioritizing design and implementation objectives for Aadhaar in India', *Government Information Quarterly*, 37(2), https://doi.org/10-1016/j.giq.2019.101442.

Theodore Modis (2005). 'The end of the internet rush', *Technological Forecasting and Social Change*, 72(8), 938–943, https://doi.org/10-1016/j.techfore.2005.06.004.

Martin J. H. Mogridge (1997). 'The self-defeating nature of urban road capacity policy: A review of theories, disputes and available evidence', *Transport Policy*, 4(1), 5–23, https://doi.org/10.1016/S0967-070X(96)00030-3.

Majid Mohammadi (2019). *The Iranian Reform Movement: Civil and Constitutional Rights in Suspension*, Cham: Palgrave Macmillan.

Evgeny Morozov (2011). *The Net Delusion: How Not to Liberate the World*, London: Allen Lane.

Evgeny Morozov (2019a). 'Digital socialism? The calculation debate in the age of big data', *New Left Review*, 116–117, 33–67.

Evgeny Morozov (2019b). 'Capitalism's new clothes', *The Baffler*, 4 February 2019, https://thebaffler.com/latest/capitalisms-new-clothes-morozov.

Vincent Mosco (2004). *The Digital Sublime: Myth, Power and Cyberspace*, Cambridge, MA: MIT Press.

Karen Mossberger, Caroline J. Tolbert, & Ramona S. McNeal (2008). *Digital Citizenship: The Internet, Society, and Participation*, Cambridge, MA: MIT Press.

Last Moyo (2018). 'Rethinking the information society: A decolonial and border gnosis of the digital divide in Africa and the Global South', in Massimo Ragnedda & Glenn W. Muschert (eds.), *Theorizing Digital Divides*, Abingdon: Routledge, 133–145.

Milton Mueller (2013). 'Internet addressing: Global governance of shared resource spaces', in Ian Brown (ed.), *Research Handbook on Governance of the Internet*, Cheltenham: Edward Elgar, 52–70.

Milton Mueller (2017). *Will the Internet Fragment?* Cambridge: Polity Press.

Milton Mueller & Farzaneh Badiei (2020). 'Inventing Internet governance: The historical trajectory of the phenomenon and the field', in Laura DeNardis, Derrick L. Cogburn, Nanette S. Levinson, & Francesca Musiani (eds.), *Researching Internet Governance: Methods, Frameworks, Futures*, Cambridge, MA: MIT Press, 59–83.

Chandrababu Naidu & Sevanti Ninan (2000). *Plain Speaking*, New Delhi: Viking.

Arvind Narayanan & Vitaly Shmatikov (2010). 'Privacy and security: Myths and falla-cies of "personally identifiable information" ', *Communications of the ACM*, 53(6), 24–26, https://doi.org/10.1145/1743546.1743558.

John Naughton (2016). 'The evolution of the Internet: From military experiment to General Purpose Technology', *Journal of Cyber Policy*, 1(1), 5–28, https://doi.org/10.1080/23738871.2016.1157619.

Gianluigi Negro (2020). 'A history of Chinese global Internet governance and its rela-tions with ITU and ICANN', *Chinese Journal of Communication*, 13(1), 104–121, https://doi.org/10.1080/17544750.2019.1650789.

Nicholas Negroponte (1995). *Being Digital*, New York: Alfred A. Knopf.

Nóra Ni Loideain (2019). 'A port in the data-sharing storm: The GDPR and the Internet of Things', *Journal of Cyber Policy*, 4(2), 178–196, https://doi.org/10.1080/23738871.2019.1635176.

Sabine Niederer & José van Dijck (2010). 'Wisdom of the crowd or technicity of con-tent? Wikipedia as a sociotechnical system', *New Media & Society*, 12(8), 1368–1387, https://doi.org/10.1177/1461444810365297.

Rasmus Kleis Nielsen & Lucas Graves (2017). *'News You Don't Believe': Audience Perspectives on Fake News*, Oxford: Reuters Institute, https://reutersinstitute.politics.ox.ac.uk/our-research/news-you-dont-believe-audience-perspectives-fake-news.

Nandan Nilekani & Viral Shah (2015). *Rebooting India: Realizing a Billion Aspirations*, London: Allen Lane.

Dawn C. Nunziato (2009). *Virtual Freedom: Net Neutrality and Free Speech in the Internet Age*, Stanford, CA: Stanford University Press.

Pippa Norris (2001). *Digital Divide: Civic Engagement, Information Poverty, and the Internet Worldwide*, Cambridge: Cambridge University Press.

Sten Nyberg (1997). 'The honest society: Stability and policy considerations', *Journal of Public Economics*, 64(1), 83–99, https://doi.org/10.1016/S0047-2727(96)01608-8.

Joseph S. Nye (2011). *The Future of Power*, New York: PublicAffairs.

Carly Nyst & Nick Monaco (2018). *State-Sponsored Trolling: How Governments Are Deploying Disinformation as Part of Broader Digital Harassment Campaigns*, Institute for the Future, http://www.iftf.org/statesponsoredtrolling/.

Kieron O'Hara (2009). ' "Let a hundred flowers bloom, a hundred schools of thought contend": Web engineering in the Chinese context', in Xiaoling Zhang & Yongnian Zheng (eds.), *China's Information and Communications Technology Revolution: Social Changes and State Responses*, London: Routledge, 121–135.

Kieron O'Hara (2011). *Conservatism*, London: Reaktion Books.

Kieron O'Hara (2012). *Aldous Huxley: A Beginner's Guide*, Oxford: Oneworld.

Kieron O'Hara (2013). 'The technology of collective memory and the normativity of truth', in Diane P. Michelfelder, Natasha McCarthy, & David E. Goldberg (eds.), *Philosophy and Engineering: Reflections on Practice, Principles and Process*, Dordrecht: Springer, 279–290, https://doi.org/10.1007/978-94-007-7762-0_22.

Kieron O'Hara (2014a). 'The information spring', *IEEE Internet Computing*, 18(2), 79–83, https://doi.ieeecomputersociety.org/10.1109/MIC.2014.34.

Kieron O'Hara (2014b). 'Enhancing the quality of open data', in Luciano Floridi & Phyllis Illari (eds.), *The Philosophy of Information Quality*, Cham: Springer, 201–215, https://doi.org/10.1007/978-3-319-07121-3_11.

Kieron O'Hara (2014c). 'The fridge's brain sure ain't the icebox', *IEEE Internet Computing*, 18(6), 81–84, https://doi.ieeecomputersociety.org/10.1109/MIC.2014.122.

Kieron O'Hara (2015a). 'Data, legibility, creativity . . . and power', *IEEE Internet Computing*, 19(2), 88–91, https://doi.org/10.1109/MIC.2015.34.

Kieron O'Hara (2015b). 'The right to be forgotten: The good, the bad, and the ugly', *IEEE Internet Computing*, 19(4), 73–79, https://doi.org/10.1109/MIC.2015.88.

Kieron O'Hara (2018). 'Pity the poor engineer', *European Journal of Communication*, 33(3), 338–343, https://doi.org/10.1177/0267323118775779.

Kieron O'Hara (2019). *Data Trusts: Ethics, Architecture and Governance for Trustworthy Data Stewardship*, Web Science Institute White Paper #1, Southampton: Southampton University, http://dx.doi.org/10.5258/SOTON/WSI-WP001.

Kieron O'Hara (2020a). 'The contradictions of digital modernity', *AI & Society*, 35(1), 197–208, https://doi.org/10.1007/s00146-018-0843-7.

Kieron O'Hara (2020b). 'Explainable AI and the philosophy and practice of explanation', *Computer Law and Security Review*, 39, https://doi.org/10.1016/j.clsr.2020.105474.

Kieron O'Hara (2020c). 'Data-driven government: The triumph of Thatcherism or the revenge of society', in Antony Mullen, Stephen Farrall, & David Jeffrey (eds.), *Thatcherism in the 21st Century: The Social and Cultural Legacy*, Cham: Palgrave Macmillan, 55–73.

Kieron O'Hara (2021). 'Personalisation and digital modernity: Deconstructing the myths of the subjunctive world', in Uta Kohl & Jacob Eisler (eds.), *Data-Driven Personalisation and the Law*, Cambridge: Cambridge University Press, 37–54.

Kieron O'Hara, Noshir S. Contractor, Wendy Hall, James A. Hendler, & Nigel Shadbolt (2013). 'Web Science: Understanding the emergence of macro-level features on the World Wide Web', *Foundations and Trends in Web Science*, 4(2–3), 1–165.

Kieron O'Hara & Wendy Hall (2010). 'Web Science as reflective practice', in Moira Cockell, Jérôme Billotte, Frédéric Darbellay, & Francis Waldvogel (eds.), *Common Knowledge: The Challenge of Transdisciplinarity*, London: EPFL Press, 205–218.

Kieron O'Hara & Wendy Hall (2013). 'Web Science', in William H. Dutton (ed.), *The Oxford Handbook of Internet Studies*, Oxford: Oxford University Press, 48–68.

Kieron O'Hara & Nigel Shadbolt (2015). 'The right to be forgotten: Its potential role in a coherent privacy regime', *European Data Protection Law Review*, 1(3), 178–189, https://doi.org/10.21552/EDPL/2015/3/5.

Kieron O'Hara, Nigel Shadbolt, & Wendy Hall (2016). *A Pragmatic Approach to the Right to Be Forgotten*, Global Commission on Internet Governance, Paper Series no. 26, https://www.cigionline.org/publications/pragmatic-approach-right-be-forgotten.

Kieron O'Hara & David Stevens (2006a). *inequality.com: Power, Poverty and the Digital Divide*, Oxford: Oneworld.

Kieron O'Hara & David Stevens (2006b). 'Democracy, ideology and process re-engineering: Realising the benefits of e-government in Singapore', in Jinpeng Huai, Vincent Shen, & C. J. Tan (eds.), *Workshop on e-Government: Barriers and Opportunities, World Wide Web Conference (WWW '06)*, https://core.ac.uk/download/pdf/1505819.pdf. .

Nuria Oliver, Emmanuel Letouzé, Harald Sterly, Sébastien Delataille, Marco De Nadai, Bruno Lepri, Renaud Lambiotte, Richard Benjamins, Ciro Cattuto, Vittoria Colizza, Nicolas de Cordes, Samuel P. Fraiberger, Till Koebe, Sune Lehmann, Juan Murillo, Alex Pentland, Phuong N. Pham, Frédéric Pivetta, Albert Ali Salah, Jari Saramäki, Samuel V. Scarpino, Michele Tizzoni, Stefaan Verhulst,

& Patrick Vinck (2020). 'Mobile phone data and COVID-19: Missing an opportunity?' *arXiv*, https://arxiv.org/abs/2003.12347.

Mathieu O'Neil (2010). 'Shirky and Sanger, or the costs of crowdsourcing', *Journal of Science Communication*, 9(1), https://doi.org/10–22323/2.09010304.

Jonathan Corpus Ong & Jason Vincent A. Cabañes (2018). *Architects of Networked Disinformation: Behind the Scenes of Troll Accounts and Fake News Production in the Philippines*, Newton Tech4Dev Network, https://newtontechfordev. com/wp-content/uploads/2018/02/ARCHITECTS-OF-NETWORKED-DISINFORMATION-FULL-REPORT.pdf.

Ana Maria Pacheco Huamani & Sébastien Ziegler (2019). 'GDPR compliance tools for Internet of Things deployments', in Sébastien Ziegler (ed.), *Internet of Things Security and Data Protection*, Cham: Springer, 119–128, https://doi.org/ 10.1007/978-3-030-04984-3_8.

Claudia Padovani & Elena Pavan (2007). 'Diversity reconsidered in a global multi-stakeholder environment: Insights from the online world', in Wolfgang Kleinwachter (ed.), *The Power of Ideas: Internet Governance in a Global Multistakeholder Environment*, Berlin: Land of Ideas, 99–109.

William H. Page & John E. Lopatka (2007). *The Microsoft Case: Antitrust, High Technology, and Consumer Welfare*, Chicago: University of Chicago Press.

Brian Parkinson, David E. Millard, Kieron O'Hara, & Richard Giordano (2018). 'The digitally extended self: A lexicological analysis of personal data', *Journal of Information Science*, 44(4), 552–565, https://doi.org/10.1177/0165551517706233.

Lisa Parks & Nicole Starosielski (eds.) (2015). *Signal Traffic: Critical Studies of Media Infrastructures*, Urbana: University of Illinois Press.

Alex Pentland (2014). *Social Physics: How Good Ideas Spread—The Lessons from a New Science*, New York: Penguin.

Clement Salung Petersen & Thomas Riis (2016). 'Private enforcement of IP law by internet service providers: Notice and action procedures', in Thomas Riis (ed.), *User Generated Law: Re-Constructing Intellectual Property Law in a Knowledge Society*, Cheltenham: Edward Elgar, 228–251.

Bilyana Petkova (2019). 'Privacy as Europe's First Amendment', *European Law Journal*, 25(2), 140–154, https://doi.org/10.1111/eulj.12316.

Valentin M. Pfisterer (2019). 'The right to privacy—a fundamental right in search of its identity: Uncovering the CJEU's flawed concept of the right to privacy', *German Law Journal*, 20(5), 722–733, https://doi.org/10.1017/glj.2019.57.

Timothy Pitt-Payne (2007). 'Access to electronic information', in Chris Reed & John Angel (eds.), *Computer Law: The Law and Regulation of Information Technology*, 6th edition, Oxford: Oxford University Press, 505–550.

Gabriel Pogrund & Patrick Maguire (2020). *Left Out: The Inside Story of Labour under Corbyn*, London: Bodley Head.

Karl Polanyi (1944). *The Great Transformation: The Political and Economic Origins of Our Time*, New York: Farrar & Rinehart.

Eugenia Politou, Efthimios Alepis, & Constantinos Patsakis (2018). 'Forgetting personal data and revoking consent under the GDPR: Challenges and proposed solutions', *Journal of Cybersecurity*, 4(1), http://doi.org/10–1093/cybsec/tyy001.

Peter Pomerantsev (2015). *Nothing Is True and Everything Is Possible: Adventures in Modern Russia*, London: Faber & Faber.

Peter Pomerantsev (2019). *This Is Not Propaganda: Adventures in the War against Reality*, London: Faber & Faber.

Alison Powell (2013). 'Argument-by-technology: How technical activism contributes to internet governance', in Ian Brown (ed.), *Research Handbook on Governance of the Internet*, Cheltenham: Edward Elgar, 198–217.

Maria Priestley, Timothy J. Sluckin, & Thanassis Tiropanis (2020). 'Innovation on the web: The end of the S-curve?' *Internet Histories*, 4(4), 390–412, https://doi.org/10.1080/24701475.2020.1747261.

William L. Prosser (1960). 'Privacy', *California Law Review*, 48, 383–423.

Pierre-Joseph Proudhon (1923). *General Idea of the Revolution in the Nineteenth Century*, London: Freedom Press.

Aare Puussaar, Ian G. Johnson, Kyle Montague, Philip James, & Peter Wright (2018). 'Making open data work for civic advocacy', in *Proceedings of the ACM on Human-Computer Interaction*, Article No. 143, https://doi.org/10.1145/3274412.

Nripendra P. Rana, Sunil Luthra, Sachin Kumar Mangla, Rubina Islam, Sian Roderick, & Yogesh K. Dwivedi (2019). 'Barriers to the development of smart cities in Indian context', *Information Systems Frontiers*, 21, 503–525, https://doi.org/10.1007/s10796-018-9873-4.

Jacob Ratkiewicz, Michael Conover, Mark Meiss, Bruno Gonçalves, Snehal Patil, Alessandro Flammini, & Filippo Menczer (2011). 'Truthy: Mapping the spread of astroturf in microblog streams', in *Proceedings of the 20th International Conference Companion on World Wide Web: WWW '11*, New York: ACM, 249–252, https://doi.org/10.1145/1963192.1963301.

Eric S. Raymond (2001). *The Cathedral and the Bazaar: Musings on Linux and Open Source by an Accidental Revolutionary*, 2nd edition, Sebastopol, CA: O'Reilly Media.

Abbas Razaghpanah, Rishab Nithyanand, Narseo Vallina-Rodriguez, Srikanth Sundaresan, Mark Allman, Christian Kreibich, & Phillipa Gill (2018). 'Apps, trackers, privacy, and regulators: A global study of the mobile tracking eco-system', in *Proceedings of The Network and Distributed System Security Symposium (NDSS 2018)*, http://eprints.networks.imdea.org/1744/.

Ian K. Reay, Patricia Beatty, Scott Dick, & James Miller (2007). 'A survey and ana-lysis of the P3P protocol's agents, adoption, maintenance, and future', *IEEE Transactions on Dependable and Secure Computing*, 4(2), 151–164, https://doi.org/10.1109/TDSC.2007.1004.

Ian Reay, Scott Dick, & James Miller (2009). 'A large-scale empirical study of P3P privacy policies: Stated actions vs. legal obligations', *ACM Transactions on the Web*, article 6, https://doi.org/10.1145/1513876.1513878.

Merten Reglitz (2020). 'The human right to free Internet access', *Journal of Applied Philosophy*, 37(2), 314–331, https://doi.org/10.1111/japp.12395.

Hilde Eliassen Restad (2012). 'Old paradigms in history die hard in political science: US foreign policy and American exceptionalism', *American Political Thought*, 1(1), 53–76, https://doi.org/10.1086/664586.

Thomas Rid (2020). *Active Measures: The Secret History of Disinformation and Political Warfare*, London: Profile.

Huw Roberts, Josh Cowls, Jessica Morley, Mariorosaria Taddeo, Vincent Wang, & Luciano Floridi (2021). 'The Chinese approach to artificial intelligence: An ana-lysis of policy, ethics, and regulation', *AI & Society*, 36(1), 59–77, https://doi.org/10.1007/s00146-020-00992-2.

Sarah T. Roberts (2019). *Behind the Screen: Content Moderation in the Shadows of Social Media*, New Haven, CT: Yale University Press.

Jean-Charles Rochet & Jean Tirole (2003). 'Platform competition in two-sided mar-kets', *Journal of the European Economic Association*, 1(4), 990–1029, https://doi.org/10.1162/154247603322493212.

Colin A. Ronan & Joseph Needham (1978). *The Shorter Science and Civilisation in China*, Cambridge: Cambridge University Press.

Arnold Roosendaal (2012). 'We are all connected to Facebook . . . by Facebook!' in Serge Gutwirth, Ronald Leenes, Paul De Hert, & Yves Poullet (eds.), *European Data Protection: In Good Health?* Dordrecht: Springer, 3–19, https://doi.org/10.1007/978-94-007-2903-2_1.

Eric Rosenbach & Katherine Mansted (2019). *The Geopolitics of Information*, Defending Digital Democracy Project, Belfer Center for Science and International Affairs, Cambridge, MA: Harvard Kennedy School, https://www.belfercenter.org/publication/geopolitics-information.

Beate Rössler (2005). *The Value of Privacy*, Cambridge: Policy Press.

Thorsten Ruprechter, Tiago Santos, & Denis Helic (2019). 'On the relation of edit behavior, link structure, and article quality on Wikipedia', in Hocine Cherifi, Sabrina Gaito, José Fernendo Mendes, Esteban Moro, & Luis Mateus Rocha (eds.), *Complex Networks and Their Applications VIII: Volume 2, Proceedings of the Eighth International Conference on Complex Networks and Their Applications COMPLEX NETWORKS 2019*, Cham: Springer, 242–254, https://doi.org/10.1007/978-3-030-36683-4_20.

RUSI (2015). *A Democratic Licence to Operate: Report of the Independent Surveillance Review*, London: Royal United Services Institute for Defence and Security Studies, https://rusi.org/sites/default/files/20150714_whr_2-15_a_democratic_licence_to_operate.pdf.

Carolina Alves De Lima Salge & Elena Karahanna (2018). 'Protesting corruption on Twitter: Is it a bot or is it a person?' *Academy of Management Discoveries*, 4(1), 32–49, https://doi.org/10.5465/amd.2015.0121.

Pamela Samuelson (2001). 'Anticircumvention rules: Threat to science', *Science*, 293(5537), 2028–2031, https://doi.org/10-1126/science.1063764.

Larry Sanger (2006). 'The early history of Nupedia and Wikipedia: A memoir', in Chris DiBona, Danese Cooper, & Mark Stone (eds.), *Open Sources 2.0: The Continuing Evolution*, Sebastopol, CA: O'Reilly Media, 307–338.

Hans Schaffers, Nicos Komninos, Marc Pallot, Brigitte Trousse, Michael Nilsson, & Alvaro Oliveira (2011). 'Smart cities and the future Internet: Towards co-operation frameworks for open innovation', in John Domingue, Alex Galis, Anastasius Gavras, Theodore Zahariadis, Dave Lambert, Frances Cleary, Petros Daras, Srdjan Krco, Henning Müller, Man-Sze Li, Hans Schaffers, Volkmar Lotz, Federico Alvarez, Burkhard Stiller, Stamatis Karnouskos, Susanna Avessta, & Michael Nilsson (eds.), *The Future Internet: Future Internet Assembly 2011: Achievement and Technological Promises*, Berlin: Springer, 431–446, https://doi.org/10.1007/978-3-642-20898-0_31.

Quirin Scheitle, Taejoong Chung, Jens Hiller, Oliver Gasser, Johannes Naab, Roland van Rijswijk-Deij, Oliver Hohlfeld, Ralph Holz, Dave Choffnes, Alan Mislove, & Georg Carle (2017). 'A first look at Certification Authority Authorization (CAA)', *ACM SIGCOMM Computer Communication Review*, 48(2), 10–23, https://doi.org/10.1145/3213232.3213235.

Eric Schmidt & Jared Cohen (2013). *The New Digital Age: Reshaping the Future of People, Nations and Business*, New York: Random House.

m. c. schraefel, Richard Gomer, Enrico Gerding, & Carsten Maple (2020). 'Rethinking transparency for the Internet of Things', in Mireille Hildebrandt & Kieron O'Hara (eds.), *Life and the Law in the Era of Data-Driven Agency*, Cheltenham: Edward Elgar, 100–116.

Theresa Schumilas & Steffanie Scott (2016). 'Beyond "voting with your chopsticks": Community organising for safe food in China', *Asia Pacific Viewpoint*, 57(3), 301–312, https://doi.org/10.1111/apv.12127.

Joseph Schumpeter (1950). *Capitalism, Socialism and Democracy*, 3rd edition, New York: Harper & Row.

Klaus Schwab (2016). *The Fourth Industrial Revolution*, Geneva: World Economic Forum.

Paul M. Schwartz (2019). 'Global data privacy: The EU way', *New York University Law Review*, 94(4), 771–818.

James C. Scott (1998). *Seeing like a State: How Certain Schemes to Improve the Human Condition Have Failed*, New Haven, CT: Yale University Press.

Jean Seaton, Amy Sippitt, & Ben Worthy (2020). 'Fact checking and information in the age of Covid', *Political Quarterly*, 91(3), 578–584, https://doi.org/10.1111/1467-923X.12910.

Meera Selva (2019). 'Reaching for the off switch: Internet shutdowns are growing as nations seek to control public access to information', *Index on Censorship*, 48(3), 19–22, https://doi.org/10.1177/0306422019876438.

Amartya Sen (2005). *The Argumentative Indian: Writings on Indian Culture, History and Identity*, London: Penguin.

Nigel Shadbolt (2013). 'Midata: Towards a personal information revolution', in Mireille Hildebrandt, Kieron O'Hara, & Michael Waidner (eds.), *Digital Enlightenment Yearbook 2013: The Value of Personal Data*, Amsterdam: IOS Press, 202–224.

Nigel Shadbolt, Tim Berners-Lee, & Wendy Hall (2006). 'The Semantic Web revisited', *IEEE Intelligent Systems*, 21(3), 96–101, https://doi.org/10.1109/MIS.2006.62.

Nigel Shadbolt & Kieron O'Hara (2013). 'Linked data in government', *IEEE Internet Computing*, 17(4), 72–77, https://doi.ieeecomputersociety.org/10.1109/MIC.2013.72.

Nigel Shadbolt, Kieron O'Hara, David De Roure, & Wendy Hall (2019). *The Theory and Practice of Social Machines*, Cham: Springer.

Saif Shahin & Pei Zheng (2020). 'Big data and the illusion of choice: Comparing the evolution of India's Aadhaar and China's social credit system as technosocial discourses', *Social Science Computer Review*, 38(1), 25–41, https://doi.org/10.1177/0894439318789343.

Jesse M. Shapiro (2006). 'Smart cities: Quality of life, productivity and the growth effects of human capital', *Review of Economics and Statistics*, 88(2), 324–335, https://doi.org/10.1162/rest.88.2.324.

Dinesh C. Sharma (2015). *The Outsourcer: The Story of India's IT Revolution*, Cambridge, MA: MIT Press.

Katie Shilton (2018). 'Engaging values despite neutrality: Challenges and approaches to values reflection during the design of Internet infrastructure', *Science, Technology, and Human Values*, 43(2), 247–269, https://doi.org/10.1177/0162243917714869.

Sergio Sismondo (2010). *An Introduction to Science and Technology Studies*, 2nd edition, Chichester: Wiley-Blackwell.

Ganesh Sitaraman (2020). 'Too big to prevail: The national security case for breaking up big tech', *Foreign Affairs*, 99(2), 116–126.

Brad Smith & Carol Ann Browne (2019). *Tools and Weapons: The Promise and the Peril of the Digital Age*, London: Hodder & Stoughton.

Timothy Snyder (2018). *The Road to Unfreedom: Russia, Europe, America*, London: Bodley Head.

Andrei Soldatov & Irina Borogan (2017). *The Red Web: The Kremlin's War on the Internet*, updated paperback edition, New York: PublicAffairs.

John T. Soma & Stephen D. Rynerson (2008). *Privacy Law: In a Nutshell*, St Paul, MN: Thomson/West.

Alina Sorescu (2017). 'Data-driven business model innovation', *Journal of Product Innovation Management*, 34(5), 691–696, https://doi.org/10.1111/jpim.12398.

Patricia Spiccia (2013). 'The best things in life are not free: Why immunity under Section 230 of the Communications Decency Act should be earned and not freely given', *Valparaiso University Law Review*, 48(1), 369–416.

David Stevens & Kieron O'Hara (2015). *The Devil's Long Tail: Religious and Other Radicals in the Internet Marketplace*, London: Hurst.

Randall Stross (2008). *Planet Google: How One Company Is Transforming Our Lives*, New York: Free Press.

John Suler (2004). 'The online disinhibition effect', *CyberPsychology and Behavior*, 7(3), 321–326, https://doi.org/10.1089/1094931041291295.

Sindy R. Sumter, Laura Vandenbosch, & Loes Ligtenberg (2017). 'Love me Tinder: Untangling emerging adults' motivations for using the dating application Tinder', *Telematics and Informatics*, 34(1), 67–78.

Cass R. Sunstein (2007). *Republic.com 2.0*, Princeton, NJ: Princeton University Press.

James Surowiecki (2004). *The Wisdom of Crowds: Why the Many Are Smarter than the Few*, London: Little, Brown.

Tian Tao, David De Cremer, & Wu Chunbo (2017). *Huawei: Leadership, Culture, and Connectivity*, New Delhi: Sage Publications.

Don Tapscott & Anthony D. Williams (2006). *Wikinomics: How Mass Collaboration Changes Everything*, New York: Portfolio.

Don Tapscott & Anthony D. Williams (2010). *Macrowikinomics: Rebooting Business and the World*, New York: Portfolio.

R. H. Tawney (1938). *Equality*, 3rd edition, London: George Allen & Unwin.

Linnet Taylor (2016). 'From zero to hero: How zero-rating became a debate about human rights', *IEEE Internet Computing*, 20(4), 79–83, https://doi.org/10.1109/MIC.2016.88.

Richard H. Thaler & Cass R. Sunstein (2008). *Nudge: Improving Decisions about Health, Wealth, and Happiness*, New Haven, CT: Yale University Press.

William I. Thomas & Dorothy Swaine Thomas (1928). *The Child in America: Behavior Problems and Programs*, New York: Alfred A. Knopf.

Kirsi Tirri (2014). 'The hacker ethic for gifted scientists', in Seana Moran, David Cropley, & James C. Kaufman (eds.), *The Ethics of Creativity*, 221–231, London: Palgrave Macmillan, https://doi.org/10.1057/9781137333544_13.

Alexis de Tocqueville (2011). *The Ancien Régime and the French Revolution*, New York: Cambridge University Press.

Anthony M. Townsend (2013). *Smart Cities: Big Data, Civic Hackers, and the Quest For a New Utopia*, New York: W. W. Norton.

Paul Triollo (2020). 'China's 5G strategy: Be first out of the gate and ready to innovate', in Scott Kennedy (ed.), *China's Uneven High-Tech Drive: Implications for the United States*, Washington, DC: Center for Strategic and International Studies, 21–28, https://www.csis.org/analysis/chinas-uneven-high-tech-drive-implications-united-states.

Milena Tsvetkova, Ruth García-Gavilanes, Luciano Floridi, & Taha Yasseri (2017). 'Even good bots fight: The case of Wikipedia', *PLoS One*, 12(2), e0171774, https://dx.doi.org/10.1371/journal.pone.0171774.

Sherry Turkle (2011). *Alone Together: Why We Expect More from Technology and Less from Each Other*, New York: Basic Books.

UN Secretary-General's High-Level Panel on Digital Cooperation (2019). *The Age of Digital Interdependence*, https://www.un.org/en/pdfs/DigitalCooperation-report-for%20web.pdf.

United States Pirate Party (n.d.). *No Safe Harbor: Essays about Pirate Politics*, United States Pirate Party.

Lachlan Urquhart, Neelima Sailaja, & Derek McAuley (2018). 'Realising the right to data portability for the domestic Internet of Things', *Personal and Ubiquitous Computing*, 22, 317–332, https://doi.org/10.1007/s00779-017-1069-2.

Narseo Vallina-Rodriguez, Srikanth Sundaresan, Abbas Razaghpanah, Rishab Nithyanand, Mark Allman, Christian Kreibich, & Phillipa Gill (2016). 'Tracking the trackers: Towards understanding the mobile advertising and tracking eco-system', *arXiv*, https://arxiv.org/abs/1609.07190.

Shannon Vallor (2016). *Technology and the Virtues: A Philosophical Guide to a Future Worth Wanting*, New York: Oxford University Press.

Barbara van Schewick (2010). *Internet Architecture and Innovation*, Cambridge, MA: MIT Press.

Tommaso Venturini & Richard Rogers (2019). '"API-based research" or how can digital sociology and journalism studies learn from the Facebook and Cambridge Analytica data breach', *Digital Journalism*, 7(4), 532–540, https://doi.org/10.1080/21670811.2019.1591927.

Ingo Vogelsang (2018). 'Net neutrality regulation: Much ado about nothing?' *Review of Network Economics*, 17(3), 225–243, https://doi.org/10.1515/rne-2018-0051.

Luis von Ahn (2006). 'Games with a purpose', *Computer*, 39(6), 92–94, https://doi.org/10.1109/MC.2006.196.

Luis von Ahn & Laura Dabbish (2004). 'Labeling images with a computer game', in *CHI '04: Proceedings of the SIGCHI Conference on Human Factors in Computing Systems*, New York: ACM, 319–326, https://doi.org/10.1145/985692.985733.

Luis von Ahn & Laura Dabbish (2008). 'Designing games with a purpose', *Communications of the ACM*, 51(8), 57–67, https://doi.org/10.1145/1378704.1378719.

Soroush Vosoughi, Deb Roy, & Sinan Aral (2018). 'The spread of true and false news on-line', *Science*, 359(6380), 1146–1151, https://doi.org/10.1126/science.aap9559.

W. Gregory Voss & Kimberley A. Houser (2019). 'Personal data and the GDPR: Providing a competitive advantage for U.S. companies', *American Business Law Journal*, 56(2), 287–344.

Sandra Wachter (2018a). 'Normative challenges of identification in the Internet of Things: Privacy, profiling, discrimination, and the GDPR', *Computer Law and Security Review*, 34(3), 436–449, https://doi.org/10.1016/j.clsr.2018.02.002.

Sandra Wachter (2018b). 'The GDPR and the Internet of Things: A three-step transparency model', *Law, Innovation and Technology*, 10(2), 266–294, https://doi.org/10.1080/17579961.2018.1527479.

Peter Wagner (2012). *Modernity: Understanding the Present*, Cambridge: Polity Press.

Marc Waldman, Lorrie Faith Cranor, and Avi Rubin (2001). 'Trust', in Andy Oram (ed.), *Peer-to-Peer: Harnessing the Power of Disruptive Technologies*, Sebastopol, CA: O'Reilly & Associates, 242–270.

M. Mitchell Waldrop (2001). *The Dream Machine*, New York: Viking Penguin.

Dennis Wang (2020). *Reigning the Future: AI, 5G, Huawei, and the Next 30 Years of US-China Rivalry*, Potomac, MD: New Degree Press.

Dingkun Wang & Xiaochun Zhang (2017). 'Fansubbing in China: Technology-facilitated activism in translation', *Target: International Journal of Translation Studies*, 29(2), 301–318, https://doi.org/10.1075/target.29.2.06wan.

Noah Wardrip-Fruin (2004). 'What hypertext is', in *HYPERTEXT '04: Proceedings of the 15th ACM Conference on Hypertext and Hypermedia*, New York: ACM, 126–127, https://doi.org/10.1145/1012807.1012844.

Rolf H. Weber (2010). 'Internet of Things: New security and privacy challenges', *Computer Law and Security Review*, 26(1), 23–30, https://doi.org/10.1080/23738871.2017.1366536.

Rolf H. Weber (2013). 'The legitimacy and accountability of the internet's governing institutions', in Ian Brown (ed.), *Research Handbook on Governance of the Internet*, Cheltenham: Edward Elgar, 99–120.

Rolf H. Weber (2015). 'Internet of Things: Privacy issues revisited', *Computer Law and Security Review*, 31(5), 618–627, https://doi.org/10.1016/j.clsr.2015.07.002.

Rolf H. Weber (2020). 'A legal lens into Internet governance', in Laura DeNardis, Derrick L. Cogburn, Nanette S. Levinson, & Francesca Musiani (eds.), *Researching Internet Governance: Methods, Frameworks, Futures*, Cambridge, MA: MIT Press, 105–121.

Rolf H. Weber & Romana Weber (2010). *Internet of Things: Legal Perspectives*, Berlin: Springer.

Mark Weiser (1991). 'The computer for the 21st century', *Scientific American*, 265(3), 94–104.

Antony Welfare (2019). *Commercializing Blockchain: Strategic Applications in the Real World*, Chichester: John Wiley & Sons.

Tom White (2015). *Hadoop: The Definitive Guide: Storage and Analysis at Internet Scale*, 4th edition, Sebastopol, CA: O'Reilly Media.

James Q. Whitman (2004). 'The two Western cultures of privacy: Dignity versus liberty', *Yale Law Journal*, 113, 1151–1221.

Elizabeth Williamson, Alex J. Walker, Krishnan J. Bhaskaran, Seb Bacon, Chris Bates, Caroline E. Morton, Helen J. Curtis, Amir Mehrkar, David Evans, Peter Inglesby, Jonathan Cockburn, Helen I. Mcdonald, Brian MacKenna, Laurie Tomlinson, Ian J. Douglas, Christopher T. Rentsch, Rohini Mathur, Angel Wong, Richard Grieve, David Harrison, Harriet Forbes, Anna Schultze, Richard T. Croker, John Parry, Frank Hester, Sam Harper, Rafael Perera, Stephen Evans, Liam Smeeth, & Ben Goldacre (2020). 'OpenSAFELY: Factors associated with COVID-19-related hospital death in the linked electronic health records of 17 million adult NHS patients', *medRxiv*, https://doi.org/10.1101/2020.05.06.20092999.

Karen Li Xan Wong & Amy Shields Dobson (2019). 'We're just data: Exploring China's social credit system in relation to digital platform ratings cultures in Westernised democracies', *Global Media and China*, 4(2), 220–232, https://doi.org/10.1177/2059436419856090.

Wendy H. Wong & Peter A. Brown (2013). 'E-bandits in global activism: WikiLeaks, Anonymous, and the politics of no one', *Perspectives on Politics*, 11(4), 1015–1033, https://doi.org/10.1017/S1537592713002806.

Heather Suzanne Woods (2018). 'Asking more of Siri and Alexa: Feminine persona in service of surveillance capitalism', *Critical Studies in Media Communication*, 35(4), 334–349, https://doi.org/10.1080/15295036.2018.1488082.

Samuel C. Woolley & Philip N. Howard (2017). *Computational Propaganda Worldwide*, Oxford: Oxford Internet Institute Working Paper 2017.11, http://

comprop.oii.ox.ac.uk/wp-content/uploads/sites/89/2017/06/Casestudies-ExecutiveSummary.pdf.

Joshua D. Wright, Elyse Dorsey, Jonathan Klick, & Jan M. Rybnicek (2019). 'REQUIEM for a paradox: The dubious rise and inevitable fall of hipster antitrust', *Arizona State Law Journal*, 51, 293–369.

Angela Xiao Wu (2020). 'The evolution of regime imaginaries on the Chinese Internet', *Journal of Political Ideologies*, 25(2), 139–161, https://doi.org/10.1080/13569317.2020.1750759.

Tim Wu (2003). 'Network neutrality, broadband discrimination', *Journal on Telecommunications and High Technology Law*, 2, 141–175, http://www.jthtl.org/content/articles/V2I1/JTHTLv2i1_Wu.PDF.

Jost Wübbeke, Mirjam Meissner, Max J. Zenglein, Jaqueline Ives, & Björn Conrad (2016). *Made in China 2025: The Making of a High-Tech Superpower and Consequences for Industrial Countries*, Berlin: Mercator Institute for China Studies, https://kritisches-netzwerk.de/sites/default/files/merics_-_made_in_china_2025_-_the_making_of_a_high-tech_superpower_and_consequences_for_industrial_countries_-_76_seiten_1.pdf.

Xu Xu (2020). 'To repress or to co-opt? Authoritarian control in the age of digital surveillance', *American Journal of Political Science*, https://doi.org/10.1111/ajps.12514.

Eryong Xue & Jian Li (2019). *The Chinese Education Policy Landscape: A Concept-Added Policy Chain Analysis*, Singapore: Springer Nature.

Yi Yang, Wencui Han, & Michael Shaw (2016). 'A framework for disruptive innovation diffusion', in *Proceedings of Adoption and Diffusion of Information Technology (SIGADIT)*, http://aisel.aisnet.org/amcis2016/Adoption/Presentations/4/.

Elliott Zaagman (2018). 'China's computing ambitions', *Communications of the ACM*, 61(11), 40–41, https://doi.org/10.1145/3239534.

Andrea Zanella, Nicola Bui, Angelo Castellani, Lorenzo Vangelista, & Michele Zorzi (2014). 'Internet of Things for smart cities', *IEEE Internet of Things*, 1(1), 22–32, https://doi.org/10.1109/JIOT.2014.2306328.

Fabio Massimo Zanzotto (2019). 'Human-in-the-loop Artificial Intelligence', *Journal of Artificial Intelligence Research*, 64, 243–252, https://doi.org/10.1613/jair.1.11345.

Tal Z. Zarsky (2017). 'Incompatible: The GDPR in the age of big data', *Seton Hall Law Review*, 47(4), 995–1020.

Yue Zhang (2008). 'The effects of perceived fairness and communication on honesty and collusion in a multi-agent setting', *Accounting Review*, 83(4), 1125–1146, https://doi.org/10.2308/accr.2008.83.4.1125.

Yingqin Zheng & Ai Yu (2016). 'Affordances of social media in collective action: The case of Free Lunch for Children in China', *Information Systems Journal*, 26(3), 289–313, https://doi.org/10.1111/isj.12096.

Malte Ziewitz & Ian Brown (2013). 'A prehistory of internet governance', in Ian Brown (ed.), *Research Handbook on Governance of the Internet*, Cheltenham: Edward Elgar, 3–26.

Jonathan Zittrain (2006). 'The generative Internet', *Harvard Law Review*, 119, 1974–2040, https://doi.org/10–1145/1435417.1435426.

Jonathan Zittrain (2008). *The Future of the Internet: And How to Stop It*, New Haven, CT: Yale University Press.

Shoshana Zuboff (2019). *The Age of Surveillance Capitalism: The Fight for a Human Future at the New Frontier of Power*, London: Profile.

INDEX

For the benefit of digital users, indexed terms that span two pages (e.g., 52–53) may, on occasion, appear on only one of those pages.

Tables and figures are indicated by *t* and *f* following the page number

China (*cont.*)
    Communist Youth League, 136
    data, policy, 81, 201, 202, 205, 211, 212, 227
    effectiveness of government, 126, 127–28, 129, 212, 227
    e-RMB, 139
    Fifty Cent Army, 165–66
    food supply, 232
    geography, 127, 130, 134
    geopolitical ambition, 127, 129, 135–36, 140, 146, 207–8, 228
    Great Firewall, 130, 134, 138, 143
    Hangzhou, 137–38
    history, 127–28, 129
    Hong Kong, 128, 145, 241
    Hubei, 137–38
    India, tensions with, 183, 188–89, 191–92, 194, 201
    ITU, use of, 37, 132–33
    local government, 212, 226
    Made in China 2025 130–31, 145–46, 150, 207–8, 212
    Mandarin, 178
    Ministry of Commerce, 201
    national security, 43*t*, 130, 158–59, 201
    nationalism, 127, 129
    one child policy, 140
    outreach, soft power, 130, 134, 135, 137*t*, 143, 152
    People's Liberation Army (PLA), 145–46, 147
    privacy, surveillance, 90, 96, 133, 213, 232
    Provisions on the Governance of the Online Information Content Ecosystem, 136, 137*t*
    public opinion, 135–36, 137–38, 142–43
    public opinion, government influence on, 136
    Shaanxi, 143
    Skynet, 226–27
    smart/safe cities, 214, 226–27
    social aspects of Chinese Internet, 67–69, 74, 135–40, 165–66, 232
    social credit, 139–40, 191, 226–27
    social machines in, 232–33
    State Council, 139–40
    Taiwan (*see* Taiwan)
    technological autonomy, self-sufficiency, 130–31, 152–53, 212, 228
    Tibet, 128, 130, 211–12
    United States, tensions with, 9, 11–12, 116, 130–31, 145–47, 148, 149–51, 152–53, 162, 174–75, 178, 201, 214, 228, 238–39
    Wuhan, 135–36, 137–38, 139, 226
    Xi'an, 143
    Xinjiang, 128, 130, 139, 144, 145, 211–12
China Mobile, 146
China Telecom, 146
chips, computer chips, silicon chips, 130–31, 148, 151–52, 211
Christian Democratic Union. *See* CDU
citizen science, 230–32
Citizendium, 63
civil society, 7–8, 11–12, 37, 38, 71, 81, 111, 116, 132, 134, 169–70, 198, 204–5, 210, 223, 224, 238, 242
civilizational states, 11–12, 127–28, 183–84, 188, 189
CJEU. *See* European Union: Court of Justice of the European Union
Clark, David, 25–26
Clegg, Nick, 123, 179, 194
climate change, renewable energy, 96, 104, 122, 125, 130–31, 178–79, 203, 214, 221
    denial, 156
Clinton, Hillary, 160, 161, 164, 167–68
closed circuit television. *See* CCTV
closed world assumption, 18–19, 76
cloud computing, 19, 32, 35, 120, 132, 143, 150, 152, 175, 186–87, 200, 203, 204, 205, 207, 218–19, 226–27, 234–35
CloudWalk Technology, 144
CNCERT/CC, 43*t*
Coase, Ronald, 104
Coker, Christopher, 183–84, 188
Cold War, 27, 167, 188, 198–99, 203
collaboration, collaborative methods, 33–34, 48, 53, 60–62, 63–64, 139–40, 162–63, 209, 229–33
collective action problems, 72, 82, 111, 221
collective intelligence, 34, 60, 156, 229–33

digital interdependence, 242

digital modernity, 4–5, 20–23, 76, 85, 93, 94–96, 120–21, 129, 168–69, 174, 181, 206, 212, 224, 227–28, 243–44

Digital Object Architecture. *See* DOA

Digital Object Identifier. *See* DOI

digital omniscience, 221–22

digital rights management. *See* DRM

digital twins, avatars, 19–20, 35, 93, 94–95, 221, 239

discrimination, 80, 94–95, 177–78, 215, 243

disinformation. *See* misinformation

disintermediation, 21, 22, 76, 121

disruption, technological, 22–23, 61–62, 80, 81, 82–83, 119, 120–21, 122, 129, 130, 162, 242–44

dissent. *See* protest, online

distributed denial of service attacks. *See* DDoS

diversity, 63–65, 72, 76, 210, 211–12, 242, 246

Djibouti, 3t

DNS, 38–41, 43t, 111, 132–33, 174, 176, 241

Do Not Track, 83–84

DOA, 132–33, 152, 227, 228, 254n.17

Doctoroff, Dan, 224

DOI, 132–33

Dolmans, Maurits, 52

Domain Name System. *See* DNS

Dostoyevsky, Fyodor, 157

DPD. *See* European Union: Data Protection Directive

DPI, 72, 74–75, 110, 130, 162

DRM, 111

Drones, 112, 122–23

DTP, 236

Durov, Pavel, 163–64, 175–76

Duterte, Rodrigo, 165–66

Dutton, William, 78

Dyson, Esther, 39

eBay, 34, 57–58, 139–40, 143–44

ECHR, 82, 84

e-commerce, 17, 32, 33–34, 96, 118, 119–20, 131–32, 138–39, 143, 186–87, 201, 202, 218, 244–45

economy, digital economy, knowledge economy, 8, 52, 53, 55, 114–15, 132, 146, 174–75, 182, 195, 200–1, 207–8, 240–41

economies of action, 220

Ecuador, 164–66

education, 1, 112, 113, 128, 137–38, 143–44, 168, 170, 184, 196–97, 212, 213, 232, 243–44

EEA, 84–85, 86, 204

Eggers, Dave, 56, 116

e-government, 32, 98, 157–58, 218, 244–45

Egypt, 3t, 10–11, 176, 202, 214

e-Health. *See* healthcare

Einstein, Albert, 244

Ekbia, Hamid, 233

El Salvador, 3t

Elastos, 234–35

elections, referendums, 123, 161
  Andhra Pradesh Legislative Assembly 1994, 184–85
  Andhra Pradesh Legislative Assembly 2004, 185
  Andhra Pradesh Legislative Assembly 2019, 185–86
  German CDU leadership 2018, 97
  German CDU leadership 2021, 96, 97
  German federal 2021, 96
  Indian general 2014, 184
  Indian general 2019, 184, 188, 189, 193
  Iranian Parliamentary 2016, 175–76
  Iranian Presidential 2009, 176
  Iraqi Parliamentary 2018, 166
  Scottish independence referendum 2014, 160
  UK Brexit referendum 2016, 160
  UK general 2019, 170–71
  US Presidential 2016 (including primaries), 56, 122–23, 152, 157, 160, 161, 164, 166–67
  US Presidential 2020 (including primaries), 120, 124, 166–67, 170

email, 25, 43t, 45, 72, 73–75, 103, 108, 130

emergence, 7–9, 26, 178–79

encryption, 19, 33–34, 45, 83–84, 141, 147, 163–64, 175–76, 194, 197–98, 204–5, 219–20
  crypto wars, 204–5

Encyclopaedia Britannica, 61

human rights, dignity, 51–52, 72, 76, 77, 80, 82–83, 92, 102, 107–8, 112, 113, 114–15, 126–27, 128, 136, 141, 152, 170, 203–4, 216, 217, 225, 237, 238, 240–41, 246
Hungary, 10–11
Huxley, Aldous, 116
Hypertext, 33, 61
Hypertext Markup Language. *See* HTML
Hypertext Transfer Protocol. *See* HTTP

IAB, 32, 47
  Internet Architecture Board Network Working Group, 32
IANA, 39, 43*t*
IBM, 30
ICANN, 39–41, 43*t*, 67–69, 113–14, 120, 125, 132, 174, 241
  GAC, 39–40, 67–69, 132
Iceland, 3*t*
IDEMIA, 197, 198
identity, 39, 103, 190–91, 196–99, 235
IEEE, 43*t*
IETF, 30, 31, 36–37, 43*t*, 46–47, 52, 113, 241, 254n.2
IFTF, 164–66
Ilyin, Ivan, 157
image tagging, 120, 213, 230–31
IMDb, 34, 61–63
inclusion, 22, 37, 43*t*, 64–65, 72, 82–83, 191, 198, 244–45
India, 2–3, 3*t*, 72–73, 181, 183–99, 237
  Andhra Pradesh, 184–86, 190
  artificial intelligence, 213, 227–28, 240–41
  Assam, 195
  authoritarianism, 142, 165–66, 187–93, 214
  Bengaluru, 183
  BJP (Bharatiya Janata Party), 165–66, 184, 185–86, 187–88, 192, 193–94, 196
  bureaucracy, 184–85, 189, 220, 227–28
  business environment, 186–87, 189–90, 192, 213, 268n.30
  China, relations with, 143–44, 150, 174, 183, 188–89, 191–92, 194, 201
  Citizenship Amendment Act 2019 188–89, 193–94

civilizational state, Axis of Incivility, 10–11, 183
colonial experience, 188, 195, 202–3
conflicts, 194
Congress Party, 185, 188, 192, 193
data, cross border flows of, 201–3, 205
Data Protection Bill, 192, 201, 204, 213
Delhi, 191–92, 194
diversity of, 183–84, 188, 196
Gujarat, 166, 187–88
Hinduism, Hindus, 188–89, 193–94
HITEC City (Cyberabad), 185
Hyderabad, 183, 185–86
Jammu and Kashmir, 188–89, 194–95
Kashmir, 192–93, 194–95
kirana, convenience stores, 187
Ladakh, 189
Maharashtra, 193
Mumbai, 183, 187
Muslims in, 166, 187–89, 193–94, 195–96
nationalism, 174, 227–28
New Delhi, 195–96, 242
Noida, 195
Pune, 183
Reserve Bank of India, 189–90
Sikhism, 188
smart cities, 221, 227–28
Spoiler model, 165–66, 193–96
Supreme Court, 192–93, 194–95
Tamil Nadu, 191–92
TDP (Telugu Desam Party), 184–86
technology sector, 183, 184, 185–86, 188–89, 196, 198–99, 201–2
Telangana, 185–86
traditions, 188–89
Tripura, 193
Uttar Pradesh, 195
Vadodara, 191–92
West Bengal, 195
See also Aadhaar; MOSIP
individualism, individuality, 77, 95–96, 120, 126–27, 157
Indonesia, 202
information, 8, 18–20, 45, 86–87, 212–13, 239–40
  definition and basics, 12–18
  flow, 18, 25, 67, 104, 162, 164–65, 169, 234, 239, 240–41, 245
  quality, 18–19, 54, 59, 61, 64–65

information intermediaries, 38, 43*t*, 72–73

Infosys, 183, 190

innovation, 22–23, 37, 48, 49, 53–54, 56–58, 74, 80, 90–91, 103, 104–5, 106, 108, 109, 116, 117, 118, 119, 120–21, 122, 124, 151–52, 197, 210, 213, 217, 224, 231, 233, 234, 242–44

Instagram, 35, 60, 119–20, 124, 229–30

instant messaging. *See* messaging

Institute for the Future. *See* IFTF

Institute of Electrical and Electronics Engineers. *See* IEEE

Institute of Information Technology Bangalore, 197–98

intellectual property, 10, 33, 40, 46, 52, 55–56, 61, 71, 73, 109, 111, 113, 125, 134, 142, 151–52, 155, 245

International Organization for Standardization. *See* ISO

International Telecommunication Union. *See* ITU

Internet, passim
  alternative visions of, 177–78, 244–45, 246
  binary (China/US) view of, 9, 11–12, 178, 208, 214–15
  Clean Network, 152
  .com, 39, 40–41, 43*t*, 88, 174
  country code top-level domains, 43*t*, 174
  .edu, 108
  exceptionalism, 47, 51–52, 177
  fragmentation, 8–10, 12, 73–74, 152–53, 173–76, 177, 194, 228, 239
  fragmentation, definition of, 10
  future of, 181–82, 228, 237–46
  governance of, 25–26, 30, 36–44, 43*t*, 46, 48, 52, 57, 67–69, 72, 73, 76, 104–5, 106, 111–14, 126, 132, 133, 135–36, 145, 179, 181, 182, 189, 198–99, 200–1, 203, 209, 237, 238, 242–43
  halal internet (*see* Iran: National Information Network)
  history of, 26, 29–32, 52, 119, 237
  mobile internet, 35, 46–47, 125, 129, 146
  .org, 39, 43*t*, 113–14, 238

precursors of, 27–29

privatization of, 30, 39–40, 88, 111–14, 136

protocol stack, 44–45, 47, 49, 51, 74, 82–83

regulation of (by governments), 8–9, 25–26, 35, 40–41, 46, 52, 57, 72–74, 82, 90–91, 104–5, 107, 109, 117–18, 120, 123, 124, 130, 132, 171, 210, 233, 241–42, 245–46

resilience of, 28, 45, 48–49, 73, 237, 238, 244

root zone, 40–41, 43*t*, 174

scaling of, 25, 31, 32–33, 48–49, 59–60, 72, 76, 238, 245, 246

shutdowns, 130, 175, 176, 192–93, 194–95

social aspects of, 31–32, 33–34, 36–38, 41, 45, 63, 67–69, 71–73, 74, 75, 181, 218–19, 229–33, 244

sovereign, sovereignty, 73–74, 173–76, 177, 205, 239, 245–46

subconsciousness of, 156

top-level domains, 39, 40–41, 43*t*, 114, 174

transport layer, 45, 47–48, 49, 51, 74, 82–83, 132–33, 208, 245–46

values of/in, 45, 46, 47, 48–49, 51, 71–76, 177, 228

virtual political layer, 45, 245–46

Internet Architecture Board. *See* IAB

Internet Assigned Numbers Authority. *See* IANA

Internet Corporation for Assigned Names and Numbers. *See* ICANN

Internet Engineering Task Force. *See* IETF

Internet Exchange Points. *See* IXPs

Internet Movie Database. *See* IMDb

Internet of Things, 16–17, 35, 75, 96, 125, 130–31, 132, 133, 145–46, 147, 152, 181, 185–86, 218–28, 229, 239

Internet Protocol. *See* IP

Internet Protocol Suite. *See* TCP/IP

Internet Research Agency. *See* IRA

Internet Service Providers. *See* ISPs

Internet Society. *See* ISOC

interoperability, 25, 45, 48, 52, 53–54, 58, 75, 100, 101, 105, 108, 114–15,

Murdoch, Rupert, 111–12
Musk, Elon, 56–57
Myanmar, 166, 168–69, 171
MySpace, 35, 122

Naidu, Chandrababu, 184–86, 190
Nardi, Bonnie, 233
NASA, 30, 150
NASDAQ, 103
Nash, Johnny, 182
Nashi, 157–58, 165–66
National Science Foundation, 30
national security, 134–35, 137t, 145, 147, 148, 149, 150, 151, 152, 174–76, 200, 201, 204–5, 212, 240–42, 244–45
NATO, 149
Naxalites, 185, 194
NEC, 152
Needham, Joseph, 128–29
Negro, Gianluca, 135–36
Negroponte, Nicholas, 121
Nelson, Ted, 33
Nemtsov, Boris, 159–60
net neutrality, 48, 57–58, 58f, 71, 72–73, 74–75, 82–83, 83f, 105–6, 105f, 108–10, 112, 113, 131f, 179
Netflix, 57–58, 97–98, 193–94, 201, 210
Netherlands, the, 101, 149–50
  Amsterdam, 214–15
  Rotterdam, 143–44
Netscape Navigator, 33
network effects, 9–10, 12, 37, 46–47, 48–49, 52, 103, 104, 118, 120, 121–22, 133, 187, 190–91, 210, 229, 236, 238, 245–46
  definition, 6
Network Information Center, 28, 39
networks, 5–6, 7–8, 20–21, 22–23, 61, 93, 136, 181
  cellular telecommunications networks, 145–46
  closed networks (see walled gardens)
  connected and unconnected networks, 5, 8–10
  directed and undirected networks, 5
  economics of, 103–4, 210
  efficiency, 28–29, 31, 45, 46, 48, 51–52, 57–58, 72, 81, 103–4, 109, 234
  fragmentation, 8–10, 160

graphs, 5, 35
Internet/ARPANET as a network, 4–5, 8–10, 12, 28, 29–31, 32, 45, 46–47, 48, 85, 219, 238, 242
New Zealand, 286n.17
news, 2–3, 12, 83–84, 103, 138–39, 163, 168, 184, 229
  algorithms, 162–63, 167
  See also fake news
Nextdoor, 231
Nigeria, 197
Night Wolves, 157
Nilekani, Nandan, 190
Nokia, 145–46, 151, 152
Non-Aligned Movement, 188, 198–99, 203
North Korea, 3t, 9, 59–60, 73–74, 147–48, 174–75
Norway, 101
NSFNET, 30
NSINET, 30
Nupedia, 60–61, 63
Nye, Joseph, 11–12

Obama, Barack, 18, 111, 166, 178
  See also United States: Obama administration
objectivity. See epistemology
OECD, 240–41
Ofcom, 57
Office, The (TV show), 59
O'Hara, Kieron, 8, 82, 135–36
Onde Tem Tiroteio, 229–30
onion routing, 130
Open Internet. See Silicon Valley Open Internet
Open Network Architecture, 57
open source software, 53, 99, 115, 197, 198, 236
open standards, 25, 30, 33, 37, 46, 48, 52–53, 54, 58, 58f, 72–73, 82–84, 83f, 105–6, 105f, 107–8, 130, 131f, 133, 152, 197–98, 204–5, 234, 246
Open Standards Identity API. See OSIA
Open Systems Interconnection model. See OSI
openness, 20–21, 23, 33, 34, 41–44, 45, 46, 48–49, 51–56, 60, 62, 64, 65, 67, 69, 71–76, 77, 106, 107, 111, 114–15, 116, 124, 125, 129, 150–51, 154, 155–56, 162–63, 178–79,

Project Maven, 122–23
property, property rights, 52, 103–5, 106, 107–8, 110, 111, 116, 122
  See also intellectual property
protest, online, 93, 126, 135–36, 138, 156, 162, 165–66, 244
Proudhon, Pierre-Joseph, 20
pseudoscience. *See* epistemology
public goods. *See* social value(s)
public health. *See* healthcare
Public Interest Registry. *See* PIR
public space, sphere, 77–79, 81, 136, 138, 164–65
Pushkin, Alexander, 157
Putin, Vladimir, 157, 159, 162–63, 164, 173, 207–8, 241

Qatar, 3*t*
Qualcomm, 151–52
quantum computing, 143, 244

racism, racial issues, sectarianism, 52, 75, 76, 125, 137*t*, 141–42, 156, 160, 169, 170, 187–88, 193, 198, 215
Rakuten, 152
Rasbhari, 193–94
Raymond, Eric, 7
RDF, 34–35, 235
reason. *See* epistemology
Reding, Viviane, 84–85
reflexivity, 95–96
Regional Internet Registries. *See* RIRs
registries, 30–31, 40–41, 43*t*, 111, 174
relativism. *See* epistemology
Relcom, 173–74
Reliance. *See* Jio Platforms
Ren Zhengfei, 145–46, 147, 148–49
Reporters Without Borders, 111
Republican Party (US). *See* United States: Republican Party
Request For Comments. *See* RFC
resistance. *See* protest, online
Resource Description Framework. *See* RDF
RFC, 32
RFID, 218–19
right to be forgotten, 82, 86–88, 113
rights. *See* human rights
RIRs, 43*t*, 125

Roberts, Sarah, 113
Robertson, Pat, 166–67
robot.txt standard, 54
robotics, 130–31, 207–8, 214
Rohingya, 168–69
Roldugin, Sergei, 164
Romania, 3*t*, 204
routers, routing, 30–31, 43*t*, 73
  See also onion routing
RSS, 33–34
RT, 159, 163–64
rumour, 78, 136, 137*t*, 138, 140, 141–42, 169, 193, 194, 195–96
Russia
  civilizational state, exceptionalism, Axis of Incivility, 10–11, 157
  Estonia, cyberattack upon, 157–58, 163
  Georgia, invasion of, 157–58, 162–63
  Ingushetia, 175
  Internet governance, 37, 39–40, 43*t*, 133, 173–74, 202
  media, 160–62, 163–64
  misinformation, 157–65, 169–70, 178, 237, 238
  National DNS, 175
  national security, 174–75
  nationalism, 157–58, 175
  Roskomnadzor, 162, 175
  rule of law, 157, 170
  RuNet, Russian Internet, 173–76, 205
  secret services, 158, 163–64
  Skolkovo, 162–63
  sovereign internet, 174–75, 205, 245–46
  sovereignty experiment 2019, 9, 73–74, 173–74, 175, 239
  Strategy of Information Society Development, 174–75
  Ukraine, invasion of, 157–58, 159–60, 162–63, 173, 238–39
  United States, tensions with, 37, 39–40, 166–67
  values, 67, 157–64, 174–75, 237
Russia Today. *See* RT
Rwanda, 198

Safari, 33
safe cities. *See* smart cities
Safe Harbor, 85–86, 90